APPEASEMENT AND GERMANY'S LAST BID FOR COLONIES

Appeasement and Germany's Last Bid for Colonies

Andrew J. Crozier

Lecturer in Modern History
University College of North Wales, Bangor

679498

St. Martin's Press   New York

First published in the United States of America in 1988

Printed in Hong Kong

ISBN 0–312–01546–1

Library of Congress Cataloging-in-Publication Data
Crozier, Andrew J.
Appeasement and Germany's last bid for colonies/Andrew J.
Crozier.
p. cm.
Bibliography: p.
Includes index.
ISBN 0–312–01546–1: $30.00 (est.)
1. Germany—Colonies. 2. Germany—Politics and
government—1933–1945. I. Title.
JV2018.C76 1988   87–23060
325'.343—dc19   CIP

For my Mother and to the memory of my Father

Contents

Preface

This book inevitably owes much to the efforts of many besides those of the author himself. I should, however, like to record here my particular gratitude to three outstanding historians, D. C. Watt, R. F. Leslie and C. L. Mowat, who supported and encouraged me at various times. Thanks are also due to Wolfgang Michalka and Eckhard Most for very many stimulating conversations during the early days of the project. The research was made very much easier by the courtesy and helpfulness of the staffs of the Public Record Office, the Churchill Archive Centre, the British Library of Political and Economic Science, the University of Cambridge Library and the Library of the University College of North Wales. Regarding the last named institution, I am especially in the debt of Mrs D. Jones whose assistance has been invaluable on more than one occasion. The prosecution of historical research is these days an expensive business. I am, therefore, very grateful to the Research and Conference Grants Committee of the University College of North Wales which has from time to time made funds available for visits to the Public Record Office and other archive centres. I am obliged to Mike Dockrill for his continual prodding and to Miss L. M. Oyler and Mrs J. Hughes for their many kindnesses over the years. This book is largely based upon original sources and for permission to consult and quote from them my thanks are due to the Master, Fellows and Scholars of Churchill College in the University of Cambridge regarding the Phipps and Hankey Papers; Sir Colville Barclay regarding the Vansittart Papers; David Higham Associates Limited regarding the Cadogan Papers; Lord Croft regarding the Croft Papers; the University of Birmingham Library regarding the Dawson and Neville Chamberlain Papers; the University of Cambridge Library regarding the Templewood Papers; and the Clerk of the Records, the House of Lords Record Office regarding the Lloyd George Papers. All Crown Copyright material has been reproduced by permission of the Controller, Her Majesty's Stationery Office. Finally, I thank Gwen for having so often provided a roof and food during my visits to the capital and Andrea, Ian and David without whom the book would never have been written.

ANDREW J. CROZIER

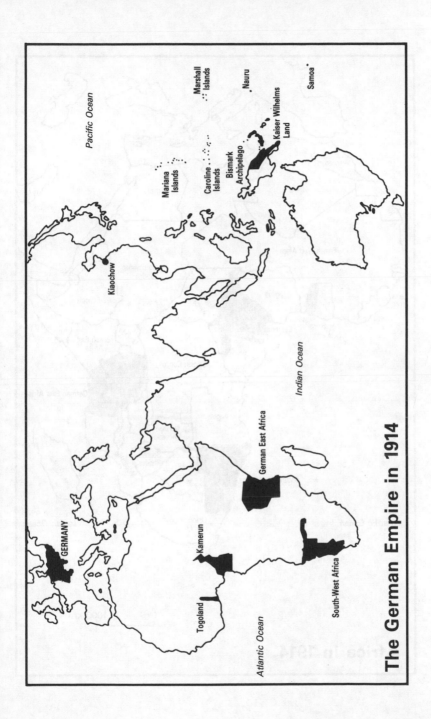

The German Empire in 1914

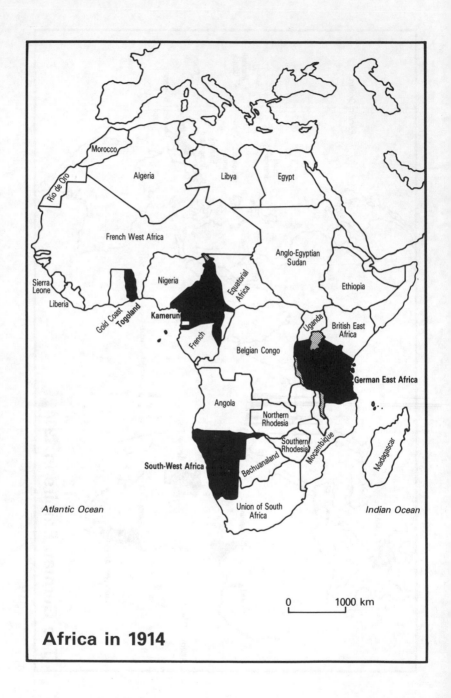

Morocco

Algeria

Libya

Egypt

Rio de Oro

French West Africa

Anglo-Egyptian Sudan

Sierra Leone

Nigeria

Equatorial Africa

Ethiopia

Liberia

Gold Coast

Togoland

Kamerun

French

Uganda

British East Africa

Belgian Congo

German East Africa

Angola

Northern Rhodesia

South-West Africa

Southern Rhodesia

Moçambique

Madagascar

Bechuanaland

Atlantic Ocean

Union of South Africa

Indian Ocean

0   1000 km

Africa in 1914

1
Introduction

On 3 March 1938 Sir Nevile Henderson, the British ambassador at Berlin, presented Hitler a plan, which it was hoped by the British government would satisfy Germany's colonial aspirations; the ambassador asked what in return Germany was prepared to contribute towards an atmosphere of *détente* in Europe. Hitler's response was derisory. Nothing could be done to improve Anglo–German relations until the press campaign against him in Britain was brought to a halt; Germany would not permit the interference of third parties in her relations with central European states. As for colonies, they were not a pressing issue; Germany could wait as much as ten years for satisfaction in the colonial sphere.[1]

Despite Hitler's dismissive treatment of possible colonial satisfaction, this meeting was in a very real sense the culmination of an orchestrated campaign for colonial restitution that had been conducted in Germany, officially and unofficially, ever since the signature of the Treaty of Versailles. Why Hitler decided to respond negatively at this stage is an issue that will be addressed later, but the fact is that the British had been given to understand that the restoration of Germany's former colonies formed part of Germany's wider aspirations and they were prepared to respond sympathetically in the broader interests of the maintenance of peace in Europe and the world. Beyond the narrow issue of Germany's colonial demands, this, after all, was what Henderson's meeting with Hitler was about. Unfortunately the meeting of 3 March 1938 has received scant attention from historians in the post-war era and, in general, has been lost in the welter of Munichology, but it is of vital importance for an accurate appreciation of British foreign policy during the 1930s and, in particular, for an understanding of British policy towards Germany in that period.[2] It was essentially the first and last attempt by the British government to deal with Germany on a broad basis prior to the outbreak of war in 1939.

From the end of 1935 onwards the British government had assiduously sought to solve the problem created by the resurgence of German power in a European context, the object being to achieve

1

a *general settlement* that would put an end to political and economic uncertainty throughout the continent. Such a policy, however, proved difficult to apply. The Rhineland crisis of 1936 and the diplomatic elusiveness of the German government during its aftermath were responsible for this. But, after much deliberation, the Chamberlain Cabinet felt, at the beginning of 1938, that the situation was sufficiently auspicious to make an approach. That the approach proved abortive does not detract from its significance, for it was the only occasion on which the policy of *appeasement*, as understood by Neville Chamberlain and his colleagues, namely the policy of bringing about a European and general settlement by negotiation, was put formally, directly and fully to Hitler. While the *Anschluss*, that was shortly to follow, made the application of this policy even more difficult,[3] it should not be imagined that the fundamental aspirations of British policy were thereby altered: the policy of trying to achieve a general settlement remained un-changed. In a way the Munich conference represented an aspect of this ideal; the final irritant – the Czech question – was to be removed as a prelude to an Anglo–German understanding and thence a European settlement. Admittedly, as the international situation worsened, the effort to obtain German co-operation in a general settlement became a diminishing fundamental, but the ideal of a general settlement continued to animate a British policy until the start of war.

For many years after 1945 an assessment of the importance of the British colonial offer of 3 March 1938 was hampered by the lack of documentary evidence relating to its background. Moreover, the memoirs of statesmen, politicians and diplomats made only fleeting reference, if any, to the matter.[4] Given this state of affairs it was easily assumed that the colonial question was in fact an issue of trifling importance during the 1930s. As Lord Duncan-Sandys remembers 'being very active in opposing the idea in the minds of Baldwin and Chamberlain that the return of the German colonies in Africa might be considered', but little else about the matter, it could be argued that this lends substance to the assumption.[5] On the other hand, it is an incontrovertible fact that almost two-thirds of the material circulated to the British Cabinet Committee on Foreign Policy in the period July 1936 to February 1939 related directly to the colonial question. Moreover, it is equally indisputable that during 1937 and 1938 the issue was discussed in the House of Commons on no fewer than seventeen occasions. Whatever, therefore, the recollections of contemporary politicians, it would seem that consideration and discussion of the colonial question played a considerable part in the events of the 1930s. It has even been suggested, with some justice, that these discussions had an important bearing on the future of British colonial policy, for those who wished to refute Germany's colonial claims had to do so 'on grounds that were clearly acceptable to world opinion; there had to be a sound moral case'. In putting the British government and British public opinion 'on the defensive', Hitler 'unwittingly' became 'the trail-blazer for the British policy of Colonial Development'.[6]

An obvious reason why the colonial question has been so long ignored by historians and commentators alike lies in the fact that it never became an issue of practical politics in Anglo–German relations during the 1930s. But even had they wished to investigate the subject progress would have been difficult until comparatively recently. Although Anthony Eden, then Foreign Secretary in Churchill's War Cabinet, announced in March 1944 that 'the most important documents in the Foreign Office archives between 1919 and 1939' were to be published, nothing was done until the 1970s to complete the second series of *Documents on British Foreign Policy*. This meant that a gap in the published documentary record existed covering the years 1934 to 1938 when the third series begins, which has now been closed. The years 1934 to 1938 were, however, vital for the formation and development of British foreign policy as it was to emerge under the Chamberlain government: they were also the years during which Anthony Eden served his first term as Foreign Secretary and during which the colonial question reached the peak of its importance in the foreign policy deliberations of the British government. Despite the significance of certain developments in these years, very little was known about them until the introduction of the Thirty Year Rule in 1968; indeed an attempt was made during the course of the war to suppress knowledge of them.

In July 1943 Sir George Gater, the permanent under-secretary at the Colonial Office, wrote to his opposite number at the Foreign Office, Sir Alexander Cadogan, suggesting that publication of material relating to the British proposals of 3 March 1938 in the postwar period might be embarrassing for British policy in Africa. Gater informed Cadogan:

Out of fear of Germany, we were prepared to hand over large tracts of colonial empire to Germany without consulting the wishes of the inhabitants . . . playing straight into the hands of those sections of the colonies that wish to throw off Downing Street control.

The 'sections' to which Gater referred were the white settlers in Southern Rhodesia whose advocacy 'of local administration of African peoples' had been turned down by Whitehall on the grounds of the paramountcy of native interests. Such revelations would have provided excellent propaganda for the settlers who could have argued that, as far as Nazi Germany was concerned, the British government had by no means been over-solicitous about the interests of African peoples. Churchill, to whom Cadogan referred the matter, thought that the Colonial Office was making too much of the issue and later commented: 'I really do not see much in these references to the colonial question and it is not very clear what was actually meant.'[7] Nevertheless, the fact remains that the papers relating to the background of the British offer of March 1938 have only been published or made available for inspection in recent years and some are still closed.[8]

It is, however, now possible to give a complete picture of the unfolding of British foreign policy in the period 1934 to 1938. In this picture the colonial question emerges as one of the central issues in the formulation of British foreign policy towards Germany. As such it had considerable ramifications, intimately connected as it was with all the other major issues, including economic appeasement,[9] that affected Anglo–German relations during the 1930s. A study of the colonial question reveals that *appeasement* was not a hastily constructed policy of surrender, but rather a broadly based policy of conciliation, the object of which was to procure a new European and *general settlement* that would replace the settlement of Versailles and open up a new era of certainty and prosperity in Europe and the world. It also illustrates the incipient decline of Britain as an imperial power.[10] Finally, the colonial question and its handling by the Foreign Office, it will be shown, played a crucial part in forming Neville Chamberlain's attitude towards that department on the eve of his assumption of the premiership.[11]

Colonial issues in Anglo–German relations have a long history and much has been written about them.[12] As a complication in relations between Britain and Germany they began to have an effect in 1884 with the German annexation of South-West Africa.[13] Nonetheless, the attitude of Britain and Germany towards one another in colonial policy prior to 1914 was not one of complete and uncompromising hostility; there existed on both sides a willingness to co-operate, especially if it meant the prevention of French domination in Africa. In 1898 the British and German governments were able to agree upon the division between themselves of the central African possessions of Portugal, if the Portuguese had to abandon their title to them. It was, of course, the real object of Lord Salisbury, the British Prime Minister, to shore up the decrepit Portuguese colonial empire, but should it collapse the agreement 'divided the spoils before the arrival of the French . . . meant the abandonment of the Transvaal by the Germans; and . . . strengthened the British hold over Delagoa Bay' considered essential for the conquest of the Boers.[14] This agreement was revised in 1913 during the foreign secretaryship of Sir Edward Grey. It favoured Germany more than the original agreement, quite deliberately as evidence of Britain's goodwill, but it was never signed.[15]

While opposition to German colonialism was founded in Britain on considerations that were fundamentally strategic, there were in certain quarters serious objections on humanitarian grounds. Although it has since become clear that German colonial administration was by no means bad and in many cases excellent, particularly after the colonial crisis of 1906–7 and the subsequent reforms in German colonial administration associated with Bernhard Dernburg, the events connected with the *Maji-Maji* rising in East Africa and the Herero rebellion in South-West Africa were fresh in the minds of British officials.[16] When, however, war came in 1914, it was security and not humanitarianism that prompted the offensive sub-committee of the Committee of Imperial Defence (CID) to recommend that military operations against the German colonies begin.[17]

In 1914 the German colonial empire extended over 1 000 000 square miles of the globe's land surface. The colonies were situated in two groups: those in Africa and those in the Far East and the Pacific. On entering the First World War, Germany entertained grandiose war aims that included a vast expansion of the African part of her colonial possessions. In his celebrated memorandum of September 1914, the German Chancellor, Theobald von Bethmann Hollweg, listed the 'creation of a cohesive Central African colonial empire' among aims such as the acquisition of Luxemburg and southern Belgium, the reduction of the rump Belgian state to 'vassal' status, the destruction of France as a great power, the removal of

Russia 'as far as possible from the German frontier', and the establishment of a huge central European economic federation (*mitteleuropäischen Wirtschaftsverbandes*) under German leadership which would in turn serve to maintain Germany's hegemony in Europe. The nature of Germany's colonial aims was more precisely delineated by the colonial secretary, Wilhelm Solf. Although Portugal was neutral, she was to surrender Angola and the northern half of Mozambique: Belgium was to cede the Congo and France its equatorial territories as far north as Lake Chad. In addition, Dahomey was to be attached to Togoland with the northern frontier of the new colony extended into the Upper Volta region as far north as Timbuctu and the banks of the river Niger. From the economic point of view, 'the . . . most important objectives in this plan were the occupation of the mining areas of Katanga, the domination of the rail route between Katanga and the Atlantic Ocean and the securing of the Angolan ports'. Later Solf speculated that the defeat of Britain could lead to the complete unification of Germany's African possessions by the transfer of part of Nigeria.[18] In the minds of both Bethmann Hollweg and Solf the concept of *Mittelafrika* was complementary to the concept of *Mitteleuropa*. They 'advocated a large Central African colony (*Mittelafrika*) that . . . would supplement Central Europe as a reserve area and market for industrial Germany'. These ideas received a wide measure of support within and without government and formed the basis of even more ambitious schemes that were developed as the war progressed, particularly after Bethmann Hollweg fell from power in 1917 when the economic imperialist thinking that had prevailed until then was replaced by the excessive and almost undiscriminating *annexationist* views of men such as Heinrich Class of the Pan–German League.[19]

The creation of *Mittelafrika* was always contingent upon German victory in Europe and Germany's defeat in 1918 meant not only the end of the colonial dream, but also the loss of those colonial territories she had possessed in 1914. By the end of the war they had all been subjugated by the allies with the exception of German East Africa, where Paul von Lettow-Vorbeck and the remnants of his army did not surrender until after the armistice.[20] In most of Africa, however, the collapse of German resistance was rapid. In Togoland the German forces capitulated almost immediately; following the Afrikaner revolt led by Colonel Maritz, South-West Africa was in the possession of Union forces by July 1915; and the Cameroons were in the hands of British and French forces by February 1916.[21] Nevertheless, despite the deployment of some 300 000 men, the British were unable to inflict a decisive defeat upon the troops under Lettow-Vorbeck.[22] Although, it is true, German East Africa had been cleared of Germans by the end of 1917, Lettow-Vorbeck was able to continue the struggle against the British by retreating into Mozambique; at the time of the armistice he was conducting an invasion of Northern Rhodesia. In his aim of pinning down as many allied troops as possible, through the East African 'side-show', he was brilliantly successful and his achievements were widely respected.[23]

But, however heroic the defence of the German colonies had been, they were all in the hands of the allies at the conclusion of hostilities in Europe and there was a determination in the allied camp to maintain possession of them.[24] In Britain ardent imperialists such as Curzon, Milner and Leo Amery had looked upon the war as a means of furthering and securing the advance of British imperialism besides the containment of Germany in Europe.[25] On the other hand, there was a considerable complication for imperialists in Britain in that there was strong dissent on the left of British politics from the imperialist view. To a generation so near to the African scramble, it was axiomatic that colonial rivalry over economic opportunities was a cause of war.[26] Men such as G. Lowes Dickinson, Norman Angell, H. N. Brailsford, J. A. Hobson and H. G. Wells argued that imperialism had been an important element in bringing about the outbreak of war.[27] At first the argument in favour of internationalising colonial areas had as its central feature the belief that all undeveloped regions of the world should be available on equal terms to all nations desiring access to their 'markets, resources and investment facilities'. In due course 'concern for the protection of colonial natives developed into an integral part of the argument' and so 'the doctrine of tutelage or trusteeship became the pivot of "progressive" thinking on the colonial question'.[28] The notion of trusteeship had its greatest impact on the Labour movement in Britain and once the concept was established it was the British Labour movement that became the major driving force behind the principle.[29]

Although these notions might have been odious and unacceptable to imperialists, they had to be taken into account by the British government. With the entry of the United States into the war the British radicals at last acquired a formidable means of impressing their opinions on the political leadership in Britain.[30] President Woodrow Wilson shared their beliefs. He too thought that foreign policy should be subjected to public control; that the war was not a disaster for which one party alone could be entirely culpable; and that, at the end of it, there should be no 'exemplary triumph and punishment'.[31] Moreover, he was an opponent of imperialism: every nation, he believed, had a prescriptive right to self-government. Point Five of President Wilson's Fourteen Points of 8 January 1918 called for

A free, open-minded and absolutely impartial adjustment of all colonial claims, based upon a strict observance of the principle that in determining all such questions of sovereignty the interests of the populations concerned must have equal weight with the equitable claims of the government whose title is to be determined.

It is, of course, quite reasonable to argue that this statement is not anti-colonial and that at this time Wilson was merely concerned with securing a fair balance of the colonial interests of the European powers in which Germany could 'expect a "just" consideration of her claims'.[32] Furthermore, it is even possible to claim that this statement did not rule out and even 'implied annexation'.[33] However, in the circumstances of the time and in the context of Wilson's known attitudes, the British did not interpret it in this way.

The influence of Wilson, the growing impact of the Union for Democratic control, the British Labour movement and the effect on British opinion of the Bolshevik *Decree on Peace* and the revelation of the secret treaties all conspired therefore to force Lloyd George into a moderate statement of British war aims on 5 January 1918.[34] On the issue of the post-war colonial settlement he declared:

With regard to the German colonies . . . they are held at the disposal of a Conference whose decision must have primary regard to the wishes and interests of the native inhabitants of such colonies. None of these territories are inhabited by Europeans. The governing consideration, therefore, in all these cases must be that the inhabitants should be placed under the control of an administration acceptable to themselves, one of whose main purposes will be to prevent their exploitation for the benefit of European capitalists or Governments. The natives live in their various tribal organisations under chiefs and councils who are competent to consult and speak for their tribes and members and thus to represent their wishes and interests in regard to their disposal.[35]

The British government had, thus, by the beginning of 1918, publicly declined a straightforward annexationist colonial settlement and had admitted the principle of self-determination.

Nevertheless, the British government was determined not to allow acceptance of the principle of self-determination to interfere with its imperial aims.[36] The governments of the Dominions were instructed to produce evidence of the desire of indigenous populations of conquered colonial territory to live under British rule; as a result the notorious Blue Books were published in 1918, which purported to demonstrate the brutality of German colonial rule and the reluctance of the colonial peoples in question to submit to the continuation of the former regime.[37] Furthermore, during 1918 a scheme was evolved, which, it was hoped, would make British colonial war aims acceptable to American opinion. In July Smuts produced a memorandum in which he put forward the idea of a *Development Board* for Africa, established under international convention: the area under the board's authority would be subjected to the principles of demilitarisation and free trade. A scheme of this type, Smuts thought, would commend itself to President Wilson, and furthermore, reassure Britain against a possible German re-entry into Africa.[38]

The broad outlines of the colonial settlement had, therefore, been established by the governments of Britain and the Dominions when the war ended and the British and French governments had also agreed between themselves the division of Togoland and the Cameroons.[39] Germany was not going to be reinstated as a colonial power under any circumstances; the Dominions were going to retain their conquests (Lloyd George informed Colonel House on 29 October 1918 that unless they did Britain would be confronted with revolution in the empire);[40] an international supervisory system was to protect Britain from the charge of imperialist annexation; and the whole settlement would be justified and accomplished on the basis of self-determination. During December 1918 the Imperial War Cabinet more precisely defined the envisaged form of international supervision. Each colony would be administered by 'a single Power', which would govern in accordance with principles and rules drawn up by the putative League of Nations. The captured territories would thus be governed in a 'mandatory capacity', as

opposed to outright possession, and there would be no international administration of any kind.[41] This, however, was not to
apply to South-West Africa or the Pacific Islands.[42] Hughes, the
Australian Prime Minister, was doggedly hostile to any form of
international interference.[43]

The mandates system as outlined by the Imperial War Cabinet at
the end of 1918 was essentially that adopted by the Paris peace
conference and later the League of Nations. Under it the governments of Britain and the Dominions achieved virtually all their
imperial war aims at the expense of conceding a minimal amount of
international supervision of their administration of captured colonial territories. The Dominions were ultimately compelled to place
their conquests under mandate at the insistence of President
Wilson,[44] but even so this was understood to mean virtual
annexation.[45] It is therefore difficult to disagree with the assessment
of the mandates system made by Robert Lansing, American
secretary of state until 1920, in his memoirs, where he wrote:

> It seemed obvious from the very first that the Powers which under
> the old practice would have obtained sovereignty over certain
> conquered territories would not be denied mandates over these
> territories. The League might reserve in the mandates a right of
> supervision of administration and even of revocation of authority,
> but that would be minimal and of little if any, real value, provided
> that the mandatory was one of the Great Powers, as undoubtedly
> it would be.[46]

The former German colonies were split into two categories of
mandate, being designated as class 'B' and class 'C' mandates (the
former Arabian provinces of the Ottoman empire being classified as
'A' mandates). In accordance with Article twenty-two of the League
covenant, 'C' mandates could be 'administered under the laws of
the Mandatory as integral portions of its territory', ostensibly on the
grounds of 'sparseness of population', 'small size', or 'geographical
contiguity to the territory of the Mandatory'.[47]

Although the division of Germany's former colonial possessions
amongst the allies had for all practical purposes been determined
long in advance of the opening of the Paris peace conference, no
formal decision was made until 7 May 1919 when the council of four
decided that Britain should hold a 'B' mandate for German East
Africa; that 'C' mandates should be held by the Union of South

Africa for South-West Africa, by New Zealand for Samoa, by Australia for all other German possessions in the Pacific south of the equator and by Japan for all German possessions in the Pacific north of the equator; and that Britain and France should jointly make a recommendation to the League of Nations regarding the future of Togoland and the Cameroons, which were both eventually partitioned between the two countries as 'B' mandates. It was not stated, but presumably understood, that all mandates were subject to ratification by the League.[48]

The views of the German government were not sought concerning the colonial settlement prior to the presentation of the draft terms of peace to the German delegation on 7 May. They contained the following articles:

Article 119: Germany renounces in favour of the Principal Allied and Associated Powers all her rights and titles over her overseas possessions.

Article 120: All movable and immovable property in such territories belonging to the German Empire or to any German State shall pass to the Government exercising authority over such territories.

Article 122: The Government exercising authority over such territories may make such provisions as it thinks fit with reference to the repatriation from them of German nationals and to the conditions upon which German subjects of European origin shall, or shall not, be allowed to reside, hold property, trade or exercise a profession in them.

Germany was, therefore, to be unequivocally stripped of her colonies and her material possessions in them were to be confiscated. Neither the German state nor any of its nationals were to have any legal standing in them whatsoever. Given the substantial degree of publicity that the colonial question had received in Germany during the course of the war, along with the widespread belief at the time that colonies were essential to economic well-being and great power status, these terms were bound to be something of a shock. Besides which, until the end of the war, the German government had been pursuing over a long period a policy which was ultimately designed to turn Germany into a 'world power', with perhaps the ultimate object of world domination, which would have involved the acquisition of further colonies.[49] Count Bernstorff, the

German ambassador at Washington, all but acknowledged this on 31 January 1917 when he informed Secretary of State Lansing of Germany's renewed submarine campaign and preferred peace terms. Amongst them was the 'restitution of Colonies in form of an agreement which would give Germany colonies adequate to her population and economic interest'.[50]

It is with the communication of the draft terms of peace to the German delegation that the colonial question, as it affected Germany's relations with Britain in the inter-war years, might be said to have begun. As early as 1918 the colonial secretary, Solf, had warned that Britain was preparing to exclude Germany from the task, that should be shared by all the civilised powers, of developing the peoples and resources of backward lands, for the British press was comparing the German colonial record with that of Leopold's Congo. There was already too much colonial territory in the possession of France, Britain and Portugal, he argued, and even if the principle of the *open door* was accepted universally this would not guarantee the supply of raw materials required by Germany. There would, Solf thought, be very little prospect of peace in the future unless the forthcoming peace settlement embraced a more equitable redistribution of colonial territory.[51] Within Germany there was general approval for the idea that Germany should retain her colonies after the war among all political parties, with the exception of the Independent Socialists, and even for the view that a colonial redistribution should leave Germany with a substantial and consolidated tract of African territory.[52]

It was, however, clear to the foreign minister, Brockdorff-Rantzau, that by February 1919 such aspirations were under the gravest threat. In an interview with the Berlin press he claimed that the allies were organising the division of Germany's colonies amongst themselves after having conquered them in violation of international treaties.[53] Germany, he declared, would not endorse any settlement made without her agreement and in contravention of the fifth of Wilson's Fourteen Points. There should, he suggested, be a redistribution of colonies and *Mittelafrika* should be internationalised. Individual powers should continue to undertake the responsibility of administering the territories allotted them, but the region as a whole should come under the supervision of the League of Nations. Only in this way would the best interests of the native inhabitants be served.[54]

The colonial terms of 7 May thus confirmed the worst fears of the

Germans. The German response was one of the utmost dissatisfaction. The responsibility of the League of Nations regarding colonies, it was felt in Germany, should be total and not merely confined to the colonial conquests of the war. All colonies should be subject to international regulations issued by the League, which would cover the protection of indigenous peoples against abuses such as 'slavery, alcohol, arms and munitions traffic, epidemics, compulsory labour and forcible expropriation'; would promote 'the health, education and well-being of the natives'; and would secure the neutralisation and demilitarisation of colonial territories. Freedom of economic and religious activity in all colonies should be permitted to all citizens of the League's member states.[55]

In its observations on the peace terms the German delegation to the peace conference announced the readiness of Germany 'to subject all her colonies to administration by the community of the League of Nations if she is recognised as its mandatory' and then went on to rehearse many of the arguments that were to become familiar over the next 20 years regarding the desirability of continued German colonial activity. Article 119 was 'irreconcilable' with Wilson's Fifth Point, for there had not been an 'open, frank and absolutely impartial solution of all colonial claims'; because of 'the unfavourable rate of exchange' Germany needed the facility of being able to acquire raw materials from territory under her control; Germany required an 'outlet for exports for her industry' and 'a field of activity for her commerce'; and Germany needed an area for the settlement of her surplus population. Moreover Germany as a civilised nation had a moral claim to continue her scientific and development work in Africa, which was not vitiated by the inevitable errors in colonial administration in the past. The demand that all property of the German state in the colonies be surrendered without compensation and without the assumption of Germany's debts in the colonies was 'unacceptable'. It defied 'all principles of international and public law' that the private property of German nationals in the colonies be surrendered 'to the arbitrary control of the Mandatory States'.[56]

Before the allies replied to the German observations, the colonial terms were not really discussed at all in the light of the German objections and no alterations were made in the allied proposals concerning the colonial settlement. On the contrary, the reply of the allied and associated governments to the German observations contained a savage rebuke. They were satisfied that the indigenous peoples of Germany's former colonies did not want to return to German rule. The essence of the reply was contained in the following words:

> Germany's dereliction in the sphere of colonial civilisation has been revealed too completely to admit of the Allied and Associated Powers consenting to make a second experiment and of their assuming the responsibility of again abandoning thirteen or fourteen millions of natives to a fate from which the war has delivered them.

It was also pointed out that the allied and associated governments wished to secure themselves and the world by denying suitable bases to a 'military imperialism' that had pursued 'a policy of interference and intimidation against the other Powers'.[57] Eventually a German government was formed that agreed reluctantly to sign the Treaty of Versailles which contained some minor amendments to the original terms, but which also incorporated the colonial settlement unaltered, amongst the other unpalatable conditions.[58]

To suggest, as one historian has done, that colonialism or imperialism were never very popular in Germany, or that colonies did not feature as a priority in governmental or party thinking in Germany, is to belittle the significance of the colonial question in German politics and German foreign policy.[59] It is certainly true that during the 1920s matters such as reparations, the military occupation of the Rhineland and territorial questions more cognate with Germany's historic territories were paramount in foreign policy considerations and were correspondingly more frequently discussed, but these were issues that touched the average German most directly, both in a material and psychological sense. Had the colonies, however, been the only territorial loss sustained by Germany, they would doubtless have received a higher priority. Subsidiary the colonial question might have been; unimportant it was not, being, as it was, intimately bound up with the problem of Germany's post-war psychology and the trauma of Versailles. It remained a grievance that demanded redress and, for a matter of 'unimportance', remarkably live throughout the inter-war period. Even Hitler, supposedly the most indifferent of Germany's politicians towards the colonial question, has been shown recently, if one accepts the thesis of the essential continuity of German foreign policy under him, to have included colonies in his ultimate world political goal.[60]

This is not to deny that colonial enthusiasm as such was a predominant preserve of the upper classes and those with personal and material interests in the former colonies,[61] or that the colonial enthusiasts were disappointed by the general response of the German government and opinion in Germany to their case.[62] But, at the same time, it would not be to go too far to suggest that that case had never been more vociferously and expertly presented, or more widely supported. The American student of German colonialism, Mary Townsend, was obviously impressed. In her opinion the Treaty of Versailles had given a real impetus to German colonialism. It had stimulated 'an effort . . . never perhaps . . . quite so intense in that nation'. Germany abounded with colonial literature and propaganda 'telling the Germans more about their former colonies than they ever knew when those lands were German soil'.[63] Activities on such a scale had to enjoy a wide measure of at least passive support.

After 1918 a number of organisations were formed in Germany whose common object was the revision of the Versailles colonial settlement. In 1920 an extraordinary meeting of the *Deutsche Kolonialgesellschaft* (DKG), founded in 1887, decided to continue its existence and resolved that its aim in the future should be 'to maintain the German character of the former German colonies and to strive to regain them'.[64] By 1926 the DKG had some 30 000 members and by 1924 it was powerful enough to appeal to the general public by organising a colonial congress to commemorate the fortieth anniversary of the founding of Germany's colonial empire. Its leader throughout the 1920s was Theodor Seitz, who was succeeded by Heinrich Schnee, the former governor of German East Africa, until 1936 when the DKG was absorbed into a new organisation under the aegis of the NSDAP. Other organisations were Paul Leutwein's *Kolonialer Volksbund*; the *Bund für Koloniale Erneuerung*; the *Deutsche Kolonialverein*, which affiliated to the DKG in 1933; and the *Kolonialkriegerdank*. These societies and groups were in turn associated with the *Koloniale Reichsarbeitsgemeinschaft* (KORAG), an umbrella organisation that co-ordinated their various activities. KORAG also included among its membership firms with shipping and overseas interests and the colonial sections of agricultural and economic societies such as that of the *Deutsche Landwirtschaftgesellshaft*. These business connections were important because of the funds they supplied.[65]

Within the Reichstag the colonialists formed an effective interparty group which pressed the colonial question whenever an opportunity occurred. In 1925 the *Interfraktionelle Koloniale Vereinigung* was formed under the leadership of Heinrich Schnee, who represented the German People's Party (DVP). The DVP, which tended to represent finance, industry and the upper middle classes, was the most persistent and concerned advocate of colonial revision. Less active in the colonial field were the nationalists (DNVP), who by and large represented the landed interest, but were willing to lend their support to any 'national cause'. The Democratic Party (DDP) was split on the colonial question: some of its members opposed colonies and colonialism *per se*, but it also included among its members important figures from the world of banking such as Hjalmar Schacht, the principal advocate of German colonialism on economic grounds, and the former colonial secretary, Bernhard Dernburg. The attitude of the Socialists (SPD) was somewhat equivocal. A majority of the party, whose spokesman was Rudolf Breitscheid, felt that there were more important matters for Germany's foreign policy, but it was equally held that Germany should receive equal treatment in everything and this included colonies. The trade unions, however, were especially noted for their support of the colonial claim, and throughout the Weimar period the NSDAP added its voice to the demand for colonial revision. Only the Centre and the Bavarian People's Party (BVP) were indifferent, while the Communists remained ideologically opposed.[66]

That the German government itself was not going to allow the League or the mandatories to do as they wished in the former German colonies without protest was made clear in November 1920. A memorandum addressed to the secretary-general of the League and the governments of League members contested the validity of the Hymans report on mandates which had been approved by the League Council the previous August.[67] The Hymans report had stated that the responsibility for the allocation of the mandates rested with the principal allied and associated powers and that, owing to the impracticability of negotiating the conditions of the mandates with all members of the League, the determination of these conditions should be undertaken by the principal allied and associated powers in the first instance. The German memorandum disagreed, arguing that League control, which should be real, would be reduced to a formality. Some sympathy for this view was shown in the British Foreign Office. Mr S. P. Waterlow minuted that it would be hard to deny the German contentions:

The only answer [he wrote] is that it was only on such conditions that it was possible to introduce the mandate system at all, and that something is gained by even so attenuated a form of League of Nations control that cynics may regard as a sham. Whether that is a good answer is another question.

Sir Eyre Crowe, the permanent under-secretary, remarked: 'Fortunately, we are not called upon to reply.'[68]

But however much Foreign Office officials might sympathise with the German point of view the attitude of the British government towards the responsibility of the League regarding mandates was one that was radically opposed to it and intransigently held. It was perhaps best defined by Balfour in an address to the League on 17 May 1922, in which he said:

Mandates are not the creation of the League, and they cannot in substance be altered by the League. The League's duties are confined to seeing that the specific and detailed terms of the Mandates are in accordance with the decisions taken by the Allied and Associated Powers. In carrying out these mandates the Mandatory Powers shall be under the supervision – not the control – of the League. A Mandate is a self-imposed limitation by the conquerors on sovereignty which they exercise over the conquered territory. In the general interest of mankind the Allied and Associated Powers have imposed this limitation on themselves and have asked the League to assist them in seeing that this policy is carried out.[69]

Implicit in the British interpretation of the mandates system was a determination not to surrender control of mandated territory now that it had been acquired. The British empire 'had reached its greatest territorial extent, and the peak of its influence on world politics'.[70] Throughout the 1920s belief in and commitment to the imperial mission remained undiminished.

Although German colonialism in the post-war years did not find a very encouraging response in Britain, there were, however, men of influence who were prepared to support its claims if only in a negative sense and who dissented from the interpretation of the mandates system supported by the government. In the House of Commons men such as Kenworthy, Wedgwood Benn and Bottomley found it deplorable that Germany had not received a mandate and cast doubt on the credibility of the mandates system.[71] Furthermore, as early as February 1919 J. L. Garvin, the editor of the *Observer*, was writing that the war had been about raw materials and food supplies. He thought that the whole of central Africa and the Middle East should be subjected to the 'principle of the open door', the suzerainty of the League should extend over all the territories and the League itself should be charged with the function of appointing mandatories.[72] Two years later, Norman Angell, the journalist and politician, condemned the hypocrisy of the attitude of the allies. They had claimed to be fighting to abolish the moral justification of might, but now they asserted that their 'power' gave them 'access to the wealth of the world' from which others were to be excluded. Germany should, he thought, be invited to participate in a system of international colonial government. He argued: 'By developing the mandate system into something really international we could then give Germany a large share in administration.'[73]

The most enthusiastic and persistent advocate of German colonialism in Britain, however, was the distinguished scholar of German history, W. H. Dawson.[74] The peace settlement, he thought, had been 'ill-considered and shortsighted', particularly in its colonial aspects, and had maintained in existence 'the vicious principle of violent annexation'. Nevertheless, he considered that South-West Africa should remain in the possession of the Union government. This situation could, on the other hand, be regularised morally if the Union government elected to buy the territory from Germany, and he urged upon Smuts the virtues of this course of action which would 'set the whole world an example'.[75] From an early stage after the war Dawson was in close touch with leading figures in Germany's political, economic and social life, and he became their principal spokesman in Britain for the cause of the revision of the colonial aspects of Versailles.[76] In August 1920 he discussed revision of the peace settlement with Friedrich Sthamer, the German ambassador at London. He suggested that 'the impracticality of the treaty must be shown by experience' and that the colonial question should be kept open. Germany ought to press for the mandate for East Africa, but should simultaneously abandon the rest of her former colonies. Sthamer endorsed these sentiments.[77] Such aspirations, however, were not practical at the beginning of the 1920s.

But during the course of the decade that succeeded the peace settlement the colonial question did begin to figure quite significantly in the diplomatic exchanges that accompanied the process of treaty revision in the period that Gustav Stresemann acted as Germany's foreign minister. The issue was particularly in the air at the time of the Locarno negotiations, Germany's entry into the League and the negotiations regarding the Young Plan. Moreover, it also became the subject of unofficial Anglo–German contacts involving the Von der Ropp brothers and British politicians of widely diverging views such as Major A. G. Church of the Labour Party and the Conservative, Sir Henry Page Croft. The response, however, of the notably empire-minded Conservative government of Stanley Baldwin from 1924 to 1929, containing as it did the imperial enthusiast Leo Amery as both Colonial Secretary and Secretary of State for the Dominions,[78] was predictably and emphatically negative to all German entreaties concerning the colonial question.[79] The attitude of the French government was similarly uncompromising. In Paris it was felt that Germany's entry into the League would be especially menacing for those powers that acted as mandatories and an intense 'offensive' by the German government on the colonial question was anticipated. A Quai d'Orsay memorandum of October 1926 argued that it was necessary 'to organize the defensive without delay'.[80] By the time that Hitler came to power the only successes that the German government could point to in the colonial field were the inclusion of a German national on the permanent mandates commission of the League of Nations and the frustration of British plans for the 'closer union' of the east African territories under their control, namely, Kenya, Uganda and the Tanganyika mandate.[81]

The disappointments experienced by the Germans in the colonial question did not dampen the ardour of the colonial party in Germany. Stresemann clearly believed that the acquisition of colonial possessions by Germany would be popularly received. Asked in 1928 by the British ambassador at Berlin, Sir Ronald Lindsay, why there should be such a clamour in Germany and Italy for colonies when it could not be justified 'by mere matters of trade, or necessarily by the needs of emigration' and when 'past experience' had shown 'clearly that colonies were generally only a burden on public finance', the German foreign minister replied:

the reasons were mainly psychological. The more highly developed any civilization became, the stronger would be the desire in considerable classes to escape from it. If in the stormy periods of the past few years Germany had possessed some colony, much trouble would have been saved to everyone because all the hotheads would have emigrated to it. But there was more than that. Since he himself had been to school, the whole basis of education had been changed. He himself and all his contemporaries had been brought up in the classical tradition, on thoughts of ancient Greece and Rome. To-day the basis of education was modern thought, scientific invention, the broad horizon of the aeroplane. The youth of to-day was seeking always a wider outlook . . . The result was a general desire to get outside the limits of society as defined by the conceptions of the home state. If by chance Germany were to-morrow to gain possession of a colony, by the day after to-morrow it would be over-populated with Germans. He himself, he said, had in his public speeches made only very few references to Colonies, but they had always been received with enthusiastic applause, especially where his audience was mainly composed of young people.[82]

Easy as it was, however, to refute the premises on which Stresemann based his arguments, the fact was that the colonial question refused to disappear as an issue.[83] From 1929 onwards the revision of the colonial settlement of 1919 was included in all British estimates of German foreign policy aims. Moreover, there was a discernible softening in the posture of British officials towards Germany's colonial demands and on the eve of Hitler's assumption of power the transfer to Germany of Liberia as a mandate was being actively considered.[84]

2
British and German Attitudes in 1933

The colonial question in Anglo–German relations was the point at which Britain's imperial and European interests intersected. As such, the perceptible moderation that had crept into the attitude of British officials by the end of the 1920s towards German colonial claims illustrates an increasing tendency in British governmental circles towards involvement in Europe and a corresponding steady decline in commitment to empire.[1] This more flexible posture regarding German colonialism is thus an indicator of the general problem that faced the formulators of British foreign policy at the beginning of the 1930s. The political scene in Europe, and more particularly in Germany, had not stabilised and showed no signs of doing so. Was Britain, therefore, to involve herself further in Europe, or was she to leave Europe to her own devices?

The alternatives were clearly outlined by the permanent under-secretary at the Foreign Office, Sir Robert Vansittart, in two Cabinet papers. He wrote:

> For us European politics are mostly other people's feuds and grievances. We have espoused some foreign causes, but a point has come where we can go no further than 'according to plan' in political bigamy. We have been taken for granted and we are not granted. Beyond a certain point, the quarrels of Europe are not our quarrels, and the point may now be reached when, failing agreement on our contribution, we must say so.[2]

There was, nevertheless, another side to the European problem. If Britain counted the achievement of stability on the continent as more important than the benefits of isolation and imperial commitment, the key to the pacification of Europe lay very much in her hands. And if Britain was to take upon herself the leadership of Europe, she would have to make a 'practical contribution'.

21

Here I think [Vansittart stated], Great Britain can have a concrete policy. It has long been in my mind that eventually nothing short of some form of treaty revision will enable Europe to settle down – by consent. The proposition is unpalatable to me as to anyone else, but I think one must have the courage of one's own previous conviction.[3]

Ultimately the British government found itself compelled by events and by conviction to play a dominant role in the affairs of Europe.

In this process the reaction of the British government to German colonial demands is significant. Whereas during the 1920s the issue was treated by British ministers as virtually 'not discussable', this intransigence of attitude gave way to a willingness to admit that the resolution of the central issue in international relations in the inter-war period, namely the role that Germany should play in Europe, might require a colonial dimension. Thus, the peace and security of Europe, and hence of the world, might be worth the price of the restoration of colonies to Germany. This, naturally, would always be more painlessly accomplished at somebody else's expense and in June 1934 Sir John Simon, the Foreign Secretary, who thought that a 'great claim for the restoration of their colonies' was imminent from the Germans, raised again with Lord Cecil the possibility of transferring Liberia to Germany.[4] The important point, however, is the fact that Germany's assumed colonial demands were very much alive in the minds of British ministers as an issue in contemporary international politics and this ultimately led the British government to consider transferring to Germany territories under direct British control. In retrospect this can be seen as symptomatic of Britain's imperial decline, but it would be wrong to suggest that this was consciously perceived at the time. Rather, the fact that the British government from the mid-1930s onwards sought persistently to bring about a *general settlement* in Europe[5] demonstrates the growing conviction in Britain that active involvement in the affairs of Europe was the precondition of the protection of British world and imperial interests. It was precisely on these grounds that one Foreign Office official defended the avoidance of war represented in the Munich agreement: 'If we lose, the whole Empire goes, if Germany loses, she can recover.'[6] Within the context of this *general settlement* a colonial deal with Germany was always a possibility.

Yet it would be misleading to imply that there was any change in the basic aim of British foreign policy during the inter-war years.

The fundamental aspiration of British policy – the organisation and maintenance of world peace – remained constant throughout the 1920s and 1930s and essential to any global regime of peace was a settled Europe free from tension and strife. Moreover, the means of attaining that end – revision of the peace settlement as and when necessary – remained unchanged. As one French writer commented in 1922, Britain was 'revisionist from the moment the Treaty of Versailles was signed'.[7] What happened after 1930 was that the British government increasingly envisaged the necessity of revision on an hitherto unprecedented scale, deemed that an active role on its part was essential to this process and perceived that the time for enacting these revisions was short. In doing this, the British government was not merely reacting to events in Europe, but also acting on the advice of those in Britain who had condemned the deficiencies of the Treaty of Versailles and their impact on European stability from the beginning.

British unease about Versailles surfaced prior to its signature. Sir John Maynard Keynes, who attended the Paris peace conference as one of the representatives of the British Treasury, resigned his position over the terms of the draft treaty. For Keynes the draft treaty contained 'much that' was 'unjust and much more that' was 'inexpedient': its imposition would be 'disastrous in the extreme'. He contemplated a 'morass of destruction', with Europe disrupted economically and depopulated 'by millions of persons'.[8] Although he castigated Lloyd George for this, the British Prime Minister's position concerning the peace settlement was not that far removed from his own. In his now famous *Fontainebleau Memorandum* he warned that Germany could turn Bolshevik and much worse if she was treated unfairly and he urged moderation in the peace terms such as would 'commend itself to all reasonable opinion as a fair settlement of the European problem'.[9]

Lloyd George was unsuccessful in his plea.[10] The Treaty of Versailles was ultimately imposed upon Germany without discussion and virtually unaltered from its draft form. This not only led to an outburst of indignation in Germany, but also provoked feelings of dissatisfaction in Britain, where 'the English sense of fair play . . . led to the fairly speedy abandonment of the more melodramatic modes of vindictiveness'.[11] Such a reversal was well in train before the signature of the peace treaty. In April 1919 H. N. Brailsford was in Germany for three weeks where he discovered a mood of penitence that was not reciprocated in the allied camp by a more tolerant attitude towards Germany. With the allied blockade still in force and a strong desire on the part of the victors to make the German authorities confess to war guilt, he considered that the infant Weimar Republic was not being helped. He believed that those who signed the treaty would be stigmatised as traitors; consequently, 'the [German] government, discredited as well as disarmed, would be incapable of coping with *revanchiste* militarism or revolutionary strikes'.[12] Brailsford gave vent to his gloomy prognostications at greater length in his *After the Peace*, published in 1920.[13]

Following the conclusion of peace with Germany, a reaction set in in Britain in academic and journalistic circles that began to doubt atrocity stories, the theory of German war guilt and to question the whole climate of anti-Germanism. A good example of this process is the historian W. H. Dawson, not least because he was the foremost British advocate of the return of Germany to colonial activity. Dawson appears to have been genuinely convinced that Germany was mainly responsible for the outbreak of the First World War and that the system of dictatorship had been the source of her troubles. Consequently he believed that the best safeguard for the future peace would be the introduction of true parliamentary government and the subordination of the military to parliamentary control in Germany. In his view: 'let the German nation enter at last into full possession of its long-withheld political rights, and an incubus will be removed from Europe and thus from the whole world'.[14] Nevertheless, this did not mean that those who had led Germany into war should go uncensured. He argued:

> It is not less important that when the time for peace negotiations comes . . . the Powers shall resolutely refuse to treat with the band of military criminals, or any of them, who made this war, and who already have flung at Europe in advance the deliberate challenge that they would represent at the council-board neither the voice of the German nation nor the wishes of the German Parliament, but only the interests of the army. To parley with such men were to accept them at their own insolent valuation.[15]

Dawson, therefore, was a 'fight-to-a-finish man', but he coupled with this an advocacy of 'a real world settlement on great, broad, world principles'.[16]

These lofty goals, Dawson felt, did not find fulfilment in the Treaty of Versailles. It was 'full of pitfalls and occasions of future mischief'. This was not the fault of the British and Americans, whom he praised for their moderation, but rather the result of the fact that it had been necessary to compromise with the French. Britain and America, he suggested, had only agreed to the treaty because they knew 'it to be unworkable' and were biding their time until the French became convinced of this.[17] There was, neverthless, 'one clear ray of light' and this was the League of Nations.[18] In his evaluation of the peace settlement Dawson was nourished and sustained by Lady Wester Wemyss, the wife of Baron Wester Wemyss, First Sea Lord 1917–1919. She regarded it with 'the greatest misgivings' and believed 'that if we made war to end war, we have certainly succeeded in making peace to end peace'.[19]

The rapid revision of the peace settlement that Dawson deman-ded was not realised. This he attributed to the French. In May 1921 he protested to Lloyd George in very strong terms over the handling of reparations, suggesting that a clause could be inserted in the reparation settlement that would 'at least give the Germans hope' and that something could be done about the withdrawal of the occupation forces. Pointing out that the Prime Minister himself had observed during the war that only Britain would be able to help Germany, he predicted that the *entente* with France would not last and that Britain would one day 'be glad of the friendship of the now humiliated and enfeebled German nation'.[20] Following the Genoa conference of 1922, Dawson was more hopeful of the future. A *modus vivendi* between the French and Germans was possible, but it would have to be established on one-sided concessions by France and Britain as Germany had nothing left to concede. He envisaged a 'tri-partite treaty of reconciliation between Britain, France and Germany which would do away altogether with reciprocal pledges' and include concessions to the Germans relating to reparations and territorial, economic and commercial issues. If this was done 'the national sentiment of' Germany 'would at once undergo a peaceful transformation and the outlook for all Europe improve as a consequence as by magic'.[21]

Dawson's views represented, although in many instances in extreme form, the convictions of many members of the policy-making élite in Britain.[22] These convictions, however, as they expressed themselves ultimately in governmental policy, were not solely rooted in altruistic considerations of fair play and sentiment. As a trading nation, Britain's economic recovery during the 1920s and after the depression was closely linked with the economic recovery of the rest of the world and without general peace there could be no general economic recovery. In 1935 the British white paper on defence bluntly stated: 'The first and strongest defence of the peoples, territories, cities, overseas trade and communications of the British Empire is provided by the maintenance of peace'.[23] The importance of a revived Germany to a revived world economy and peace was axiomatic to J. L. Garvin. Writing in 1919 he urged that war indemnities ought to be reasonable, for the imposition of 'an amount huge enough to ruin Germany would defeat its purpose by making life intolerable in that country'.[24] Although Germany had failed to gain a world empire by war, her citizens had to feel that they could 'be associated on equal terms with that economic system of the League which would influence the whole world's work'. To insist that Germany should become an economic outcast as regards her 'industrial dependence on supplies of food and raw materials from territories under other flags' would be 'irreconcilable with the spirit of interests of a permanent peace-system'.[25] Garvin warned:

> The central race in Europe must have normal outlets, or compression must make it a volcanic agency. To suppose that it can be dealt with permanently by mere compression and repression is like proposing to keep Vesuvius quiet for ever by trying to fill up the crater.[26]

Norman Angell harmonised on the same theme. He alleged that Europeans were starving in the midst of plenty because of the deliberate victimisation of Germany and the refusal of the European states to co-operate in putting Europe on her feet again. This situation had reached the limits of absurdity in the fact that Germany was not even allowed to export toys. But Germany was the industrial heart of Europe and if Germany was denied so would be the rest of Europe. The entire continent was 'in the position of an ill-disciplined child that cannot bring itself to swallow the medicine that would relieve its pains'. The moods of the war years had to 'be indulged, whatever the ultimate cost'.[27] The most important and influential subscriber to this line of thought was Keynes. His 'epoch-making book', *The Economic Consequences of the Peace*,[28] was a devastating attack upon the terms of the Treaty of Versailles. In it he pointed out that European economic prosperity was contingent upon German economic prosperity, but concluded that in the Treaty of Versailles little had 'been overlooked which might impoverish Germany now or obstruct her development in future'.[29] His

argument may have been simple,[30] but it was compelling and
provoked a 'revolution in British thought'. Within the educated
section of society in Britain, the peace settlement soon found few
supporters and many opponents.[31]

In the years after 1919 it became the aim of British policy to secure
international co-operation with a view to establishing a peaceful
atmosphere in Europe that would in turn provide the right
conditions for economic activity to resume on a normal basis.[32] This
consequently led the British government into a revisionist posture,
at least as far as the financial and economic aspects of the peace were
concerned.[33] Thus, however much some politicians might regret any
form of British involvement in Europe, some degree of involvement
was inevitable. But the involvement and the revision were limited,
certainly after Locarno when the British government demonstrated
an increasing aversion towards taking initiatives in Europe: Britain
had done what she could and Europe should now sort out her
problems. As one historian has put it: 'The Dawes Plan and Locarno
had been given great publicitly as the panaceas for European ills.
The time seemed therefore to have come to allow these panaceas to
work undisturbed'.[34] The objectives of British policy, however,
could not be attained by detachment. The condition of Europe grew
worse: *faute de mieux* Britain had to involve herself in the affairs of
Europe.

The implications of this involvement were spelled out by two
Foreign Office officials, Orme Sargent and Ashton-Gwatkin, in a
Cabinet paper of November 1931. They pointed out that the security
of Europe could be left to the French and their allies, who would
attempt to achieve it by entrenching 'themselves in their present
position', by maintaining the 'peace settlement intact', and endeavouring 'by economic and military pressure to extort further
guarantees from Germany'. But this would not result in security or
confidence. The most it could do would be to establish momentarily
the paramountcy of France, while, in the long term, the continued
friction and tension in Europe would create more insecurity. There
was, however, the possibility of 'international agreement and
action'. The whole of Europe, and particularly Britain, would have
to make 'further contributions' towards the creation of confidence
and the establishment of security. The authors did not minimise the
risks of British involvement in Europe, but it seemed to them that
Britain was 'already committed' by virtue of geographical and
economic factors.

The underlying theme of this paper, which had been written with the opening of the disarmament conference in 1932 in mind, was that the issue of disarmament could not be approached in isolation. Political questions were now 'inextricably involved with economic and financial questions as well' and the following diagnosis was offered:

> The present world 'confidence crisis' can be analysed as a series of interlocking problems, ranging from the purely financial and monetary problem at the one end to the purely territorial problem created by the Peace Settlements at the other end. The links in the chain fall together more or less in the following order: The *monetary crisis* leads inevitably back to the *economic chaos* in Europe. The economic chaos and all attempts to deal with it, involve in their turn the political questions of *reparations and war debts*. These are linked by the United States with the question of *disarmament*, and the latter, in the eyes of the French Government, depends upon the problem of *security*. The problem of security in its turn raises the question of the *territorial status quo* in Europe . . . which brings us to the *maintenance of revision of the Peace Settlements*. We thus have a whole range of interlocking problems, and, no matter at what link we touch the chain, we cannot find any satisfactory halting place until we have reviewed this whole series of problems.

Thus the British government ought to welcome any broadening of the discussion, for, unless it was prepared 'to embrace the whole complex' of problems, there was the risk of 'failure from the very start'. The aims of British policy were peace and the restoration of confidence and world trade; the aim of French policy was security. The success, however, of the policies of the British and French governments hinged upon the future of Germany – indeed, 'the future of "civilisation" itself depended upon it'. Germany, they warned, was the fulcrum of the European economic machine and unless she had the capital necessary to activate her own economy there could be no improvement. They continued: 'World recovery (the aim of our policy) depends on European recovery: European recovery on German recovery; German recovery on France's consent; France's consent on security (for all time) against attack.'

German policy was thought to be aimed at the total cancellation of reparations, equality of treatment in disarmament, *Anschluss* with Austria, rectification of the eastern frontier, the re-acquisition of colonies (a dormant, but 'not necessarily dead' aspiration), and investment in the German economy. But capital was Germany's most urgent necessity and it was argued that 'her consent to a general settlement should be forthcoming in return for a promise of financial help, on an international basis'. The French problem of security should be confronted boldly by consideration of a system such as had been adumbrated in the Geneva protocol. There would be hazards for Britain in this, but clearly the French policy of coercing Germany could not be pursued with success and the only alternative was an international agreement. Therefore the two officials urged: 'Our aim should be an "all-in" settlement; and it is for an "all-in" settlement that we must prepare during the short time we may still have for preparation.' The minimum required for a satisfactory settlement would be a drastic reduction in reparations, disarmament, guarantees of security and the rectification of frontiers.[35]

The views outlined in this paper received strong support from Vansittart. For him treaty revision was the key to the success of the policy put forward by his subordinates. He believed that 'real disarmament' could only be achieved by 'moral disarmament', which in effect implied treaty revision. It was 'at the root of everything'. He did not share the view of Sargent and Ashton-Gwatkin that the disarmament conference would ultimately involve financial and economic issues, but he did believe that it would be used to set in train events that would lead to the general revision of the peace settlement. In this respect, the obstruction of the French was one of the central difficulties. He thought that it should be impressed upon the French that their military strength and alliances left them a sufficient margin of safety to make concessions. Should France continue to be recalcitrant, the possibility of her isolation ought to be hinted. To encourage future German co-operation France should concur in the abrogation of the naval clauses of Versailles and Franco–German naval equality; in addition, she should agree to the abolition of the military clauses of Versailles and permit German military aircraft and tanks, although on a limited basis. Germany should also be allowed conscription and European armies should eventually be fixed on a population ratio. In essence, it should be urged upon France that a sufficient concession, enabling the German government to justify itself in front of the German people, was in her own interest.[36]

The connection between these ideas and those that had been

advanced by publicists in Britain from 1919 onwards is self-evident. Extremism in Germany was the consequence of her deliberate economic strangulation and the economic depression. It was believed that 'Hitlerism in Germany and Fascist bellicosity in Italy' were 'the symptoms of an economic disease'.[37] Cure the disease and you would eradicate its political manifestations. This was the essence of what was to become known as *economic appeasement*. As Tom Jones, Baldwin's close friend, later observed, the situation would become dangerous if Germany's economic situation became so parlous as to make war a 'preferable alternative'.[38] And thus Eden, drawing upon the experience of the Italo–Ethiopian war, observed that economic weakness could encourage a dictator to embark upon a foreign adventure to divert the attention of a dissatisfied populace from internal policy failure; therefore, he urged, 'we should be wise to do everything in our power to assist Germany's economic recovery, thereby easing the strain upon the German rulers and making the outbreak [of war] less likely'.[39]

But however popular such ideas were in the Foreign Office,[40] and however logical and insistent the policies advocated on them, their immediate impact upon the attitude of the British government was limited. That is not to say that the relationship between the various problems in Europe was obscure to British ministers. Ramsay MacDonald, the Prime Minister, was clear in his mind in September 1932 that if Germany walked out of the disarmament conference the work of the cancellation of reparations at the Lausanne conference would 'be largely undone'.[41] Moreover, he believed that nobody could any longer 'rigidly resist the German claim that the Treaty of Versailles must in some respects be reconsidered'.[42] And he was also aware that qualities of leadership were required from Britain if Europe was to emerge peacefully from the climate that existed by the beginning of the 1930s.[43] The kind of leadership, however, that British foreign policy tended to represent under the guidance of an 'instinctive isolationist'[44] such as Sir John Simon, inclined all too easily to lapse into the category, as Neville Chamberlain observed, of the 'honest-broker'.[45] Thus, while by the time Hitler gained power Britain was *involved* in Europe in a way she had not been during the latter half of the 1920s, the involvement did not at this stage imply the role of forceful leadership and complete acceptance of the grand policies for peace then being encouraged in the Foreign Office.

In any case, the advice emanating from the Foreign Office was not all of a type. At the end of 1931 Sir Walford Selby, Simon's principal private secretary, attempted to emulate Sir Eyre Crowe's celebrated anti-German memorandum of January 1907,[46] when he warned of the dangers of being too solicitous with regard to Germany. He wrote:

> In the last few years, experience has . . . tended to show that the method of approach to the problem of Germany favoured by Sir Eyre Crowe is productive of better results, whether for Germany herself or for the well-being of Europe as a whole, which we must continue to regard as an essential British interest, than the generally sympathetic attitude which is taken up towards every claim Germany may care to put forward.

The policy of combining co-operation with France with willingness to revise the peace settlement and firmness towards Germany pursued by Sir Austen Chamberlain was the correct approach. But Chamberlain's policy had not been popular and since 1929 genuine co-operation between Britian and France had ceased, creating the impression in Paris that Britain was 'seeking a settlement of Europe apart from France'. The breach had been readily exploited by Germany. The mood and intentions of Germany, however, were plainly manifest and there was 'no rhyme or reason' in the public attitude in Britain which was based on a total misconception of Germany and her aims. There was 'behind the facade of weakness and injured pride', that Germany liked to present to the world, 'a strong and calculating nation freed already, by the now expert manoeuvring, from many of the shackles which embarrass her competitors as a result of war'. British public opinion had to be educated out of its antipathy towards France and it was worth examining Britain's relationships with both France and Germany before Britain drifted, 'perhaps inadvertently and carelessly', into intimacy with a state whose policy it had 'been the proud tradition of the people of these islands to oppose and confound for 300 years past'.[47]

Interestingly, the Selby thesis received warm support from Sargent. In the disarmament negotiations Britain would have to co-operate with one power at least. The United States, Sargent believed, was ruled out because of her unreliability and Germany because 'open co-operation' with her would 'take the revolutionary form of concerted attack on the *status quo* of Europe'. This left France. Selby had shown that no progress could be made except when France and Britain worked in harness and he urged that a special effort be made to ensure Anglo–French co-operation. Nevertheless, this did 'not preclude a policy of sympathy with German sufferings and encouragement of her aims, and a more or less platonic advocacy of Treaty revision'.[48] Selby remained sceptical. Following the withdrawal of Germany from the disarmament conference at the end of 1932, he commented that the 'first objective' of German policy was the 'reversal of the Eastern frontier' and that the 'more remote objectives' of German aspirations could not be overlooked once 'that small issue' had 'been disposed of'. He warned that 'the German agitation for overseas expansion which directly touches our position' had to be borne in mind. Finally, he considered that 'the question of "concession" to Germany in the matter of armaments' could not be contemplated without having due regard to its impact on the peace settlement as a whole. The British government should stand by its policy of discouraging the disregard of treaty obligations and refusal to sanction material increases in German armaments.[49]

Although British ministers were conscious of the dangerous and uncertain dimension that Hitler's assumption of power added to the European situation,[50] this did not predict an abrupt and immediate transformation in the style or content of British policy. Under the direction of Simon the strategy of cautious involvement in Europe and cautious concession to Germany was logically and prosaically continued and was 'pragmatically decided on a case-by-case basis'.[51] The aims of Hitler's Germany were anticipated as being much the same as the aims that German governments had traditionally pursued, although it was recognised that they were now being more urgently and vigorously advanced. Nevertheless, the British government was eventually forced to reconsider its approach to the European problem as the international crisis of the 1930s deepened. It was soon apparent that Hitler had brought the totality of the peace settlement into question in an unprecedented manner and British policy had to respond to this fact. Encouraged by the Foreign Office yet again, it became the basic principle of British foreign policy from the end of 1935 onwards to seek a *European* and *general settlement* that would in effect replace the peace settlement of 1919 and bring all European states into satisfactory treaty relations with one another.[52]

This policy was first introduced by Eden at the beginning of 1936: it aimed at 'a return to the normality of the twenties and the creation of conditions in which Hitler could behave like Stresemann'.[53]

Fundamental to the policy was the notion that Nazi belligerence could be defused by offering Germany economic prospects that would lead her to prosperity,[54] a course thought to be attractive because of the suspected imminent collapse of the German economy.[55] It was, therefore, anticipated by Eden that Germany could be induced to agree to a disarmament convention, to return to the League and to renounce all 'further territorial claims in Africa and Europe, in return for the remilitarisation of the Rhineland, colonial satisfaction and 'economic priority along the Danube'.[56] In the subsequent development of this policy Neville Chamberlain played a significant part and he continued it during his premiership.[57] Moreover, in its evolution the consideration of colonial restoration to Germany played a crucially important role.

But there were serious flaws in this strategy by the mid-1930s. It presupposed, firstly, that Hitler would be susceptible to the traditional bargaining and compromise of international affairs.[58] Secondly, it assumed that Nazi extremism was at bottom economically motivated. On both counts the formulators of British foreign policy miscalculated badly. The Nazi party might have been carried into power on a tidal wave of economic discontent, but in essence it was a purely political movement[59] and its political objectives were strikingly different from those of its immediate predecessors. Economic concession could never have deflected it from its course, nor political concessions diverted Hitler from the path he had rigidly prescribed German foreign policy should take under his leadership: the nostrums of the 1920s could no longer apply. That British policy makers did not perceive this becomes clear if their reactions to the German claim for colonies under the Third Reich is examined. They responded to it as a straightforward demand in exactly the same way as they had responded to similiar claims advanced during the period of the Weimar Republic, except that they were now more favourably disposed towards colonial restoration. They were incapable of seeing in Hitler's statements relating to the issue anything other than revisionism pure and simple. Lord Halifax was indeed more right than he knew when he wrote during the Munich crisis 'that we cannot possibly tell . . . what is going on inside the brains of the one man who matters'.[60] Few could, for, despite the abundant evidence readily available at the time of Hitler's bizarre and far-reaching foreign policy goals, they were – perhaps because of their radical and outlandish nature – easily discounted or misunderstood.[61]

There was, however, a little more to it than that. Hitler's obsessive secrecy and deceitfulness concerning his plans and policies served to obfuscate the reality of his aims, even those he had published, to his advantage. A good illustration of this trait is the following exchange between Hitler and Halder, the recently promoted army Chief of Staff, in September 1938. Hitler told Halder that he would only discover his 'thoughts and intentions' when they were issued 'as an order'. To Halder's observation that soldiers generally worked together, Hitler, with a dismissive gesture, rejoined: 'No, things are quite different in politics. You will never learn what I think and those who publicly proclaim to know my thoughts I lie to all the more.'[62]

For many years after the collapse of Germany in 1945 the nature of the foreign policy of the Third Reich thus remained obscure. It was, of course, recognised that Germany under Hitler had fundamental expansionist drives, but these were not seen as being part of any coherent plan or system. The expansion was 'haphazard', the methods Machiavellian. This view, principally associated with Alan Bullock,[63] was modified in 1960 when H. Trevor-Roper published an article in which he suggested that Hitler did have a specific objective in view for Germany's expansion and that the method of achieving it was quite closely defined.[64] According to this interpretation Hitler's foreign policy plans could be described as: 'alliance with England (and Italy) in order to subdue France . . . with the ultimate aim of a subsequent march of conquest to win fresh *Lebensraum* in the East on the ruins of Bolshevik Russia'.[65] Hitler's foreign policy, therefore, was seen as centred on Europe with the creation of a land empire in the east of the continent being the main purpose of National Socialism.[66] It is now generally accepted that the creation of German hegemony in Europe by the subjugation of France and the destruction of the Soviet state was the central purpose of Hitler's foreign policy, but what a group of German scholars during the 1960s and 1970s have established is that this represented only the first stage, albeit the most crucial and important one, of a foreign policy that was intended to result in German domination of the world.[67] As the leading exponent of this line of thought puts it: 'geograpically' National Socialist foreign policy 'was designed to span the globe; ideologically, too, the doctrine of universal anti-Semitism and social Darwinism, fundamental to his programme, were intended to embrace the whole of mankind'.[68]

It was the discovery and publication of *Hitler's Secret Book*,[69] along with the use of other material such as his speeches, which made it possible to see in Hitler's somewhat desultory comments on foreign policy in *Mein Kampf* the emergence of a coherent programme of German expansion that was to be completed in definite stages. Eventually, it became apparent that by 1928, when the *Secret Book* was written, Hitler had gradually arrived at concepts about his 'future foreign policy . . . to which he then single-mindedly adhered until his suicide in the Reich Chancellery'.[70] The essence of these concepts was to be found summarised in one sentence in *Mein Kampf*: 'Germany will either be a world power or there will be no Germany.'[71] After the creation of her empire on the continent of Europe, which would provide Germany 'with a solid and strategic power base', she would then be in a position to consolidate further her position as a world power by the acquisition of colonies in Africa and the establishment of naval bases in the Atlantic region. Hitler expected this stage of his plans to be completed by the time of his death when Germany would have arrived at the position in which she would be a world power alongside the British empire, Japan and the United States. Of these four, Germany and the United States would be the most powerful and it would be the task of the generation that succeeded Hitler to compete with the United States for the domination of the entire world. In this struggle it was anticipated by Hitler that the British would ultimately find it to be in their interest to side with Germany. Should Germany fail in her mission to achieve world dominion, he was emphatic that she would be 'condemned to insignificance in world politics'.[72]

In the years immediately succeeding 1919, there was very little in Hitler's utterances to differentiate his thinking on foreign policy from that of the Wilhelmine conservatives. His single aim was to remove the 'disgrace of Versailles and bring about the resurrection of the mighty empire of the Hohenzollerns'. Moreover, until 1923 Britain, France and the United States appeared to him as the 'absolute enemies' of Germany.[73] But gradually Hitler incorporated into his thinking fresh influences that radicalised his ideas. As late as 1920, for example, his anti-Semitism was limited in scope to Germany where he believed the instinctive anti-Semitism of pogroms should be replaced by a governmental policy of reason that would first remove from the Jews in Germany their civic rights with a view to their ultimate deportation. In 1920, however, he came into contact with the *Thule Gesellschaft* in Munich, composed of white Russian *émigrés*. From these he learnt of the *Protocols of the Elders of*

Zion and a secret plan of Jewish world domination. His anti-Semitism now took on a universal dimension, for the removal of the Jews from Germany could not alone, he perceived, solve the Jewish problem for Germany. Working through the agencies of capitalism, freemasonry, workers movements and Bolshevism, the Jewish scheme for world domination would still continue to threaten Germany. From this time onwards, therefore, he was 'animated' by the 'relentless resolution to strike at the root of the evil and destroy it root and branch'. In this way anti-Semitism became a cardinal point in his foreign policy concepts,[74] together with anti-Bolshevism, for it was 'with the help of the Marxist creed' that 'the Jew' aimed 'to be victorious over the other peoples of the world'.[75]

Similarly, it seems that Hitler's ideas about *Lebensraum* evolved progressively until in the 'involuntary leisure of Landsberg prison' he came to a final conclusion. There the ideas of the Munich geo-politician, Karl Haushofer, were impressed upon him by Rudolf Hess, which enabled him finally to construct a 'doctrinaire' foreign policy programme that replaced his earlier revisionist concepts. In Hitler's mind, the open spaces of Russia now became the main focus of Germany's foreign policy: 'there was the necessary *Lebensraum* to be won, Bolshevism smashed, and Jewry destroyed'.[76] Finally, by 1924 Hitler was no longer convinced that Britain needed to be treated as a perpetual German enemy, observing in the unen-thusiastic British reaction to the occupation of the Ruhr the possibility that Britain could be detached from the enemy front.[77] This was to be of major importance for the practical implications of his future foreign policy.

By the time Hitler came to write *Mein Kampf,* he was thoroughly critical of the foreign policy of the Wilhelmine Reich. Prior to 1914 the German government had sought to solve the problem of the increasing incapacity of German territorial and soil resources to sustain Germany's burgeoning population through industrialis-ation, world trade, sea power and colonies. This represented to Hitler a 'belief . . . that the world could be peacefully opened up to', and perhaps 'conquered for, the German people' by economic means. It was also 'a classic sign of the loss of real state-farming and state-preserving virtues and of all the insight, will power, and active determination which follow from them'.[78] The consequence of this 'lunacy' was 'industrialisation as boundless as it was harmful'. It led inexorably to the 'weakening of the peasant class' and a correspond-ing increase in the size of the urban proletariat until 'the balance was completely upset'. This was fatal, because it was impossible to overrate the value of a 'healthy peasant class' as the basis of national life. The cause of Germany's 'sufferings' lay in the imbalance between the urban and rural populations. With the growth of industrialisation and urbanisation it was inevitable that spiritual decay would set in. Hitler wrote:

> As economic life grew to be the dominant mistress of the state, money became the god whom all had to serve and to whom each man had to bow down. More and more, the gods of heaven were put into the corner as obsolete and outmoded, and in their stead incense was burned to the idol of Mammon.

For Germany, this 'malignant degeneration' occurred at the precise moment when she 'needed the highest heroic attitude'.[79]

These ideas remained with Hitler. In his *Secret Book* he referred to cities as 'abscesses in the national body' in which 'all evil, vice and disease' were united. They were places in which miscegenation was rife, leading to the dilution of racial qualities, and 'purulent infection centers in which the international Jewish racial-maggots thrive and finally effect further destruction'.[80] The virtues of the rural life were again expanded upon in the *Table Talk*. The peasant was 'the solid backbone of the nation', for the uncertainties of making a living from the land taught 'energy, self-confidence and the readiness to make swift decisions', whereas the city dweller had to have everything done for him.[81] Such was Hitler's abhorrence of urban contamination that he prescribed that the soldier-peasant who was to colonise the Crimea should 'not marry a townswoman, but a countrywoman who, as far as possible, will not have begun to live in a town with him'.[82]

The spiritual decay of Germany, attendant upon the policy of commercial expansion under the Wilhelmine Reich, was also accompanied by the gratuitous creation of a dangerous enemy. Hitler believed that it had been the objective of British policy for three centuries to prevent the rise on the continent of Europe of any power that might threaten Britain's world interests and it was in the industrial, commercial and overseas expansion of Germany that Britain perceived the resurgence of exactly such a threat. Thus British politicians began to organise the resistance against Germany.[83] Indeed the 'peaceful economic struggle for the conquest of a place in the sun' could only have continued 'for just as long as

England could count on bringing about the collapse of German competition with purely economic means . . .' Had the Wilhelmine policies been successful, there could be no doubt that war with Britain would have ensued.[84] As it was British statesmen took their chance in the First World War and with the defeat of Germany in 1918, and her following internal political and social collapse, 'the British concern over a threatening Germanic world hegemony found an end'.[85]

There had, on the other hand, been an alternative policy to which the Wilhelmine Reich could have turned as a means of solving the problem of surplus population, which not only would have avoided conflict with Britain, but would also have led to the spiritual regeneration of the German people. This was the acquisition of fresh territory.[86] To Hitler it was a basic premise that 'the bread which a people requires is conditioned by the living-space at its disposal' and that a 'healthy people' would 'always seek to find the satisfaction of its needs in its own soil'. The numerical population of a nation might vary, but it did not follow that the national territory would vary accordingly. An expanding population, therefore, that wished to remain sound had to extend its territorial limits forcibly by war. For Hitler, this was not a moral issue.[87] What was an issue for him was the fact that, in his estimation, if a people did not guarantee for itself a livelihood out of its own territorial resources, it was certain that sooner or later this would result in the 'injury if not annihilation of the people'.[88]

It was equally clear to Hitler that the only area in which Germany could satisfactorily seek the realisation of her territorial needs was in Europe. Unless the new territories lay in close proximity to the mother country, the expansion of the German population would become an emigration.[89] And as to the specific direction in Europe that German territorial expansion should take, there was the clear example of the medieval Teutonic Knights who had been behind the German drive eastwards in that period.[90] Had the Wilhelmine Reich pursued such an expansionist policy, Hitler argued Germany need never have feared the enmity of Britain. It would have meant the renunciation of German industrial, naval and colonial competition with Britain, but in turn it could also have implied an alliance with the British who would have protected Germany's rear while the 'new Germanic march' began.[91] That Britain would have acquiesced in this development was historically self-evident to Hitler, because Britain's relations with Prussia proved that she would not oppose a

European power of superlative military strength provided that the scope of that power's ambitions remained confined to the continent.[92]

In *Mein Kampf* Hitler was adamant about the path that National Socialist foreign policy would take. He stated:

> We National Socialists consciously draw a line beneath the foreign policy tendency of our pre-War period. We take up where we broke off six hundred years ago. We stop the endless German movement to the south and west, and turn our gaze towards the land in the east. At long last we break off the colonial and commercial policy of the pre-War period and shift to the soil policy of the future.

The soil that was to be conquered was to be found in Russia. There the Bolshevik revolution had removed the creative, Germanic element that had ensured Russia's survival as a state and replaced it with 'the Jew'. The Russians were themselves incapable of throwing off the Jewish yoke, but this did not mean that the task Hitler had allotted Germany was impossible. 'The Jew' himself was a 'ferment of decomposition' and could not for any length of time sustain the organisation of a great empire. The Russian empire, therefore, was ripe for dissolution. The German nation had been 'chosen by Fate as witness of a catastrophe which will be the mightiest confirmation of the soundness of the folkish theory'. Hitler continued:

> Our task, the mission of the National Socialist movement, is to bring our own people to such political insight that they will not see their goal for the future in the breath-taking sensation of a new Alexander's conquest, but in the industrious work of the German plough, to which the sword need only give soil.[93]

In the above paragraph may be seen the elements of a policy that had crystallised by the time the *Secret Book* was written. The suggestion here is that once the objective of *Lebensraum* had been achieved, further foreign adventures should cease. In the *Secret Book* Hitler elaborated further and spoke of a period of a hundred years – which has been suggested means 'for some considerable time to come'[94] – as being the period of time which Germany would need to develop her fresh territorial acquisitions. That this pre-supposed a period of peace can be seen in the fact that Hitler believed that 'the

obligation to be a naval power' would recede during this time.[95]
Moreover, in his *Political Testament* he later claimed significantly that
a peace with Britain in 1941 would have been essential to the
fulfilment of his life's work and the mission of National Socialism,
namely 'the destruction of Bolshevism and the simultaneous
securing for the future of our people of the necessary *Lebensraum* in
the east'.[96] Thus it seems indisputable that the dismantling of
Bolshevik Russia and the colonisation of her territory west of the
Urals were the central features of Hitler's foreign policy, and that the
subsequent peaceful development and consolidation of the conquered lands was for him a question of critical importance.[97]

Equally critical for Hitler in the achievement of this end was an
alliance with Britain, or, at least, the benevolent neutrality of the
British. As long as Germany conducted a policy which no longer
contradicted Britain's 'sea and trade interests' he thought this
possible.[98] An alliance, however, with Britain and in conjunction
with Italy would be the most favourable development from the
German standpoint. It would isolate France, which country was to
be first destroyed,[99] and offer Germany a favourable strategic
position.[100] Until well into the Second World War the hope that
Britain would eventually see it as being in her interests to come to an
understanding with Germany never left Hitler. In January 1942 he
informed his listeners:

> One thing may seem improbable, but in my view it's not
> impossible – that England may quit the war. As a matter of fact, if
> to-day every nation were to reckon up its own private balance,
> England would to-day still be best off . . . if there's one nation that
> has nothing to gain from this war, and may lose everything by it,
> that's England.[101]

In the twilight of the bunker he even explained his decision to attack
Russia, and thus engage in the war on two fronts that he had always
sought to avoid, as being motivated by the desire to compel the
British to make peace. The British, led by 'blockheads', had refused
to recognize the leading role of Germany in Europe and there was
the increasing threat of the might of the Americans in the background. Time was working against Germany and it had been
necessary to stake everything on a lightning strike against the
Russians in order to bring the conflict to a speedy conclusion. Only if
it had been proved conclusively to the British that they could not

rely upon a continental ally to resist the march of Germany would they have been forced to make the peace so urgently required by the Third Reich.[102]

Peace with Britain, therefore, was a pivotal element in Hitler's strategy for the conquest of *Lebensraum*, the elimination of the Marxist 'world plague',[103] and the shattering of world Jewry. It is indicative in this connection that all the passages in *Mein Kampf* and the *Secret Book* that deal with the renunciation of overseas and colonial interests do so with the overriding aim in focus of removing any cause for conflict between Germany and Britain. Did this, however, imply a renunciation for all time of extra-European activity on the part of Germany? The answer to this would seem to be in the negative. In the passages relating to *Lebensraum* in *Mein Kampf* there appears the revealing comment that 'the German nation can defend its future only as a world power'.[104] It was not so much the striving after world and sea power in themselves that was absurd, but rather the 'orientation of the German national strength towards this aim, without the most thoroughgoing previous securing of our position in Europe'.[105] As Hitler told Carl Burckhardt on the eve of the attack upon Poland: 'I need the Ukraine, so that no one can starve us out again as in the last war.'[106] Again, in his *Table Talk*, he emphasised that the key to the 'hegemony of the world' lay in 'possession of the Russian space', which would convert Europe into 'an impregnable fortress, safe from all threat of blockade'.[107] Once the German organisation of Europe was complete the time would come to 'look towards Africa'.[108] Furthermore, he speculated on the splendours of Berlin 'as a world capital', comparing them with Babylon and Rome,[109] and one cannot escape the force of the following sentence in *Mein Kampf*: 'A state which in this age of racial poisoning dedicates itself to the care of its best racial elements must some day become lord of the earth.'[110]

The establishment of Germany as a world power inevitably entailed the possibility of a conflict with Britain. Hitler hoped, nevertheless, that this aim could be achieved with Britain's acquiescence[111] and he argued that there were good grounds for believing this to be possible. Although as a result of the First World War Britain had removed the German challenge to her world interests, 'the American threat, with a considerably stronger base', had replaced it.[112] The defeat of Germany had, in fact, been a 'Pyrrhic victory' for Britain.[113] The threat which America posed could not, Hitler surmised, remain purely economic indefinitely, for: 'In proportion as the American people fulfil the tasks of internal colonization, the natural, activist urge that is peculiar to young nations will then turn outward.' When this occurred, he claimed that 'only the state which has understood how to raise the value of its folkdom and to bring it to the most expedient state form for this, through its inner life as well as through its foreign policy, will be able to face up to North America'.[114]

Ultimately, the British would realise that their world interests could only be maintained 'with a strong continental power at their side'[115] and they would forge an alliance with Germany. Hitler envisaged nothing less at the end than a titanic struggle between Europe, led by Germany, and the United States for the entire mastery of the globe.[116] This Germany would win, because during the period of 'friendship' with Britain the German nation would have developed itself 'racially into the most superior people in the history of the world'. In this way, 'world history would have fulfilled its racial purpose and, in culmination, the dynamic process was to fuse into the biologically static equilibrium of Utopia'.[117]

In most respects the parameters of the foreign policies Britain and Germany were to pursue towards one another were set by the time Hitler came to power. Although Hitler was compelled by events to compromise and compress his programme – not least because Britain refused to play the part assigned to her in his world melodrama – it is evident that he attempted to implement the foreign policy plan that he had formulated by 1928 and resorted to tactical expedients from time to time in order to maintain the course that he had precisely outlined. When, for example, his tactic of colonial renunciation in the period 1933 to 1935 seemed no longer capable of securing an alliance or understanding with Britain, he altered his posture to one of colonial claims and threats as a means of bringing Britain to see 'reason' and to enter into the relationship with Germany that he so much desired. Despite, however, the disappointments of his British policy during the 1930s, his confidence and conviction that a friendship with Britain was attainable remained against the clearest evidence to the contrary. Herein, along with his grotesque underestimation of the strength of the Soviet state, lay his essential miscalculation. Had British ministers ever perceived the vast scope of the reality of Hitler's intentions, they would never have been seduced, for his concept of German continental hegemony alone offended 'Britain's interest in the continental balance of power'.[118]

As it was, the symptoms of Hitler's intentions were enough by 1939 to convince the British government that Hitler had to be resisted. What saved the British government from their miscalculation, that even the demands of the Hitler regime could be satisfied by fair treatment and Germany brought into normal relations with the rest of Europe, was the recognition, after the occupation of Bohemia and Moravia in March 1939, that Hitler might be 'seeking European or world domination'.[119] This did not mean that Hitler's programme had finally been unravelled, but rather that Britain had 'reached the crossroads'. While Hitler had been 'incorporating Germans into the Reich' it had been possible to justify his actions, but now that he had started to engulf other nationalities the time had come to stop him.[120] It had come primarily because the British saw in Hitler's actions a German threat to themselves, which Hitler had always sought to avoid.[121]

3

The Colonial Question and the Reaction to Hitler 1933–35

On Hitler's appointment as Chancellor the major preoccupation of the British Cabinet in the field of foreign policy was the future of the disarmament conference, then at a critical stage. Indeed, the desire of the British government to bring the disarmament conference to a successful conclusion was the major element of its policy towards Germany. Hitler's accession to power did not alter this strategy; it merely made it more difficult to pursue. There is, therefore, some substance in the argument that British policy in respect of the disarmament conference during 1933 was as much motivated by the desire that Britain should not be blamed for its breakdown, should that occur, as by the desire for its success *per se*.[1] But the wish that it should end positively was real enough as it was realised that failure 'would have incalculable consequences for Europe and the League'.[2]

The disarmament conference, which opened in February 1932, had in fact almost collapsed by the end of that year and was only saved by the five-power declaration of 11 December that recognised Germany's claim to 'equality of rights in a system which would provide security for all nations'. Nevertheless, it was clear in London that 'a mere theoretical recognition of Germany's equal status' could 'solve nothing'. Where possible states should give up their right to weapons forbidden to Germany and as a last resort Germany should be allowed weapons previously denied her.[3] It proved, however, difficult to translate such recommendations into reality. By 1 March 1933 Sir John Simon felt that the international situation was deteriorating seriously and he told the Cabinet that the disarmament conference 'might break down within the next ten days or a fortnight'.[4] At the end of February he had outlined his anxieties in more detail in a Cabinet paper. He believed that there were a series of undeclared wars going on throughout the world.

Moreover, Europe had 'continued without interruption the tendency, evident three years ago, and now becoming more crystallized, of falling into antagonistic groups'. There had so far been no agreement on any important subject at the disarmament conference; unless there was a change in approach and more vigour in discussion the conference was doomed. If no disarmament convention was produced, Germany would attempt to achieve equality outside one and this meant her rearmament. This would result in the French building up their armaments on a massive scale with a world-wide armaments race as the corollary. Simon observed:

In such an atmosphere, even if peace is nominally preserved, political relations will rapidly deteriorate yet further. The restoration of political confidence, on which all the economic as well as political experts insist, will be postponed to the Greek Kalends. In such an atmosphere the World Economic Conference would have a poor chance of producing any useful result. In such an atmosphere what trade barriers will come down, what Governments will extend the much needed credits to Central Europe? It will be an atmosphere of hostility, if not hostilities, which will militate with full force against that financial and economic recovery which is essential not only to peace but to the very existence of civilisation. And the number of years for which real hostilities can be staved off would, in all European opinion, be doubtful.

Simon felt that if Britain could do anything to save the disarmament conference she should do it. A breakdown would result in Germany re-establishing herself 'as the armed menace of Europe', a contingency of which the French were 'terrified'. The British delegation at Geneva was, however, preparing a draft convention and Simon concluded: 'Whether we can save the Disarmament Conference by some such means I do not know. But I do not believe that it can be saved by any other means.'[5]

In spite of his pessimism[6] the Prime Minister went to Geneva personally to present the British plan to the disarmament conference. Under the terms of the British draft convention Germany was to be permitted a certain measure of equality.[7] First reactions to it were encouraging and Ramsay MacDonald reported to his Cabinet colleagues that he thought the outlook was now not so bleak. He had been uneasy after it had been decided 'to launch the draft

Convention, but he was now well satisfied'.[8] Yet within two months
the disarmament conference was again in trouble. The Germans
were objecting to the 'standardisation of continental armies' as
proposed in Part II of the draft convention, and demanding for
themselves a professional regular army which Simon considered
Geneva would not accept. In addition, they were claiming equality
in the air and in the matter of guns. At a Cabinet meeting on 10 May
Simon 'did not conceal his feeling that . . . Germany was likely to
walk out of the disarmament Conference'.[9] Simon's views were very
much strengthened by a report from Brigadier A. C. Temperley of
the War Office. He stated that Hitler had carried out a revolution in
Germany and was now the master of a country which had 'given
itself up to a delirium of reawakened nationalism and of the most
blatant and dangerous militarism'. Goering, regarded as 'the most
violent, the most stupid and the most reckless' of Hitler's entourage,
had been 'nominated Minister for Air, with the mission of raising a
military air force'. This was an integral part of the process of
establishing military training organisations and the drive towards
rearmament, manifest in the hardening of the German attitude at
Geneva. Temperley wrote:

> The German delegate has reiterated his refusal to accept the
> cardinal points of the British Draft Convention, and has, in
> particular, declined to give up the Reichswehr and accept the
> uniformisation of European armies on a militia basis. The increas-
> ing insolence of the Germans has brought discussion on effectives
> to a complete standstill. When material is discussed, there are
> strong indications that the demands for samples of military
> aeroplanes, tanks and navy guns will be very large.

In the circumstances, Temperley felt that disarmament would be a
very dangerous proceeding. But there was 'one bold solution' to the
problem of Germany. She should be warned by Britain, France and
the United States that unless Germany's military preparations and
inclinations were brought to a complete halt there could be 'no
disarmament, no equality of status and no relaxation of the Treaty of
Versailles'. This naturally entailed the risk of an international crisis
and the possibility of war, but Germany was in no condition to fight
and it was essential to 'call her bluff'. It was admitted by Temperley
that this course might appear 'forceful', but 'the only alternative'
was 'to carry out some minimum measure of disarmament and to

allow things to drift for another five years', when, failing a 'change of heart' in Germany, war would appear unavoidable.[10]

Such a programme of action, however, was too dramatic for Sir John Simon. While he thought that any moderation in Hitler's attitude towards armaments would merely be a temporary retreat, and while he considered that the time had come when he and his colleagues in the Cabinet 'should consider all possible contingencies', he confined his action to a request to Hitler that Germany should not denounce the disarmament clauses of the Treaty of Versailles unilaterally on the grounds that this 'might exacerbate the European situation'.[11] Indeed, a similar injunction was directed at the British Cabinet on 17 May when Ramsay MacDonald asked ministers 'to be particularly careful in any unavoidable public references to matters of foreign policy which by the force of circumstances they might find themselves compelled to make'.[12] Presumably the disarmament conference was to be saved by a conspiracy of silence.

Hitler temporarily revived the hopes of the British government by a moderate speech on 17 May,[13] but he was temporising. There was no willingness on the part of Germany to disarm; only a willingness to use the disarmament conference, while convenient, as a cloak for surreptitious rearmament.[14] In any case, the French, whose accumulated evidence of German rearmament made them justifiably sceptical of German good faith,[15] were to render further discussion at the conference virtually worthless by their evolution, during the summer of 1933, of proposals whereby Germany would only be allowed quantitative and qualitative equality in armaments after she had demonstrated a positive disinclination towards rearmament in a preliminary trial period, during which an effective scheme of supervision would also be tested.[16] Anthony Eden, then parliamentary under-secretary of state for foreign affairs, was quick to grasp the fact that 'no Franco–German settlement could be reached' on the basis of the French proposals.[17] Simon, confronted with clear evidence of German rearmament, had some difficulty in deciding the right course of policy,[18] but eventually it was decided to support the French attitude. Informing the German foreign minister, von Neurath, of this on 23 September, Simon made it clear that Germany would not even be permitted samples of prohibited weapons during the trial period. He was convinced that British opinion 'would not tolerate it' and there would be difficulties in persuading 'British opinion to tolerate the idea . . . in the second period'.[19]

This posture on the part of the British government ensured the end of Germany's participation in the disarmament negotiations. It had been clear in London for some time that Germany would spin out the discussions for just so long as it suited Hitler's policy of gradual rearmament.[20] Now it was no longer convenient for Germany to participate in them, or in the League of Nations, and, in advance of Sir John Simon's formal statement of the British position at Geneva on 14 October, it was decided by the German government to leave both the League and the disarmament conference.[21]

In the wake of Germany's departure from Geneva, Simon presented the Cabinet with a paper concerning the future course of British policy. He clearly felt Hitler to be the main impediment to the reaching of any kind of agreement and accused the Nazi party of preaching a doctrine 'which seemed to regard preparation for war as in itself a noble ideal pervading every aspect of national life'.[22] This had not helped the attitude of the French government, which had become more and more suspicious and intransigent. But the main thrust of British policy was the maintenance of peace in Europe, which was dependent upon improved relations between France and Germany and which Britain had to strive to achieve. Furthermore, Britain desired 'to allay the ruffled feelings of Germany towards ourselves, and to bring her back into the circle; and to prevent by every possible means, a new race in armaments'. The following was suggested as the basis for future policy:

1) A policy of isolation is not practicable.
2) Our policy is still to seek by international co-operation the limitation and reduction of world armaments, as our obligation under the Convenant and as the only means to prevent a race in armaments.
3) It is dangerous to seek this by continuing the Conference in its present form without Germany.
4) It is important to maintain contact with Germany, both because her assent is essential to a Convention and as the best means of securing that she does not commit herself to rearmament in isolation or to a denunciation of the Treaty of Versailles.

These recommendations were accepted by the Cabinet.[23]

Following the events of October 1933, therefore, British policy toward Germany continued to be dominated by the disarmament conference and its questionable future. Indeed, the remainder of Simon's foreign secretaryship was almost exclusively concerned with the consequences of Germany's withdrawal from it. It is here perhaps that Simon's deficiencies as a foreign minister are most clearly revealed. He was not incapable, but he tended to react to events rather than to take initiatives.[24] He seemed unable to embark upon a fresh course of action once a previous line had proved fruitless and inclined rather to make the best of a bad job. Outside the Cabinet he was regarded as catastophic and 'morally incapable'[25] and during the early months of 1934 there was much criticism of him in the press and speculation about his removal. Public dissatisfaction was matched by disapproval of Simon within the Cabinet. Neville Chamberlain wrote of him:

> He can always make an admirable speech in the house – to a brief – but he is a bad F. S. for nobody trusts him. This is doing him an injustice, but the fact is that his manner inspires no confidence and that he seems temperamentally unable to make up his mind to action when a difficult situation arises. I am bound to say that such action as he has been able to propose has often seemed unwise and unthoughtout.

It appears that Ramsay MacDonald, who was not happy with Simon's performance, considered replacing him with Chamberlain, but took no action in the end.[26] Thus the British government remained saddled with a Foreign Secretary whose main aim was to probe the relics of disarmament. To be fair to Simon, the conduct of British policy at this time has to be seen in the context of the intelligence picture which did not seem overwhelmingly threatening. It was assumed that Germany would rearm to a level only consonant with the needs of national security. Moreover, it was anticipated that the German rearmament programme was designed to produce efficient armed services with strength in depth and that the process would take time.[27] In the circumstances Simon could perhaps be forgiven for not perceiving a need for urgency.

Despite reservations on the part of ministers as to how far Britain should go in the role of 'honest broker',[28] the British government throughout the winter of 1933–4 attempted to reconcile the German and French points of view until Simon came to the view that the total collapse of the disarmament negotiations was imminent.[29] It was at this point that he suggested a new tactic. In November 1933 Sir Maurice Hankey, in a letter to Sir Eric Phipps, Britain's new ambassador at Berlin, wrote:

> I think that Ministers are beginning to see that the rearmament of Germany is not likely to be stopped except by the most drastic measures, – for which I do not believe public opinion either here or in France would stand. If Germany intends to re-arm she will re-arm. Some kind of agreed re-armament is probably better than none. The difficulty here, however, is that the Government have repeatedly proclaimed from the housetops that there must be no re-armament of Germany. That is the dilemma, but not an unescapable one for the adroit politician.[30]

This was precisely the course that Simon now proposed. Rather than seeking to salvage a disarmament convention, should not Britain attempt to circumscribe the scope of Germany's rearmament by sanctioning it within limits in an international agreement? Rather than aiming at a disarmament convention, would it not be more prudent to aim at a convention that would recognise Germany's so far illegal rearmament? In short, 'if there' was 'to be a funeral, it' was 'clearly better to arrange it while Hitler' was 'still in a mood to pay the undertakers for their services'.[31] Little was done, however, to make progress on this basis until the closing months of 1934.

The palpable failure of the disarmament conference and the continuing evidence of German rearmament caused the British government, at the end of 1933 and during 1934, seriously to consider the rectification of the deficiencies in Britain's defences.[32] By November 1934, however, the situation was regarded as so alarming as to prompt the formation of a Cabinet Committee on German Rearmament which was to advise upon 'the desirability of re-considering our policy as regards the legalisation of German rearmament'.[33] Within two days the committee had completed its labours. The report, written by MacDonald, made it clear that Germany was not only in breach of part V of the Treaty of Versailles, but that in addition she was 'exceeding the limits which were suggested in the Draft Disarmament Convention' submitted by the British government in March 1933. This represented a clear threat to the future peace of Europe and it was recommended that a government statement in the Commons during the forthcoming debate on 28 November should make it apparent that the British government was aware of the fact of German rearmament.

Prior to this, however, it was proposed that the German ambassador and the governments of France and Italy be contacted, for it was important 'that the issue should not be allowed to develop as one between ourselves and Germany, but that it must be raised to the place of a European issue'.[34] The recommendations of the report were speedily accepted by the Cabinet. During the discussions it was agreed that Simon should not disclose the full extent of Britain's knowledge of German rearmament when he spoke to the German ambassador and it was also agreed that the views of the German government should not be invited. Within the Cabinet it was felt that: 'If our object was "controlled" re-armament by Germany it would be dangerous to be drawn into discussions with her until the question had been examined with France, and Italy, and possibly other powers'.[35]

Following the Commons debate the Cabinet Committee on German Rearmament reconvened to consider further recommendations. The basis of their deliberations was a memorandum by Simon. The Foreign Secretary pointed out that von Neurath had now admitted the fact of German rearmament and that it had been learnt from German military authorities that the period of concealment was almost at an end. It was, therefore, likely that Germany would present a demand for the legalisation of the action after the Saar plebiscite. The prevention of German rearmament by force had to be ruled out and the only alternative to legalisation was 'for German re-armament to continue just the same, with the added complication that further increases are secret and that the sense of injustice and resentment continued to be stimulated'. Clearly, any agreement on armaments had to be preceded by the concession of genuine equality. Simon accepted that it could be argued that the abrogation of the disarmament clauses of the Treaty of Versailles would merely encourage the Germans to advance their claims regarding territorial boundaries and colonies sooner rather than later, but he doubted 'whether we should really be hastening the pace by recognising the inevitable and getting such terms as we can while we recognise it'. It was proposed that recognition of German rearmament was the best course to pursue now in spite of the strain it would place on Anglo-French relations and Simon justified his view in the following manner:

Germany would prefer, it appears, to be 'made an honest woman'; but if she is left too long to indulge in illegitimate practices and to find by experience that she does not suffer for it, this laudable ambition may wear off.

Simon, however, was not prepared to contemplate legalisation without something in return and he thought that the main condition should be the return of Germany to Geneva 'for the Disarmament Conference and for League purposes'.[36] These suggestions were immediately approved by the committee and later endorsed by the Cabinet. It was also decided to invite French ministers to London with a view to a coordinated Anglo–French approach in these matters.[37]

The French eventually agreed to an early visit and on 31 January 1935 the French Prime Minister, Pierre-Etienne Flandin, and his foreign minister, Pierre Laval, arrived in London for talks.[38] Although Simon was informed before their arrival that 'reasonable Frenchmen' shared his view regarding the desirability of legalising German rearmament, it was also intimated that there would be considerable problems in reconciling French opinion with such a course.[39] In the event, the British objective of getting a joint Anglo–French declaration favouring the legalisation of German rearmament in principle did, indeed, prove more difficult to achieve than had been anticipated, for the French wished Britain to agree to an agreement on air attack as a *quid pro quo*. The French proposals required that the victim of an air attack would be immediately assisted by all the other signatories to an agreement, who would automatically attack the aggressor. The suggested signatories were the Locarno powers and it was proposed that Britain and France should immediately sign a pact of mutual assistance against air attack without waiting for the other signatories to adhere.[40] Despite strong opposition within Whitehall to the proposals for an air pact,[41] Simon persuaded his colleagues to adopt a sympathetic attitude towards them. The French desired a further assurance from Britain to present to French opinion and unless Britain was prepared to be forthcoming in this matter it would not be possible to obtain French consent in principle to the cancellation of part V of the Treaty of Versailles.[42] Thus it was that an air pact was mentioned in the communiqué that ended the visit of the French ministers. The Anglo–French communiqué of 3 February 1935 proposed the negotiation of a general settlement of limited type composed of regional security pacts, Germany's return to the League, a 'reciprocol agreement' against air attack that would be supplementary to the Locarno pact, and the legitimisation of German rearmament.[43]

The communiqué remained the basis of British policy towards Germany for the next twelve months and its publication led directly to the visit to Berlin on 25 and 26 March by Simon and Eden, who went there with the specific intention of gauging Hitler's response to the Anglo–French proposals. The visit, however, was almost fated not to take place. First, the German government had decided to announce the existence of the *Luftwaffe* on 1 March,[44] which effectively amounted to the unilateral denunciation of the Treaty of Versailles that it was the object of British policy to avoid. Secondly, on 30 January it had been decided by the British Cabinet to issue a white paper on defence for a debate in parliament that would precede the debates on the service estimates.[45] While attempts were made to tone down the language of this document on the grounds that 'if you want to do business with a fellow it is a bad plan to start by slinging mud in his face',[46] the views of Sir Warren Fisher, the permanent under-secretary at the Treasury, and Vansittart prevailed. The document proved 'downright in expression' and unequivocally named Germany as the source of European tension and the cause of British rearmament.[47] The publication of the defence white paper infuriated Hitler, who postponed the visit of the British ministers by the fabrication of a 'diplomatic' illness.[48] Matters were further complicated by the announcement of the reintroduction of conscription in Germany.[49] This could, of course, have been used by Simon to cancel altogether his visit to Germany. He did not, however, take that view. There should be a protest, but, in his opinion,

We should not retort by saying that now we will not go to Berlin. After all, what *ultimate* end would that serve? It will not alter the German decision and it will break down whatever contact is left and destroy finally any prospect of agreeing about anything. It would be quite a different matter if excommunicating Germany would lead to a combination to stop her. On the contrary, it would have quite the opposite effect.[50]

Thus at the end of March 1935 Simon and Eden proceeded to Berlin to examine the views of Hitler on the main objectives of British policy.

Immediately prior to the visit of the British ministers to Berlin, British policy toward Germany might be described as a last attempt to rake a few embers from the cinders of the disarmament conference, namely to bring Germany back to the League of Nations and to secure thereby the limitation of her rearmament. As such the policy had emerged from Britain's preoccupation with disarmament as the main means of removing tension and stabilising relations between the European powers. The nature of the new Germany had become increasingly apparent as the Cabinet discussions over Austria and the decision to commence the rearmament process show,[51] but it had been felt right to explore every possibility to the last. In this period from 1933 until the Simon visit to Berlin, therefore, the colonial question played virtually no part in the formulation of British policy.

This fact might seem to confound the statement made by Logan that 'after Hitler's assumption of power the colonial question was discussed in connection with almost every major development in Western Europe',[52] but it is clear that from 1933 onwards the Foreign Office monitored every development in colonial agitation in Germany and by the beginning of 1935 the officials there, not least among them Sir Robert Vansittart, were urging serious consideration of this issue on the Cabinet. Moreover, although the colonial question was mentioned infrequently in the Cabinet in this period, the fact that it was mentioned when general considerations regarding Germany were discussed indicates the conviction on the part of some ministers at least that the issue would appear *sur le tapis* sooner or later. When, for example, the Cabinet considered the British attitude towards German aspirations in Austria in September 1933, Hailsham, the Secretary of State for War, argued strongly in favour of maintaining Austria's independence, otherwise Germany – 'already too strong' – 'would be encouraged to take the next step in tearing up the Treaty of Versailles, dealing first with the [Polish] Corridor as a prelude to other parts of the Eastern frontier and then Alsace–Lorraine and the Colonies'.[53] Six months later, during a Cabinet discussion regarding the first report of the defence requirements sub-committee the air minister, Lord Londonderry, commented that the chiefs of staff had estimated that Germany might become a threat in five or six years' time and that within that period 'she might even make a demand on us for colonies'.[54]

Nevertheless, the official attitude of the British government in this matter was still firmly negative.[55] This emerged in the negotiations for a four power pact, proposed by Mussolini on 18 March 1933. The Italian leader had had this idea for some time and had indicated to the French that his mind was working in this direction as early as the beginning of August 1932.[56] He later put forward his ideas publicly in a speech at Turin in October of that year,[57] but it was not until MacDonald and Simon visited Rome, immediately after the presentation of the British draft disarmament convention at Geneva, that he promoted them with any vigour.[58] The precise details of the four power pact have been dealt with elsewhere,[59] but what is of immediate relevance to the colonial question is the fact that the fourth and final article stated: 'In all political and non-political European questions, as well as in the colonial sphere, the four Powers undertake to adopt, as far as possible, a line of common conduct.'[60]

The revelation of this article provoked speculation in the British press that MacDonald had indicated in Rome a 'willingness to cede British Colonies to Germany', which the British Prime Minister hastened to point out in Cabinet, was 'totally untrue'. Even though the reference to colonies in Article IV had been 'vague', he and Simon 'had been at pains to get the reference deleted'.[61] On 23 March 1933 Sir Philip Cunliffe-Lister, the Secretary of State for the Colonies, attempted to provide reassurance in the House of Commons by stating that 'His Majesty's Government have never contemplated any surrender of the Tanganyika Mandate'.[62] Definite reassurance was given when it was revealed that the final terms of the four power pact contained no reference whatever to colonies.[63]

The most significant development in the colonial question during 1933 was, however, the raising of the issue at the world economic conference by the German minister of economics, Hugenberg. The Foreign Office had, in fact, anticipated the possibility that the Germans would use this forum to raise such an issue and a memorandum was prepared so that British representatives could counter the German arguments. Significantly, it was not Hugenberg who was expected to push the matter, but rather, and for very good reasons,[64] Schacht, the president of the *Reichsbank*. The author of the memorandum was M. H. Huxley of the central department. He wrote that Schacht was one of the most persistent advocates of colonial redistribution, and that

He may well raise this question at the Economic Conference either on the grounds that German industry, faced with an increasingly nationalistic attitude on the part of the colonial powers (e.g. the extension of imperial preference to the dependent Empire), needs its own sources of raw materials, or on the ground that the payment of Germany's debts would be facilitated if she could draw supplies from within her own currency area instead of having to purchase them with her exports across the exchanges.

Huxley recited the usual counter-arguments that were to become even more familiar as the decade progressed. The transfer of a mandate was not a question for Britain alone; it would require also the consent of other powers. Germany had in the past extracted little economic benefit from her colonies, and the notion that the Germans were by nature suitable for colonising activity was irrelevant. Moreover, the German colonies had never attracted many German immigrants. Huxley thought that

> The most that could be argued would be that the possession of colonies within the German currency area would enable Germany to draw from them at least a part of her supply of raw materials without having to purchase them with her exports across the exchanges, and that her 'export surplus,' available for the payment of . . . her foreign debts, would thus be increased.

It is also of some interest that in commenting on Schacht's refutation of Germany's alleged bad colonial record Huxley observed that 'Jews and coloured people' were now the objects of racial discrimination in Germany.[65]

The fact, therefore, that the colonial question became an issue at the world economic conference came as no surprise to the British government, although the individual responsible clearly did. From the start, however, the entire proceeding was shrouded in mystery. No sooner had the Foreign Office received information that the matter had been raised by Hugenberg than it proved impossible to acquire the text of his 'famous Memorandum'. It was known that the Dutch Prime Minister, Colijn, had a copy, but Hugenberg himself had asked for it to be suppressed.[66] On 20 June Rumbold, the British ambassador at Berlin, was asked to procure a text. According to the ambassador the original draft had been produced in the Nazi office of economics and had had the approval of Rosenberg, the Nazi ideologist and recently appointed Director of the NSDAP's *Aussenpolitisches Amt* (Foreign Policy Office). Hugenberg had subsequently submitted his memorandum to the German delegation which had 'criticised it, but came to no agreement.' Acting on the assumption that he had at least obtained negative approval Hugenberg had subsequently handed a copy of it to Colijn.[67]

Transmitting to London, the following day, a translation of the Hugenberg memorandum, as published by Wolff's Telegraphic Bureau, Rumbold emphasised that the German press had gone to considerable lengths to make it clear that it was purely a statement of Hugenberg's personal views. The offending paragraph stated:

From Germany's point of view, an intelligent and amicable co-operation between creditor and debtor countries could result in two unprejudiced steps as a result of which Germany could once more be restored to her international capacity to pay. The first of these steps would be that Germany should be given back a colonial Empire in Africa, a great new continent in which she could produce considerable activity and schemes of work which otherwise would not be developed. The second step would be to open up to the 'people without space' territories in which it could find room for settlement of its active people and do great works in the interests of peace.[68]

The 'territories' in question were clearly understood at the time to refer to land within the Soviet Union. As a result the Soviet government reacted strongly through the normal diplomatic channels,[69] and through the columns of *Pravda* and *Izvestiya*, but the western governments, and the British government in particular, hardly reacted at all.[70] This, however, was not an indication of British complicity with the schemes advanced by Hugenberg, as Karl Radek asserted, but, on the contrary, the result of clear evidence that the German government had no intention of supporting its minister of economics. On 21 June Duncan Sandys, then an official at the Foreign Office, informed his colleagues that von Neurath and the entire German delegation 'had been taken by surprise' by Hugenberg's action and were 'indignant'. Moreover, now that Hugenberg had lost the sympathies of von Neurath, von Papen and the NSDAP, it seemed that his 'position in the [German] Cabinet' was 'growing daily more precarious'.[71] And, indeed, so it proved, for on 28 June Hugenberg resigned. Thus, when Mr G. L. M. Clauson of the Colonial Office asked Orme Sargent if it was 'worthwhile pursuing the matter', the view of the Foreign Office was that it was not, and there it rested.[72] The Germans had themselves disavowed the man responsible and there was no point in upsetting the delicate negotiations on disarmament at Geneva by creating a fuss over colonies. In any case, *The Times*, evidently more able to acquire a copy of the Hugenberg memorandum than the Foreign Office, spoke for England on 19 June in an editorial which declared: 'There can be no question whatever of the restoration to Germany of her former overseas possessions; and in any case her claim for mandates is one which can properly be brought up only before the League.'[73]

As the Hugenberg episode indicates, the negative attitude of the British government in the matter of colonial revision at this time, was evidently matched by a disinclination on the part of Hitler to push the issue into the forefront of Anglo–German relations, although it would appear that his major preoccupation, with what was after all only a minor lapse on the part of Hugenberg, was to dish the minister of economics and the nationalists in order to further consolidate his position in Germany.[74] It is, however, clear that in the early years of his regime his attitude towards the colonial question was one of publicly declared disinterest with a view to realising the Anglo–German understanding predicated as the foundation of his foreign policy in his writings of the 1920s. To describe his position as one of colonial renunciation would seem to claim too much.[75] It may well be that that was the impression he wished to convey to the British government; but, even if he himself wished to abandon overseas interests for all time, which it seems he did not, he could not openly renounce colonies without damaging the coalition of interests that his government and movement represented.

Although in Feburary 1933 Hitler informed a correspondent of the *Daily Express* that Germany had 'by no means given up colonial desires' and that the issue would 'have to be solved justly', as there were 'a great many things which Germany' had to 'import from the colonies',[76] it is evident and incontestable that from 1933 until 1935 he avoided reference to the colonial question whenever he could.[77] But he could not avoid making some comment when the problem was put to him by British journalists and visitors. In his answers he always did his best to reassure British opinion without denting the aspirations of his own supporters. Sometimes he went too far. For instance, the *Daily Telegraph* on 5 May 1933 carried an account of an interview between Hitler and Sir John Foster Fraser under the heading 'Colonial Dream Abandoned'. Hitler was reported as having stated that Germany had no wish to acquire overseas possessions or to enter into naval competition with Britain and that her fate was 'bound up with . . . the east of our frontier'. This compelled the *Völkischer Beobachter* to issue a carefully worded correction some days later;[78] but even before that the official communiqué that followed the Fraser interview made no mention of the disclaimer in the *Telegraph*, merely reporting that it had been stated that Britain's overseas interests would be respected. An old hand like Rumbold was not very easily deceived and he commented perceptively: 'Herr Hitler, like his predecessors in office, must now be experiencing the difficulty of addressing to the outside world remarks intended for foreign consumption, without raising protests at home and vice-versa'.[79]

More characteristic of his response to questions regarding colonies put to him by Britons was that accorded to Ward Price of the *Daily Mail* in an interview of 18 October 1933. Asked point-blank if Germany intended to pursue the recovery of her former colonies, Hitler stated that Germany was overpopulated and 'should not be deprived of the conditions of existence'. She was fully capable and worthy of colonial administration and development, but this was not a matter for war and rather one 'for negotiation'.[80] The *Völkischer Beobachter*, however, in reporting this interview described Hitler as saying that the 'apportionment of colonial territories, it doesn't matter to me where' would never be a war issue, the words, '*it doesn't matter to me where*' clearly indicating Hitler's preoccupation with mollifying the British and his corresponding desire to keep a low profile on the colonial question.[81]

Undoubtedly, therefore, Hitler would have been embarrassed when Price's paymaster, Lord Rothermere, entered the fray in March 1935 with an article headlined 'Germany Must Have Elbow-Room'. This rehearsed all the usual German arguments in favour of colonial revision. Germany had been stripped of assets from which she acquired 50 per cent of her imported raw materials; German nationals were denied the right to emigrate to areas under German sovereignty; and Germany had been wrongly accused of being unfit to govern African and Asian peoples. Germany, Rothermere continued, had already started the process of treaty revision by getting rid of reparations and by rearming; it was now up to the British government to recognise facts and assist that process further by being positive over colonial revision. Versailles, which had supposedly been constructed to make the world safe for democracy, was now making it less safe than ever. As for the mandates, they were only a burden on the British exchequer and the money spent in them was merely benefiting those German settlers and plantation owners who had returned. Moreover, 'ambitious, vigorous, hard-working German youth' needed areas into which to expand, and it was imperative to restore to Germany her former colonies for this purpose.[82]

Whether or not this caused embarrassment in Berlin, it certainly caused embarrassment in Buckingham Palace. King George V enquired through Sir Clive Wigram 'if it would not be possible to get a parliamentary question asked next week on our attitude to proposals to restore the German colonies'. This appealed to the head of the central department at the Foreign Office, Ralph Wigram, who thought 'the stiffer the answer the better', the German government only understanding 'stiff language'. Orme Sargent concurred, but the permanent under-secretary demurred. Vansittart thought it best to let the matter pass in 'contemptuous silence'. Rothermere flew 'from topic to topic' and 'it would be a waste of time – and not very dignified – to follow him with denials'. Secondly, 'Rothermere had been behaving rather more satisfactorily of late'. Finally, and most importantly, Vansittart did not 'feel that the moment may be best chosen for a reply that will call forth much foaming and abuse in Germany'. Sir John Simon endorsed this view.[83] It is arguable, therefore, that just as Hitler wished at this stage to play down the colonial question in order to fulfil his wider aims, so the British government did not wish finally to damage its major and immediate aim of securing an agreed limitation of Germany's rearmament by raising a colonial storm.

Nevertheless, the *Daily Mail* would not leave the issue alone. Granting Ward Price a further interview on the occasion of his assumption of the headship of state in Germany, following the death of Hindenburg and the blood-letting of the summer of 1934, Hitler was once again forced to comment on an issue he would rather have avoided. Reiterating to Price his desire for Anglo–German friendship, he concluded by stating: 'I say to you as an Englishman, if England does not attack us, we will never have a quarrel with England, whether it is on the Rhine or elsewhere. We want nothing from England.' Replying to Prices's enquiry as to whether or not this also covered colonies, Hitler declared: 'I would not demand the life of a single German in order to acquire any colony in the world. We know that the former German colonies in Africa are a costly luxury even for England.' The revelation of Hitler's remarks provoked a chorus of conservative dissatisfaction throughout Germany and he was obliged to issue a modification of this statement through Hess at the following month's Nuremberg rally. While colonies were a luxury for Britain, it was explained, this did not mean that they were a luxury for Germany.[84] In a sense this interview between Ward Price and Hitler marked the end of the 'policy of interviews', but that Hitler wished his efforts to secure an agreement with Britain to remain untrammelled by colonial red herrings is demonstrated by the fact that the *Deutsche Kolonialschule* in Witzenhausen was informed by the Leipzig Fair Office in January 1935 that the Reich government would value it if there was to be no colonial propaganda at its display.[85]

There was, however, an interesting postscript at the end of 1934 which indicates how little an impression Hitler's stategy in the interviews had made upon the conception that responsible British officials had of German policy. On 15 December Sir Eric Phipps met Lord Rothermere in Berlin at a luncheon given by Ribbentrop. At the end of the function Goebbels, who was also present, thanked Rothermere for having written in the *Daily Mail* that the Saar, the future territorial status of which was soon to be determined in a plebiscite, was essentially Germanic and for having supported the return of the German colonies. Phipps immediately interjected that neither the British government nor public opinion would support such an occurrence. Replying to Goebbels, who claimed that the German government was very grateful for such 'objective' pronouncements in the British press even if the return of colonies was not currently a major item of German policy, Phipps stated categorically that he 'could not think such pronouncements served any useful purpose, for they might merely arouse German hopes that were destined to be dashed'.[86] It may well be that Hitler, seen from his point of view, could not have made his intentions plainer, without provoking internal political difficulties, than in the interviews with Foster Fraser and Ward Price,[87] but even these disinterested utterances combined with evidence of quiet, but active, colonial agitation in Germany conveyed to British officials the impression that the colonial question was still alive and still to be suppressed. In a minute of September 1933, Mr J. V. Perowne of the central department of the Foreign Office encapsulated the thinking there on the colonial question at this time when, commenting on the fact that a squadron of German light aircraft was to tour the former German colonies to advertise the forthcoming Berlin Olympiad, he wrote:

More 'showing of the flag'. Hitler's policy is to keep up the colonial movement *unofficially* until he has the leisure to take it up

officially – with HMG rather than *against* HMG – and the Germans
are busy establishing prescriptive rights and keeping interest
alive in their former colonies.[88]

It has been somewhat dismissively suggested that both Robert
Vansittart and Sir Eric Phipps completely misread Hitler's pronouncements on the colonial question as they were delivered in the
press interviews.[89] This would be a largely justified criticism if the
rather simplistic assumption were valid that the only material on
Germany and the colonial question reaching the Foreign Office and
the British embassy in Berlin came from the columns of the *Daily
Telegraph* and the *Daily Mail*. Hitler's remarks, however, were
always seen in the context of a wider activity regarding the colonial
question in Germany. For example, the assertions of Schnee, the
president of the DKG, were reported to and filed in the Foreign
Office.[90] It was also noted that on 24 April 1935 a number of articles
appeared in the German press to commemorate the fiftieth anniversary of the founding of Germany's first colony and that the occasion
was celebrated in Prussian schools.[91] In June 1935 Phipps reported
extensively on a meeting of colonial enthusiasts at the *Sportpalast*
which took place in conjunction with a colonial gathering at Kiel.[92]
Finally, in connection with a colonial exhibition that ran throughout
the months of July and August 1934, it was reported to the Foreign
Office that although the attendance at the exhibition was 'meagre',
indicating an indifference on the part of the German general public
towards the matter, when it came 'to the moral issue, popular
support' was 'not lacking', popular opinion being that 'the colonies
were stolen and that the mandatory system was merely designed to
give the act a semblance of decency'.[93]

Given the fact that colonial propaganda, albeit at a low ebb,
continued in Germany during the first two years of the Third Reich it
was accepted in the Foreign Office that the return of the colonies
remained an issue on which Germany would demand satisfaction at
some stage.[94] If Hitler found the colonial agitation really embarrassing he increasingly had the means at his disposal to stop it. That it
continued strengthened the impression that, whatever Hitler said,
the colonial question was still alive and, in addition, it remained a
part of the NSDAP's official programme.[95] The problem for the
Foreign Office was that of ascertaining when the German government was likely to raise the issue. In this, it can be argued, the
officials read the signs quite accurately. At the end of 1933, it was

minuted that there were 'good indications' that Schnee's vapour-
ings would 'not receive very active official support'.[96] And in May
1934 Cunliffe-Lister informed the Cabinet that he did not see much
point in responding to outbursts by Goering on the colonial
question, as he 'gathered that Herr Hitler himself was not keen on
the return of the German colonies' and thought that Rothermere's
articles on the subject had embarrassed the German government.[97]
In the light of the evidence, therefore, it was accepted that the
German colonial enthusiasts were 'beating the air', although it was
also recognised that in those days such a prophecy was 'unsafe'.[98]
Subsequently, at the beginning of 1935, a perceptive Foreign Office
minute predicted that Hitler might raise the colonial question when
Germany's return to the League was discussed.[99]

In the circumstances, it should not really provoke too much
astonishment that, when in April 1934 Vansittart presented his
paper, 'The Future of Germany', to the Cabinet, a discussion of the
colonial question featured in it. The purpose of Vansittart's memorandum was to justify the defence requirements sub-committee's
assessment of Germany as 'the ultimate potential enemy'. It was
argued that Germany's attitude had never altered and that even the
Weimar Republic had only veiled her real intentions: the militaristic,
expansionist and chauvinistic spirit continued unchanged. Vansittart wrote:

> To Hitler militarism and Prussianism are not terms of reproach,
> but signal titles of honour. It is a matter of naive and implicit faith
> that the German people are, by this divine jackbooted means, the
> predestined rulers of Europe. In time the best of Europe will be
> peopled and dominated by innumerable and irresistable
> Germans, who will have settled some old scores for good.
> Therefore, nationalise the masses; only brute force can ensure the
> survival of the race: the ultimate aim of all education is to produce
> a German who can be converted with a minimum of training into a
> soldier.

German youth was being inculcated with these views by a systematic educational policy and the ultimate objective was expansion,
an issue that Britain could not avoid. When Germany was ready,
Austria, Czechoslovakia, Poland and Memel would come under
threat, but there was also the matter of colonies. Every German
government since 1919 had demanded their return and Stresemann

had proved no exception.[100] Agitation and propaganda for the
return of the colonies was on the increase, openly encouraged by
von Neurath.[101] Furthermore, Hitler himself in the press interviews
had not indicated an abandonment of colonial aspirations.[102] The
permanent under-secretary concluded:

> Here is a cause for increase in bad blood. There are two views now
> in Germany on the 'colonial question'. I think it may roughly be
> said that the elder party would like to solve it 'with England', and
> the younger 'in spite of England'. But they both want colonies.[103]

That Vansittart and others saw in the German references a more
immediate threat than was in fact warranted is not open to doubt,
but presumably his thesis that Germany was aiming at European
hegemony cannot be challenged.[104] In any case, the purpose of the
paper was to convince British ministers of the need to rearm against
Germany, and an imperial 'frightener' in this respect could be more
than adequately justified. If, moreover, one of the distant aims of
Hitler was that Germany should become a world power, and the
mood of Germany and Hitler's statements suggested this, then
Britain and Germany were going to come into conflict at some stage.
In drawing attention to this Vansittart was only doing his job.

Substance was lent to the anxieties in the Foreign Office towards
the end of 1934 and the beginning of 1935 by the Voretzsch affair. In
March 1934 Dr I. F. Voretzsch, the former German ambassador at
Tokyo, wrote to Lord Lugard asking if he could talk to him about
colonies when he visited Britain.[105] Meeting for lunch at the
Athenaeum the following June, Voretzsch explained that Germany
did not want 'sovereignty or the German flag' in order to achieve
colonial satisfaction, 'but only something like a Chartered Company'. Lugard gave a discouraging answer. Germany already had
complete commercial and economic equality in the mandates and
any scheme that he proposed for mandated territory would also
have to be open to all member states of the League to be acceptable.
Furthermore, since a chartered company administered territory
under its control as the 'delegate' of a sovereign power, the creation
of such an organisation in mandated territory would be inadmiss-
ible. Lugard, however, thought that Voretzsch should put his ideas
on paper.

The latter amplified his views in a letter to Lugard of 8 September.
The term 'chartered company' had perhaps implied more than he

meant. He then proceeded to outline what seemed very much like the idea of a chartered company. The sort of colonial undertaking he had in mind would be required to produce colonial products, to use German currency, to settle civil litigation by arbitration and to levy minor taxes in order to defray the costs of administration. There was no 'intention whatever to acquire sovereign rights like those of a Chartered Company or to maintain an army nor a navy, nor the political representation, nor to exercise the right of jurisdiction and inflict sentences'. The undertaking was to be 'a purely private affair', the purpose of which was to relieve European economic and financial problems, 'to mitigate the bad feeling rampant in Germany on account of the colonial question', and to enable the acceleration of the payment of Germany's foreign debts. In reply, Lugard thought it would be impossible to introduce German currency into a mandate or colony in the manner proposed. It might be possible for a company to levy 'rates', but he did not see how the organisation envisaged could be private with all the privileges demanded. Lugard, however, now felt that Voretzsch should see somebody in authority at the Colonial Office. There was a danger that he might 'mislead' the latter, as he had 'no locus standi' and could not 'be of any real use'.

Lugard's suggestion was taken up, but, before arriving at the Colonial Office unannounced in the middle of October, Voretzsch specified to Lugard more exactly where he thought the German company should operate. Not in Tanganyika, as had been anticipated, but rather in a territory comprising the Cameroons and a small portion of Nigeria. Ominously, Voretzsch remarked: 'it will come one day and the sooner it comes, the better it will be for all concerned and the peaceful development of Europe'.

At the colonial office Voretzsch was given short shrift by Sir John Shuckburgh, the deputy under-secretary of state, who told the former German ambassador that his proposals would eventually have to be transferred to the diplomatic channel. This was something that Voretzsch wished to avoid:

He had been very careful up to the present to avoid transferring the proposal to the diplomatic plane; in fact, the German Embassy were not aware that he was at present in London and did not know that he was proposing to discuss the proposals with the colonial office. On the other hand, he had had conversations with Herr Hitler and other influential persons in the German Government. Herr Hitler had always been opposed to any attempt on the part of Germany to re-acquire tropical Colonies; and apparently it had taken a good deal of persuasion to bring Herr Hitler round to a favourable view even of Dr Voretzsch's proposal for a colonial enterprise of a mainly economic character.

Schuckburgh, however, confining his remarks to the proposals as presented by Voretzsch, pointed out that it had been the policy of the Colonial Office for some time to eliminate anything resembling a chartered company and his proposals, therefore, contained many difficulties. Voretzsch was not impressed by the problems, arguing that it was really a question of the sovereign power having 'confidence in the intentions of the concessionary company'. He and his confidants had originally had it in mind to test the practicability of his scheme in a Portuguese colony, but they had been dissuaded by the inferior nature of Portuguese colonial administration, particularly in the sphere of justice. Voretzsch stated that a reply to his enquiries would not be necessary if it was unfavourable.

Transmitting the record of these proceedings to the Foreign Office, E. B. Boyd stated that an *'imperium in imperio'* as presented by Vortezsch was 'open to the gravest objections in principle' and 'unworkable in practice'. But the Colonial Office was anxious that the impression should not be given to the Germans that was it not for the practical objections to the Voretzsch scheme it would otherwise have been politically acceptable and the views of the Foreign Office were requested.[106] The Colonial Office was not disappointed. Within the Foreign Office the Voretzsch scheme was regarded as 'utterly objectionable' and 'contrary to the policy of "keeping Germany lean"'. The 'whole transaction' with Lugard was 'a typical example of German backstairs kite-flying'. In addition, Voretzsch's claim to have acted on his own behalf was disbelieved. It was probable that the German government had been aware of his actions 'at every step' and had undoubtedly instigated the approach. It was 'a typical German manoeuvre'. Thus Voretzsch had to be decisively rejected and it was to be regretted that the 'C.O. did not knock the whole thing on the head from the very start'. Voretzsch should be advised not to continue with his proposals, but if he did he should be diverted to the diplomatic channel. Nevertheless, the Foreign Office did not want 'this tiresome question raised diplomatically' if it could be avoided.[107] Voretzsch would not be baulked. He returned to the Colonial Office and at an interdepartmental conference on 19 October 1934 it was decided that he was to be given a blunt negative and that the governors of the various crown colonies should be warned 'against allowing German globe-trotters to draw them into discussions.'[108]

Voretzsch was nothing if not persistent. Writing to Sir John Schuckburgh in February 1935, he regretted that his scheme, which he 'had considered to be a fortunate '*Zwischenlösung*' between the restoration of the German colonies and the present unbearable situation', had not found favour. It was a decision 'to avoid a decisive step along the path of reconciliation between the nations in the question of colonies'. But he presumed that the British government would still 'welcome some German colonial collaboration and enterprise' and he asked Schuckburgh to communicate to him a scheme that was unobjectionable and practicable and would meet the German requirements.[109] Schuckburgh was tired of this 'irregular and inconvenient' correspondence: would it not be better, he asked the Foreign Office, for the Germans to bring this matter into the open if they had 'serious proposals?'[110] The Foreign Office disagreed. The British government had no 'interest at all in raising' the colonial question. Schuckburgh, therefore, was advised merely to ignore Voretzsch's 'impudent' letter.[111]

The Voretzsch affair was not the only indication that the Foreign Office had at this time of prominent German personages dabbling in the colonial question. In 1933 S. C. Wyatt, the chairman of the Ottoman Debt Commission, had informed the Foreign Office of a conversation with a German acquaintance 'well informed of his own country's policy and in touch with the powers that be'. The individual concerned had informed Wyatt that Germany required facilities for immigration into Angola and Tanganyika and that this for Germany was 'more important' than the issue of 'administration prestige', meaning full sovereignty over a colony.[112] The identity of Wyatt's acquaintance was clarified in March 1935 when Wyatt revealed to the Foreign Office that he frequently had talks with Dr Weigelt, a director of the *Deutsche Bank*, who often mentioned mandates. According to Wyatt, Weigelt was of the following opinion:

Germany is bent on getting her colonies back, and that a settlement of this question, in one way or another, is an essential factor for improved friendly relations with Mandatory Powers, a condition of Germany's return to the League, and to any general peace settlement.[113]

The views of Weigelt were not only relayed to London through Wyatt, but also through an anonymous British naval officer who had visited Berlin. There the hapless mariner had been told by the importunate Weigelt that Germany required colonies for raw materials. Germany could be satisfied by the transfer of Angola to her sovereignty and the establishment of an Anglo–German regime in one of the east African colonies in which the currency would be the German mark. Both he and Dr Schacht agreed upon the necessity of this. Nevertheless, realising the hostility that would be aroused in Britain by such a measure, Weigelt felt that it could be linked with the currency question which would come up with disarmament. It is also of some interest that he took the view that the return of the German colonies would enable Britain to 'influence German policy, both internal and external, to a marked degree'.[114] These remarks were treated by the Foreign Office as 'yet further evidence of the colonial storm . . . blowing up in Germany'.[115]

It is unlikely that Voretzsch or Weigelt represented any official move in the matter of the colonial question, but the similarity of their remarks to those by now frequently made by Schacht and Weigelt's open acknowledgement of association with him do indicate a possible collaboration, perhaps conspiracy, with the recently appointed German minister of economics. At Nuremberg Schacht claimed that from as early as 1931 he had attempted to divert Hitler's preoccupation with eastward expansion by suggesting the colonial alternative.[116] In this connection, Weigelt's assertion that Britain could exercise a significant influence over German policy by coming to a colonial settlement with Germany is of some importance, for undoubtedly a positive move by Britain in this direction would have put Hitler in a difficult position. He could not have declined a colonial offer, however inconvenient, without looking ridiculous and once having accepted a colony he would have had great difficulty in pursuing European territorial demands, without appearing insatiably voracious.[117] That is to say that a colonial deal could have precluded the eastward drive of German policy which was the ostensible object of Schacht's manoeuvrings. But that Schacht wanted colonies come what may, regardless of his view of Hitler's priorities, is revealed in the fact that he told the American ambassador in September 1934 that he wanted them without war for preference, but with war if necessary.[118]

As the British apprehension that it would be Schacht rather than Hugenberg who would open up the colonial question at the world economic conference of 1933 illustrates, it was Schacht whom the British feared in this matter more than anyone else in Germany. Consequently, when Phipps informed the Foreign Office early in January 1935 that Schacht's influence was 'growing steadily' on Hitler and that he was urging the Führer 'to press for return of Germany's colonies', it created considerable alarm.[119] Three possible courses of action were examined by the Foreign Office. The matter could be allowed to drift until the Germans raised it when they would be told 'nothing doing'. Phipps could be instructed to intimate personally to Hitler that the British government would deprecate the raising of the issue. Finally, the government might make its views clear in parliament in a speech by the Prime Minister, or through the means of a parliamentary question.[120]

Vansittart favoured the personal approach to Hitler, but for the time being Simon was not prepared to come to any decision. Without the approval of the Foreign Secretary, it was decided to canvass the opinion of Phipps with a view to assisting Simon's deliberations, although it was admitted that a parliamentary statement on 29 January might be rather late if Hitler really meant to make an issue of colonies in his speech scheduled for the following day.[121] It was, therefore, noted with some relief in the Foreign Office on 26 January that Phipps now inclined to the view that Hitler was unlikely to make a statement on 30 January and, moreover, that it was 'doubtful whether the German Government' was 'anxious to raise [the] colonial question officially at the present moment'. In these circumstances it would be an error to take up the colonial issue with the Germans. On the other hand, Phipps felt that a statement in the Commons would be useful, although in the event it was decided not to pursue this line of action pending further discussions between Vansittart and Simon.[122]

The issue, however, refused to die down and it was not expected that it would do so. Following Hitler's agreement in February 1935 to see Simon and Eden in Berlin it was even assumed that he would probably raise the colonial question with the British ministers.[123] Phipps was not altogether certain that he would do so, but notwithstanding this he felt that: 'these rumbles of colonial activity warn us to be prepared for all eventualities'.[124] Within the Foreign Office they were looked upon as 'straws' that illustrated 'how the wind' was 'blowing'.[125] Moreover, while the Foreign Office still maintained a negative attitude in general towards Germany's colonial claims, it should be noted that Vansittart himself doubted if this posture could be maintained indefinitely unless the government was prepared to confront force with strength. In an interesting minute of 8 January he commented that even if Hitler was dissuaded from bringing up the colonial question it would merely constitute the postponement of the 'evil day'. He continued:

> I have been pointing out for some time that this matter was bound to intrude itself within very measurable time into Anglo–German relations, with all its consequences to them. It will probably replace the naval question of pre-war days. H.M.G. must therefore realise that they will eventually be in a position where a continued negative may have the most dangerous consequences to peace and to our very existence – *unless* they pursue the policy of cooperation with France (and Italy) which may enable them to get Germany back to the League and tied to an upper level of armament, which we ourselves must equal in the air and of course far surpass at sea. That will only be obtainable at a great price. H.M.G. must realise this in time.[126]

During the first two years of the Third Reich the colonial question played little part in the public relations between Britain and Germany. This was deliberate. Hitler had no wish to broach a subject that might prove prejudicial to his hopes of an Anglo–German understanding considered essential to his long term plans. Neither did the British want to jeopardise the prospects of securing some limitation of German rearmament by the intrusion of a colonial diversion. Nonetheless, while the colonial question was not publicly in the forefront, it was increasingly in the forefront of the minds of responsible British officials who believed that it would ultimately have to be faced. This stemmed partly from the experience of the 1920s, when colonial revision had been raised on several occasions in connection with other aspects of revision, and partly from the experience of the unofficial contacts during 1934 and the early months of 1935. Simon tended to regard the attitude of the Foreign Office as premature. As, however, the Berlin talks of March 1935 were to show, Hitler was capable of using the colonial question to avoid unwelcome commitments. They also demonstrated the weaknesses of Simon's one-dimensional approach to the German problem.

4

German Irredentism in Africa

That Vansittart and the Foreign Office should have thought it probable by the early months of 1935 that Hitler was positively inclined towards raising the colonial question at an early date is understandable enough in the light of the evidence reaching them from Germany. This impression, however, was reinforced by evidence supplied by the Colonial and Dominions Offices. Just as Hitler's assumption of power in Germany was accompanied by 'mass desertion to the Nazi camp' and expressions of a 'spontaneous desire to give up old prejudices, ideologies and social restrictions', so the mood of nationalist exultation found its counterpart in German communities overseas, particularly in the Tanganyika mandate and South-West Africa.[1]

Perhaps the most curious example of this came from the French mandate of Togoland, where, in February 1933, a group, describing themselves as the *Bund der Deutscher Togoländer*, addressed a letter to the governor of the Gold Coast which complained of French misrule and attested the veracity of reports of recent shootings and floggings of Africans. What apparently provoked this outburst was an incident on 4 February 1933 when a deranged black soldier from the Ivory Coast posted himself outside a latrine on the outskirts of Lomé and then proceeded to shoot Africans one by one as they emerged from it. This incident, though, came at the end of a period of unrest occasioned by the introduction of a new system of taxation, which was probably the underlying reason why the 'German Togolanders' proclaimed: 'We are crying to get the Germans back.'[2]

This bizarre occurrence, however, was not typical of the information reaching the Foreign Office about German agitation overseas. More so was the evidence emanating from the Tanganyika mandate. In September 1933 the Governor, Sir G. S. Symes, reported that while relations between the German and British communities had been and continued to be satisfactory, the coming to power of Hitler had certainly made an impact.[3] National and

71

'even chauvinistic' feeling had been stimulated amongst the Germans and there was a revival of expectations concerning the mandate's return to Germany. New German organisations had sprung up in the territory, but it was difficult to estimate the extent of their political inspiration. A recent visit to the mandate by the former colonial governor, von Lindequist, had, however, passed off without incident. In these circumstances, Symes proposed to take no counter measures, although he felt that the whole situation had to be 'carefully watched'.[4]

Nevertheless, there was a continuation of loose talk among the German community regarding the imminent retrocession of the mandate to Germany which led to rumour and speculation among the native populations of Tanga and Iringa provinces. On the other hand, this was matched by anxiety too, lest Germany's withdrawal from the League should result in British annexation of the territory.[5] Sir J. Sandeman Allen, MP, the chairman of the Joint East Africa Board, following a visit to Tanganyika, believed that the British community in the mandate was as much responsible as the German community there for the creation of an atmosphere, as a result of their attempts 'to force a closer political union' with the neighbouring British possessions, which was not, in fact, a 'live issue', but which the Germans regarded as tantamount to annexation. Allen thought that the Germans would 'always be simmering because of the excitable nature of our own people', although he also considered that, with the rise of the Nazis, there was in the background 'the danger of the younger Germans becoming troublesome'. [6]

Undoubtedly, German aspirations in the mandate were stimulated by the foundation of the *Deutscher Bund für Ostafrika*. In April 1933 this organisation distributed a circular which justified its existence on the basis that the hitherto 'self-effacement' of Germans in the territory had been disadvantageous to their interests. The objectives of the *Bund* were stated to be the promotion of unity among the German community, the securing of their representation in the government of the mandate, and the prevention of 'British attempts to attenuate the character of the Mandate'. In April 1933 it claimed to have over 400 members.

The leader of the *Bund* was Captain W. Schoenfeld, a Moshi planter, who was confirmed in office by Oberstleutnent Bauszus of the Berlin office of the NSDAP's *Kolonialpolitisches Amt*.[7] Schoenfeld was something of a firebrand having, in a book, described non-German residents in Tanganyika as 'robbers and bloodsuckers'.[8]

That he was a potential troublemaker was clear to Syme's successor, Sir Harold MacMichael, who wanted, if possible, to exclude him from the mandate. Moreover, there was, it seems, even support among the moderate Germans for such a course, Schoenfeld being regarded by them as a 'menace'.⁹

Ultimately more significant, and even more in accord with the moderate attitude of most Germans living in the mandate, was Ernst Troost. Besides being the chairman and acting chairman respectively of the Sanya and Moshi branches of the *Bund*, he was also the leader of the Moshi group of the NSDAP. That he was found to be a more congenial associate by his compatriots probably lies in the fact that he clearly expressed the wishes of Hitler, who did not want colonial complications with Britain while he pursued the central objective of an Anglo–German understanding. In a letter to all German nationals resident in the Moshi district of November 1933, he asked them to refrain from intimating to Africans that the mandate would soon be returned to Germany. He emphasised the importance of the white community maintaining a united front towards the Africans, but, more pertinently, remarked: 'The members of the NSDAP . . . are especially reminded that every member of the party abroad is expressly forbidden to involve himself in the politics of the country in which he is a "guest".' It was not, however, until Oberstleutnent Bauszus came to Tanganyika in January 1934 that there was any significant decline in the nationalistic activities of the German community.¹⁰

The importance of Troost in Berlin is evident in that he accompanied Bauszus throughout the latter's tour of the mandate.¹¹ Quite apart from the purpose of organising Nazi activity in Tanganyika, the object of the Bauszus mission appears to have been to stamp out anything that would offend the British authorities. He was reported as having stated publicly at Moshi that:

Certain misguided persons had of late been making themselves conspicuous by their ridiculous antics. That sort of nonsense must cease. He had come from Germany to tell them that such behaviour was an abuse of hospitality, for they must remember they were only guests in Mandated Territory and owed respect and courtesy to their hosts. The crazy doings of a certain section of Germans in Tanganyika were affecting the good name of the whole nation.

He hoped everyone present clearly understood to what he was

referring and what he meant to convey. If Tanganyika, or any other of the former German colonies of Germany were ever restored to her, that was a matter which could be settled between the Chanceries of London and Berlin. Local agitation, such as certain hot-heads had been indulging in recently, only hindered the cause of treaty revision.

Moreover, at Arusha Bauszus was reported as having spoken words to the effect that Britain 'was Germany's best friend in the world'.[12] That he had comported himself in this manner throughout his sojourn was later confirmed by the Tanganyika commissioner of police. Consequently, the governor drew the conclusion that Bauszus's visit 'had had a beneficial effect on community relations'.[13]

But extremist agitation could not altogether be stopped. On 20 May 1934 MacMichael received from the acting head of the *Bund*, Captain Wolfersdorff, a letter from Schoenfeld, who was at that time on leave in Germany, suggesting that the three seats on the mandate's legislative council due to become vacant the following July should be filled by Germans. Furthermore, two German scholars made remarks of a political nature concerning the future of Tanganyika while on a 'purely scientific' visit, which alarmed the British community.[14] By September evidence was also coming to light that Africans working for the Usagara Company on the Makyumbi estate were being paraded daily, compelled to raise the Nazi salute and to cry 'Heil Hitler'. The director of the company, Herr Gaehde, was instructed to ensure the discontinuance of this practice with the warning that 'any attempt to tamper with the native population would not be tolerated for a moment'.[15]

More alarming, however, to the British authorities were reports that Schoenfeld's return to the mandate at Mombasa on 6 October was to mark the beginning of a new phase of German agitation. According to the 'moderate' Count von Stillfried, this 'would be on a large scale and . . . would lead to political difficulties similar to those which' had 'arisen in South West Africa'. It was also learnt from the commissioner of police that Erich Schiller, the salaried secretary of the *Bund*, had received letters from two highly placed officials in Germany who supported Schoenfeld's activities and stressed that all German nationals in the mandate must join the *Bund* under his leadership. Besides this, anti-British propaganda among the African population continued unabated. In the Tanga province adverse comments were being made about the British administration and on one estate Africans were being urged to refuse to pay taxes. Finally, a circular issued by the president of the Tanga branch of the *Bund*, Herr Frauenholz, contained a report of a speech by Wolfersdorff in which he claimed prescriptive rights for the *Bund* over the entire German community in Tanganyika: all Germans were members of it unless they specifically requested exclusion. And in the same circular Frauenholz stated that henceforth all German disputes of honour were to be submitted to the arbitration of the *Bund* before being submitted to British courts.[16]

MacMichael and Cunliffe-Lister became alarmed. The governor thought all these activities were being orchestrated from Germany. He was not certain whether the agency concerned was official or not, but, presuming it was official, he wondered if the German government could be prevailed upon 'to deter it from its activities and prevent unauthorised individuals from lending colour to the suspicion that an official agency' was behind the agitation.[17] By November the Colonial Secretary was taking a 'most serious view' of these developments and had begun to doubt if active membership of the NSDAP was compatible 'with the duties and loyalty of citizens in a Territory under British Mandate'. He hoped that MacMichael would inform him the moment 'that action similar to that taken against the Nazi Movement in South-West Africa' was 'justified and called for'.[18] MacMichael, however, considered anything resembling a ban on any German organisation in the territory premature: unless its leaders were simultaneously deported, it would drive the movement underground doing, thereby, 'more harm than good'.[19] In spite of the return of Schoenfeld, he was prepared to wait and see if the majority of Germans would 'conform to the Baussusz [sic] formula'.[20]

There were signs that they would and, in retrospect, signs that, when they could, the German authorities in Berlin would take immediate steps to curtail the activities of any individual that were deemed inconvenient. Thus in November 1934 Horst Frehse, who had only some months before been appointed leader of the German Youth Movement in Tanganyika, was deprived of his post and ordered back to Germany on the grounds that his excessive enthusiasm had offended local German feeling and the British authorities.[21] Moreover, by the end of 1934 Schoenfeld was a discredited force in the German community, for a split had occurred between him and Ernst Troost. The split promised a possible easing of the situation for MacMichael. It resulted in the supremacy of the Nazi movement among the German community in Tanganyika with the possible implication that any action the government proposed to take against it might 'command sympathy and even the open support of a section of the local German population'.[22] The circumstances of the split possibly indicate the determination of authoritative bodies in Berlin to break any individual or organisation likely to embarrass the aims of the German government. That is to say that *Gleichschaltung* was undertaken in Tanganyika not thereby more effectively to threaten the British authorities, but with a view to reassuring them.[23] This, of course, was not quite so evident in Whitehall.

After having attended a course at an NSDAP training institute in Germany, Troost arrived back in the mandate at the end of 1934 at the same time as Schoenfeld. On his arrival he assumed the territorial leadership of the NSDAP and was simultaneously appointed *Ehrenrichter*.[24] Thereafter a rivalry commenced between the two men, Troost claiming that the NSDAP should have priority over and 'command obedience' from the *Bund*, while Schoenfeld argued that, the interests of his organisation being purely local, it would not submit to Troost's dictates. On 12 December a meeting was held at Moshi to reconcile the differences, but it was there that the break 'became open and complete'. Schoenfeld, who was heckled by Troost and his supporters, claimed that if German representatives on the legislative council of the mandate were compelled to follow the orders of the NSDAP 'they would be unable to give their individual attention to the interests of the German community in East Africa as they would become the mouthpiece of a party whose interests were not local but universal'.[25] Possibly sensing that he had lost command, he appealed to his compatriots to reject the NSDAP, to establish friendly relations with other national-ities and work towards the 'aim of forming a United Free State in Tanganyika'. Thereafter he also resigned the territorial leadership of the *Bund*.

Troost's performance at the meeting was quite a revelation. He was now 'the direct representative of Hitler and the German Government' in the mandate and the *Deutscher Bund* had to come 'under the direct and absolute control of the Nazi Party'. He accused Schoenfeld of having been a failure and of having alienated many Germans from the *Bund*. At a subsequent meeting Troost adminis-tered the Nazi oath of obedience and ordered all party members to join the *Bund* as a means of ensuring the final eclipse of Schoenfeld and his supporters. He asserted that 'all orders given by the leader in Germany to his representative in East Africa must be obeyed even to the extent of going against the Mandate Government', although, of course, such a contingency was unlikely. MacMichael, however, understandably saw Troost as a threat: 'the man to be reckoned with' and whose objective was 'the prosecution of an active Nazi policy'. He now clearly envisaged a situation in which Troost would have to be deported and the Nazi movement banned.[26] Cunliffe-Lister promised his full support if he considered such a course essential, although the governor was to notify the colonial office in advance of any proscription 'since . . . the general political situation might make it desirable to take such action at a particular time or to defer it a little to some time more opportune'.[27]

In the event it proved unnecessary for MacMichael to resort to drastic action of the type he anticipated, for overt political action on the part of the German community died down fairly rapidly. Dr Paul Zitzlaff, who replaced Schoenfeld as the leader of the *Bund*, acted as a restraining influence. On a tour of the mandate he emphasised that his 'main endeavour . . . was to instil into his compatriots the need to maintain friendly relations with all sections of the community'.[28] The *Bund*, however, was now confined to non-political activities with the NSDAP taking the lead in covert political activity. The half yearly Tanganyika intelligence report for June 1935 stated:

> The scarcity of information and reports received concerning the activities of the various German societies in the Territory, are due possibly to meetings being held less frequently in some districts, but also due to the fact that in others the strictest secrecy is maintained. In support of the latter, it is reported that the Germans in the Moshi district hold a mass meeting every month at Sanya. These meetings, at which attendance is compulsory, are held behind closed doors and no information concerning discussions has yet been obtained.

There is also evidence that young Germans of the 1914 class were being forced to return to Germany to do one year's military service.[29]

MacMichael, therefore, still considered the position to be sufficiently disquieting to justify the consideration of precautionary measures should a deterioration of the political situation in Europe

suggest a worsening of the difficulties in the mandate. Should a
crisis arise, he proposed to augment the company of the King's
African Rifles stationed at Arusha, where most Germans in the
north of the mandate were resident, with one of the companies
stationed at Tabora. Granting MacMichael the necessary discretion
for such action, the new Colonial Secretary, J. H. Thomas, requested
that he be consulted if possible before any drastic measures, such as
the 'arrest of leading Germans' were taken, 'in view of fact that such
action might have embarrassing repercussions on general sitiation
[sic]'. Thomas, however, thought the danger of war in Europe
remote.[30]

Significantly, this exchange took place in the immediate aftermath
of the remilitarisation of the Rhineland, which led to unease
amongst the British population in Tanganyika where speculation
about the possible retrocession of the mandate began to spread. This
unease, which had always been present in the business
community,[31] manifested itself in requests to the Colonial Office for
further government statements asserting the permanence of the
mandate on the grounds that the present uncertainty was killing
business confidence.[32] The more sophisticated elements among the
African population also began making representations opposing the
return of German rule.[33] Unrest among the British population and
the native Tanganyikans concerning the future of the mandate
seems, however, to have been more stimulated by events in Europe
than by the activities of the German community. According to
MacMichael, there were rumours that the German section was
armed and prepared for hostilities, but they could not be substan-
tiated by 'any reliable evidence'. Moreover, the leadership of the
NSDAP was still preaching the virtues of moderation, Major Paul
Rheinbaben, the new deputy leader of the party in Tanganyika,
having informed his fellow countrymen that Britain and Germany
should remain 'on good terms' and that the colonial question would
be settled satisfactorily in the fullness of time. The governor felt that
any renewal of political activity was best regarded as a normal
response to what was happening in Europe, concluding that: 'Its
extent and its importnce have probably been magnified unduly
amongst the "settler" community by the rumours which inevitably
feed on such situations.'[34]

The attitude of the German community following the ousting of
Schoenfeld at the end of 1934 was probably best summarised in a
despatch from MacMichael of March 1937. He wrote:

The general policy of the German community, dictated no doubt from Berlin, directly or indirectly, appears to be cardinally concerned with the prevention of any action, corporate or individual, which might provide His Majesty's Government or this Government with reasonable excuse for counter-action of a kind which would bring the German name into disrepute and so weaken the force of their colonial claim. Briefly, they are on their best behaviour; nor does any dubiety of motive that may be alleged or suspected alter the fact that no cause of official complaint arises in consequence on our part.[35]

MacMichael's estimate of the situation was publicly confirmed the following August at a meeting of the German community at Oldeani. In a speech a certain Herr Buchsel stated that the Germans wanted the mandate returned to Germany, while the British wanted it to become a formal part of their empire. He went on:

We fully realise that this problem can and will only be settled one day in EUROPE between the responsible statesmen of our two nations and that meanwhile it is our duty to refrain here from anything which might jeopardise the most necessary good understanding between our two nations in general and our two communities here in Tanganyika Territory. I am giving away no secret when I mention that this our attitude here is not only approved by our Home Government but clearly wished by it.

MacMichael's deputy, D. M. Kennedy, who attended this meeting, had a low opinion of the British settlers in the mandate and inclined to the view that it was their activities rather than those of the Germans that provoked unrest.[36] Thus, while at the end of 1937 there was some discussion about introducing a 'permissive' ordinance in the mandate that would enable the governor to ban the wearing of political and paramilitary uniforms, it was decided in the end to take no action.[37]

In his dispatch of March 1937, however, MacMichael had noted that the Germans in the mandate were still continuing to build a self-contained, 'home from home' community. Their policy appeared to be one of 'self-contained agricultural colonies reserved, so far as may be, for their own nationals and financed by their own companies'. Many of the German settlers held substantial mortgages from large German companies, some having 'a status little

removed from that of unpaid managers'.[38] In the period prior to
Simon's visit to Hitler in March 1935 it was precisely this evidence of
organised German economic penetration of the mandate and the
increased German immigration that attended it that caused most
alarm in the Foreign Office.[39] Indeed, by the middle of 1934 certain
sections of British public opinion were also showing concern.[40]

In May 1934 the Colonial Office was informed of the following
statistics on European immigration into Tanganyika:

Year	British	German	Greek	Others
1929	442	283	142	149
1930	321	279	74	131
1931	256	200	25	96
1932	249	244	20	66
1933	226	248	18	114[41]

Within the Foreign Office these figures created considerable anxiety.
It was even suggested that, while all recent information had
indicated South-West Africa as the main centre of German unrest,
should German immigration into Tanganyika be maintained the
position could be reversed.[42] On the other hand, the governor of the
mandate was not quite so worried. Reporting the number of
German holdings in Tanganyika as 517 on 19 May 1934 with a total
acreage of 453 082, he felt that these statistics did not 'suggest in
themselves any special activity in the acquisition of estates by
Germans during recent months', when the steady flow of Germans
into the territory and the low price of land there were taken into
consideration.[43] He did, however, report shortly thereafter that the
capital of the *Deutsche Ostafrikanische Gesellschaft* (DOAG) had been
greatly increased in 1931, that that company was under the direct
control of the German Foreign Office, and that DOAG in turn
controlled the activities of the other two German companies in the
mandate, namely, the General Investment and Development Co.
Ltd. (GID) and the Usagara Company.[44]

Notwithstanding the views of MacMichael, the situation was
considered sufficiently serious by the Colonial Office to merit
soliciting the views of the Treasury and the Department of Overseas
Trade regarding the possibility of circumscribing German economic
activity in the mandate. The Treasury was not very helpful. It was
admitted that it was morally unsatisfactory that the German

government should be providing foreign currency funds through DOAG to Germans for the purchase of land at a time when it was claimed that Germany was too poor to meet the interest payments on her foreign debts, but Britain did not have, and should not seek to possess, any kind of control over the way in which the German government disposed of its foreign exchange.[45] The Department of Overseas Trade was equally unable to offer much constructive advice, but it did at least share the anxieties of the Colonial Office and observed that 'the question of the diversion to Germany, of orders for equipment' for the German estates had already been considered. This was not a serious and immediate threat, but the situation required 'careful watching'.[46]

The Foreign Office not only believed that these developments in Tanganyika required close and continued scrutiny, but also considered methods of putting a stop to the German activities. In a memorandum, J. V. Perowne outlined the history of German settlement in the mandate from the time of its foundation. Following the ending of restrictions on German entry into Tanganyika in 1925, Germans had begun to return to the territory, buying back their old properties at low cost. The GID had been incorporated in 1929 for the specific purpose of assisting in this. Any German who wished to buy land in the mandate could apply to the company for an advance which was readily forthcoming at an uneconomic rate of interest (5 per cent). It was rumoured that cash was available within as little as 48 hours, with the account of the GID being 'fed by telegraphic transfers from Berlin'. As a result of foreclosures on mortgages, the GID was already a substantial landowner, Perowne estimating that in time it would control considerable areas of the mandate and be in a position to dominate the real estate market. The other German undertaking, the Usagara Company, dealt exclusively in sisal. Some 30 per cent of the mandate's annual sisal crop was now being shipped direct to Germany with a corresponding loss to London's *entrepôt* trade. Perowne confirmed the dominating role of the DOAG. Its articles of association specifically laid down that its activities were to be subject to the supervision of the German Foreign Office and, if this was effective, it was evident 'in view of the connection . . . between the DOAG, the GID and the Usagara Co. that the German companies operating in Tanganyika [were] under the more or less direct control of the German Government in Berlin'.[47]

In an accompanying Minute, Perowne observed that whatever

'the ultimate concealed aims' of the German government, it was clear that they wanted to play down the colonial question. The political aspect of the problem, therefore, was not pressing. But the economic activities were 'undoubtedly more serious' and 'likely to contribute much more effectively to achieve the ultimate aim in view'. The problem was that they were all legal and there was nothing that the Foreign Office could do by way of representations to stop them. Nevertheless, Perowne did believe that there was one course of action that could be taken to combat German activities in Tanganyika: 'to spend more money and to have a definite policy of encouraging suitable British settlers'. Moreover, once Germany's withdrawal from the League became effective it would be possible to investigate the cessation of German immigration into Tanganyika altogether.[48]

Vansittart was less circumspect. A 'very ugly problem' would arise if the situation was allowed 'to drift' and got 'out of hand'. He asked: 'Cannot immigration *as a whole* be checked (i.e. without discrimination) until we are free to deal with the Germans, when they have finally left the League?'. He went on:

If we are to continue to keep Germany from recovering her colonies, we have got to have 2 kinds of policy, local ones (such as I here suggest) and a national one (which involves much more definite reequipment than has yet been contemplated either by HMG or the supine and misled British public). At present we have practically no semblance of either kind of policy. To go on repeating that we will never hand back the German colonies, while doing nothing to make their retention sure, or even feasible, is not a policy at all. It is simply blindness. Personally I would prefer to adopt the more virile policy of the two, which is the logical consequence of our repeated declarations. But if we are to take no steps in time, the alternative policy is to follow the courses of the craven Lord Rothermere.[49]

As a result of these observations, Perowne visited the Colonial Office for a discussion about Tanganyika. There he was told that a policy of stopping immigration generally was ruled out by the terms of the mandate. Moreover, the astounded Perowne was informed that the Colonial Office was no longer so anxious about the German problem in Tanganyika. The Germans had only established themselves in two small areas of the mandate and in any case the amount of land they could acquire was limited by government ordinance to that which was in private hands before the war. In general, the Colonial Office seemed 'well content with the situation' and even welcomed 'German enterprise and penetration in Tanganyika'. Perowne, however, put this down to official optimism on the grounds that the problem had never been thoroughly considered. While at the Colonial Office, he had been shown a letter from MacMichael which was quite concerned regarding 'the possibility of German expansion into native areas'. The opinion of the governor was that: 'the only real remedy was to find British settlers of the right sort to take up the land in Tanganyika; at present it was the German settlers who were of the right sort, the British settlers, with one or two exceptions, being very poor stuff indeed'.[50] Perowne drew the conclusion that the Foreign Office had merely been consulted in the expectation that it 'could work some magic on the German Government'. Accordingly, Perowne informed the Colonial Office that, on the basis of the information they had supplied, there was no possibility of making 'any formal protest'.[51]

The officials in the Foreign Office, however, were not to be deterred. It was felt that developments in the mandate could not be allowed to continue unchecked and it was intimated formally to the Colonial Office that a blanket ban on immigration into Tanganyika was feasible pending Germany's formal withdrawal from the League, when the ban could be restricted to German nationals only. But MacMichael considered such a strategy impracticable. This attitude provoked frustration in the Foreign Office. The Colonial Office had no policy in the mandate: they were afraid of the permanent mandates commission and 'quite unwilling to grasp any genuine nettles'. For Perowne, 'the only really effective policy [was] to spend money by encouraging the right kind of British settler'.[52] During the first two months of 1935 a thorough examination of the legal issues involved in restricting German immigration into the mandate was undertaken by the Foreign Office. These were quite complex but, simply reduced, the view of the Foreign Office was that German immigration could be prohibited under Article 122 of the Treaty of Versailles, which provided that the administering authority could 'make such provisions as' thought 'fit' concerning the repatriation and terms of residence of Europeans. A letter to the Colonial Office along these lines was eventually drafted, but was never sent. Even so, the more bold passages of the draft were deleted, with Vansittart observing that, much as he disliked having to remove these constructive suggestions, they were matters of policy on which Sir John Simon would have to decide.[53] Simon, however, proved very reluctant to come to any decision in the colonial question.[54]

If the position in Tanganyika caused the Foreign Office alarm, events in South-West Africa were altogether more tempestuous. Although there was nothing the Foreign Office could do there, the mandatory power being the Union of South Africa, which conducted its own external affairs, it did take note of what was going on in the mandate and was regularly informed by the Dominions Office. By the beginning of 1933 South African opinion was already showing distinct signs of anxiety. It was noted that 'the effort to stimulate fresh interest in the former German colonies' was a feature of the renewed nationalist and militarist spirit in Germany and that, while Germans on the whole were disinterested in the colonies, the 'mainly aristocratic groups', who were conducting the colonial agitation, were 'unceasing' in their propaganda and might 'produce a popular movement in time'.[55]

The German settlers in South-West Africa had proved a serious problem from the inception of the mandate. Generally recalcitrant, they held that mandatory status was a temporary phenomenon that would be ended once Germany joined the League. In the early days the problem became acute in 1922 when the advisory council of the mandate passed a resolution calling for a form of representative government. The major difficulty here was that the German community would be excluded from the electoral processes suggested unless its individual members opted for voluntary naturalisation. This the German community consistently refused to do for fear of losing its German nationality. The advisory council, therefore, proposed that the Union government should pass an act which would confer Union nationality automatically on all German residents in the mandate.[56] Thereafter, the De Haas–Smuts agreement between the Union and German governments was concluded in October 1923 and passed into law in the mandate the following September. Under its terms German schools and the German language were to be protected, German rights were guaranteed and German residents in South-West Africa were automatically to become naturalised Union subjects unless exemption was specifically requested.[57] In an open letter De Haas encouraged the German community not to exclude itself from Union citizenship: the future of South-West Africa was now bound up with that of the Union of

South Africa and it would be prudent for German nationals there to co-operate with the Union authorities.[58] It should be noted that as an undoubted act of conciliation the advisory council in the mandate rejected the proposal made by a Union commission in 1920 that South West Africa would best be governed as the fifth province of the Union.[59]

By 1925 the overwhelming majority of German residents had passively accepted Union nationality with only 261 opting for exemption.[60] Thus the way was clear for reconciliation between the white communities in the mandate and the introduction of limited self-government for them. Until 1928 the Union and German factions, as they were represented in the legislative assembly, appear to have worked well together, the knowledge that the white community as a whole constituted only 10 per cent of the population acting as a catalyst in maintaining a united front.[61] Inevitably, however, the profound differences between the two communities began to reassert themselves. These related to the future status of the mandate. Not unnaturally, the Union section developed an inclination towards close cooperation with the Union government with the ultimate end in view of the realisation of the fifth province concept.[62] This had some support in the Union itself;[63] and the attitude of the Union section was dramatically exposed during the early months of 1927 when their representatives in the legislative assembly, in response to growing suggestions that South-West Africa would ultimately be returned to Germany, introduced 'a resolution expressing formal disapproval of the idea of any restoration of the Mandated Territory to Germany'. It was carried in the absence of the German members, who walked out when it was put to the vote.[64]

Given the fact that the realisation of the fifth province concept was possible provided that a majority in the mandate desired it, the numbers game was important. That the German community was aware of this was revealed in their refusal to provide the necessary two-thirds majority for the financing of the settlement in the mandate of the Angolan Boers. Moreover, they wanted equal naturalisation rights for new German immigrants in the mandate.[65] The reduction in the time for naturalisation from five years to one, as was the case for immigrants from the Union, would have had considerable political significance for the Germans, for, from 1923 until 1928, German immigration had outnumbered that of all others by six to one.[66]

Nevertheless, by 1932 there were distinct signs that reconciliation between the Union and German communities was possible. It was agreed, in principle, that German should become a third official language, that all unnaturalised Germans resident in the mandate on 31 December 1931 should be automatically naturalised, and that the period of naturalisation for subsequent German immigrants should be reduced from five years to two years. But disputes broke out again. The German party wanted the elections due in December 1933 postponed for a year so that their supporters could take full advantage of the proposed new legislation, while the Union party remained opposed. Eventually, the administrator secured a compromise whereby the elections were postponed and the operation of the reforms delayed until the Germans had proved their good faith, but blatant antagonism persisted. The Union party was now firmly wedded to the fifth province concept and the Germans continued to advocate the maintenance of the mandate pending its return to Germany.[67] The unity of the white population, a condition of the introduction of reforms, could not be sustained.

That it could not be sustained was very much the consequence of the impetus given to German nationalism in the mandate by Hitler's accession to power in Berlin. By the middle of 1933 the Postmaster General in South-West Africa, Colonel Venning, considered the position to be sufficiently grave to address a lengthy memorandum to the British High Commissioner in South Africa, Sir H. J. Stanley. Venning considered that all the efforts of the administration in the mandate to accommodate the wishes of the Germans had had no impact and that, 'the growing nationalist spirit in Germany has been deliberately transplanted in South West Africa over the heads of the older German population'. Official and private visits to South-West Africa by German naval detachments, journalists and former officials of the German colonial regime were principally responsible for stimulating unrest. This activity, which was increasing, had caused the older and more moderate section of the German population to lose its grip on the rest of its compatriots. It was, in any case, already being swamped by new arrivals from Germany, thus making the problem of assimilating Germans in the mandate more intractable than ever. The younger group of Germans wanted nothing less than the full restoration of South-West Africa to German sovereignty and they were coercing their older fellow countrymen into support for this. These were utopian aims, but Venning thought it would be dangerous, in the circumstances, to make further progress with representative democracy in the mandate for the time being. Furthermore, the Union itself was not immune to developments in South-West Africa. The 'chauvinistic elements' in the mandate had made contact with the German population in the Union with the evident purpose of creating 'a homogeneous German South African political entity which . . . through their contact with a large section of the Union population [would] exert its influence in the direction desired by the German colonial circles in Germany'. Venning reported that the main German organisation in the mandate was the *Deutscher Bund*, which organised and controlled all 'lesser organisations' and constituted the 'actual political organisation ruling the Germans' in the territory. Its chairman was Alfred Voigts. In forwarding this memorandum to the Dominions Office, the High Commissioner confirmed that what it contained was substantially correct.[68]

The anxiety felt by Venning was reflected by opinion in the Union. By July 1933 the South African press was regularly reporting on the Nazi-inspired activities of the German community in the mandate.[69] On 31 July the *Cape Times* stated that Nazism was rife in the mandate, with every town having its own cell which tried 'to live up to the traditions of Hitlerism in Germany'. The most public manifestation of the movement was the appearance of anti-Semitism. The swastika was scribbled into the books of Jewish children and the Jewish members of a gymnastics society had been expelled. The *Cape Times*, however, thought that the totality of German society in South-West Africa was in a political dilemma:

> While many of them sympathise with the [Nazi] movement, they feel that to do so openly would create a distinct and everlasting breach between the British and German sections.
> On the other hand, if they do not support the views of the Nazis, they will be ostracised by their German friends and customers.[70]

An indication of the moderate nature of a large proportion of the German settlers in South-West Africa might be found in the fact that the *Schulverein* there voted to remove its chairman, Dr Brenner, who, after a visit to Germany, attempted to introduce Nazism into the mandate's German schools.[71]

There can be little doubt that the activities of German organisations in South-West Africa and the Union were all coordinated from Pretoria by Dr Emil Wiehl, the German consul-general. From the beginning of his appointment he was a controversial figure, almost his first action being the dismissal of a Jewish typist, Regina Kessel, from the offices of the German consulate.[72] Such an event naturally profoundly offended the powerful Jewish community in the Union. It also stimulated nascent anti-Semitism in South Africa, which in turn provoked a violent and deserved Jewish reaction culminating in a riot.[73] But if Wiehl's presence in the Union and his public statements, many of which enjoyed the 'specially sympathetic support' of Dr H. D. J. Bodenstein, the Union Secretary for External Affairs,[74] encouraged Nazi supporters and fellow-travellers in South Africa, his impact in South-West Africa was even more telling on the German community there. In August 1933 Whitehall was informed that the *Bund* was referring to Pretoria on matters of policy,[75] and in October and November of that year Wiehl, in the company of Oberstleutnent Bauszus, played an important role in organising the political activities of the Germans in the mandate.[76]

The main objective was to ensure that the main vehicles of German expression, the *Bund* and the NSDAP, in existence in South-West Africa since 1929, worked in harmony and in accordance with instructions from Berlin. These reflected Hitler's current preoccupation with keeping German colonial agitation at a low level. In May 1933, therefore, Major Weigel, the leader of the South-West African Nazis, was informed that Hitler's attitude 'towards the colonial problem is, at present, a very circumspect one'.[77] Wiehl's publicly stated aspiration of securing a compromise between the German and Union sections on the occasion of his visit to Windhoek on 1 November 1933 was perfectly in line with this.[78] Presumably Dr Schwietering, appointed Führer of the *Bund* following the Wiehl–Bauszus mission, was encouraging movement in the same direction in a crude sort of way when he announced that the intentions of the *Bund* were not aggressive and that it was recognised that South-West Africa could only prosper by co-operation. He coupled this, however, with statements claiming that the 'Fatherland' had 'shown the way for the unification of the German people' and that, 'as Germany' refused 'to be treated as a second-class nation, so the Germans in South-West Africa' would 'relentlessly strive for equality' to which they were entitled owing to their numbers and standing in the mandate.[79] Such pronouncements were not very well calculated to allay the apprehensions of the Union section.

These had become considerable by the end of 1933. In August the legislative assembly voted for the Criminal Law Amendment

Ordinance which was designed to forbid persons or organisations disturbing the peace, but its application was suspended by the Union government in the hope that political stability would return to the mandate.[80] There was little prospect of this. The suspicions of the Union section were now so firmly entrenched that quiescence of the German population, even if that had been possible, would only have been treated with more suspicion. Speaking to the press in Cape Town in November 1933, J. P. Niehaus, leader of the United Party in South-West Africa, opined that South-West Africa would inevitably become German again unless more moral support from the Union was forthcoming.[81] Eventually, the Union government was forced to allow the application of the Criminal Law Amendment Ordinance at the beginning of 1934. From that time onwards the administrator, Dr Conradie, and the executive committee of the mandate were empowered to suppress subversive organisations, proscribe the wearing of badges and instruct the police to search any premises.[82]

The effect of the measures taken by the government of the mandate and the preferences indicated from Berlin was a decline in overt nationalistic activity on the part of the German community.[83] But this did not lead to a more trusting attitude among the Union section. Mr L. Taljaard, a member of the legislative assembly, pointed out that the absence of parades and uniforms did not in itself indicate the cessation of Nazi activity.[84] And he was right to have been suspicious. A letter from Bauszus, delivered by Wiehl to Schwietering and Weigel, indicates quite clearly that both the *Bund* and the NSDAP were acting on instructions from Berlin and that differences of interpretation regarding these instructions were to be submitted to Germany for arbitration.[85] Moreover, Weigel, in March 1934, informed the *Auslandsorganisation* that he thought it would be possible to increase the German population in the mandate until it constituted a majority amongst the white settlers. In connection with this he noted that Afrikaner farms were being sold off by the Land Bank at a price below their bond value. There existed, therefore, the possibility 'of acquiring through cleverly concealed manipulation comparatively cheap farms for German settlement purposes'.[86]

It was, however, given the history of organised German settlement in South-West Africa and the constitutional developments of the 1920s, difficult for the NSDAP and its front organisations to maintain a low profile indefinitely. The events of 1933 had hardened the resolve of the Union section to pursue the fifth province concept and they were determined to push it by constitutional means through the legislative assembly.[87] The German community was, as a corollary, obliged to declare its opposition. Its position was that it wanted the abolition of the constitution of the mandate and a return to the administrative system as it had been in the beginning, namely, by an administrator and an advisory council, which would maintain the distinctive nature of the territory.[88] In May 1934 the Union Prime Minister, Hertzog, arranged a conference for the purpose of reconciling the two communities, but it proved abortive. The Union section would only participate in discussions if their basis was to be closer union with South Africa.[89] The German position was now unequivocally stated by Schwietering: unless German became an official language and Germans were given equal franchise and naturalisation rights, they would henceforth refuse to contest elections.[90]

During the summer of 1934 this political crisis was overtaken by an outburst of Germanic enthusiasm that was to lead to the full application of the Criminal Law Amendment Ordinance. As early as March 1934 Professor Bohle, the leader of the Union NSDAP, had warned Weigel of the dangers of rowdyism on the part of the German community. Having recently spoken to von Neurath, he had been confirmed in his view 'that the colonial problem' would 'ultimately be decided in Europe and not in the various Mandated Territories'. Consequently, he thought that loose talk about the return of South-West Africa to Germany was undesirable and that 'it would do no harm if the people of South-West Africa were to take a broader view of matters'. He did, however, recognise that indiscipline was a difficult problem.[91]

Bohle was justified in being apprehensive. In the first week of July 1934 a large number of young Germans descended upon Windhoek, 'which had been transformed by German flags flying all over the town – both the black, white and red and the Hakenkreuz', in order to celebrate a German youth week.[92] During the course of the following week the administrator took firm action. The Hitler Youth were banned and its organiser, Erich von Losnitzer, was deported. In addition, a search of the NSDAP's headquarters was undertaken, which revealed that a list of Jews resident in the mandate had been compiled.[93] At the beginning of October further searches of the NSDAP's offices were carried out which resulted in a complete ban on the party in the mandate and the deportation of Major Weigel.[94] It was the evidence found during these raids that made this step necessary. Colonel Venning and the Windhoek town clerk, Mr Kerby, later informed Mr P. Liesching of the British High Commission in the Union that they had seen the relevant documentation, which had been bound into a volume, and that:

> it contained convincing proof that the German community, strongly supported by the German Government in Europe, were pursuing a time honoured policy . . . of flattering the Dutch community in South Africa with promises of assistance against British political and commercial influence, in the conviction that if they succeeded in their scheme of reducing or eliminating British influence, the Dutch South Africans would be easy prey.[95]

Flattery of the Dutch community, however, did not produce much of a result.

Although the United Party split in September 1934, with the splinter group, the Economic League led by General De Jager, forming an electoral alliance with the *Deutscher Bund* for the purpose of contesting the elections in the mandate due the following October,[96] the elections proved a total disaster for the Germans and the Economic League. The only United Party candidate to lose his seat was Mr Niehaus. Of the elected seats on the legislative assembly, the United Party won eight and had the support of the successful independent, Mr Lardner Burke.[97] With the appointment of three other United Party members, the Union section now had the necessary two-thirds majority to enable the Union government to act upon the basis of a resolution passed in the mandate's legislative assembly.[98] Thus on 29 November the Hamman resolution was passed which called for the 'administration of the territory as a fifth province subject to the terms of the Mandate'.[99]

By the beginning of January 1935 Hertzog had arrived at the conclusion that the whole situation in the mandate demanded investigation[100] and the relevant commission was appointed the following April.[101] It reported in March 1936. The commission found that there had been continual interference by the *Auslandsorganisation* in the affairs of South-West Africa, to such an extent that the basic democratic rights of Germans who were Union subjects had ceased to exist. In the circumstances, the existing form of government in the mandate had become impracticable, but the commission was unable to agree upon a system to supersede it. It could only be agreed that: 'there is no legal obstacle to the government of the territory as a province of the Union subject to the Mandate'. From March until December 1936 the situation in South-West Africa continued to deteriorate owing partly to an increase in colonial agitation in Germany.[102]

There was constant talk of the imminent return of the mandate to the Reich which eventually provoked the 'Declaration of the Administration of South West Africa'. This document stated that there was no intention of changing the system of government; that the government of the mandate as a fifth province of the Union would not conflict with the terms of the mandate; that the mandate had been conferred upon the Union government irrevocably and that the Union government would not even consider its transfer to another power; that in future aliens would not be able to become members of political organisations or similar institutions in the mandate; that the Union government did not recognise dual nationality in the territory; and that German would not be recognised as an official language except at the request of the majority of South-West Africa.[103]

The report of the South-West African commission and the Declaration, both of which elicited strong German protests,[104] were followed in April 1937 by a Proclamation of the Union Government. This provided that:

> No person who is not a British subject shall . . . be eligible for membership of, or employment of, a public body; that no person who is not a British subject shall . . . become a member or employee of any political organisation; and that any British subject within the territory who takes an oath or promises to be faithful to or bear allegiance to, or obey the orders of (a) any sovereign or head of state other than His Majesty the King, or (b) the government or any member or official of the government of any state other than the Union, or (c) any foreign political organisation shall be guilty of an offence.

The application of this proclamation to South-West Africa was evidently a 'drastic' measure, placing 'considerable power in the hands of the administration'.[105] It did not, however, put a stop to German activity[106] and right up until the war the atmosphere within the mandate remained fraught.[107]

The situation in South-West Africa was very embarrassing for the

Union government. It wanted to maintain control over the mandate but, at the same time, it wanted to maintain good relations with its 'spiritual' kin in Berlin. Thus, until the appointment of the South-West Africa commission, it pursued a policy of non-interference in the mandate's political affairs. In August 1934 Dr Bodenstein favoured Mr Liesching with his views. He thought that if the German community carried out a boycott of the forthcoming elections and as a result the Union section passed a resolution calling for closer union between the mandate and South Africa, this would not be regarded by the Union government as 'a constitutionally valid basis for the drastic intervention for which it asked'. Liesching believed that the most the Union would do, on the basis of Bodenstein's remarks, was 'to cause the Territory to revert to a constitutional position in which the Administrator would govern with some form of Advisory Council'. This, of course, was precisely what the German section wanted! Questioned by Liesching as to the permanence of the mandate for South-West Africa, Bodenstein returned an interesting reply. He observed that:

> a Mandate was, in essence, not permanent, and that there must therefore be a reluctance to take any step, such as the administration of the Territory as a fifth province, which would give the appearance of greater permanence.

On the other hand, the South African foreign minister indicated that the Union government had not considered, and was not likely to consider in earnest, 'the possibility of surrendering the mandate within the measurable future'. As far as Bodenstein was concerned, the major preoccupation of the Union government in South-West Africa was the deadlock between the two white communities which had to be broken. He had been for a number of weekend walks with Wiehl, now elevated to the rank of *chargé d'affaires*, and had warned him of the consequences of continued German intransigence. Nevertheless, Bodenstein felt strong sympathy with the Germans, as on many points their views coincided with those of Afrikaner nationalism.[108]

If anything, therefore, the attitude of the South African government was more favourable to the German community in the mandate than to the Union section, although nothing would be permitted there that was likely to jeopardise the security of the Union. The egregious Wiehl, however, was sufficiently confident in his relations with the South African government to utter publicly, on the occasion of his further elevation to the rank of envoy extraordinary and minister plenipotentiary, characteristically tactless remarks. The existence of blood ties between South Africans and Germans, he claimed, was very important now that the South-West African mandate was under the control of the Union, for it meant that the Union government had been charged 'with the protection and care of the numerous German nationals domiciled therein'. He hoped that Germany and South Africa would move closer together culturally and commercially. The *Cape Times* responded to this indiscretion with typical candour. In a leading article it commented:

> the use of the word 'nationals' by the German Minister . . . is neither tactful nor justifiable in our opinion. It implies a claim on behalf of the German Government to retain the allegiance of the German section of the population of South-West [Africa] . . . and it will certainly be taken by them as a hint that when the time comes, Germany will demand the return of the territory.

In the opinion of the *Cape Times*, Wiehl had missed an excellent opportunity of telling the German community in South–West Africa that it was their duty to co-operate with other communities in the mandate.[109] A public row ensued between the Union government and the *Cape Times*, in which the former defended Wiehl and the latter the freedom of the press, although not without cost.[110] The British High Commissioner later reported that Mr B. K. Long, the editor of the *Cape Times*, had been compelled to resign, possibly as a result of his outspokenness over incidents concerned with the presentation of Wiehl's new credentials. He had heard on 'good authority' that it had been governmental pressure that had secured Long's demission and that the pressure had been exerted through the acting Minister for Native Affairs, who was a member of the newspaper's board of directors.[111]

This information, which was regularly fed to the Foreign Office by the Dominions Office, was very interesting and illuminating, but, as Orme Sargent had observed in August 1933, the Union government had its own relations with Germany and they were no concern of the British government.[112] The most that the Foreign Office could do was to take note. When, however, Oswald Pirow, the Union defence minister, made his famous speech to the crew of the

German cruiser *Emden* in January 1935, the implications were seriously considered.

Whitehall had had some forewarning of Pirow's views. In November 1934 the British High Commissioner in the Union had availed himself of an opportunity to talk to Pirow about South-West Africa. According to the latter there was emphatically no prospect of the Union administering the mandate as an integral part of its territory. There was 'no advantage . . . that could possibly accrue to the Union from the assumption of a greater responsibility than it already had for the administration of the finances of the Territory'. In fact, said Pirow, there were distinct disadvantages which would be incurred 'from the additional liabilities'. There were already enough undesirables on the electoral rolls in the Union without adding to their number and South-West Africa was a 'wretched' country where the quality of the colonists was exceptionally low. He referred mainly to the German and Afrikaner sections. In Pirow's estimation:

> There were a few decent Germans, but they dared not assert themselves. The people were not fit for representative institutions, and the proper thing to do would be to abrogate the Constitution, and let the administrator govern with some assistance from an Advisory Council.

The defence minister did not say that this was actually contemplated, but it is interesting that, like Bodenstein, he inclined to a view of the constitutional future of the mandate that accorded with the preferences of the German section. Even from the strategic aspect, Pirow doubted the value of the mandate, which caused the High Commissioner to conclude:

> His references to South West were so depreciatory as to cause me to wonder whether he might be toying with the idea of a return of the mandated territory to Germany, though he did not say anything implicitly indicative of such a policy.[113]

When Pirow finally made his view of Germany and the colonial question public, he did not specify a territory, but he did argue that Germany should once again become a colonial power. Addressing the crew of the *Emden*, he stated:

Germany as a civilised State, is one of the chief exponents of our Western culture, which can be maintained only by white peoples, and preserved only by the united co-operation of all. To-day more than ever, when the rising tide of the coloured races is reaching higher and higher, the active help of a strong Germany is more than ever necessary. For us in South Africa the maintenance and the spread of white civilisation is a question of life and death. In this sense I express the hope that Germany will again soon become a Colonial Power in Africa.[114]

This statement at first went unreported in the South African press[115] until the *Cape Argus* reported that Ward Price had raised the issue of Pirow's statement in an interview with Hitler. Hitler's response had been characteristic. He said: 'Until it is confirmed I should not like to pass any opinion. I will only say that if South Africa or any other Government would offer to give us back any of our colonies we should accept them willingly'.[116] There then followed parliamentary questions in South Africa to which Pirow responded by stating that what he meant was quite clear in its context and that it merely represented his personal opinion.[117]

Within the Foreign Office, however, it was considered that Pirow's remarks implied much more than that. The South African defence minister had been in Germany the preceding summer, but it was not known what he had been doing and he had done 'his best to avoid H. M. Embassy'. It now seemed that the German government might be testing 'the weaker vessel first' and hoping, in the field of colonial concessions, to find 'HMG in the Union of S.A. more *coulant* than HMG in the U.K.', with a view to using 'the example of the former to impress & nag at the latter'.[118]

Vansittart, who was at first inclined to rank Pirow with Lord Rothermere,[119] was obliged to think again when the Berlin chancery informed the central department of a conversation between the Dutch and South African ministers in Berlin. According to the latter, Pirow's statement had not been a collection of casual remarks. The defence minister had rather taken advantage of an opportunity to enunciate a policy to which the Union government attached great importance. For South Africa, the presence of Germany in the continent was essential 'for the future safety of the white population'. Nonetheless, the Union government was not contemplating the retrocession of South-West Africa and neither did they think Tanganyika or the Cameroons should be returned:

But if it were possible for Germany to be given possession of the Portuguese colonies, that would be the ideal. For strategical reasons South Africa could not give up the central and southern portion of South-West Africa but they would gladly hand over the tropical belt of the northern portions if Angola were to be German.[120]

Simultaneously, the Foreign Office learnt that the French had been approached by the Germans about Angola and that the British Consul-General in Loanda was firmly of the opinion that German 'intrigue' was 'rife in that colony'.[121]

This information, together with the approach made by Voretzsch and secret information of a 'German endeavour to arouse Nordic race-consciousness among the German half-castes in New Guinea and Samoa', conspired to prompt Mr J. V. Perowne into the preparation of a memorandum on 'German Colonial Aspirations'. Clearly, Perowne anticipated an imminent attempt on the part of the German government to revive its old aspirations to the possession of Angola. In this respect, he thought that the connection between South Africa and Germany was very significant. The Union government had long coveted Mozambique, which was important to them for two reasons; the port of Lourenço Marques and the Labour which supplied the Rand mines. Perowne commented:

Given the Union desire for Mozambique, a fear of the 'rising tide of colour' of Union politicians like Mr Pirow and the recently revealed fact that the German appetite for Angola is still alive . . . it seems far from impossible that during Mr Pirow's visit to Berlin last summer the agreeable possibility should have been discussed of Union support for Germany in obtaining Angola and possibly other Portuguese possessions in West Africa, in return for German support in securing Mozambique for the Union.

Such an eventuality would be very embarrassing for Britain. Quite apart from the fact that Britain did not wish to see Germany once again installed in Africa, if it was in any way avoidable, Britain was bound to defend the integrity of Portugal's overseas possessions by a number of treaties. Consequently, there existed the danger that: 'Two of His Majesty's Governments might . . . find themselves involved in a serious conflict arising, in part at any rate, out of German territorial appetites in Africa'.[122] Vansittart was adamant

over such a set of circumstances: Britain could 'have nothing to do
with this ancient and dirty game'. It had been a mistake to
encourage Germany in this way previously and 'the time for it' was
'long past'. The League of Nations now existed and some of its
members had 'League principles'.[123] He thought, however, that
Simon might 'receive feelers' over the whole range of the colonial
question when he visited Berlin.[124]

5

The Colonial Question and a General Settlement

The widespread feeling in the Foreign Office, prior to the visit made by Simon and Eden to Berlin at the end of March 1935, that Hitler might raise the colonial question in his talks with British ministers was confirmed. Thus the pressure that had built up in the Foreign Office for the government to define its attitude towards the colonial claim before March intensified in the succeeding months, until the point was reached by the beginning of 1936 where the British government was prepared to countenance colonial satisfaction for Germany in return for her agreement to participate in a general settlement of outstanding European problems.

By February 1935 the Foreign Office was trying to elicit the views of the Dominions and Colonial Offices regarding policy towards Germany's colonial claims, but there was little response.[1] The Dominions Office suggested that the matter could be informally discussed by the Dominions Prime Ministers when they attended the King's silver jubilee celebrations the following May,[2] but the attitude of the Colonial Office was not helpful at all. The Colonial Secretary, Sir Philip Cunliffe-Lister, thought the preparation of a memorandum justifying Britain's administration of the mandates against German colonial demands unnecessary and he had the support of Sir John Simon, who wrote:

> Secret [My own view is that we ought *not* to treat the German claim as requiring that we need to justify ourselves. But at the same time I don't think we should be so obdurate about the claim as some people affect to be. If we are ever going to yield at all, let us yield when the concession is *worth* something & will get us something in return].[3]

His officials, however, disagreed. Wigram thought the attitude of the Colonial Office short-sighted. In the past they had declined to prepare memoranda on the mandates and Britain's title to them

99

because 'they chose to believe that the colonial question would never be raised by the Germans' and they had been vacillating over issues connected with Tanganyika, arguing one minute that there was danger from the German settlers and the next that there was none. He wanted a letter sent to Cunliffe-Lister explaining why the Foreign Office thought it necessary to produce a statement about the former German colonies and a parliamentary question and answer about them.[4] Some days later he went even further, demanding that a decision regarding the method of restricting the impact of German immigration into Tanganyika be taken.[5] By the beginning of March he was insistent that a 'full and adequate' memorandum should be composed for the meetings of the dominions premiers at the King's silver jubilee in order that the colonial question could be 'reviewed and some common policy concerted'. The Foreign Office had no instructions and time pressed.[6]

All the relevant papers relating to the colonial question were with Simon by mid-March; Vansittart hoped for a speedy decision on the outstanding issues, but it was not forthcoming.[7] Eventually, however, a decision does seem to have been reached, on the intervention of Sir Maurice Hankey, that the preparation of a memorandum for the dominions Prime Ministers could go ahead, although the exercise was hampered by inter-departmental disagreements as to whose responsibility the preparation of such a memorandum should be.[8] Moreover, Simon continued to be 'doubtful about the necessity of preparing any document'. Almost a month, therefore, after Simon's return from Berlin J. V. Perowne could indicate that four issues pertaining to the colonial question still remained for decision: that of immigration by Britons and Germans into Tanganyika; that of whether or not a letter should be sent to the Colonial Office suggesting that the preparation of a statement on the colonial question was their province; that of whether or not the Dominions and Colonial Offices should prepare a memorandum on colonies for the dominions Prime Ministers; and the nature of the reply, if any, that should be sent to a letter from Sir John Sandeman Allen regarding the position of Tanganyika.

Orme Sargent observed that these issues were all connected with one 'major question of policy', namely, 'the policy which H.M. Government . . . should adopt towards the German colonial claims'. He considered that the time had come 'when this major question might well with advantage be put to the Cabinet' and he thought that 'it would certainly be convenient if it could be definitely settled' before the dominions Prime Ministers arrived. Vansittart, too, felt that there should be no 'further delay', for the policy of continually resisting the German colonial claim was bound up with Britain's ability to resist it, which at present was insufficient. No decisions, however, were taken and neither was a memorandum submitted to the Prime Ministers of the dominions, it being decided by Vansittart and Simon that it would be 'impossible . . . until the matter had been discussed in the Cabinet'. Thus the dominions premiers went 'home without the matter having been gone into'.[9] Nevertheless, it is clear that by the end of April 1935 the Foreign Office was exhibiting considerable urgency in the matter of the colonial question and that this had been stimulated by the fact that Hitler had raised the matter with Simon during the March talks.

During Cabinet discussions immediately preceding Simon's visit to Berlin, only fleeting mention was made of the colonial question. On 20 March Simon told the Cabinet that he proposed to make the basis of his talks the topics set out in the Anglo–French communiqué of 3 February 1935. But it was the presentation of the British case that was crucial:

> He thought it should be presented crisply, but firmly. Herr Hitler should not be allowed to take charge from the outset, as was his wont. His idea, therefore, was to present firmly that there were two directions in which the European situation might develop.

There could either be a system of regional pacts, such as Locarno, in which the participation of Germany was essential to achieve security, or security could be achieved by the division of Europe into blocs. Simon would point out that the British government would deprecate the latter development, but he would give no indication of what the British attitude was likely to be if that was to occur. He would, however, make it clear that in the British estimation it was very much Germany's responsibility as to how things evolved.

That British ministers had international conciliation and co-operation as their primary objectives was made very plain by Neville Chamberlain who stated that if suggestions that had been made by Ribbentrop and Goering that 'the German idea was to get closer to this country at the expense of other countries' really represented Hitler's policy then the sooner he was disabused of this the better. It 'ought to be brought home to Hitler what were likely to be the consequences to himself and his country if he refused to co-operate'.

Simon, however, recognised that the Anglo–French communiqué only offered Germany equality in the field of armaments. In response, Hitler might well raise some large issues such as the demilitarised zone, Memel and colonies and argue that Germany did not have equality in these matters. Chamberlain thought that the answer here was to indicate that these questions could be discussed once security was achieved. It was also felt within the Cabinet that Germany would have to return to the League before further moves in the direction of *Gleichberechtigung* could be considered. If Hitler stated that Germany could not return to the League under its present constitution, Simon would suggest that Germany rejoin 'and see what could be done to alter its constitution'.[10]

In essence, what the British contemplated as a desirable consequence of the talks was clearly stated in the British note of protest of 18 March against the unilateral abrogation of the disarmament clauses of the Treaty of Versailles, namely, 'a general settlement freely negotiated between Germany and the other Powers' and 'agreements regarding armaments, which in the case of Germany would replace the provisions of Part V of the Treaty of Versailles'.[11] What, however, the British government meant by a *general settlement* at this time was a rather limited concept confined to security pacts in central and eastern Europe, an armaments agreement, an aerial agreement and the return of Germany to the League. At bottom it remained an attempt to repair the damage of October 1933.

Hitler's hopes of the talks were not fixed upon any international agreement, but rather, as Chamberlain had speculated, on an Anglo–German understanding. Indeed, Phipps reported that Hitler's fury over the British defence white paper was based upon the fact that he had contemplated making 'an appeal' during the talks for exactly this.[12] Such a possibility now seemed to have been placed in jeopardy. There is further evidence of Hitler's ambitions in this respect in the early months of 1935. At the end of February he seems to have expressed a wish for a personal meeting with Vansittart, because he was 'convinced' that the permanent under-secretary was 'opposed to him'.[13] Presumably Hitler intended to reassure Vansittart that Germany had no hostile intention towards Britain, thereby weakening what he ragarded as a powerful anti-German influence in the counsels of the British government.[14] Moreover, on 27 February Phipps was informed by Hitler's private secretary that it would be 'easy . . . for Great Britain and Germany to come to an agreement on all subjects' but, 'regretfully' it appeared that the British government did not want 'any separate agreement'. Phipps replied that this indeed was the position, because Britain 'felt peace and "apaisement" must be general'. It was, however, Phipps's view that the notion of an Anglo–German understanding was supported to a considerable extent by 'many highly placed persons in the Nazi party, in the army and in official circles'.[15]

The constant iteration of these desires for an agreement with Britain at this time may well be an indication of a certain frustration on the part of Hitler that the policy pursued in the period of the interviews had not come to fruition. It is possible that rumours of Schacht's ascendency over Hitler in matters relating to Germany's colonial claims that reached the Foreign Office at the end of 1934 and the beginning of 1935 were the first stages leading to Hitler's decision to use the colonial claim as a means of blackmailing the British into an understanding.[16] This did not mean that he was listening to Schacht and his sympathisers because he wanted to push the colonial question as a concrete issue, but rather because he was interested in using their arguments as a means of duping the British into thinking that he wished to do so. Thus, any rumours that were created to the effect that he had been converted to colonialism in the traditional sense would be advantageous from this point of view.

In this connection, it is of some interest that on 19 and 20 March 1935 Hjalmar Schacht and Heinrich Schnee sent their views on colonial policy to Hitler.[17] It is at least certain that Schacht's statement was sent at the request of Ritter von Epp, the head of the NSDAP's *Kolonialpolitisches Amt* (KPA). While this does not automatically suggest that von Epp had acted at Hitler's behest, it is noteworthy that his copy of Schacht's statement was submitted fairly speedily to the Führer. It is, therefore, not beyond the bounds of possibility that the views to Schacht and Schnee had been deliberately solicited with a view of using them in the imminent talks with British ministers in order to compel the British government to be amenable to his real aim of an Anglo–German understanding.[18] It may be that Hitler was confirmed in his intentions by the fact that the British note of protest against the introduction of conscription in Germany resembled more a routine act than definite opposition. And that the British ministers were still prepared to come to Berlin after the events of March perhaps demonstrated that the British would only react in the way he wanted if they were confronted forcefully.[19]

An examination of the record of the talks that took place between

Hitler and Simon and Eden indicates in retrospect just how far apart
the German and British standpoints were and also illustrates for the
first time Hitler's use of the colonial question in order to threaten the
British into a favourable posture regarding an Anglo–German
understanding. In opening the talks on 25 March, Simon pointed
out that it was the object of British policy to secure peace by the co-
operation of all European countries. The British government,
despite the disturbance to British public opinion created by Germany's conduct, was prepared to accept Hitler's word that he
wanted peace, but wanted to know if 'there was any line of action
which Germany would find it possible to take' that could persuade
'friendly peoples and Governments' that the energetic pursuit of
European co-operation was worthwhile. In reply, Hitler evaded the
issue that had been put to him by claiming that co-operation without
equality was impossible. Moreover, he lied about his long term aims
by claiming that National Socialism was not for export and that
Germany, therefore, did not threaten any state. In blatant contradiction with what he had written in *Mein Kampf*, he stated with
disarming frankness that: 'His problem was to find an economic
basis for the life of 60 million people. Annexation of territory would
merely add to the political and economic difficulties with which he
was faced.' Concerning the League, Germany's withdrawal had
received overwhelming support from German opinion, but Germany would return under conditions of equality. On Austria, Hitler
asserted that Germany presented no threat. The government of that
country was, however, opposed by the mass of opinion and
Germany could not co-operate with a government that offended the
'German ideal'.

Dealing with accusations that he had violated the Treaty of
Versailles, Hitler observed that he had not signed the treaty and
would never have done so. The territorial settlement would be
respected, but the clauses of the treaty that involved Germany's
'moral defamation' would never be accepted and he would liberate
the German people from them. There was, however, Hitler emphasised, no desire on his part to sabotage European collaboration.
Germany would make concessions, but she could not do so where
her honour was concerned. Should 'he make concessions on this
latter point, he would no longer be Chancellor, and he was not sure
whether this would be a help to European pacification'.

These rather negative statements from the British point of view
were reinforced as the discussion began to extend over the substan-

tive points that Simon wished to raise. On the question of an eastern pact, Hitler declared that he thought the possibility of a war in eastern Europe slight. Security in that area, he believed, would best be achieved by the conclusion of non-aggression pacts and he 'could give the British ministers the assurance that Germany would never declare war on Russia'. He was himself disinclined to favour multilateral, mutual assistance systems such as that enshrined in Locarno. For him they were redolent of the pre-war system of blocs and 'he feared that the only result of mutual assistance would be better to organise war'. Furthermore, if Germany was to avail herself of the assistance of the Soviet Union it would be akin to 'opening a box of pestilence germs at the front'. The purpose would be to destroy the enemy, 'but the germs would destroy one's own troops as well'.

Likewise Hitler argued that the Austrian problem could best be solved by a non-aggression pact, rather than a central European, multilateral one. Concerning the question of military armaments, Eden asked if Germany still wanted an arms limitation agreement. If so, Germany's recent behaviour made this difficult to achieve. Were Germany's effectives to total 500 000, a figure which had been mentioned by the British ambassador, this would be an army larger than any other west European power could produce and Germany would have military superiority. Hitler countered that this was not so. Germany had a vast frontier to defend and the total superiority of the surrounding nations was overwhelming. Although at the end of this part of the talks Hitler expressed a willingness to participate in an arms agreement, if a satisfactory system of supervision could be worked out, the general nature of his comments and those of von Neurath were discouraging. Not least Hitler's claim that Germany already had parity in the air with Britain.[20]

Equally discouraging were Hitler's comments when Simon turned the discussion towards Germany's return to the League. Significantly, it was in these comments that Hitler for the first time used the threat of the colonial question in conjunction with the objective of securing an Anglo–German understanding, which, of course, was what he wanted to see emerge from the talks. According to Hitler the Treaty of Versailles imposed a condition of inferiority upon Germany and, given that the League was associated with Versailles, this made it impossible for a German to participate in the League. Simon suggested that the separation of the League covenant from the Treaty of Versailles could perhaps

help and Hitler agreed that this was part of the problem. Nevertheless, while Germany had rectified the military aspect of her
inferiority, other matters remained. Thus, at this point, Hitler
referred to colonies. If Germany returned to the League she would
have no colonies; yet Japan, remaining outside the League, would
still be administering a former German colony. He

> did not know the economic value of these colonies. Perhaps they
> had little economic value for the British Empire. Probably they
> caused financial loss to the British Empire and would cause
> financial loss to Germany too. But it was the moral and legal
> aspect of the question, and the whole position which Germany
> occupied in the world was affected by it.

Hitler then produced a diagram showing the British empire and
other colonial empires, illustrating what he meant by inferiority. He
continued: 'If a satisfactory solution of this question was found then
Britain would have engaged Germany; and Germany would blindly
and loyally fulfil her undertakings.' Germany wanted an agreement
with Britain and also with France, but there were special difficulties
in regard to the latter. However, 'an understanding with Britain
would be a valuable asset' for Germany, and one day the British
empire might be glad of Germany's help. Simon immediately
retorted that Britain could not support a policy that meant a close
relationship with Germany at the expense of general co-operation in
Europe. What Hitler had implied was an 'invitation to Britain' to
regard France as less associated with her than Germany'. While the
British government wanted close co-operation with Germany, they
wanted this 'without prejudice to the relations with France'. Simon
felt he had to make that clear. Regarding the colonial question, he
stated that the mandated territories were not a question for Britain
alone; other countries were involved. As for the extensive areas of
the British empire to which the Führer had referred, he was bound
to point out that they were not colonies, but self-governing
dominions. The Foreign Secretary went on:

> He did not wish to leave the Chancellor under any misapprehen-
> sion that he held out any hope whatever that the British
> Government could do anything about the colonial question. He
> took note of what had been said and he would report. But he did
> not wish to leave the Chancellor under any mistaken impression.
> It was best to be frank.[21]

At the end of the talks Simon made his disappointment evident. It was the intention of the British government to promote a 'general agreement'; he was sorry that it had not proved possible to make progress in that direction.[22] Neville Chamberlain was similarly disappointed. No clear picture of what the Germans wanted had emerged and it was impossible to tell 'whether their protestations of peaceful intentions were genuine or only a means of gaining time while they built up their strength'. He was also irritated that Simon had not pressed Hitler strongly enough over the alternatives to an eastern pact.[23] In fact, Simon had virtually come to the end of the line with his *reactive* policy. Hitler could make recourse to all manner of convenient expedients to avoid suggestions for improving the situation in Europe created by Germany's actions and Simon was unable to contemplate an alternative strategy. He had 'had a whiff from the bottomless pit', but he was not convinced that holding hands with France and Russia 'around the smouldering crater' would 'necessarily stop the explosion'. Moreover, he deprecated 'anything which could be treated as abandoning all hope of a general agreement', and a mere closing of ranks against Germany until this became '*absolutely* inevitable'.[24]

The disappointment that the British felt after the Berlin talks does not seem to have been totally reciprocated on the German side. Phipps considered that Hitler was in 'rather chastened mood' following the failure of his 'little plan' to inveigle Britain into collaboration with Germany 'to the exclusion of other Powers', but simultaneously emphasised his strong regard for Britain, a country which had won and held an empire.[25] On the other hand, the official view in Berlin was that the discussions had gone 'according to plan and came well up to expectations'. Differences had surfaced, although none 'such as to provide an insuperable obstacle to a general understanding'.[26] What, however, the German government meant by a general understanding was essentially a general understanding with Britain alone and within three months of the talks it seemed to Hitler that he was well on the way to achieving this with the Anglo–German naval agreement.

During the Berlin talks Hitler had appeared vaguely encouraging on two issues, namely, naval limitation and an air pact. In accordance with his policy of doing nothing to provoke the antagonism of Britain, Hitler, responding to Simon's suggestion that Germany might attend a naval conference which it was proposed to convene in 1935, stated that as a matter of principle

Germany did not wish to involve herself in a naval race on the pre-war scale. It was not 'politically necessary' and Germany did not have sufficient resources. Simon observed that the figure of 35 per cent of the British fleet had been mentioned as the size of fleet demanded by Germany[27] and this seemed so large to him as effectively to preclude a general naval agreement. Hitler, however, emphasised that Germany had no hostile intent towards Britain in naval matters: the German claim, if met, 'would be for ever'. Eventually Simon took note of Hitler's agreement in principle to naval discussion in London. Regarding an air pact, Hitler averred that the German government was very much in favour, although it was a matter for regret that the British view required the conclusion first of an international agreement on the limitation of air forces.[28]

Although, therefore, during April 1935 the British government, along with the Italian and French governments, condemned Germany's action in reintroducing conscription at the Stresa conference,[29] this did not mean that British ministers thought further discussions with Germany precluded. On the contrary, prior to MacDonald's departure for Italy, it was agreed in the Cabinet that should the French and Italians attempt to prevent the continuation of the Anglo–German dialogue they would be resisted. The object of British policy should be to gain the confidence of France and Italy 'without isolating Germany at Stresa'.[30] But while British ministers spoke in commendably idealistic terms about bringing Germany into a general agreement, they had a more pressing and particular interest in maintaining contact with Germany, for Hitler's offer to limit the German navy to 35 per cent of the British fleet had, in the event, proved more attractive than Simon had indicated during his talks with Hitler.

Thus at the beginning of June negotiations opened in London for an Anglo–German naval agreement with Joachim von Ribbentrop, minister plenipotentiary of the German Reich, representing the German government. They were crowned with success on 18 June in an exchange of notes in which it was agreed that Germany should have 35 per cent of the surface tonnage of the British fleet and parity with the total submarine tonnage of the British empire.[31] Although the Anglo–German naval agreement was in reality the concluding event of Sir John Simon's foreign secretaryship, it was his successor, Sir Samuel Hoare, who signed the British note and who later justified the whole proceeding in a memorandum, which was 'not in all cases suitable for publication'. Both the Italian and French governments had severe reservations about the British action, the French considering that it contravened the Anglo–French communiqué of 3 February and the Stresa declaration. Hoare's memorandum, however, argued that the naval agreement was vital to British interests, that it did not necessarily affect French naval construction and that it was not prejudicial to an ultimate general naval settlement.[32]

It is hard to dispute that the fundamental British motive in concluding the naval agreement with Germany was a self-interested one, but it is clear that it was never intended to be the first stage in a growing intimacy with Germany at the expense of other powers.[33] Rather, Britain still sought to make progress towards the general settlement envisaged in the London communiqué of 3 February. In this Hoare considered the proposals for an air pact, to which Hitler had responded positively in the Berlin talks, as the key to success. But in spite of concessions to the German viewpoint over the negotiation of such an instrument – it could, for instance, be negotiated independently of the other elements in the London communiqué – it proved impossible to make progress.[34] On 1 August Hoare explained the position about an air pact to the German ambassador, von Hoesch, but no reply was ever forthcoming.[35] When Orme Sargent addressed a reminder on the subject to the counsellor of the German embassy, Prince Bismarck, three weeks later, he was told that there could be no reply until after the holidays.[36]

By the end of 1935 it was clear to the British Cabinet that the unco-operative German attitude owed much to the eruption of the Abyssinian crisis.[37] The German government was quite happy to sit back and watch the disintegration of the Stresa front, which removed from them the pressure to appear conciliatory.[38] This in itself was unsatisfactory, but even more unsatisfactory was the continuing evidence of German rearmament. At the beginning of December, Hoare circulated his Cabinet colleagues with correspondence from Berlin concerning this and he wrote:

These despatches emphasise the tremendous efforts and sacrifices which are being made in Germany in the cause of rearmament. They point out that the peace which Germany desires is a German peace; that in certain National Socialist quarters the possibility is contemplated of successful action for the ratification of the German frontiers before even rearmament is complete; and that the present imbroglio in Abyssinia is mere child's play compared to the problem with which these German claims will in some not very distant future confront His Majesty's Government.

Hoare urged the necessity of hastening the completion of the British defensive preparations, but it is also of importance that he stated:

That is not to say that defensive measures and counter-armaments are the only reply which we can make to what is in progress in Germany. But they are the essential accompaniment and, so far as possible, preliminary of any agreement to discuss with the German Government the changes which, in Herr Hitler's own words, are almost certainly necessary to prevent 'an explosion in the future'.[39]

What Hoare was referring to essentially was the fact that the Anglo–German naval agreement and the abortive negotiation for an air pact had brought to a close a phase of British policy towards Germany which had been *reactive and piecemeal*. Its origins lay as much in the years immediately preceding Hitler's assumption of power as in the events which had accompanied the *Machtergreifung*, and in practice it had entailed dealing with situations as they arose. What, however, was being proposed in the Foreign Office at the end of 1935 was an active and positive policy towards the redress of Germany's grievances as a whole, which would remove from her any grounds for future refusal to co-operate. In the formulation of this policy the colonial question featured significantly.

Indeed the colonial question had already begun to intrude prominently in a public manner, for it had not proved possible to keep secret the fact that the subject had been raised during Simon's visit to Berlin.[40] The result was that Duncan Sandys, now resigned from the Foreign Office in favour of a parliamentary career, asked the Prime Minister in the Commons if it would not be advisable for the government to state categorically that the transfer of mandates was out of the question in order to dispel any misunderstandings. In reply MacDonald asserted that there was no confusion and that the government's position had been clearly stated by its predecessors.[41] On the same day, however, Simon did reveal the nature of the exchange that had taken place on colonies in the Berlin talks.[42] On 2 April 1935, Sandys, the bell-wether of imperialism in retreat, again raised the issue. He hoped that it would be possible for the government to satisfy Germany's honour 'in other fields', in exchange for her renunciation of colonial and naval ambitions.[43]

With a view to allaying the evident anxiety that was building up in the Commons, Sir John Simon observed that during the Berlin talks Hitler had merely cited the colonial question as an illustration of the inequality to which Germany would still be subject if she rejoined the League. Unfortunately, he also offered the observation that the question of the distribution of mandated territory was an issue for the League of Nations and not for its individual members. This earned an immediate rebuke from Sir Austen Chamberlain, who claimed that if Simon had stated this to Hitler without qualification it would indicate a new departure in British policy. He stated: 'It has never been held or pretended that it was within the power of the League to transfer a mandate from one country to another.' Simon hastened to assure Chamberlain that he had not misled Hitler, which was strictly true.[44] Nevertheless, there were those who were not averse to giving Germany a position in the world 'appropriate to a nation that normally would be regarded as the most powerful single State in Europe'. In the view of Lord Lothian, there were four main issues to be confronted concerning Germany: the status of the Rhineland, the Polish corridor, *Anschluss* and the colonial question. Unless Britain was prepared to discuss the colonial question, it was possible that it would be solved in an inconvenient way.[45] Simultaneously, the Prince of Wales expressed to the German ambassador his sympathy for Germany's colonial claims.[46]

Meanwhile, further evidence was being received of Germany's alleged increase in colonial interest. In his May Day speech Hitler referred to Germany's lack of colonies[47] and Phipps learnt from Cerruti, the Italian ambassador to Berlin, that not only would Germany require colonies before returning to the League, but that this position was supported by Italy.[48] Subsequently, the ambassador reported that Ribbentrop and Schacht had turned Hitler in this direction: the colonial claims, in his opinion, were 'the dragons' teeth sown by Lords Rothermere, Lothian and Allen', despite all his efforts.[49]

Such was the anxiety in the Foreign Office over the German attitude in this matter that in June 1935 it was decided to revise and print the memoranda which J. V. Perowne had written the previous March, as a basis for a possible submission to the dominions premiers when in London for the silver jubilee. The first of these was an extensive analysis of the background of the German claims and the situation regarding them since Hitler's accession to power. Although the British government had frequently made its attitude clear on several issues, namely, that mandates derived not from the League, but from the peace treaty, and that Britain had no intention of returning the mandates, Perowne concluded that 'the transfer of an existing mandate to Germany or to some other Power' was 'not technically or legally an impossibility'. In addition, he thought that the actual means by which a transfer could be effected – the assent of the donor, the recipient and the League council – were 'somewhat academic' because it was evident that 'Germany's colonial ambitions would not now be satisfied by the transfer to her of a mandate over one or even more of her former colonies'. What Germany wanted, and what he thought the government would be confronted with, was a demand for 'the actual *retrocession* to Germany of some or all of her former colonial Empire' [in full sovereignty]. The motivation behind the claims was, Perowne believed, fundamentally emotional. The economic arguments were, on the whole, trivial and none of Germany's former colonies was suitable for emigration.[50]

The second memorandum and its supplement dealt with past German designs on the Portuguese colonial empire and possible future ones. This, according to Perowne, was not a matter that could easily be disregarded. The acquisition by Germany of territory in Africa would stimulate German naval expansion, cause 'a widespread *malaise* throughout a continent' where British interests were 'virtually paramount', encourage rather than satisfy Germany's territorial appetite, and, if Germany was given colonial satisfaction at the expense of the Portuguese, 'raise the question of the special treaty relations existing between Portugal and Great Britain in an acute form'. Perowne did not rule out the possibility of an armed rising by German settlers in Angola in collaboration with sympathisers in the Union and South-West Africa. He examined, however, in more detail the contingency that Germany might acquire Angola by 'exerting pressure on the Portuguese Government with the assistance of some other Government with special African interests'. The Union government had wanted to gain control of the Mozambique port of Lourenço Marques for a long time, it 'being the natural outlet for the Johannesburg mines' and Portuguese East Africa being the major labour resource for the Rand mines. It was not inconceivable, Perowne thought, that an agreement already existed between the Union and German governments providing for

South African help in German acquisition of Portuguese colonial territory in return for German recognition of the Union's primary claim to Lourenço Marques and a complete German renunciation of any title to the mandate of South-West Africa.[51]

In a minute of 29 March Perowne presumed that Britain's attitude in the colonial question remained what it had always been. However, as Hitler seemed to have placed the item on the agenda, he felt that the government would be well advised to ascertain what line of action it could take in conjunction with the dominions, France, Portugal and Italy in order to prevent the retrocession of the mandates to Germany. He observed: 'A mere reiteration of our intention not to surrender any of these territories to Germany will not, it is to be feared, deter that country from pressing her claim in and out of season, in the most inconvenient manner.'[52] By July 1935 Wigram was not so convinced of the need for haste. Germany had indicated that she wanted colonies in connection with her return to the League; for the present that was a remote contingency. Furthermore, consideration of the matter would be difficult 'until the Abyssinian question' had 'developed further'. It is important, nevertheless, that Wigram believed that the colonial question ought to be 'considered at leisure in connection with the whole of our attitude to . . . the reconstituted Germany'. He continued:

> For a long time a large part of our business in the Foreign Office has been to show to those who are not aware of all the facts that Germany is rapidly becoming, and will be in a very short time, a Power of great strength, and in certain circumstances perhaps a dangerous Power even to ourselves. That task is now almost complete for the reappearance of Germany as a mighty Power in the forefront of Europe is now obvious to almost everyone.

It now behoved the British government to consider its future relationship with this 'great Power and potential rival'. What had to be determined was whether Britain was capable of resisting Germany's expansionist tendencies in north-east Europe, the Danube basin, south-east Europe and overseas, or if a wiser course would be 'to divert her energies to certain of these points rather than to certain of the others'. It was in this light that the colonial question had to be examined.[53]

In this Minute may be seen the origins of the very significant review of Britain's attitude towards Germany that took place in the

Foreign Office at the end of 1935. From the beginning it was emphatically encouraged by Vansittart, who disagreed with Wigram that the colonial question should be considered at leisure. For him it was as urgent as ever and on 26 July he requested a meeting with Hoare to discuss it.[54] In his opinion Germany, 'encouraged by the examples & the methods of Japan and Italy', would soon put forward colonial claims. If she was opposed she would threaten force and, if that was not enough, she would use it.[55] It was, however, in a Minute of 4 August, in which Vansittart commended Perowne's major memorandum on Germany's colonial claims to Hoare, that he laid out his thoughts most clearly. It is worth quoting extensively. Perowne's paper was 'timely', he wrote:

> because we ought really to be thinking out a comprehensive policy towards this new-old Germany, which has rearisen with all tricks, and threats and violence . . . I have long thought it time for this serious stock-taking by HMG, but hitherto there has been some governmental reluctance to face a menace now visible and nearing. The ultimate intention of Germany to reconstitute and *enlarge* her colonial empire is obvious to anyone. This can only lead to an era of increasingly strained relations, and very possibly to war [in the margin: It will almost certainly lead to an eventual ultimatum if the present spirit and teachings of Germany continue], if we maintain our present attitude of complete and absolute negation. (That attitude seems at present the popular one in this country, and recent German violences & persecutions will not have made it less popular.)
>
> That, however, is not a *policy*. If we are to maintain such an *attitude*, it imposes the necessity of a very full and further measure of self-defence not only in the air but at sea, and a policy which will go to considerable lengths to keep in the closest collaboration with France. (We have practically lost Italy out of the combination.)
>
> In any case I do not believe that we shall avail to hold in this highly aggressive & bellicose Germany full of a vast superiority-complex – a far more dangerous Germany than even before 1914 – at all points of the compass where she means to break out by force. Nor do I believe the British taxpayer will think the extra taxation, or anyhow outlay, justified by our hold on the German colonies alone.
>
> On the other hand a return of the colonies to Germany in her

present mood will not appease her megalomania, or buy her off much less avowable designs in central & Eastern Europe. (This particular colonial design must in fairness be admitted to be perfectly comprehensible and, in some respects, just. We are really over-fed colonially.)

Vansittart concluded that for the construction of a coherent policy there was 'time, but not too much time'.[56] Hoare, though, was not to be rushed in the colonial question. He admitted that the subject required thought, but it should not be raised 'prematurely'. He was also mindful, as Perowne's memorandum illustrated, that: 'The more we did for the Germans, the more they stuck us in the back'.[57] He agreed, however, to discuss the colonial question with Vansittart after the recess.[58]

Meanwhile, further impetus was added to the colonial question as it affected Germany by the Abyssinian crisis, which dominated and finally destroyed Hoare's brief foreign secretaryship. As Pierre Laval put it to the French colonial minister, Rollin: 'The daily exposition of the colonial aspirations of Mussolini, the most noisome of the "have nots", has made the [colonial] question the order of the day.' Laval had also learnt from the French embassy in London that 'a high official in the foreign office' had remarked that a visitor from the stars, if he landed on Earth, could not fail to be struck by the injustice of the current division of the world.[59] Observations about justice did not necessarily predict action, but on 27 August 1935 the Foreign Office did receive advice from Geneva that suggested that the need for areas into which surplus populations could move and the problem of the availability of raw materials lay at the root of the Abyssinian affair. It was also indicated that it would be excellent if the British delegation at Geneva could show that it was alive and sympathetic to these problems and initiate an enquiry into them.[60]

Ashton-Gwatkin, head of the economic section of the Foreign Office, was not convinced. If these matters were discussed they would lead inevitably to colonial redistribution which the government wished to avoid. Eden's under-secretary of state, Lord Cranborne, disagreed. He did not think anything should be done immediately as any admission that Italy had a surplus population problem might be taken by her as justification of her case. But these matters would have to be discussed and he saw no objection to a study of the availability of raw materials. This view received very strong support from Sir George Mounsey, the head of the western department of the Foreign Office, and from Vansittart.[61] Despite requests from the Board of Trade for caution[62] and anxiety on his own part,[63] Hoare spoke on the subject of raw materials when he addressed the League assembly on 11 September 1935. His purpose was to suggest that the economic and political parts of the colonial question could be separated and that countries without colonies might be assured and satisfied by guarantees of access to raw materials. Ashton-Gwatkin remained doubtful. Assurances of this kind would be meaningless to a country like Germany if she was involved in a war with a colonial power. And, in any case, in time of peace colonial producers were desperate to sell. Lack of foreign currency was Germany's 'only impediment' in this respect.[64] Nevertheless, with the endorsement of Neville Chamberlain and Baldwin, Hoare stated at Geneva that, while the advantages accruing to powers possessing large areas productive of raw materials could be exaggerated, the British government did realise the reality of the problem. Therefore, he continued: 'the wise course is to investigate it, to see what the proposals are for dealing with it, to see what is the real scope of the trouble and if the trouble is substantial, to try to remove it'. The British government, Hoare emphasised, was willing to participate fully in an enquiry.[65]

Within Britain Hoare's statement unleashed a wave of comment.[66] In two articles in *The Times* Lord Lugard dismissed the economic bases of the Italian and German colonial claims. Africa, by and large, was unsuited to white settlement; and there should be no difficulty in the procurement of raw materials because the fall in commodity prices meant that they were being produced in excess. Moreover, as primary products were not being bought, this meant that a continent such as Africa could not for the present be treated as a potential market by the industrial powers. Lugard did admit that the suzerain power in a colony had an advantage in that it could use its own currency, but currency would not be a problem for Germany and Italy if those countries lifted their embargo on the export of their currencies. The notion of colonial redistribution was not, he believed, feasible, and neither was there much point in Britain placing all her colonies under the mandate system. Mandatory principles already applied to the British colonies, besides which, such a gesture would not be welcomed by other colonial powers and would not be regarded by Germany and Italy as meeting their needs. A 'collective Mandate' imposed on some or all territories in

Africa would be impracticable. The nationality of the governor of an individual territory would determine the *de facto* mandatory, creating 'several Nazi and Fascist autocracies in Central Africa'. Nevertheless, Lugard 'heartily' supported an enquiry into the problem of the distribution and acquisition of raw materials.[67]

The Economist thought that the figures for the proportion of the world's raw materials controlled by the British empire were 'deceptive'. But they did make the 'Have-not' psychology understandable and showed that the 'Haves' stood in a relation of quasi-trusteeship to the world as a whole.[68] It was felt by this journal that apprehensions over access to raw materials could best be dissipated by the application of the 'open door' in all colonies. The simplest method of doing this would be for the colonial powers to place all their tropical possessions under a League mandate.[69] Taking up the issue again in January 1936, Lugard repeated his hostility to this idea even though it was now supported by the Labour Party. As a gesture of willingness to do all that was possible for Italy and Germany in the colonial sphere, he recommended that Britain return to the 'open door' policy in all her colonies which she had abandoned in 1932.[70]

The debate in the national press was accompanied by parliamentary comment. The 'open door' was very widely supported across the Commons, but there was very little support for George Lansbury's idea of a general conference that would re-examine the Treaty of Versailles.[71] In the debate on the King's speech which followed the general election of 1935, Hoare affirmed that he stood by the statement he had made at Geneva. He thought, though, that when the issue of raw materials came to be investigated, it would be revealed that the problem was 'one of selling raw materials rather than buying raw materials'. He hoped, however, that there would be an investigation, although he and the government took the view 'definitely that an investigation of this kind must take place in a calm, dispassionate atmosphere' and not 'in an atmosphere of war'.[72]

In his Commons speech Hoare intimated that the government had already instituted its own enquiry into the matter. What he was referring to, in fact, was an interdepartmental committee on freedom of acces to raw materials which had been constituted to consider the implications of his Geneva statement. This committee was set up on the initiative of the Colonial Office.[73] It took almost a month for the Foreign Office to respond to the initial enquiry. In an interesting minute of 7 October 1935, Vansittart indicated that while it was the Italian action that made this issue immediately pressing, it was its long term implications for Anglo–German relations that had priority in his mind. He agreed that a committee should be organised, but, he continued: 'I fear that *Italy* has made, and will for long make, progress impossible. What we have really to prepare for is our delaying action when *Germany* raises the Colonial question. So we may as well begin now.' Hoare minuted on the same day that he concurred and on 9 October Ashton-Gwatkin wrote to G. L. M. Clauson of the Colonial Office asking for a meeting.[74] By early November the Colonial Office had completed a draft report. Within the Foreign Office opinion favoured an international and public enquiry into the matter, the only problems being whether the initiative should be taken after the settlement of the Abyssinian question and whether other governments should be consulted in advance.[75] The reason for the enthusiasm was evident in that the draft report demonstrated that there was no economic grievance that the 'hungry' powers could logically sustain. Nevertheless, it was felt that care would have to be exercised in the preparation of any enquiry lest it should stray into the political field.[76]

Before the final submission of the interdepartmental report as a Cabinet paper, considerable discussion was prompted in the Foreign Office by Professor J. T. Shotwell, who paid Hoare a personal visit.[77] Shotwell underlined the importance of the raw materials issue to the future of the League and the attitude of the United States. The League should not be seen as a rigid protector of the *status quo*. If it was made the agency responsible for safeguarding 'the unrestricted distribution of raw materials', this would do much to improve its image. According to Shotwell, the co-operation of Britain in such a scheme could result in the lowering of trade barriers, the return of Germany to the League and the reconciliation of liberal opinion in the United States towards co-operation with the League. Hoare found this argument 'attractive' and he was impressed 'with the need for our maintaining and pushing the initiative with the question of raw materials'. He now considered that there was something to be said for raising it at Geneva before the conclusion of the Italo–Abyssinian war.[78]

Wigram, however, did not think there was much to commend the idea: Germany could not be induced to return to the League by it and France and Belgium would take exception to the notion. However, Mr L. Collier, the head of the northern department, inclined to value it as a tactical move, 'not because it would . . . "offer a real carrot" to that supreme donkey, Signor Mussolini', but because 'it would expose, once and for all' the hollowness of the Italian and German colonial claims. For Ashton-Gwatkin a League enquiry into raw materials would merely lead to the obvious statement that in time of peace raw materials were freely available. But, if an enquiry was to lead anywhere, Shotwell, in his opinion, might have indicated the right direction. An offer to place the entire British colonial empire under the tutelage of the League might well silence the Italian and German demands forever. Furthermore, if, on reflection, Britain wished to withdraw the offer, the predictable opposition of the French would provide the perfect excuse.[79]

In an undated and characteristically lengthy minute, Vansittart observed that he was told frequently by Sir Maurice Hankey and MPs that a transfer of colonies by Britain would cause a split in the country. He was not certain that this was so but, if it was true, he thought that putting the British colonial empire under the League would create a *'double-split'*. Reform of the League in this sense, he considered, could not be approached until after the Abyssinian crisis and he was certain that it would satisfy neither Italy nor Germany. They wanted territory pure and simple; there was no point in 'exposing' what was already evident. And he doubted if such action would make much impact in the United States. In his words: 'We should be making the worst of all worlds a present.' He concluded:

> We should not think of putting down so large a contribution till we are more sure of the future. Must there not be a territorial redistribution of some limited nature at least? When we talk of reform of the League, are we sometimes really not talking of reform of the map, not a system, without perhaps admitting it.[80]

Hoare, however, seems not to have been deflected from his course. Before departing for his ill-fated confrontation with Laval at the beginning of December 1935, he left instructions that he wanted a memorandum on the raw materials question ready for his return from abroad. Within the Foreign Office it was felt that the Colonial Office memorandum would suffice.[81]

Throughout December discussion over the merits and demerits of a raw materials enquiry and cognate matters continued in the department and ultimately it led to a decision on the matter which to the minds of the officials had been outstanding for almost a year. Was Britain going to compromise with Germany in the colonial question or not? Sir George Mounsey considered that the existing international political grievances were rooted in economic problems and that their discussion was intimately bound up with Article nineteen of the League covenant. The questions posed by the situation were 'whether Article nineteen of the Covenant' could 'be made into a living factor for the solution of world affairs' and whether alteration of the League would be necessary 'before any advance' could 'be achieved in the redress of the political-economic balance'. Mounsey favoured a course by which the League would set up a permanent commission under Article twenty-nine whose duty would be to forecast future grievances and recommend remedies. Orme Sargent agreed with Mounsey's general approach, although it seemed to him a little like trying to resurrect the world economic conference. Victor Wellesley and Lord Stanhope, under-secretary of state for foreign affairs, demurred. For them raw materials were only 'the fringe' of the much wider matter of territorial redistribution. Neither did Stanhope feel that France would be very grateful for an enquiry into raw materials. He wrote: 'France's methods in her colonies would inevitably be investigated & she would hardly thank us for having put her in the pillory.' Vansittart concurred with Wellesley and Stanhope. There was no point in holding world economic conferences until Britain had determined her attitude in the colonial question as a whole, which for him was now 'concrete and imminent'.[82]

At the beginning of the New Year Anthony Eden, the newly-appointed Foreign Secretary, supplied the answer. In a Minute of 3 January 1936 he stated that as Britain had raised the raw materials question she was likely to be asked why she had not pursued it. It was possible to reply that the time was not auspicious, but the problem would soon become troublesome. He argued, therefore:

> In my own view the future of colonial territories should form some part of final settlements with Germany which would include her return to the League and an arms agreement, but such a settlement will not be realisable until we are stronger in a military sense, and it would be useless to offer Germany concessions piecemeal, for such sops would only stimulate the appetite that feeds upon it.[83]

Thus the decision had finally been taken in principle that Germany could once again become a colonial power in return for her clear indication of good intent. It was, in many respects, a decision forced by the circumstances of the Abyssinian crisis.

The interdepartmental report on raw materials when finally circulated to the Cabinet in January 1936 showed that there was no scarcity in the supply of colonial raw materials. Neither was there any evidence to show that raw materials from British or foreign colonies had been withheld from any potential customer. In addition, the possession of colonial territories did not automatically mean free access to all raw materials; Britain herself was heavily reliant upon external supplies of cotton, petroleum, barley, maize and tobacco. Within the British colonial empire it was generally true that foreign nationals and capital were allowed to function without restriction. Equality of opportunity to trade and exploit resources was guaranteed under 'A' and 'B' mandates and in territories governed by the Congo basin treaties. The German population in Tanganyika had increased, while the flourishing banana industry in the Cameroons was 'entirely in German hands', the entire produce being 'shipped to Germany in German boats'. There were three reasons behind the desire for freer access to raw materials: the fear of monopoly, the fear of deprivation in peace or war and the inability to pay. It was the final cause that was most important in the cases of Italy and Germany. Concerning the scope of a possible League enquiry, the authors pointed out that if raw materials from colonial areas only were to be considered this would probably result in French objections, for there was considerable evidence of French discrimination against aliens in their colonial possessions. More-over, only rubber, cocoa and tin were produced in any preponder-ating amount in colonial territories, most *colonial raw materials* being produced outside colonial areas. The report recommended that the aim of any enquiry should be to obtain guarantees of access to certain individual raw materials, but repeated that such proposals were unlikely to meet the real grievances of the Germans and the Italians. Eden felt that the report's conclusions and the existing political situation precluded immediate action at Geneva, but he thought that the report would soon have to be considered by the government 'in its relation to . . . general foreign policy', by which he meant policy towards Germany.[84]

The public debate on raw materials was brought to a temporary end in February 1936 when George Lansbury tabled a motion in the Commons calling for an international conference on the problem of access to raw materials and emigration facilities. The motion was eventually lost, but it was significant mostly because it provoked a controversial outburst from Lloyd George. According to Lloyd George it was beside the point to argue that raw materials were freely available to all nations. The difficulty for Italy and Germany lay in acquiring the foreign currency to pay for them. He was not himself in favour of the cession of British territory, but, he declared:

> I do put forward this plea quite seriously as one of the three or four who were responsible for drafting the Treaty of Versailles. Under the Treaty of Versailles, these territories [the mandates] were not given to us as British possessions; they were given to the League of Nations, and the legal right is vested in the League of Nations . . . I do not believe that you will have peace in the world until you reconsider the mandates.

Referring to the vast overseas possessions of Belgium, Portugal and the Netherlands, and contrasting them with Italy's almost complete lack of colonies, he stated that Germany's claims were not very extravagant.[85]

The imperialists in the Commons were amazed. Leo Amery could not understand the logic of Lloyd George's position. An international economic conference would only collapse in the same way as the previous one had done. Moreover, Lloyd George, by referring to the smaller colonial powers, had hinted at the redistribution of their territories. But Germany could not settle her emigrants in Africa and the only suitable area for such settlement in Europe was to be found in Russia. The Soviet Union was not going to come to any conference ready to surrender her land. The central problem for the world, Amery argued, was the disruption of trade: he asked, therefore, why Belgium, Portugal and the Netherlands could not 'enter into some mutual economic arrangement with the great markets of Central Europe for mutual trade, with mutual preference, and follow the good example which the nations of the British Empire set at Ottawa?' Sir Henry Page Croft was more direct. Any government that endeavoured 'to placate' those nations which were 'doing wrong in the world' by returning mandates would be 'kicked from power'.[86]

There were considerable international repercussions following

Lloyd George's outburst, although not in Germany.[87] The biggest fuss was made by the Portuguese, who since August 1935 had been agitated by rumours in the French press to the effect that discussions were in progress regarding the transfer of Angola to Italy and Mozambique to Germany. On 22 January 1936 the Portuguese foreign minister, Armindo Monteiro, told Eden that Portugal would not 'yield one inch of her colonial territory' and he asked if it was possible for the British government to make some statement expressing Anglo–Portuguese solidarity in these matters.[88] It is, therefore, not surprising that, in the immediate wake of Lloyd George's remarks, Monteiro again requested of Eden some public reassurance that Portugal's colonies would remain sacrosanct.[89] Similar representations were made to the British embassy in Brussels.[90]

In London the Colonial Secretary, J. H. Thomas, wished to keep the whole issue very quiet. Indeed, he went so far as to dissuade Lord Elibank from putting down a motion for debate in the House of Lords on the subject of the former German colonies. He could not, however, restrain members of the House of Commons from asking questions.[91] Thus on 12 February he told the Commons: 'His Majesty's Government has not considered, and is not considering, the handing over of any of the British Colonies or Territories held under mandate.'[92] As Thomas informed the Cabinet, this statement did not bind the government in the future,[93] which was just as well because the matter was about to receive 'serious consideration'.[94] Wigram, in these circumstances, minuted strong objection to Thomas's reply stating that it 'might well prove embarrassing in the near future'.[95] The Dutch and Belgians showed none of Thomas's finesse. They would *never* surrender any of their territory and Salazar, the Portuguese Dictator, emphasised that 'from the standpoint of force Portugal must show that she is ready'.[96] The decision of the Portuguese, therefore, to commence rearmament at this time owed as much to fear for the future of their colonial possessions as it did to the development of 'a situation in which Portugal might have again, as in 1914–18, to co-operate with Great Britain in a European War'.[97]

The reservations in the Foreign Office regarding Thomas's reply related to the fact that the British government by the beginning of 1936 was reviewing its whole posture towards Germany and that in that review the possibility of colonial concessions was under very active consideration. Although Hoare's foreign secretaryship and the beginning of Eden's were inevitably dominated by the Abyssinian crisis, the German problem was their continuing and over-riding concern. By the end of 1935 it was apparent to Foreign Office officials that the initiatives launched in the Anglo–French communiqué of 3 February had run out of steam. As a consequence an examination of the present position regarding Germany was undertaken with results not dissimilar from those which the Foreign Office had arrived at at the end of 1931.[98] Whereas, however, the government had not implemented in their entirety the policies suggested by the department in 1931, the result of these fresh endeavours was that they served as the basis of Eden's foreign policy throughout his first foreign secretaryship and, as an extension, that of the government until the outbreak of war and perhaps beyond.

That the Foreign Office included the colonial question in its deliberations was not exclusively founded in the general debate on the subject stimulated by the Abyssinian crisis. It owed as much to continued and intensifying evidence reaching London of the seeming strength and reality of the German colonial demand. Once the 'Abyssinian imbroglio' was out of the way it was feared that Germany would push her colonial claims.[99] During October and November 1935 the *Morning Post* and the *News Chronicle* reported that a big push in colonial propaganda was about to start in Germany and reports from Phipps confirmed that interest in the colonial question was growing, although he dismissed the likelihood of a colonial campaign.[100] On 10 October the ambassador lunched with General von Blomberg, who insisted that Germany must have colonies. A month later he learnt that Schacht had told an 'intimate friend':

> What Germany and Italy need is colonial expansion by mandate or chartered company. Germany wants to buy raw material with marks instead of devisen. England should divide up her West African territory, especially the Cameroons and Togoland, between Hitler and Mussolini. I recognise the special difficulties in the case of East Africa.[101]

By the end of November the Berlin embassy was receiving substantial information from its consular offices throughout Germany that the DKG was making a 'special attempt . . . to whip up interest in colonial matters'. Ill-advisedly, however, Phipps discounted rumours that the NSDAP was about to take over the DKG and argued that there was no reason 'to fear an active campaign for the recovery of Germany's colonies in the immediate future' because of 'the Chancellor's well known desire to keep on good terms with Great Britain'.[102]

During a luncheon engagement with Phipps on 6 December, Schacht dilated on Germany's colonial demands. It emerged that the German economics minister was mainly concerned with the Cameroons, from which Germany could obtain 70 per cent of her fat requirements. 'Siren-like', he 'indicated that Colonies would only be for Germany guarantees of good behaviour, as Great Britain would always be able in case of need to take them away again'. Schacht then boldly asserted that he had converted Hitler towards overseas expansion and 'took credit' for having diverted him from the 'folly' of German expansion in eastern Europe. Unless Germany's demands in the matter of colonies were met, Schacht argued, Communism in Germany or war would result. Reporting this conversation, Phipps observed that he doubted if colonial restitution would cause Germany 'to relinquish ideas of expansion in the East', but he presumed that Germany would only be satisfied colonially 'in return for certain definite undertakings of good behaviour'.[103] A week later, in an interview with Phipps, Hitler appeared to confirm Schacht's remarks, adding 'bitterly that Great Britain's present prosperity was clearly due to her "Empire"'.[104] Phipps closed his comments on German colonial claims at the end of 1935 by suggesting that the school of thought in Germany that favoured overseas expansion was gaining ground because those who favoured European expansion could only realise their ambitions by war, which contradicted the 'peaceful' thrust of Nazi propaganda. Nevertheless, those who favoured colonial expansion also argued that this would assist European expansion in the long term. Were it not for the fact that Hitler, Ribbentrop and von Neurath were so anxious for an Anglo–German understanding that they were prepared to contemplate 'a course of rigorous self-denial for some time to come', the colonial lobby would have been even more strident. In all the circumstances, the ambassador concluded, there was much to be said for 'procrastination' and 'obstruction' in this matter. He feared that 'the return of the colonies would be the prelude to bigger music'.[105]

Towards the end of 1935 the King himself mentioned to Vansittart that he would like to see progress towards an understanding with

Germany. In the light of the evidence reaching the Foreign Office it would have been surprising if the colonial question had not been prominent in the permanent under-secretary's comments. For the present Vansittart did not think there was much to be gained by making serious moves in this direction. It would be more prudent to wait until Britain was better armed and he did not like the idea of an agreement with Germany that excluded France. In addition there was the question of the terms, which might prove too high; an agreement with Germany would have to be 'handsomely paid for'. Under Hitler that country was 'highly expensive' and would become 'highly explosive' if the attempt were made 'to cramp her everywhere'. An understanding with Germany would have to be bought by allowing her to expand in Europe or Africa. Vansittart continued:

> If the expansion were to be in Europe it would be at other people's expense. If it is to be in Africa, it will be at our expense. I do not think that there can be any question that it will have to take the latter form. Any attempt at giving Germany a free hand to annex other people's property in central or eastern Europe is both absolutely immoral and completely contrary to all the principles of the League which form the backbone of the policy of this country.

In his estimation, the political fabric of Britain would be rent asunder if Germany was invited 'to satisfy her land hunger at Russia's expense'. The colonial solution, therefore, was one that had to be faced however unpalatable this might be to right-wing opinion. In any case, Vansittart did not believe that anyone would want to fight for mandates and he was convinced that 'the Left, the Left-Centre and the Churches' were 'ready for this solution'.[106]

When Orme Sargent and Ralph Wigram came to write their massive memorandum entitled, 'Britain, France and Germany', one of the conditions stipulated by Vansittart regarding an agreement with Germany seemed near fulfilment. France was showing signs of wanting an understanding with Germany in co-operation with Britain.[107] Secondly, it did not seem to Sargent and Wigram worthwhile waiting until Britain had rearmed before attempting a negotiated settlement with Germany. By that time Germany too would have rearmed further and the diplomatic position would not have been improved. Thus on two counts they argued against

Vansittart's counsel of delay. There was, however, the added dimension of Germany's economic system which was 'undergoing severe and increasing strain' and which was bound to affect her foreign policy. Finally, although France was willing to come to terms with Germany, it was feared that she might elect to do so bilaterally and not be too scrupulous about recognising her obligations to the League in the process, even to the point of abandoning her interests and allies in eastern Europe. Consequently, the two officials urged that Britain should take the lead in negotiations with Germany and determine her attitude 'without loss of time'.

In examining the alternatives confronting the British government, they dismissed 'drift' as being hardly constructive. Encirclement, they argued, would merely recreate the pre-war system of blocs and 'the anti-revisionist bloc, even if it could be formed, would probably not hold'. Therefore, they favoured a policy of coming to terms with Germany. Since the war it had been British policy 'to eliminate those parts of the peace settlement' known to be 'untenable and indefensible'. The essence of British policy was to bring about change in an orderly manner, which was the 'only constructive policy open to Europe'. In the minds of Sargent and Wigram the alternatives to renewed and vigorous pursuit of traditional British policy – drift and encirclement – were 'not really feasible'.

There was one particular factor which the officials felt compelled haste on the part of Britain: Germany was still positively orientated towards the United Kingdom. Germany's inclinations here could probably be explained by a desire to 'neutralise and stabilise' western Europe with an eye to her expansionist ambitions in the east. For Sargent and Wigram the main aims of German policy were: the remilitarisation of the Rhineland; the reacquisition of colonies; the annexation of Austria and the German districts of Czechoslovakia; the recovery of territory lost to Poland in 1919; and 'the economic penetration of the Baltic States, the Danubian Basin and of Eastern Europe'. In the west the situation was more or less settled with the exception of the demilitarised Rhineland zone, which, the officials argued, could not be maintained indefinitely. There was much, therefore, to be said in favour of settling this issue at an early date in a peaceful manner, instead of allowing Germany to settle it herself in an aggressive and threatening way.

As far as Britain specifically was concerned, colonies were the only issue outstanding between Britain and Germany. Sentiment and prestige lay at the bottom of Germany's colonial claims. She wanted colonies returned as colonies and not as mandates and she was likely to want more than merely her old colonies. It was only Germany's desire for good relations with Britain that had inhibited her from hitherto raising these demands officially. The position of the British government in this matter had been one of intransigent opposition, but a section of British opinion now appeared to support the German claim. The main argument for meeting the German demands was that the only point of conflict between Britain and Germany would be removed and, it was assumed by Sargent and Wigram, that in return Britain would require that Germany made no further overseas claims on her and that she also desisted from 'warlike adventures', promising to 'work for change only by methods of peace and agreement'. On the other hand, it had to be questioned whether British opinion would supinely accept the transfer of British territory, if it was prudent to reinstall Germany in areas of paramount British interest, and if Germany would be bound by any undertakings she gave. There were three policies which the British government could pursue in the colonial question: say no, give Germany colonies if it was felt that an advantage might thereby accrue, or follow the line adumbrated by Hoare in his speech to the League assembly. Sargent and Wigram concluded: 'Whichever policy we choose in the colonial question . . . it does not seem that we could lose by an immediate decision actively to pursue once more our traditional policy of coming to terms with Germany.'

Regarding Germany's aims in central and eastern Europe, there was no reason to suppose that the assimilation of Austria and parts of Czechoslovakia and German economic penetration of the area could not be peacefully accomplished. There were, of course, substantial objections to British acquiescence in such developments, for Britain traditionally opposed the creation of a dominant power on the continent. It had, however, to be asked if these developments could realistically be stopped; if the answer was 'no', there was much to be said for working with Germany in order to minimise her gains and to ensure that they were accomplished peacefully. The two officials thought that the process of general revision could be inaugurated through a League enquiry into raw materials, or through an Anglo–French colonial settlement with Germany. In conclusion, they urged the British government to seize what might be the last opportunity of achieving a settlement with Germany, for Europe as a whole would benefit from 'the success of a policy which' aimed 'at securing collective security and international cooperation through the reconciliation of Europe with a Germany which is at present rearmed, proud, powerful and yet aggrieved'.[108]

In an important annex to this memorandum, Ashton-Gwatkin added an economic dimension to the arguments of Sargent and Wigram. He pointed out that Germany was still the world's third greatest trading power, but that her exports were declining. He offered the following formula: 'Economic distress was the prelude to military adventure in the recent case of Japan and Italy; this must not be forgotten in connection with Germany.' Germany, he observed, was the natural trading centre for the Danubian and Balkan region and a preferential system for Germany in this region would be ideal. This area was not of great commercial interest to Britain, but 'trade with a prosperous Germany' was of 'greatest moment' to her. Ashton-Gwatkin then boldly summed up the alternatives:

The British Government now have to decide whether they wish to see a Germany that is economically strong or economically weak. There is some danger in either course; but the latter seems far more perilous. A weak, hysterical individual, heavily armed, is a danger to himself and others. From a purely commercial point of view a strong Germany would be one of our best customers.

Thus the British government should explore the possibility of assisting Germany in her financial and commercial recovery. In addition to the restoration of colonies, which Ashton-Gwatkin thought 'would be a political gesture rather than an economic boon', the creation of a special area in Europe for Germany should be contemplated that would include Poland, the Danube and the Balkans.[109]

The views of Sargent, Wigram and Ashton-Gwatkin were not greeted with universal enthusiasm in the Foreign Office. Sir L. Collier of the northern department did not believe that the proposals that had been put forward represented a 'continuance' of British policy. For him they were a clear reversal. There was no prospect of reaching a general settlement with Germany; the only grounds on which such discussions could proceed with a degree of hope were the abandonment by the Nazis of their racial views and the German colonial claims.[110] Vansittart claimed to occupy a median position. He agreed with Ashton-Gwatkin, but was not convinced that it would be desirable to strengthen Germany in her current mood. He asked: 'Surely we are entitled to expect her to sober down, before we put our hand in our pockets again to help a fraudulent debtor, for that is what Germany has been and still is.' Nevertheless, while he did not think at this stage that it would be profitable to enter into general discussions with Germany, he did not rule them out and considered that Britain should examine the price that she might be prepared to pay for a general settlement in more propitious circumstances. It was here that he differed with Collier. Germany was bound to expand and he wrote:

> If it can't be in Africa, it will be in Europe. And I would prefer it to be in Africa in regions with which we were always able to dispense. I prefer, in a word, that we should pay ourselves and honestly, rather than attempt or countenance any murky transaction at the expense of someone else. We cannot possibly be a good Member of the League in Africa and a shockingly bad one in Europe.

He did, however, admit that this might not inhibit German expansion in Europe and in that case Britain would probably have to fight. But if Britain continued to refuse to treat with Germany that in itself could be productive of trouble. Vansittart, therefore, advocated preparation for negotiations with a view to initiating them as soon as possible after the end of the Abyssinian affair. He hoped that Hoare and Eden would look at all these papers, and the former minuted that he would like to do this during the December holiday.[111]

Greater force was added to the arguments of the Foreign Office officials by a despatch from Phipps. The ambassador reported that throughout 1935 Germany's foreign policy objectives – absorption of all Germans into one Reich, expansion in the east and recovery of her former colonies – had remained unchanged. The only uncertainties concerned the methods and timing of the realisation of these aims. Friendship with Britain remained the keystone of German policy, but in some circles there was a growing disillusionment with this and a tendency towards renewing the relationship with Russia. Nonetheless, Hitler would not make any move for the time being: the Abyssinian crisis had thrown Europe into the melting pot and events were 'slowly untying his hands'. Phipps commented humorously:

> If Hitler's heart could be searched to-day his policy would doubtless be found to be very simple. He will keep his powder

dry, bide his time and put his trust partly in Wotan, but chiefly in his own mysterious good fortune that has led him, at times unexpectedly, *per aspera ad astra*.

A mood of urgency now began to manifest itself in the Foreign Office. Wigram was of the opinion that 'the sands' were 'running out' and that, if Britain was going to fight with Germany, it would be necessary 'to compose' with her soon. Sargent suggested a review of reports and telegrams from Germany since 1933.[112]

In the event it was not Hoare who took the decision as to whether or not to proceed with the suggestions emanating from the Foreign Office, but his successor, Eden. This was crucial because in his first months as Foreign Secretary he laid the foundations of a policy towards Germany that in essentials was to last until the outbreak of war in 1939 and was fundamentally his. Acting on the advice of Sargent, Eden, in January 1936, circulated his Cabinet colleagues with a collection of ambassadorial reports from Berlin since 1933.[113] In a covering memorandum he identified European hegemony, through the systematic dismantlement of the Treaty of Versailles, as the basic aim of German policy. So far Hitler had been spectacularly successful in all his ventures, excluding the 'economic and financial spheres', where he was facing possibly 'insuperable difficulties'. Eden concluded from these observations that Britain should not only rearm rapidly, but also make a positive effort to arrive at a *modus vivendi* with Germany that might reduce European tension.[114] It was subsequently agreed by the Cabinet that they would take up the question of policy towards Germany as soon as Eden was ready.[115] Eden's convictions were strengthened by the opportunity for talks that the funeral of George V afforded him. Phipps, in particular, had been in London and in consultation with him the Foreign Office began to compose a memorandum on the German situation. The Foreign Secretary was now convinced that the 'reconditioning' of the armed forces had to be 'accompanied by some attempt at an arrangement in the political sphere with Germany'.[116]

Meanwhile, at the end of January 1936, Ashton-Gwatkin, in conjunction with Gladwyn Jebb, returned to his theme of removing the economic motivation of Nazism. In their memorandum it was argued that 'German "expansion", in the sense of increased export markets', was 'essential if internal pressure' was 'to be relieved [in Germany] and the danger of war arising from such pressure to be averted'. The areas they singled out as desirable for such expansion were central and south-east Europe. It was also possible that Britain, by moderating or reversing 'her present commercial policy', could help Germany, along with the return of her colonies in full sovereignty and the 'admission of German goods to the British Colonial Empire on an equality basis'. Indeed they emphasised that if Britain wanted Germany to expand peacefully in central and south-east Europe these other steps were an essential adjunct.[117] Furthermore, Vansittart added his formidable weight to those arguing in favour of a general settlement with Germany in a mammoth lucubration, which exhorted the government to deal with Germany on a European level: it should aim, he urged, not merely at an Anglo–German agreement, but rather at a comprehensive, European settlement. Germany would, however, require the incentive of a promise of territorial expansion if her co-operation was to be secured. Europe could not provide an outlet; but a sympathetic consideration of Germany's colonial claims might provide a way out of the impasse.[118]

In a memorandum covering that of Vansittart, Eden commented that the British government was faced with a dilemma. Germany was suffering severe economic distress, which could lead to an explosion, and the obvious answer seemed to be to assist Germany's recovery. But this might not be a cure in the case of Germany. Despite this reservation, he wrote:

> On balance . . . I am in favour of making some attempt to come to terms with Germany, but upon one indispensable condition: that we offer no sops to Germany. There must be no concession merely to keep Germany quiet, for that process only stimulates the appetite it is intended to satisfy.[119]

The type of agreement that Eden and the Foreign Office had in mind was replacement of the Locarno treaty by an air pact, in which France and Germany would guarantee Britain, besides one another, and in which the demilitarised Rhineland zone would disappear; Britain and France would recognise Germany's preponderant interest in central and eastern Europe, provided her aims there were peacefully accomplished; and Britain would not deliberately impede the expansion of Germany's export trade. For the present it was thought imprudent to raise the issue of Germany's return to the League or the colonial question.[120]

Eventually, these suggestions were considered by a special sub-committee of the Cabinet constituted on Baldwin's instructions on 14 February.[121] When this committee met on 17 February colonial issues figured very significantly in the deliberations of the ministers involved. Although Eden proposed a short-term policy of supporting a League enquiry into raw materials until the Cabinet was clear in its mind as to what would constitute a long term policy towards Germany, this was rejected by the committee. Ramsay MacDonald particularly disliked it as a means of promoting general discussions with Germany. For him the air pact proposals represented a more promising opening, whereas 'the colonial raw materials suggestion would be a new opening . . . and it was a suggestion regarding the utility of which he . . . was not quite convinced'. Nevertheless, Eden feared that there could be no final settlement 'without some transfer of mandates' to which both Neville Chamberlain and J. H. Thomas rejoined that they would be happy to contemplate 'the transfer of Tanganyika . . . if a really permanent settlement could be achieved'. The problem was whether there was any settlement that Germany would regard as permanent.[122]

On 6 March 1936 Eden therefore made his opening move by suggesting to the Germans negotiations for an air pact.[123] As, however, in the previous year, when the British government was about to embark on an initiative which was intended to lead Europe to peace, the German government had already resolved upon action that was to weaken severely the force of such an attempt.[124] On 7 March Hitler remilitarised the Rhineland. Although this deprived the British government of a valuable concession, thereby placing Eden in a position of disadvantage in the negotiations which he wished to start, it did not mean that those negotiations would be dropped: on the contrary, Eden thought they were now inevitable.[125]

Thus, within three months of Eden becoming Foreign Secretary, not only had a fresh basis for British policy towards Germany been laid, but the colonial question was recognised as possibly a major part of it. It may well be that if it came to the point Eden favoured the transfer of colonial territory to Germany only under mandate, but this was beside the point. Any such action would have been gravely unpopular in Britain and even the insistence upon mandatory status could not have been guaranteed beyond the point at which the actual transfer was made. The most such insistence could have achieved would have been the preservation of Eden's image as a defender of the League.[126]

6
The Plymouth Report

At a Cabinet meeting of 5 March 1936 the possibility of the remilitarisation of the Rhineland was discussed. The clear impression from the minutes of this meeting is that ministers believed this eventuality not to be imminent and that, if it was, there was little that could be done to counteract it. As the discussion came towards a close, both Ramsay MacDonald and Neville Chamberlain articulated the view that neither Britain nor France could do much against a German violation of the Treaty of Locarno and that the French 'ought to be put up against this reality'.[1] The Cabinet and the Foreign Office had miscalculated. Not only was the remilitarisation of the Rhineland imminent, but an Italo–German *rapprochement* had begun which made such action possible. The roots of this *rapprochement* can now be seen to lie in the period before the Abyssinian war began as much as in the German action of continuing to supply Italy with raw materials during it. Under the influence of Ciano, Mussolini was gradually convinced that Italy's overseas ambitions might best be achieved and secured in alignment with Germany.[2] In August 1935 the Foreign Office learnt that the Italians had approached the German government with a request for diplomatic support in the Abyssinian question in exchange for Italian support for German colonial aspirations. Evidently, the German response indicated that Germany's colonial ambitions could only be fulfilled in co-operation with Britain, whom she had no wish to antagonise, but it is perhaps of some significance that on 30 August the *Völkischer Beobachter* published an article that went a considerable way towards meeting the Italian wishes.[3]

It was not, however, until January 1936 that relations between the two powers began to develop in such a way as to encourage Hitler to bring forward his proposed date for the remilitarisation of the Rhineland from the spring of 1937 to the spring of 1936. Using the ratification of the Franco–Soviet pact by the French Chamber of Deputies as grounds for the denunciation of the Treaty of Locarno, he proceeded towards the remilitarisation of the Rhineland, accompanying his action by offers that went some way towards meeting

British *desiderata* concerning a general settlement with Germany. There were proposals for a demilitarised zone on both sides of the Franco–German Rhine frontier; a non-aggression pact of 25 years duration with France and Belgium, guaranteed by Britain and Italy and supplemented by an air pact; and a German return to the League of Nations.[4] The British desire for a wider agreement was revealed in the reply of 19 March of the Locarno powers other than Germany, which proposed, among other things, arms limitation and economic co-operation.[5] These counter-proposals were rejected by Germany in a memorandum of 31 March, which, in essence, was an amplification of the previous German statement.[6]

While these exchanges are important from the point of view of the Rhineland crisis itself and its management, what is significant from the point of view of the colonial question is that both German memoranda linked to a putative German return to the League, 'the expectation that in the course of a reasonable period the question of colonial equality of rights . . . may be clarified through friendly negotiations'. Furthermore, in his speech to the Reichstag on 7 March, Hitler made this aspiration immediately public.[7] This, therefore, marked a clear change in Hitler's treatment of the colonial question. The open disinterest in this matter which had previously marked his utterances on the subject had now been replaced by a public, if not urgent, demand for its consideration.

This is not to say that the change in policy was sudden. The documentary evidence revealed since 1945 makes it clear that Hitler had been tending in this direction since at least the time of the Anglo–German naval agreement, and probably for some time before that. It was, nevertheless, only after June 1935 that his ideas in this respect seem to have begun to crystallise, although right up to the time of the Rhineland crisis a certain ambiguity can be detected in his private and public statements on the colonial question. For example, in a private letter to Lord Rothermere at the end of 1935, he wrote:

You ask me . . . whether I do not think that the moment has now come to put forward the German colonial wishes. May I ask you . . . not to raise this point now because looking forward to closer collaboration with Great Britain I do not want to give the impression as if I wanted to avail myself of the present situation of your Government and its many difficulties and of the British Empire to exercise a certain pressure.[8]

And yet a month later in a speech at Munich, without making any overt claims on Germany's behalf, he spoke so forcefully of the right of European powers to take colonies by force and of the destiny of the white race to rule, by virtue of a 'non-pacifist' and 'heroic conception of life', that he caused alarm in London.[9] For his part, Neville Chamberlain thought that Hitler had gone further on the subject than ever and he asked the Foreign Office for a copy of Phipps's report on the speech.[10]

But, despite these ambiguous intimations, Hitler had, by the end of 1935, decided to take steps regarding the colonial movement in Germany that would make its future activities conform more accurately with the foreign policy tactics of the German government. Until this time the German colonial movement had not been subjected to the same process of *Gleichschaltung* as had affected other institutions and organisations in Germany. It was allowed to function independently with its actions being neither opposed nor endorsed by the state or NSDAP. To some extent this arrangement was obviously to the advantage of Hitler while he pursued a policy of colonial disinterest.[11] But that such a situation could endure so long under the Third Reich also owed something to the skill of the leader of the DKG, Heinrich Schnee, for from an early stage he decided to pursue a course of purely formal and voluntary *Gleichschaltung* of the colonial movement in order to preserve its independence and prevent a genuine *Gleichschaltung* from taking place.[12] Individuals offensive to NSDAP opinion were removed from their offices in the DKG and General Ritter von Epp, head of the *Kolonialreferat* in the *Reichsleitung* of the NSDAP, was made vice-president in the organisation. In addition, the executive committee of ten, the main organ of the DKG, was to include five members of the NSDAP and it was agreed that the *Führerprinzip* should be given greater expression. Thus Schnee, the president of the DKG, was to have the right to confirm the composition of the various executive committees of the DKG's sections and in certain circumstances was able to nominate or reject their chairmen. The voluntary *Gleichschaltung* of the colonial movement was completed by the reorganisation of the umbrella organisation, KORAG, under the name *Reichskolonialbund* (RKB), but the reorganisation was almost literally nominal only.[13] The continued independence of the colonial movement is perhaps best attested by the fact that at a meeting of the DKG's executive committee one of its National Socialist members, Schulze-Wechsungen, was able to comment on the singular fact that for the first time National Socialists place themselves under the leadership of a personality other than that of the Reich Chancellor and that they are ready willingly to follow the leadership of the President [Schnee] and to struggle with him jointly for the colonial idea.[14]

The official attitude of the NSDAP on the colonial question was expressed through the KPA, which was established in May 1934 by reorganising the *Kolonialreferat*; the leadership was entrusted to General Franz Ritter von Epp. The tasks of the KPA were to undertake 'colonial indoctrination within the party' and to manage the discussion of the colonial question in the German press.[15] From the start von Epp was very clear about the limitations that Hitler wanted to put on the colonial claim. Germany, he asserted, had to proceed with caution in this matter and necessarily put it 'behind other problems' until she was in a position to raise it with success.[16] Von Epp, therefore, saw his primary function as being one of keeping the colonial question alive in Germany while, at the same time, ensuring that German colonial propaganda did not obstruct or embarrass the foreign policy aims of the German government. But for all that von Epp had a high position in the hierarchy of the NSDAP and was prominent in the cause of colonial revision, he was never one of the inner circle around Hitler. When the latter decided that the time had come to bring about a final and genuine *Gleichschaltung* of the colonial movement he did so through the agency of Joachim von Ribbentrop rather than von Epp.

Ribbentrop's rise to prominence in the Third Reich had been rapid. By 1934 he had been appointed to the rank of special commissioner for disarmament questions and had even created his own foreign policy agency, the *Dienststelle Ribbentrop*. Besides this he was also now entitled, on Hitler's instructions, to read all diplomatic correspondence 'not specially marked "For the Foreign Minister" or "For the Secretary of State"'.[17] Hitler was further confirmed in the high regard he had for Ribbentrop when in the summer of 1935 he conducted the German side of the negotiations that culminated in the Anglo–German naval agreement, 'for Hitler the first stage of his alliance policy' towards Britain.[18] Ribbentrop, however, was by no means in total accord with Hitler's foreign policy concepts. He may have slavishly carried out his master's bidding, but he did have ideas of his own which harked back to earlier Wilhelmine foreign policy traditions. Among these was a belief in the need for colonial revision:

> From the beginning of his political career onwards, the future 'Star diplomat' and foreign policy confidant of Hitler, occupied himself with the colonial question in both internal and foreign policy. And again and again he emphasized – differing from Hitler – the urgency of the return of all Germany's colonies, while referring constantly to the *Rechtsstandpunkt* and without engaging in compromise solutions.[19]

As early as December 1933, for example, he told Ivone Kirkpatrick of the British embassy in Berlin that Britain would be 'well-advised' to return Germany's former colonies.[20] He continued in this vein with British diplomats thereafter as and when the occasion arose.[21] On the other hand, it is significant that he soft-pedalled the issue in the months preceding the naval agreement.[22]

Within Germany Ribbentrop was already by 1935 closely involved in the politics of the colonial movement; indeed 'in the administrative anarchy of the Third Reich . . . he hoped to win power through the *Gleichschaltung* of the conservative colonial associations'.[23] Given, therefore, his interest, ambition and increasing stature in Hitler's eyes, it is fully understandable that between 18 June and 3 July of that year Hitler should have decided to entrust Ribbentrop with control of German policy in the colonial question.[24] During the course of the next year the total *Gleichschaltung* of the German colonial movement was subsequently brought to a conclusion, despite the remonstrations of Schnee.[25] In May 1936 the new *Reichskolonialbund* came into being. It was open to individual membership and was to monopolise all German colonial activity. *Gleichschaltung* was completed the following September when all independent colonial groups received a 'suggestion' from the *Gestapo* that they should 'voluntarily' close down.[26] The leadership of the RKB was given to von Epp, who was created *Bundesführer*, but he was to 'take steps in matters touching on foreign policy only in agreement with Ambassador von Ribbentrop'.[27]

Having dropped in volume during 1935 to its lowest point for the 1930s, colonial propaganda now rose steeply to a level approximately double that which had existed before the *Gleichschaltung* of the colonial movement and which was to be maintained until the outbreak of war.[28] The arguments deployed in justifying Germany's demand for colonial revision were by and large the familiar ones that had been common currency since the time of the peace settlement. Germany needed colonies for the satisfaction of her national honour and in recognition of her status as a great power.[29] Moreover, Germany had been deprived of her colonies on false premises[30]; the mandates were nothing less than a veiled form of annexation.[31] The German colonial movement aimed at the removal of this 'enforced control' and, therefore, the claim for colonial restitution was 'a matter of right'.[32]

It was, however, the economic argument which, in the circumstances of the time, commanded most attention. In a speech at Leipzig Fair on 1 March 1937, Ribbentrop himself argued that Germany had been compelled to adopt the Four Year Plan and pursue a policy of economic autarchy because of the lack of colonies.[33] But the economic argument was most convincingly and sophisticatedly presented by Schacht. In an article in the American journal *Foreign Affairs*, he stated that: 'The German colonial problem is not a problem of imperialism. It is not a mere problem of prestige. It is simply and solely a problem of economic existence. Precisely for that reason the future of European peace depends upon it.' The possession of colonial empires by Britain and France enabled them to survive the existing economic situation: the British empire was regarded as reasonably self-sufficient in 20 out of an estimated 25 categories of essential raw materials, whereas Germany was dependent upon outside resources for 19 of these categories. It was 'silly or cynical' to claim that Germany could freely buy raw materials in the world market. She could not because she lacked the necessary foreign currency. Schacht, of course, conveniently omitted to mention that it was the currency controls which he had introduced in Germany that were responsible for this. Nevertheless, in his view, Germany's raw materials problem could only be satisfactorily solved by German management of colonial territory which 'would form part of her monetary system'.[34]

The actual benefits that Germany could expect to derive from colonial possessions were generally stated with caution, partly in order to avoid inflating expectations. It was suggested by one writer that the capital value of Germany's former colonies was equivalent to a third of Germany's national wealth, while another writer estimated their annual productive capacity at 400–700 million Reichsmarks.[35] According to Johannsen and Kraft the former German colonies could be expected to provide at the end of a decade about one eighth in value of the Reich's annual food and raw material imports.[36] They could produce twice Germany's sisal requirements, 75 per cent of phosphates, 40 per cent of cocoa, 30 per cent of bananas, 20 per cent of tropical timber, and one sixth of her annual vegetable oil and fat needs.[37] It should also be noted that international benefits arising from the restitution of a colonial empire were stressed. As von Epp put it: 'Economic improvement [in Germany] in turn would help to ease political tension . . . the solving of the German colonial question would mean a real contribution towards the recovery of Europe, both commercially and politically.'[38]

Another argument used with caution was that relating to the need for areas for the settlement of Germany's population. This stemmed partly from the fact that some were aware of the limitations of tropical areas for this purpose, but there was also an important political reason. Nazi ideology 'demanded the concentration of German *Volkstum* in a single continental bloc' in Europe.[39] Quite apart from the fact that this was a central aim in Hitler's foreign policy calculations, it was a view that was vociferously and vigorously supported in the NSDAP by Walther Darré, the Reich minister of agriculture, and his supporters, the radical agrarians. For them the attempt to acquire colonies overseas was an 'indiscriminating "pan-world policy", endangering "racial purity"'. Germany must renounce any such endeavours until the realisation of her European aims.[40] Eventually a compromise between the two groups, the overseas expansionists and the European expansionists, was found under the slogan of *Kolonialpolitik und Ostpolitik*: overseas colonies were to provide raw materials and eastern Europe colonies for German settlement.[41]

Hitler's open demand for consideration of Germany's colonial claims, the *Gleichschaltung* of the German colonial movement and the upsurge in colonial propaganda that followed it, all marked a complete break in the treatment of the colonial question by the German government. The reasons for it seem to be founded in Hitler's disappointment that his policy of securing an agreement with Britain through publicly expressed disinterest in overseas possessions was not producing the desired results. Clearly, the Anglo–German naval agreement had from his point of view been a successful start, but its conclusion had also been accompanied by statements on the British side that could have left him in no doubt that British policy was still directed towards an international agreement rather than the exclusive Anglo–German arrangement that he sought. On 13 June 1935, for example, Hoare informed the German ambassador that 'Germany would do herself and the world a great service if she were to facilitate the settlement of the remaining questions . . . by adopting a more positive attitude to the Eastern Pact'.[42] Ribbentrop was similarly advised by Vansittart on 19 June that Germany would be wise to proceed towards the conclusion of an eastern pact in order to disarm her critics, particularly in eastern Europe, 'where . . . Germany's ultimate intentions were matters of deep suspicion'.[43] By way of contrast nothing was said about an exclusive Anglo–German agreement: 'Hitler's blueprint on bilateral lines and the multilateral policy of the British stood in irreconcilable opposition'.[44]

This impression was undoubtedly reinforced during Hitler's interview with Phipps in December 1935 and the Hoare–Laval pact evidently caused Hitler alarm concerning its implications for Britain's policy towards Germany.[45] It seems possible, therefore, that Hitler, during the winter of 1935–6, finally decided upon a course of 'colonial threats' towards Britain in order to force the British into a relationship with Germany as he desired it.[46] This policy, however, was not one of classical revision in the colonial sphere, but rather one of bluff. Significantly, the new RKB when it was formed had no special office for the preparation of a future German colonial administration.[47] Thus Hitler had no imminent colonial plans, but was rather using the colonial question as a means of bringing about the Anglo–German understanding crucial to the first part of his programme, namely, the achievement of German hegemony on the continent of Europe and *Lebensraum* in the east.[48] As the acting French colonial minister, Moutet, perceptively observed regarding the attitude of Germany in the colonial question, she

> uses this question for her political game and her claims are raised or toned down according to the needs of general German policy, especially in Europe . . . The aim of Germany has been to split England and France apart in order to draw England into an anti-Soviet campaign.[49]

The reaction of the British government to Hitler's public demand for consideration of the colonial question was not to run into the arms of Germany, but rather to set up a committee. On 8 March 1936

Eden wrote to Baldwin suggesting that the time had now come when 'a memorandum ought . . . to be prepared considering the question of the possible transfer of a colonial mandate or mandates to Germany in all its aspects'.[50] The following day the Prime Minister constituted a sub-committee of the Committee of Imperial Defence (CID) under the chairmanship of Lord Plymouth, the parliamentary under-secretary of state for colonies, to do exactly that.[51] At the first meeting of the committee Plymouth indicated that the matter was urgent because Germany might raise the issue at any time and he hoped that a report might be ready by Easter.[52] The labours of the committee took much longer than that.

The Plymouth committee was composed of representatives from the Foreign Office, the Colonial Office, the Dominions Office, the War Office, the Admiralty, the Air Ministry and the Board of Trade. At an early stage Baxter, the Foreign Office representative, made it clear that Germany was unlikely to be satisfied 'with anything less than the restoration of all her colonies except perhaps the Pacific Colonies'.[53] It was, in fact, a Foreign Office note which provided the foundation for the most contentious of all the Plymouth committee's meetings. The note, which appears to have been written by Baxter, suggested that if Britain had the strength, the support of the dominions and the resolve of British public opinion to accept the risk of war involved, there was much to commend an attitude of resistance towards colonial revision. But the Foreign Office took the view that it would not be prudent to allow 'the colonial grievance to develop into a permanent source of friction in Anglo–German relations'. The note continued: 'We cannot believe that it will be possible, by simply blocking all suggestions of peaceful change, to maintain the *status quo* in Africa indefinitely; to attempt to do so would involve a grave risk of war.'

Against this, however, it had to be realised that a positive attitude towards colonial revision on the part of Britain would be interpreted as weakness.[54] Consequently, the Foreign Office favoured a compromise policy which would begin with 'passive obstruction', but aim at 'securing in the end some sort of compromise or *modus vivendi*'. Concessions, though, should only be entertained in the framework of a general settlement and they should not put Germany in the position of being able to carry out *faits accomplis* such as converting a mandate into a colony. Therefore, concessions should not be irrevocable; in a colonial settlement African welfare should be safeguarded and the mandate system retained.[55]

The Colonial Office representative, Clauson, offered strong objections to the assumptions contained in the Foreign Office note. It had, Clauson argued, proceeded from the premises that colonies were possessions. This notion was obsolete. British colonial policy now stemmed from and was inspired by the British belief in the virtues of democratic government; the 'counterpart of democratic ideas at home was the doctrine of trusteeship in the Colonies, leading up to partnership'. This colonial policy was different from that of other powers. Moreover, it was certainly different from the policies that Germany could be expected to pursue in colonial territories if the sentiments expressed in Hitler's speeches were to be believed. Clauson agreed that the mandates stood in a different legal position from that of colonies proper, but to their relinquishment, he emphasised, there were the 'gravest objections in principle'. In general, he believed that the Foreign Office had tackled the issue in the 'wrong order'. The position of the Foreign Office was founded on the assumption that it would be unwise to do nothing in the colonial question and came to the conclusion that some appropriate action should be taken:

> He [Clauson] felt that the order should be: (i) Can we do all that Germany wants? The answer to this was no. (ii) Should we do nothing at all? The answer to this again was no. (iii) What then should we do? So far as we are concerned he thought that a transfer of Mandated Territory was inacceptable [sic], but if other countries with other views of colonial policy cared to make such concession, we should not object.

Clauson was not entirely negative. He thought that it would be possible for Britain to trade off approval of German union with Austria against colonial restoration, besides which there were the possibilities of granting Germany the same rights as League members in all colonies and of preferential trading conditions for Germany in Britain's African possessions.[56]

In effect, the contributions of the colonial office to the deliberations of the Plymouth committee throughout were of a strongly disapproving tone as far as the actual transfer of colonial and mandated territory was concerned. It was the moral considerations that were paramount. It seemed inconceivable that Nazi Germany, seized as she was by authoritarian and racist concepts, would abide by the principles of mandatory rule. The former German colonies were of very limited economic value and the possibility could not be ruled out that the Germans, in their disappointment should the mandates be returned, would resort to maltreatment of the native populations in an effort to increase productivity. It was also scarcely in the interests of native populations that the mandatory powers should be constantly changed. In every respect, the transfer of mandates to Germany by Britain would be the betrayal of a 'sacred trust'.[57] Moreover, it would contradict the wishes of the native populations[58] and the views of the British population, not only in Tanganyika, but throughout Africa, which, since the war, had become strongly supportive of the notion that 'a British bloc from the Cape to the confines of the Sudan' should be maintained.[59]

The attitude of the War Office, Admiralty and Air Ministry, except in the case of Tanganyika, was not quite as hostile towards the idea of German possession of colonies as might have been expected.[60] Generally, it was felt that German possession of Tanganyika would put the defensive position on the east coast of Africa back to what it had been prior to 1914, but the decisive consideration concerning the return of this territory to Germany was that it would break the 'all-red' Cape to Cairo route, which enabled the mobility of the Royal Air Force 'to be exploited fully in times of emergency'. These factors, however, were not held to apply so rigorously elsewhere. The possession of overseas ports and naval bases by a potential enemy had been a problem that had always confronted Britain and, it was stated,

> Provided that Germany's ratio of naval strength remains as 35% of our own, that we are not also at war with Japan, and that our fleet strength is adequate, we could view with some equanimity the possession by Germany of naval ports in one oversea territory, especially if these ports were undefended.[61]

In this connection it is interesting that Captain Syfret, the Admiralty's representative on the Plymouth committee, argued strongly that Britain should take the initiative and make a colonial offer to Germany. He supported this on the grounds that:

> A course of action whereby we gave the world the impression that whatever was eventually conceded had been wrung from us by our fear of Germany was to be deprecated while a graceful and generous offer might go far to satisfying her.

He favoured giving Germany part of Tanganyika, Britain retaining territory for her air route on the western side and areas on the Kenyan border.[62]

After considering a variety of schemes for the satisfaction of Germany's colonial demands, including proposals that had previously been made by Voretzsch[63] and one for the establishment of an international development company in Africa,[64] the Plymouth committee's findings were summarised in a report of 9 June 1936. A truly massive document, 36 pages long with 8 appendices, it was a thorough-going survey of the colonial question in Anglo–German relations until that time and fully examined all the courses open to the British government in the matter together with their advantages and disadvantages. The extent of Germany's colonial demands was now estimated as being the return of all her former colonies and probably more than that.[65] If the German government was successful in achieving this, it was accepted that it would be popular in Germany, although not corresponding to 'really deep-rooted feelings'.

The reasons behind Germany's demands were listed as economic, strategic and psychological. It was the psychological aspect that the report assessed as the most significant. It stated:

> She [Germany] regards herself as one of the greatest Powers, and she feels she has a right to colonies on that account alone. Other Powers, some of them in comparison weak and small like Belgium and Portugal, have large colonial possessions, and she does not see why she should not have them too. She feels herself to be a 'dynamic' power; she feels that she *must* expand in one direction or another. Finally and most important of all, she regards her former colonies as her own property of which she was wrongly deprived at Versailles, and her resentment is aggravated by the 'colonial guilt lie' . . . and the implication that she is not worthy to hold colonies.

The report recognised that Germany would undoubtedly derive some benefits from the return of her colonies. Psychologically, she would receive instant satisfaction, but economically the case was by no means clear cut. Under German administration and with the application of an intensive development programme, it was anticipated that the former German colonies could, over a three year period, boost Germany's exports annually by some £10 000 000.

This, however, had to be set against the cost of development projects. The degree to which Germany's raw material requirements could be met in her former colonies was believed to be wildly exaggerated. The report pointed out:

> The present exports of the former colonies amount to no more than 5 per cent. of Germany's total requirements of raw materials. They include practically none of the industrial minerals she requires, only some 4 per cent. of the oils and fats, and very small amounts of many of the other non-minerals such as wool and cotton.

Undoubtedly, as a result of heavy expenditure and development, the former colonies could be made to yield more, but the cost involved 'would add to the burden of debt already borne by the Government of the Reich'.

The report then went on to examine the problems that would be entailed if it was decided to restore colonies to Germany. The legal complexities alone were substantial. If it was decided to return to Germany a mandate in full sovereignty, this would probably require an amendment to Article twenty-two of the League covenant, its ratification by a unanimous vote in the League council and a majority in the assembly, and the consent of the United States and Japan. These procedures were held to involve 'formidable' difficulties. Apart from these legal obstacles, there were also the wishes and interests of the native populations to be considered. These had to be respected because it was fundamental to the mandates system that it was the 'well-being of the inhabitants' of the mandates and 'their development towards self-government' which were of paramount importance. The German attitude towards colonial administration, however, was 'utterly repugnant to the whole spirit of the mandates'. There were further difficulties in the way of transfer of mandates to Germany in that all the mandatory powers, including Britain, had from time to time made statements regarding the permanency of their mandates and had expressed a determination never to surrender them. Any deviation from this course was bound to lead to bitter opposition and the loss of prestige. The report stated quite bluntly:

> Events of recent months have somewhat impaired British prestige and there would be danger of the transfer appearing not as a

gesture of goodwill towards general world peace, but as a sign of weakness. Particularly would this be so in Germany itself and in the countries outside Europe and America.

In tropical Africa and other parts of the Colonial Empire, any handing over of territory would most certainly be looked upon by the natives as a sign of impotence on our part, particularly in view of our apparent failure effectively to support Abyssinia when oppressed by a powerful European state. It would be hard to persuade them that we had relinquished our hold for any other reason than weakness.

Finally, from the strategic point of view it was argued that Germany would be able to evade any military restrictions that were imposed upon her as a mandatory and that this would demand corresponding increases in Britain's imperial defence commitments.

The concluding section of the report dealt with the possible courses of action that were open to the British government in handling the colonial question. A refusal to discuss the matter with Germany was dismissed as not being feasible and the report was quite clear about this. It declared:

> We have, we think, made it clear that we are not inclined to underestimate the difficulties which any discussion will cause, but we very much doubt whether in fact a blank refusal to discuss would be practicable, if indeed a general settlement with Germany is to be reached. Whatever the rights and wrongs of the case, there can be no question that many Germans have a real sense of grievance, and to refuse to discuss the grievance would merely have the effect of increasing it. We think therefore that whatever the value put by Herr Hitler on England's friendship it is too much to hope that such a refusal on our part would be regarded in Germany as the end of the matter.

But neither was the report enamoured of the prospect of returning mandates to Germany. It was difficult to see what concessions Germany would make in return that would be as binding upon her as a transfer of territory would be upon Britain. Even if Germany accepted mandatory status she would probably only do so with an eye to escaping her commitments at the first opportunity. It was, in fact, Germany's proven unreliability in sincerely recognising her commitments that opened up special objections to the transfer to her of any territory under mandate. It should, however, be noted that the report hesitated 'to say that such action should not be contemplated', if it became clear that Germany attached such importance to the return of colonies that the issue 'would tip the scales between war and peace'. The third possibility examined by the report was a number of compromises that stopped short of actually transferring territory to Germany, but could be said to meet at least some of Germany's grievances in the colonial sphere. It was considered that an Anglo–German condominium and the chartered company idea were both unacceptable. They would lead to 'friction and inefficiency' and the chartered company proposal would 'have practically all the objections of the transfer of territory without even the advantages of satisfying German *amour propre*'.

Equally objectionable was the imposition of the mandates system on all colonial territories. This would result in severe political opposition in Britain and in the colonies, where 'devotion to the crown' on the part of both settler and native populations was 'one of the most striking characteristics' and could not be 'lightly set aside'. Most of the other compromise proposals, it was felt, were also open to various objections, not least the fact that they 'might involve an undue sacrifice of British interests', but of these guarantees of equality of treatment in immigration and access to raw materials seemed the most acceptable. Importantly, however, this section of the report concluded by observing that the totality of Germany's expansionist aims could never be satisfied in the colonial sphere: no matter how generously she was treated, she could not 'necessarily be diverted from pursuing her aspirations in Europe'.

It is evident that the Plymouth report illustrated the practical, legal, political and economic objections and difficulties that stood in the way of satisfying Germany's colonial claims. At the same time, it was quite explicit that the issue could not be avoided if Britain was to achieve a general settlement with Germany. The problem, though, was not so much a question of the satisfaction of Germany's colonial claims, but rather the willingness of Germany to participate sincerely in the terms of a general settlement in which those demands could be met. If this was possible, or if other circumstances required it, the report suggested that the most convenient way to satisfy Germany in the colonial question would be the transfer by Britain and France of the Cameroons and Togoland to her. In this case, Britain would probably have to make other 'contributions, perhaps not necessarily by the transfer of territory, to equalise the sacrifice' made by France.

It was, however, recommended by the report that Britain should in no circumstances entertain the surrender of Tanganyika.[66]

Within the Foreign Office it was already clear before the Plymouth report was ready to be circulated that Britain had little to gain by adopting a positive attitude towards Germany's colonial claims. On 27 May 1936 Baxter minuted that such a course would be 'madness', although he was not certain that a public statement explicitly rejecting the German demands would be wise. He favoured a compromise whereby Britain would issue a public negative regarding Tanganyika, while stating that as France was involved in the other mandates she would have to be consulted before any action could be taken concerning them.[67] Ashton-Gwatkin, who also served on the Plymouth committee, was equally impressed by the difficulties in the colonial question. He had gone into the committee very positively inclined towards giving Germany colonial satisfaction, but now tended to the view that the answer was 'No'. Nevertheless, he accepted that Germany was at least owed an enquiry into raw materials, which would reveal the weakness of her economic arguments.[68]

Vansittart's reaction to the Plymouth report was typically convoluted. He had 'expected no other finding from the committee' and he continued:

> My paper earlier in the year[69] advocated a colonial transfer as part, & only as a part, of a durable European settlement, *if* that could be obtained. There is no sign that such a settlement can be obtained. If therefore the Govt. adopt this report, they will also be confirming the preceding sentence – with all that it implies.
>
> What it eventually implies is this. If we are *not* going to remove the last partly legitimate grievance, we shall enter upon a period of bad relations with Germany, which will hamstring us in any mediation – on the hypothesis that any successful mediation was even possible, which I doubt, though we are doing our best. And ultimately these bad relations will be followed by war. We shall have to fight to keep Germany out of the colonial sphere. Will the nation think the game worth the dizzy taper? I wonder – when we get to the point. And unless we are both careful and clever we shall get these hostilities before we are ready.

Vansittart obviously thought, particularly in the light of Germany's diplomatic conduct since the remilitarisation of the Rhineland,[70] that a general settlement was not possible, at least for the present, and that this of necessity precluded Germany's colonial satisfaction. But a sustained negative response would require the completion of British rearmament. It seems, therefore, that he favoured a course that fell short of an outright rebuttal of the German colonial claims.[71] What he was advocating was a policy that would maintain tolerably good relations with Germany, while simultaneously gaining 'time'. He supported a raw materials enquiry as a 'time-saving device'[72] and he believed that the government ought not to be pressed into imprudence by the pressure of public opinion.[73]

Likewise, Eden supported a raw materials enquiry, but linked this with the view that Germany should be told that Britain could do nothing in the colonial question. The Foreign Secretary estimated that colonies were still a secondary consideration for Hitler and that, as the latter had not yet committed himself publicly to colonial restoration, a British *non possumus* on this issue could not offend his *amour propre* and thereby embitter Anglo–German relations.[74] Vansittart, however, still had doubts and he minuted on 24 June:

> If we *are* going to say definitely NO to the Germans . . . I am not sure that it is quite consistent with our policy of playing for time – we must assuredly re-arm faster than we are doing now. Personally I think that the moment has already passed when any firm negative to the Germans could have closed this question up. The Germans are now officially committed to the campaign, & cannot now draw back. Herein lies the danger of eventual war.[75]

In essence, it was the advice of Vansittart that the Cabinet was later to follow.

Whatever the differences in the Foreign Office, it was a universally held opinion that the Cabinet ought to define its attitude on the colonial question as soon as possible. There was some reluctance to do this, for Baldwin removed the Plymouth report from the agenda of the CID.[76] The matter, though, was eventually referred to the Cabinet Committee on Foreign Policy, which body had evolved from the earlier Cabinet Committee on Germany.[77] Almost its first task was consideration of the Plymouth report.

When the Foreign Policy Committee convened on 21 July 1936, it was reminded by the Colonial Secretary, Ormsby-Gore, that there was to be a debate in the Commons on the subject of Germany's former colonies the following week. Eden pressed for an immediate pronouncement of opposition to a retrocession of the mandates. This proposal was resisted by Neville Chamberlain with the support of Hoare, who since June had been reinstated in the Cabinet at the Admiralty. Chamberlain, who had already exhibited an interest in Germany's colonial demands[78] and had told the French the previous March that the colonial question ought to be considered if 'an all-round settlement' was in prospect,[79] thought it best to state that while Britain could not contemplate the surrender of Tanganyika she was not in principle opposed to territorial alterations. Endorsing this view, Hoare added that British willingness to participate in a raw materials enquiry should be reaffirmed. Besides this, he pointed out that as there was little opportunity for territorial revision in Europe it would be hard to tell the Germans that the same obtained in Africa. Hoare and Chamberlain were supported by the Lord Privy Seal, Lord Halifax, although he was of the opinion that it would be best to delay a decision until a draft statement had been considered. Eventually it was agreed that Eden and Ormsby-Gore should prepare one.[80]

The draft statement, when it was produced, did not truly reflect the balance of view expressed in the Foreign Policy Committee. It opened with a lengthy advocacy of a League-based enquiry into the accessibility of raw materials, concluding with a rehearsal of all the obstacles in the way of transferring mandated territory, such that 'it would be impossible for . . . [the British government] . . . to contemplate any such transfer'.[81] At the Foreign Policy Committee meeting of 27 July Halifax immediately argued that this went further than had been agreed by the committee. He continued:

The concluding sentence closed the door on any possible transfer of a mandate hereafter, and he feared that as soon as the statement was known in Germany, the German Government would decline to enter into discussions with us on any of the outstanding questions.[82] If a statement was made in these terms, Hitler could only refrain from raising the question by exposing himself to the criticism of those Germans who were pressing for a return of her Colonies to Germany that he was submitting to British dictation.

Halifax then read out a draft of his own which referred to those parts of the statement dealing with the transfer of a mandate to Germany. This stated that the British government was not prepared to add substantially to what it had already said; that the dominions and other powers were also affected; and that there were many moral, legal and political difficulties regarding the transfer of mandates which still remained hard to resolve. It was, of course, possible for any power to raise the issue and the British government would not refuse to discuss it, but it was to be hoped that with so many other outstanding problems this further problem would not be raised. Halifax believed that a statement along these lines would indicate to Hitler that 'we are not prepared to accede to Germany's demand' and that he would be able to explain to his people that the difficulties involved were great and that it would be better to defer consideration of this problem until 'more important issues of interest to Germany were disposed of'.

Eden now confessed that he was reluctant to make a statement on the subject but the parliamentary situation made it imperative, besides which the Foreign Office was in favour of as clear and definite a statement as possible. The impression of indecision would satisfy public opinion neither in Britain nor in Germany, where Hitler would be fortified in his belief that the continued exercise of pressure would bring results. It was also the view of the Foreign Office that the draft that he and Ormsby-Gore produced would not necessarily jeopardise the negotiation of a new Locarno agreement.[83] At this point Neville Chamberlain intervened in the discussion and it was decisive. He was 'gravely alarmed' by the draft that Eden and Ormsby-Gore had presented: it would have the 'worst possible effect in Germany'. Even if the Germans elected to attend the five power conference, which was then being proposed with a view to the reconstruction of Locarno,[84] 'they would come in a sulky and disgruntled frame of mind'. Despite a rearguard action by Ormsby-Gore, it was evident that he and Eden were in a minority. Ultimately the latter said that he had been persuaded by the wisdom of Halifax's arguments and that he would make a statement to the Commons that conformed with the text of the Lord Privy Seal's draft.[85] Thus, on the same afternoon, Eden informed the Commons that the government would not refuse to discuss the aspect of the colonial question relating to freer access to raw materials, but that to an actual transfer of mandated territories there were 'grave difficulties, moral, political and legal, of which His Majesty's Government must frankly say that they have been unable to find any solution'. With so many international problems still pending, it was to be hoped that there would 'in no quarter be the desire at this time to introduce further cause of serious differences between the nations'.[86]

Although the Plymouth committee was secret, it is probable that there were rumours of its existence. In any event, the fact that Hitler had mentioned colonial equality of rights in his March memoranda was sufficient to unleash a flood of questions in the Commons. Indeed, Eden's Commons statement can be seen as the culmination of this pressure. The most prominent opponent of colonial transfer in the Commons was Leo Amery who, 'as *The Times* correspondent in Berlin in 1899 . . . had come to understand the intensity of German envy of . . . [the British] . . . empire'.[87] Amery was supported by Duncan Sandys, Winston Churchill, Austen Chamberlain, Sir Henry Page Croft and others. On 6 April 1936 Sandys enquired of the government's present attitude in the colonial question, to which Baldwin replied that there had been no change.[88]

Such responses were naturally unsatisfactory to those who wished to oppose the transfer of mandated territory to Germany. On the same day further exchanges took place in the Commons on the colonial question in which Neville Chamberlain made certain remarks which were regarded as highly significant at the time, and since, as an example of his attitude towards the German government.[89] Both Churchill and Sir Austen Chamberlain requested of the Chancellor of the Exchequer a categorical statement rejecting the transfer of mandates to Germany while 'race persecution' was 'rife' there.[90] In reply, Chamberlain stated:

> Let me point out that there is a clear disinction between colonies and mandated territories. As far as I know, no one has ever asked or suggested that the British Empire should give up any of its colonies, and I need hardly say that, if any such demand were made, it could not possibly be entertained for a moment. Mandated territories are not colonies: they are in a somewhat different category, and are only part of the British Empire in what I may call the colloquial sense.

It was Chamberlain's belief that the allocation of the mandates had been procedurally muddled, but it was evident that changes in the nationality of the mandatory power had not been envisaged. Should such a transfer occur the consent of at least the League council, the donor mandatory and the recipient would be required. Nevertheless, the government had not considered and was not currently considering the transfer of a mandate. He went on:

> As to what might happen in the future, I think it would be unreasonable to ask me to predict the action of future governments, but this I will say at any rate. Mandates are not held by this country alone. I cannot conceive that any government would even discuss the question of transfer of its own mandates quite irrespective of what will happen to the mandates held by other governments.

Moreover, Chamberlain was clear in his own mind that the government would never transfer mandates, even in the pursuit of a general settlement, unless satisfaction was given 'that the interests of all sections of the population inhabiting those territories were fully safeguarded'.[91] Not surprisingly this statement led to further requests for information on the government's position, which were met effectively with the reply that Chamberlain had stated it.[92]

Speculation in the Commons over the colonial question refused to die down. After the Easter recess Chamberlain's statement was vigorously assailed from his own backbenches. This provoked an intervention from the then Colonial Secretary, J. H. Thomas. Germany, he indicated, was quite free to buy raw materials in the mandates; there were no restrictions. In addition, he rejected the idea that the inhabitants of mandates could be regarded as cattle. Nevertheless, he recognised that in the present circumstances investors in the mandates might well be disturbed by rumours of cession. To quell their anxieties he repeated the statement he had made in the Commons on 12 February 1936, but concluded: 'We have not considered and we are not considering this question, but if it is raised by any other people it will be our duty to consider the circumstances again, but not to attempt to bind anyone.' Churchill thought this most unsatisfactory. The Colonial Secretary had succeeded in creating the impression that the colonial question was not closed. He declared: 'A door should be either open or shut. It should not be flapping to and fro to see whether there is anyone pushing hard enough.' Opposition to the transfer of mandates would have to be pressed and pressed until those who desired it could no longer see any prospect of success.[93]

On 23 and 27 April Baldwin himself attempted to reassure the Commons,[94] but his statements did nothing to allay the apprehensions of the imperialists. It is also possible that by the beginning of April 1936 they had learnt something of the formation of the Plymouth committee, for in his memoirs Amery wrote that he was surprised and alarmed to discover at this time 'that the Cabinet generally, and Neville Chamberlain in particular, were bent on offering Tanganyika to Hitler'. To resist this he and others formed an imperial affairs committee of which Duncan Sandys was the 'energetic secretary'.[95] It speedily passed a resolution calling on the government to announce that in no circumstances whatever would it agree to the transfer of mandated territory.[96] Lord Winterton, the chairman of the committee, then asked Baldwin to receive a small deputation which was soon agreed.[97] The Colonial Office found it difficult to advise the Prime Minister on his response to the deputation in view of the existence of the Plymouth committee, but suggested that the best approach for Baldwin was to say that he could not add to statements he had already made, while expressing sympathy for the deputation's anxieties.[98]

The meeting between Baldwin, who was accompanied by Neville Chamberlain and the representatives of the imperial affairs committee, took place on 19 May. Amery, the main spokesman of the committee, submitted a statement and outlined their misgivings. According to Amery there was nothing in the terms of the mandates to contradict Britain's right to permanent possession of those territories. The imperial affairs committee, therefore, deprecated 'any Government statements which' drew 'any distinction between British territories whether subject to mandate or not'. In this respect, Chamberlain's statement of 6 April had been disturbing. Equally alarming had been statements made by Lord Stanhope which had implied British willingness to surrender mandates in the context of a general settlement. This, Amery argued, could only encourage Hitler.[99] Only a firm and categorical renunciation of the claims advanced in the German memoranda of the previous March could stop Germany pressing them further.[100]

Baldwin, in reply, stated that the question was not 'live' and had not been considered. In his view one of the main sources of anxiety over the issue was 'the various questions that had been put by members of the house and he strongly advised the deputation to let the matter rest for the moment'. He would not go further in the Commons on the matter and he would not commit future governments to any specific course. If the issue came up it would have to be discussed by all the mandatory powers. Chamberlain endorsed

Baldwin's comments completely.[101] In Amery's view, the deputation had 'met with evasion'.[102]

Amery and Sandys remained persistent and vigilant; they lost no opportunity of attacking the government over this issue. A good example of this was the way in which statements made by Oswald Pirow following a visit to London caused them yet again to challenge Baldwin about government policy. During his visit Pirow had had two discussions with Eden in which the colonial question was raised, but the exchange took more the form of a statement of Pirow's views than a discussion. At the first meeting, Pirow expressed a wish to see convened an African conference that would settle the future of their continent. He was against returning Tanganyika or South-West Africa, but thought that Togoland, the Cameroons and part of Angola could be ceded to Germany.[103] At their second meeting, Eden asked Pirow his views on the advisability of the British government making what was in effect a negative statement on the colonial question, but combining it with an intimation of willingness to participate in a raw materials enquiry. Pirow was favourable, but he believed Hitler should be allowed a 'back door' and that the raw materials proposal was 'too narrow'. He preferred 'some formula which showed that while refusing Tanganyika or South-West Africa we appreciated that there was a colonial problem'. Eden objected that this sounded very much like a statement that the British empire was inviolable, but that the same did not apply to the Portuguese.[104]

Nevertheless, Pirow continued in his public advocacy of a colonial settlement with Germany. Early in July 1936 he stated at Nairobi that he had discussed Tanganyika while in London, but could not reveal what had transpired. His view was that the mandate in British possession was vital to the interests of the Union and Rhodesia, although he considered it futile to believe that Germany could be kept out of Africa indefinitely.[105] Some days later he went further in a press interview, stating: 'The general feeling in Britain while desiring cordial co-operation with France is by no means unfriendly to Germany and would probably welcome a settlement of the Colonial question on a basis equitable to all parties.' It was not thought feasible to hand back Tanganyika or South-West Africa on strategic grounds, but influential quarters[106] felt that there could be no settlement unless Germany was compensated colonially.[107]

Quite apart from raising a storm in South Africa,[108] Pirow provoked unease at Westminster and a question for Baldwin to answer in the Commons. It was very quickly established by the Dominions Secretary, Malcolm MacDonald, that Pirow's remarks were not based on any comments made by ministers and it was decided by the Cabinet that this should be made clear.[109] This Baldwin did, but he was unable to satisfy his interlocutors regarding the future of British policy. Churchill and Sandys both hoped that the government would soon avail itself of an opportunity to declare opposition to the cession of mandates.[110] Matters went further: Amery, Churchill and Sir Austen Chamberlain addressed a memorial to the government;[111] and Duncan Sandys organised a parliamentary protest with 118 signatures.[112] It was to this discontent that Eden responded in his Commons statement of 27 July, but it did nothing to dispel it. Sandys demanded an immediate indication that the subject was closed to discussion: the Foreign Secretary's statement, he alleged, had made matters worse because it was quite clear, despite all that had been said, that the subject had been considered.[113]

Besides the evident disquiet at Westminster over the colonial question, it was also clear to the British government that the raising of this issue in the German memoranda of March 1936 had stimulated anxiety abroad. Indeed, British critics of their own government's handling of it never missed an opportunity of comparing the clear cut objections expressed by foreign governments with the ambiguous statements issued by the British government. In April 1936 the Dutch made enquiries about Britain's attitude. Subsequently, the Belgians made their dissatisfaction with British statements on the subject known and the Portuguese indicated their perturbation. In France a leading article in *Le Temps* argued that the colonial question was primarily an Anglo–German matter and that any colonial satisfaction of Germany would have to be at Britain's expense. All French political parties were opposed to colonial concessions, rendering it difficult to force through the Chamber such a measure without substantial concessions from Germany in other fields.[114] From within the empire equally strong resistance to the surrender of mandates to Germany was voiced.[115] It was, however, somewhat embarrassing for the British government when the Governor of Tanganyika, MacMichael, attempted to give the lead that British ministers were reluctant to undertake themselves. In a speech at Arusha on 5 August he stated quite categorically that Britain would never surrender Tanganyika. He also excoriated the arguments of colonial need based upon the premises of land for the settlement of surplus populations and areas for the exploitation of raw materials.[116] In Whitehall there was some talk of reprimanding MacMichael, but Halifax took the view that 'the least said soonest mended'. If a reprimand was sent, it would only excite MacMichael's fears and he might also tell his friends.[117]

With so much comment nationally and internationally, it was inevitable that the colonial question would become a staple for discussion in the British press and in leading political journals. A number of books were also published. Comment on this subject had never been lacking before 1936, but from that year onwards the volume of literature on the colonial question increased rapidly only to be curtailed by the outbreak of war. The German claim was not without its supporters. These were men such as Lord Lothian, Lord Rennell, Lord Mount Temple and Lord Londonderry who all favoured an outright positive response. They were supported by other 'eminent' Britons, among them Sir Evelyn Wrench and Lord Noel-Buxton, who 'expressed their belief in a serious consideration of the problem in connection with a "general settlement"'.[118]

The outstanding advocate of the German case, however, was W. H. Dawson. An intimate friend of Heinrich Schnee, he had been very active on behalf of the German colonialists throughout the 1920s[119] and at the close of that decade he had participated fully in the German campaign against the proposed 'closer union' of Kenya, Uganda and Tanganyika.[120] Within months of the installation of the Nazi regime, he was attributing Germany's internal chaos and militaristic aspect to maltreatment by the allies in the 1920s. He called for an immediate readjustment of the most glaring injustices of the Versailles settlement, from which the colonial question should not be excluded. He wrote:

> That Germany will have to be given back, if not the whole of her colonies, at least an empire in Africa corresponding to her industrial needs and worthy of her past brilliant work as a civilising force in that continent, should be taken for granted.[121]

In a eulogistic article praising Hitler's latest magnanimous offer following the remilitarisation of the Rhineland, he declared that it was 'of paramount importance that an amicable settlement [of the colonial question] should be sought on generous lines without delay'. It was 'vital to Germany, still the third greatest industrial and commercial country in the world', that she possessed 'tropical and sub-tropical territories in order to control supplies of raw materials for many of her important industries and to provide outlets for emigration and settlement'.[122]

In 1934 Schnee and Dawson attempted to bring Gilbert Murray into their cause, but without success.[123] Ultimately, Dawson found Sir Raymond Beazley a more congenial colleague in his endeavours. Following Hitler's Reichstag speech of 30 January 1937, in which he stated that Germany's colonial claim would be 'put forward again and again',[124] the two men addressed a memorial to Baldwin in which they pointed out that Hitler had also expressed his wish for 'amicable co-operation' with Britain. They were, therefore,

> profoundly convinced . . . that willingness to meet Germany on this question would do more than anything else to deepen and strengthen the foundations of our [Anglo–German] friendship, and that it would win to our side a powerful coadjutor in the service of world peace, settlement and stability.[125]

Dawson's response, however, to Hitler's claim at the Nuremberg rally of 1936 that Germany would be in a better position to cope with her economic problems with colonies[126] was more public, for he participated in the exchange of letters that subsequently appeared in *The Times* on the subject and which extended over a period of three months. An array of opinion was revealed. Vyvyan Adams, Lord Iddesleigh and F. S. Joelson argued against colonial satisfaction for Germany; men such as Brigadier General Waters and Sir Arnold Wilson for it.[127] Dawson's contribution, which received great publicity in Germany,[128] extolled Germany's colonial record, recommended her colonial demands and denounced the Treaty of Versailles.[129] His enthusiasm was matched by that of Lord Noel-Buxton, who opined that Germany had been deprived of her colonies in an insulting manner and that, while 'concession at this stage would . . . be a second best course . . . inaction may well be fatal'.[130]

In March and April 1937 Vernon Bartlett's *World Review* published a debate between Dawson and Duncan Sandys on the colonial question, which was quite intemperate in tone. Dawson deployed the usual arguments. They were dismissed by Sandys in the following manner: 'The gist of Mr Dawson's case amounts to a tearful plea of: "It ain't fair!" He relies exclusively on an appeal to what might be called "historic justice." '[131] Dawson would not let the matter rest there. The mandates had been acquired by 'foul means', resulting in jealousy, resentment and discontent throughout the world. Sandys countered, correctly, that the legal status of the mandates had never been defined. In addition, it was Germany's present attitude that made her an unwelcome potential neighbour in Africa and gave rise to unease about entrusting backward peoples to her care. In his view: 'Another twelve months and the agitation [in Britain for colonial restoration to Germany] will peter out for want of champions.'[132]

Sandys had a point. Despite the prominence in British political life of many of those who advocated colonial restoration, they represented a minority view and commanded little public opinion. This was evident to the German colonial enthusiasts from the moment that the debate began in earnest. In May 1936 Schnee informed Dawson with regret that he read on many occasions statements by British politicians who looked on Anglo–German relations from a hostile standpoint.[133] Moreover, his wife, on a visit to London, observed that there was 'still great opposition to giving up the colonies in certain quarters'.[134] By the following year it was apparent to the former colonial governor, von Lindequist, that the situation had changed little.[135]

Nevertheless, the subject continued to stimulate speculation. In 1938 Lord Londonderry published a book in which he argued in favour of a colonial settlement with Germany. He had been convinced of the strength of German feeling on this issue during two visits to Germany in 1936.[136] He was not very sure of the economic arguments, but felt that the loss of the colonies had 'hurt Germany's prestige and offended her sense of dignity as a Great Power'.[137] He also regretted that the matter had been forced into the open at the end of 1936 when it could have been avoided.[138] Comparing notes with Lloyd George on their respective visits to Germany, he wrote:

> Hitler seems most unfortunately to have committed himself to colonial possessions and as I keep telling Halifax, we should have obviated this by seeking to get hold of Germany some months ago and showing her our sympathy with her anti–communistic attitude. However, the Government have thought it best to stand completely aloof and we find the Germans gradually getting stronger and requiring our friendship and support less and less.[139]

But the colonial question now had to be faced and it seemed to him 'inevitable tht we shall have to come to some kind of arrangement with Germany as the only alternative to her taking, or attempting to take, what she wants by force'.[140]

Lord Lothian does not seem to have been very active in publishing his thoughts about colonial restoration openly, but he was ready to offer his views to a sympathetic audience. He was another visitor to Germany who was generally favourable to the totality of the German case, believing that fair treatment of Germany was the prerequisite of her moral regeneration.[141] In the wake of the Rhineland crisis, he addressed a lengthy note to Eden, following a conversation with Ribbentrop,[142] in which he put forward the view 'that if we assist Germany's escape from a position of encirclement to a position of balance in Europe, there is a good chance of the 25 years peace of which Hitler spoke'. If Britain did not do this, he forecast a German alliance with Italy and Japan. When the time came, therefore, it would be best not to stop Germany over Austria, Memel and Danzig and to agree to a frank discussion of the colonial and economic raw materials problems.[143]

At a meeting of the Anglo–German Fellowship in July he expanded further on this last point. It was for him a world question: 'The nations either had to reduce their tariffs and stabilise their currencies so that they could pay for raw materials and foodstuffs by means of exports . . . or they had to face the colonial question as an alternative to a general war.' He did not think that 'the crude transfer of territory' for the present was 'practical politics', nor did he think that the question could be satisfactorily solved merely by the restoration to Germany of her former colonies in their entirety. The issue had to be 'considered on much wider lines'. It was for all colonial nations to make a contribution. He stated: 'The new world, as well as the old, must be willing once more to re-open its doors to trade and migration.'[144] In Lothian's view the colonial question would not be relevant in a world of universal free trade.[145] During May 1937 Lothian again visited Germany, where the importance of the colonial question was impressed on him by Goering, Schacht and Hitler. He told Hitler that it was not correct to assume that Britain opposed Germany having colonies: 'colonial readjustment, though not on a large scale, was not impossible'.[146]

The balance of published opinion, however, was decidedly opposed to any question of returning colonial mandates to Germany. Opinion was broadly divided into two groups: those who opposed doing anything at all for Germany in the colonial field and those who, while not advocating the transfer of mandated territory, supported an extension of the 'open door' principle and the mandates system to all colonies as a means of guaranteeing equality of access to all colonial raw materials. The former school tended to be supported by Conservatives, the latter by Liberals and Socialists. Ferdinand Joelson's book, *Germany's Claims to Colonies*, was perhaps the most thorough criticism of the German case to appear.[147] Amery too was extensively critical when, dilating on an article he wrote in *International Affairs*,[148] he published a full-scale justification for resistance to the German demand for colonies. But Amery's attitude towards the German colonial claims formed part of his general hostility towards Nazism. Without Hitler the proposition might be altogether different, but, he wrote: 'For the moment there can be no other attitude to the German demand than a purely negative one. The issue should not be treated as open to discussion.' This, though, did not mean that 'some positive solution to what underlies that demand may not be found when the present ferment has worked itself out, and when a more normal outlook has regained its ascendency over the great German nation'.[149]

On the other hand, it was Hitler that Britain had to deal with and the colonial demand was being pursued by him as a means of increasing Germany's military, political and economic power 'for the extension of the Nazi doctrine and methods over the face of the earth'.[150] It was admitted by Amery that Germany had a raw materials problem, but colonies and mandates would provide her with few that she would require. This was the crux of the problem. If Germany wanted freer access to all the raw materials she needed, she would have to negotiate with sovereign states.[151] For Amery 'economic nationalism' was now a permanent feature of the world economy. Britain sheltered in her empire under the system of imperial preference to secure her trading interests. It was up to Germany to create for herself a similar sheltered market in eastern Europe.[152]

Generally speaking, it was not found necessary to be unfair about Germany's colonial past in order to justify the rejection of her colonial claims. Alan Bullock, for example, gave full credit to the reform and improvement in German colonial administration in the period 1906–1914, but believed that there were grounds for fearing that German colonial administration under a Nazi regime 'would approximate to the conditions of the period before 1906'.[153] Similarly, E. M. Ritchie was complimentary about Germany's colonial past, but argued that it was dangerous to trust the German state's good intentions towards Britain when embarked upon a course of *Weltpolitik*.[154] The strategic implications were spelled out by G. Roberts who pointed out that Germany, if she possessed Tanganyika, 'could dominate the Indian Ocean'. In his opinion, Tanganyika and South-West Africa provided the 'key to the peace of Africa'.[155] According to Franz Borkenau armed conflict in Africa was certain to take place. Hitler's dismantlement of the Treaty of Versailles was 'an almost insignificant incident on the road to unlimited expansion'.[156]

Likewise, Germany's colonial claims were only 'stepping stones to something else', namely 'the acquisition of a wider colonial area'. This she could only achieve by defeating Britain and France. Thus it was the strategic importance of Germany's former colonies that counted for her rather than their economic value. Borkenau thought that Germany's main target was the Union of South Africa. Once established in the African continent, she would be able to take advantage of the political situation in the dominion. With the Afrikaner element dominant there, 'to the exclusion of everything British', Germany could establish a protectorate over the Union, from where she could dominate the southern half of the African continent and one of the two sea routes to India. Furthermore, German control of South Africa would mean German control of gold production there which 'would at one stroke get rid of all the limitations imposed upon her by the lack of free exchange'.[157]

For Harold Nicolson also it was the strategic implications that were uppermost in his mind when he advocated resistance to Germany's colonial demands. But generally he was opposed to colonial restoration because it would create more problems than it would solve. It would damage Britain's prestige, when what Germany wanted in reality was power on the continent. Hitler had no fundamental interest in colonies: he would probably even allow Britain to keep the mandates in exchange for a free hand against France in eastern Europe. He wrote:

> All I wish to suggest is that those who think the Colonial Deal can be made on the basis of a little slice of the Cameroons or Togoland are subject to the most profound illusion. In other words, if we imagine we can pay the Danegeld in terms of the former colonies

we are imagining something which could only be temporarily and locally true. The price which we may have to pay for peace is infinitely heavier than that.

It would, therefore, be foolish to provide Germany with a means of embarrassing Britain overseas.[158]

The opponents of colonial restoration were represented throughout the political spectrum in Britain, but their attitude was given clearest expression in the Conservative Party. At the end of June 1936 a meeting of the Central Council of the National Union of Conservative and Unionist Associations passed two motions which were overwhelmingly endorsed. Sir Henry Page Croft's motion called upon the government to 'resist any proposals which might tend to weaken the integrity of the Empire'. Croft asserted that Germany could not be placated by a colonial deal; it was an argument that favoured placating 'the tiger tomorrow by throwing him chunks of meat to-day'. He wanted friendship with Germany, but not at the price of blackmail. Vincent Clarke then moved that no colonies or mandates be transferred to the sovereignty of the League or any other power. Seconding the motion, Duncan Sandys said that to transfer colonies to Germany would not only be strategically unsound, but morally wrong. Leo Amery emphasised that it must be made clear that Britain would never again import the German menace into Africa, or sell white or black men into Nazi slavery.[159] This mood was given wider expression at the Conservative Party conference of October 1936. Duncan Sandys and Page Croft moved a resolution that stated that the cession of British mandates was 'not a discussable question' which was carried by a large majority. A similar resolution was equally well supported at the Scarborough conference the following year.[160]

Nevertheless, opposition to the colonial satisfaction of Germany did not necessarily imply belief that existing arrangements regarding colonial administration, particularly in their economic aspects, were satisfactory. Lord Lugard, who was not averse to the return of Germany to Africa during the Weimar period, was a staunch upholder of the mandates system.[161] In his estimation, Britain had carried out her mandatory obligations 'most conscientiously'; under the mandates system Germany had 'equal commercial opportunity, and religious freedom for her missionaries, and every economic advantage enjoyed by the Mandatory itself'.[162] He did not wish to see the creation of 'international mandates', but he was prepared to contemplate the introduction of the 'open door' in all colonial territory.[163] Another authority on mandatory administration, Norman Bentwich, was prepared to go further. He believed that the best solution of the colonial question would be the extension of the mandates system, with its provisions for economic equality, to all colonies. This did not mean that Britain would have to surrender territory: rather it meant that she 'would accept international supervision over the administration of . . . [her] . . . colonies, and apply as liberally as possible liberal principles to all tropical countries under . . . [her] . . . direct administration'.[164]

Had *Round Table* remained aloof from the debate on the colonial question, it would have been strange. It did not. An article in 1934 gave some credence to the economic case advanced by the 'have-nots'. In this it was suggested that altruistic considerations had played no part in Britain's acquisition of tropical territories. Britain had wanted them to secure for herself sources of raw materials and potential markets and simultaneously to deny them to others.[165] By 1936, therefore, it is not surprising that it carried articles advocating the application of the 'open door' in colonial territories. It was accepted that German rearmament and economic autarchy were the major reasons behind Germany's incapacity to pay for raw materials. But, it was argued:

> When every allowance . . . is made for these factors, it remains true that Germany has been struck particularly hardly by the tremendous barriers to international trade, including those imposed by Great Britain, and that this has had a disastrous effect on her international capacity to buy.

World trade barriers had to come down if there was to be justice and peace. The notion that colonial territories should be private markets was 'incompatible with the acceptance of [colonial] trusteeship'. There was 'only one policy consistent with equal access to raw materials' and that was the 'open door'.[166] *Round Table*, however, was not totally seduced by the German economic arguments. They did not 'hold water': Germany's real motives were diplomatic, strategic and rooted in considerations of prestige. All the same, the abandonment of the 'open door' had been a 'grave mistake'.[167] By 1937, though, *Round Table* was striking a different note. Germany's problem in her relations with the rest of the world was seen now as political rather than economic: an economic settlement with her

could take place 'only as part of an all-round political settlement'.[168]
The arguments in favour of the extension of the principles of mandatory administration into all colonies and the rigorous application of the 'open door' in them naturally appealed to the committed Left in Britain, which had been so much responsible for bringing into existence the mandates system and which was very concerned that the concept of 'trusteeship' in colonial rule should prevail. For L. Barnes the British empire could only maintain itself on the basis of the freedom of its constituent parts and black dependencies should be included in this scheme as much as white dominions. Under the system of trusteeship backward populations were to be brought up to 'equal status with Britain'.[169] He even doubted if Britain was doing enough in this respect.[170] For men such as Barnes, therefore, the transfer of Africans to German rule would be a negation of the object of colonial administration. As Norman Angell put it:

> In the discussions of the colonial problem with Germany the protagonists of colony transfer repeatedly ask the question: 'Why, if colonies are of no particular value do you hesitate to give them up?' Nowhere have I noticed the reply that we are very steadily and consistently 'giving them up'. We are 'giving away the empire' to the only people to whom colonies ought to be 'given away' – to the people who live in them.[171]

Equally for Barnes the maintenance of the 'open door' in colonial dependencies was integral to trusteeship. The system of imperial preference could not be regarded as being in the interests of the native inhabitants of colonies because it interfered with their freedom to buy and sell in markets which were advantageous to them. But it was its threat to world peace by aggravating 'the international jealousies' which arose 'from the unequal distribution of colonial territories' that most disturbed him. The 'open door' would do much to allay the apprehensions 'of foreign industrial nations seeking a place in the sun in the form of supplies of raw materials and markets for manufactures'.[172] And it was because Norman Angell believed in free trade that he opposed the return of colonies to Germany. Those who gave support to that course were effectively agitating on behalf of the entrenchment of neo-mercantilism and economic nationalism.[173]
The spiritual and political home in Britain of those who favoured

the extension of the mandates system to all colonies and the application of the 'open door' as a means of solving the colonial question was the Labour Party, although this attitude was, of course, represented in all parties. But Labour's particular commitment in this respect was revealed in exchanges in the Commons during the summer of 1936[174] and in the pamphlet authorised for publication by the Labour Party's National Executive Committee. This pamphlet asserted that Italy, Germany and Britain acquired, in fact, only a small proportion of their raw material requirements from colonial territories, although it did accept that there were some grounds for the complaints on the part of the 'have-nots' concerning accessibility to raw materials. Tariffs also made it difficult for them to buy raw materials by impeding their exports. But Germany's contention that she had difficulty in buying in sterling areas was the result of her currency policy. Moreover, territorial transfer could not be regarded as a satisfactory solution of the problem of accessibility to raw materials which really had to be found in the establishment of an 'open door' policy. Demands for territorial transfer 'should be resisted', the pamphlet continued, for they

represent in effect an attempt to keep dissatisfied Powers quiet by paying blackmail. They are, moreover, based on a false psychological approach, since they perpetuate the notion that colonial 'swag' is a legitimate possession, only needing fair distribution among the 'robbers'. The influence of the Labour Party should be used to secure Britain's final break with this tradition.

What was recommended was the international administration of colonies through the League and the extension of the principles of mandatory administration to all British colonies.[175]

With the exception of a few influential men, any reading of the considerable literature stimulated by Germany's colonial demands and the Italian conquest of Abyssinia must lead one to the conclusion that the overwhelming majority of informed opinion in Britain was hostile to any idea of colonial transfer to Germany. There were naturally differences of view over the nature and objectives of colonial rule, but throughout the spectrum of political opinion there was a consensus that it would be undesirable to resurrect a German colonial administration overseas, at least for the duration of Hitler's regime. This was already apparent when the British government considered the Plymouth report and it was certainly so when, during 1937 and 1938, they gave serious thought to the colonial satisfaction of Germany. It can, therefore, be argued that this is one aspect of British foreign policy during the 1930s that was not devised with party political considerations in view.

7
Schacht

Following the passage of their resolution at the Conservative Party conference of 1936, Duncan Sandys congratulated Sir Henry Page Croft on his 'stirring "what we have we hold" appeal', which he thought had been crucial. In his letter he wrote: 'I agree with you that the effect will be excellent. I only shudder to think what the result would have been had we *not* carried it. It would have been an unmistakeable invitation to our friend Hitler to ask for more.'[1] The Conservative Party resolution, however, did not deter those in Germany who were bent on colonial revision. Nor did it deter the British government from consideration of the colonial satisfaction of Germany if that course promised the means of achieving their overriding policy aim of a durable European settlement. Within six months, therefore, of the Sandys–Page Croft resolution being carried the government was examining the colonial question with precisely that end in view.

Nevertheless, it would be wrong to suggest that the colonial question during the winter of 1936–1937 was a constant preoccupation of the British government in this respect. The main thrust of British policy in this period was rather dominated by the desire to create a new western pact which would replace the Locarno arrangements, rendered void as a means of maintaining peace and security by Hitler's action in the Rhineland, and which would act as the prelude to and anchor of the negotiation of a comprehensive European settlement. The negotiations conducted by the British from September 1936, until their effective termination in March 1937, for the convening of a five power conference to negotiate a western pact were the consequence of the determination on the part of the British government that the Rhineland crisis should be peacefully resolved.[2] It has been suggested by one authority that there is 'no useful purpose' in reviewing these abortive negotiations for a five power conference.[3] This would appear to be a harsh judgement as far as the evolution of British policy is concerned. Space precludes a detailed examination of these negotiations, but it is evident that they were regarded by the British government as

169

important not only because of the immediate end in view, namely, the negotiation of a western pact, but because of the implications this had for the achievement of a general settlement. This was particularly emphasised in the British note of 19 November 1936.[4] Neither the Germans nor the Italians, however, were at any stage encouraging in their responses to British promptings. As the Foreign Office had warned, French commitments in eastern Europe proved a significant stumbling block from the start.[5]

The *de facto* termination of these negotiations for a five power conference signalled in the German and Italian memoranda of March 1937 deprived the British government of the means through which to proceed to the conclusion of a general settlement, which was their real objective. In these circumstances, the suggestions that Schacht, the German minister of economics and president of the Reichsbank, had made to the French Prime Minister, Blum, the previous August, to the effect that Germany would co-operate in a European settlement in exchange for colonial satisfaction, assumed an importance which otherwise they would not have had. Until the Cabinet Foreign Policy Committee gave the Schacht proposals serious consideration in March and April 1937, it is indeed note-worthy the degree to which Foreign Office officials and ministers questioned the authority on which the German minister of economics acted in the political field, and the extent of their reluctance to treat with him is clearly manifest.

It had, nevertheless, to be assumed that there was some basis for the case presented by Schacht. Quite apart from the growing and officially orchestrated colonial propaganda in Germany, the importance that the Germans attached to the colonial question seemed to be confirmed by the way in which the issue had been intruded by them from time to time into the negotiations for a five power conference.[6] Moreover, Ribbentrop, an unequivocal colonial re-visionist, had been appointed at the end of 1936 as German ambassador at London. Urged by Hitler to 'bring . . . back the British alliance',[7] he did everything during his absentee ambassa-dorship to make the improbable impossible.[8]

In December 1936 Ribbentrop was eloquent on Germany's need for colonies in an address to the Anglo–German Fellowship, expressing the hope that a solution would soon be found.[9] But, more importantly, in February and March 1937 he spoke at length with Halifax and Eden on the subject. Visiting Halifax, during one of

Eden's absences, in order to complain about the attitude of the British press, he

> then proceeded to introduce the colonial question, prefacing it by saying that there was nothing that Herr Hitler so greatly desired as good relations with Great Britain and that there was no idea in his mind that such relations as he desired to see should be of an exclusive character. The colonial question interested Germany on both the economic and psychological side. From the economic side they had been obliged, in default of other remedies, to initiate the Four Year Plan, but . . . [Britain] . . . greatly misjudged this if . . . [she] . . . thought it connoted a desire for isolation and reluctance to take part in and develop world trade. From the other point of view he had no doubt that it would readily be appreciated how difficult it was for the German people to accept a position which said in effect that all nations except the German nation were entitled to hold colonies and that Germany alone was unfitted and unable to enjoy this privilege.

Satisfaction of the colonial claim, the ambassador argued, would 'favourably . . . affect the German outlook' and it would not augment Germany's military potential, for the Anglo–German naval agreement ensured that colonies 'would always be the Achilles heel of Germany'. Halifax replied that he could add nothing to what had been stated by Eden in the Commons on 27 July 1936. Furthermore, he regretted that Germany found herself unable to participate in the League enquiry into the raw materials question then in progress.[10] If the colonial question was ever to be discussed 'and still more if any adjustment of it was ever to be reached', this could only take place in an atmosphere in which 'British public opinion could be satisfied that the discussion and adjustment were essential to a general settlement the reality of which they could be reasonably assured'. That, however, the convention of a five power conference as a prelude to a general settlement was still the priority in British minds was made clear by Halifax.[11]

In a subsequent conversation with Eden on 16 March, Ribbentrop was informed by the Foreign Secretary that there was a danger that the colonial question 'would take a place at the present time in our relations similar to that of the naval question before the war'. Undaunted, the German ambassador rehearsed his usual arguments, adding that 'there was nothing that the Chancellor desired more' than the resolution of all disagreements between Britain and Germany, although he was 'feeling discouraged'.[12] If, indeed, it was Hitler's policy at this time to use the colonial question to bludgeon the British into submission to his will, Ribbentrop was the perfect blunt instrument.

It was not, though, Ribbentrop's representations and remonstrations that were directly responsible for the British government once again examining the colonial question as a means of bringing Germany into a general settlement, but rather the more subtle approach of Schacht, although he too could be crude. Schacht's activities during 1936 and 1937 seem to have had, in fact, some approval from Hitler; they can, therefore, be seen as part of the coercive stage of Hitler's tactical use of the colonial question. But from the point of view of the development of British policy Schacht's manoeuvres coincided with and partly prompted a belief within the Foreign Office that the German leadership was divided between groups of *moderates* and *extremists*. According to Phipps, Schacht was, indeed, the leader of the moderate party and enjoyed the support of von Neurath, the army and the bureaucracy. Furthermore, he had 'very helpful points of contact with General Goering', who had 'few Nazi proclivities in his saner moments'.[13] Hess and von Epp were similarly bracketed.[14] Generally, however, Goering was considered an extremist along with Goebbels, a view reinforced by their utterances on the colonial question during the autumn of 1936,[15] Goering even suggesting in a private conversation that the colonial question should be presented 'on the point of a bayonet'.[16]

The central dilemma for the formulators of British policy was that of estimating to which of these two groups Hitler belonged. Despite his interview with Hitler during his 'busman's holiday' in August 1936, Vansittart was unable to form an opinion and reports from Phipps were not very helpful.[17] Nevertheless, it is clear that the permanent under-secretary thought by the end of 1937 that with British assistance the moderates had an even chance of competing for Hitler's ear. In his opinion, the best form of help would be determined British rearmament. On the other hand, Britain had started her rearmament late and 'time was vital'. Given this situation, it was imperative that British policy should aim 'to stabilise the position till 1939' in Europe. The conclusion, therefore, of a colonial settlement with Germany and economic assistance for her 'as part of a political settlement' were not ruled out by Vansittart in this period if they could assist in the process of stabilisation. Only in this way did he feel that the 'moderates and moderation' might 'have a chance in Germany'.[18] Eden presented a similar view to the Cabinet in January 1937.[19] Thus, the decision of the British government in the spring of 1937 to consider the colonial question seriously has to be seen partly in the context of the failure of the negotiations for a five power conference and partly in the context of British estimates of the political situation in Germany.

Undoubtedly, Schacht's initiatives in the diplomatic field owed much to his deeply rooted belief that industrial nations needed colonial possessions in order to survive, a conviction which he maintained beyond 1945,[20] but it would seem that he was equally alarmed by the direction in which German foreign policy was tending, especially with the introduction of the Four Year Plan, and that his efforts were also directed towards gaining Hitler's support for a classical policy of 'liberal imperialism' in place of the eastern European concepts of the NSDAP.[21] In 1935 he had informed Hitler of his view that eastern policy and the conversion of Germany into a fundamentally agrarian state were 'romantic';[22] during 1936 and 1937 he appears to have been ready to fight for his foreign policy alternative and thereby his political life.

By early 1936 Schacht was becoming unpopular with the NSDAP, an organisation which he never joined.[23] Much of the conflict naturally centred upon a struggle between him and the 'party leaders, especially Goering, over the control and direction of the German economy', which was now entering a parlous state.[24] Strangely it was Schacht, with the aid of Blomberg, who was partly responsible for bringing Goering into the economic management of the Third Reich in the first instance.[25] It was hoped that the latter would curb the irregularities of senior Nazis regarding currency matters and that he would generally control the economic excesses of the Nazi radicals. It was also anticipated by Schacht that once Goering apprehended the true complexities of economic management he and the Nazi leadership would be content to leave the German economy effectively in the hands of himself and the moderates.[26] In March 1936 the *New York Times* perceptively commented:

The contest between Schacht and the radicals is not so simple. Broadly, the contest involves the issue of who is to dictate the financial and economic policies of the Third Reich and whether economics shall dominate politics or politics dominate economics.[27]

Given Hitler's desire, and one that was becoming increasingly urgent, to gear the German economy for war, it was inevitable that politics would triumph over economics and that conventional caution in economic affairs would be thrown to the wind.[28] As Goering crudely expressed it to Schacht: 'if the Führer wishes it . . . two times two is five'.[29] Goering's appointment, therefore, as head of the new Raw Materials and Foreign Exchange Office in April 1936 should not be seen as solely the consequence of Schacht's initiative, but also as an indication of Hitler's determination, at this juncture, to bring the German economy under firm Nazi control.[30]

There were, nonetheless, aspects of the political struggle that related purely to matters of foreign policy. Significantly, one of Schacht's confidants, Fritz Reuter, published an article in the *Deutsche Volkswirtschaft* in February 1936 which clearly implied that the French ratification of the Franco–Soviet pact and the reality of 'encirclement' were the inevitable consequences of German policy.[31] Subsequently, the military occupation of the Rhineland appears to have been vigorously opposed by Schacht, who contemplated resignation[32] and later advised Eden through an intermediary not to conclude any agreement with Hitler until he became 'civilised'.[33] From this time onwards Schacht became an opponent of the Nazi party, first from within the government and then from without.

In view of Schacht's record of hostility towards the Nazi regime, which culminated first in his being relieved of his ministerial post in 1937, secondly in his dismissal from the presidency of the Reichs-bank in 1939, and, ultimately, in his incarceration in Dachau concentration camp, it is perhaps surprising that he should have been arraigned at Nuremberg on the conspiracy charge. He himself was enraged at such a proceeding and evinced clear contempt for the charges he had to face and his 'criminal associates' in the dock.[34] A man of superior intelligence, he was easily able to rebut the evidence against him.[35] The British were not, it appears, primarily responsible for the decision to try Schacht: rather the Americans had been most insistent on the ground that they wished to 'make a play with economic preparation for war'.[36] In a very narrow sense there was some justification for this. On the occasion of his dismissal from the Reichsbank presidency, for example, Goering remarked to

Schacht that the whole of Germany recognised what great services he had performed, to which the latter replied: 'Other countries (*das Ausland*) know better still.'[37] Looked at in the round, however, there was very little evidence to make a case. The Treasury solicitor, Sir T. Barnes, admitted as much when he informed Sir Frederick Leith-Ross, Chief Economic Adviser to the British government during the 1930s and the war, that

> there were some statements by Schacht which would need a good deal of explaining away but the British side would see that he got a fair trial & he did not think there was any risk of his being hanged.[38]

Leith-Ross, who had more to do with Schacht than any other British official, considered, in a note of September 1937, the latter's likely departure from ministerial office as most unfortunate. Those who knew Schacht, he opined, had 'the highest regard for his character'. Schacht was a 'good German' who had worked unstintingly 'to keep the German financial and economic machine going'. There was much in Nazism that he abhorred, but he liked power and had political ambitions of his own. Thus 'he had put his abilities at the service of . . . [the Hitler government] . . . and . . . performed a remarkable *tour de force* in holding the situation'. Throughout the winter of 1936–1937 Leith-Ross believed Schacht had been working genuinely for *détente* between Germany and the western powers. His obsession with the colonial question had not helped his cause, but *pari passu* Leith-Ross wondered if it had ever been realistic to anticipate that Schacht could have prevailed against the extremists in Germany and won Hitler to his view. The British official concluded: 'Whatever people may think of him, there is no doubt that Schacht has been working for a reasonable policy and his departure from the Reichsbank would be greatly regretted by everyone in the City.'[39] The passage of years and the Second World War did not shake Sir Frederick's convictions. He believed that Schacht had always wanted a strong Germany, but one that was attained by 'peaceful economic measures'.[40] This fundamentally was what motivated Schacht in his activities from the summer of 1936 until the summer of 1937.

Although it was the proposals that Schacht made to the French premier in August 1936 that were the point of origin of the discussions that took place in the Cabinet Foreign Policy Committee the following spring, the Foreign Office had received a number of indications of Schacht's attitude in the matter of colonies before Blum officially informed Eden on 20 September 1936 of the substance of what had passed between him and the German minister of economics. While Schacht's reliability as to the course of German policy was considered suspect, his remarks, taken together with other statements and events, were regarded as possibly having some importance.[41] In March 1936 Richard von Kühlmann, who with Schacht had raised the colonial question in a most indelicate manner during the Young Plan negotiations in 1929,[42] informed Phipps that he had succeeded in convincing Hitler, through von Neurath, of Germany's need for colonies.[43] Kühlmann's claim was given more point the following May when Schacht spoke to A. L. Kennedy, a member of the editorial staff of *The Times* working in Berlin, 'with extraordinary bluntness'. According to Kennedy's record of the conversation, Schacht stated:

> Germany must have access to more raw materials and have it soon. The standard of living was steadily going down. Nothing can stop this deterioration except much freer world trade, especially the acquisition by Germany of food-stuffs and raw materials. If it is not stopped there will *inevitably be an explosion* – and the explosion, with the present regime in power, will take the form of war.

Schacht went on to argue that it was essential for Germany to be able to buy and sell in her own currency; she, therefore, required colonial markets. What Germany needed was a territory like Angola which she could develop and he 'wondered whether Germany could lease half Angola from Portugal'. Kennedy emphasised that Schacht had not been 'hysterical', even though he had suggested that without colonies Germany would be forced into a 'war of desperation'.[44]

Phipps questioned Schacht's motives in speaking in this manner. He felt that the tone of the latter's remarks was threatening rather than monitory. He did not believe Schacht to be 'a particularly reliable informant as to the probable policy of the German Government' and he rather dismissed Schacht's comments 'as an attempt to impress upon us the magnitude of Germany's "nuisance value"'. Sargent, however, in a particularly perceptive minute wrote:

> I think that these recent outbursts on the part of Dr Schacht show that he is beginning to feel the long strain of his association with

the Nazi regime, and that he is trying to discover some new means of diverting the pent-up forces which are at present threatening the economic structure which he has so laboriously built-up and defended during the last three years. For it is difficult to believe that so intelligent a man as Dr Schacht believes that the acquisition of colonies is really going to solve the economic and financial problems of Germany. He must know as well as anyone their limited value for this purpose. If so, one is driven to conclude that he is working up this colonial cry merely as a diversion for internal political purposes.

Vansittart was not so sure: even allowing for 'bluff & bluster', he thought an Anglo–German war over colonies a possibility. For his part, Gladwyn Jebb had 'little doubt' that Schacht's remarks were a 'serious warning'.[45]

That Schacht's preoccupation with the colonial question was not confined to one isolated outburst gradually became clear. In September 1936 the Foreign Office learnt from the South African legation in Berlin that Schacht was claiming to have won Hitler to his view of the colonial question. Angola still loomed large as a potential area of German colonial interest in Schacht's mind, but what was most significant from the British point of view was that the Reichsminister was asserting that, whereas the French were prepared to be complaisant in the matter of Germany's colonial requirements, it was the British who were the obstacle.[46] This information was augmented further when Dr Jäckh, 'an old personal friend' of Schacht's, informed the British embassy in Berlin that the latter, following his visit to Paris, was 'in a most optimistic mood' and talking of 'his "understanding" with M. Blum'. This centred on the colonial question, with the Cameroons now the focus of German interest. Speaking on behalf of the minister of economics, Jäckh declared that Schacht

urged that Hitler was a man of mutable ideas and that the handing over of a colony to Germany would enable . . . him . . . with Herr Hitler's help to secure the support of that section of Nazi Party [sic] which favoured a liberal policy in international economic affairs.

Furthermore, Schacht had emphasised that the Four Year Plan was the alternative to colonial restoration and that world peace depended upon the attitude of Britain. Jäckh finally expressed Schacht's desire 'to be invited to visit London', where he was certain that 'he could convince British Ministers as successfully as he convinced the French Ministers in Paris'.[47]

This was not the first occasion that a visit by Schacht to London had been mooted. In November 1935 Phipps had informed the Foreign Office that Schacht had been angling for an invitation to address the City on the 'economic and financial situation of Germany'. Sir Samuel Hoare considered then that Schacht's 'missionary journey' should be discouraged and the Foreign Office remained very much opposed to such an idea in the summer of 1936. If contact was to be made with Schacht there would have to be a political settlement with Germany first. In any case, it would be better, it was felt, for Sir Frederick Leith-Ross to visit Schacht in Germany should it be necessary to deal with him. And as for the claim that the French had been converted to colonial retrocession, the French ambassador had 'scouted the rumour, describing it as a manoeuvre'.[48] Nevertheless, the Foreign Office continued to receive information to the effect that Schacht's views had been accorded a welcome reception in Paris. B. C. Newton, minister at the British embassy in Berlin, thought that Schacht had been blackmailing the French and that he proposed to do the same to Britain by burdening her with the responsibility for any trouble that might arise as the result of a failure on the part of Britain and France to buy Germany off. He also felt that there might be lurking at the back of Schacht's mind 'the thought of sowing disagreement as to who should pay the German piper'.[49]

On 20 September the British government finally were made aware that the French had indeed been more indulgent towards Schacht's ideas than had been admitted or communicated. Although the Reichsminister's presence in Paris had only had the formal status of a courtesy visit,[50] the French from the first had attributed great importance to the event. François-Poncet, the French ambassador at Berlin, was of the opinion that it could be *'le point d'accrochage* of political action of great importance'. The ambassador wrote that if Schacht found sympathy for his views in Paris he would undertake

> with the prospect of success, an attempt to bring Hitler to the view that after the Non-Intervention Agreement in Spain, the conclusion of a new Locarno Pact and a general European settlement, the development of commercial arrangements and a European

currency alignment convention are the only valid means of avoiding catastrophe.[51]

Therefore, while it was well known in Paris that Schacht was an emphatic colonial revisionist,[52] the colonial question did not appear to be significant in what he proposed to say to French ministers. Upon his arrival in the French capital, however, he immediately broached the subject.[53] Subsequently, in his two conversations with Blum, it transpired that what he was proposing was that Germany would agree to arms limitation and a European settlement in exchange for colonial satisfaction.

At the first of these conversations Delbos, the French foreign minister, and Labeyrie, the governor of the Bank of France, were also present, together with Auriol, the minister of finance, Bastid, the minister of commerce, and Spinasse, the minister of economic affairs.[54] But the second was *à deux* at Schacht's request. The record of this meeting, drawn up by Blum, is interesting because it differs substantially from the account that the French Prime Minister later gave to Eden. From this record it seems evident that Blum was more enthusiastic about Schacht's colonial suggestions than he later admitted to the Foreign Secretary. He told the Reichsminister that he could not understand exactly how the possession of colonies would benefit Germany economically, but that, if colonial satisfaction was essential to 'Germany's adherence to a system of guarantees and armament reduction', the French government would not consider it impossible to discuss the subject and would raise it with the British.[55] Schacht had thereupon suggested that Blum contact Baldwin immediately, but the latter thought this indiscreet. Instead he asked Eden to see him while travelling through Paris on his way to Geneva.[56]

What Blum conveyed to Eden was essentially the substance of his conversation with Schacht without revealing the French attitude to a possible colonial deal. But that Blum was inclined to take a positive attitude towards Schacht's advances is to be found in the following remarks he made to the British Foreign Secretary:

Here is this German offer, underlined by the Chancellor. If we were to scan the last speeches at Nuremberg we might even find some echo of this offer. The German Government asked whether we were prepared to continue to explore the ground thus opened up. Were we to shut the door? Were we to offer a flat refusal?

The French Prime Minister concluded by asking if he had been guilty of an error in listening to Schacht.[57]

Blum's enthusaism for pursuing this entirely irregular proceeding was undoubtedly further stimulated by the fact that on receipt of Schacht's report on his Paris conversations Hitler had asked François-Poncet to visit him at Berchtesgaden. Although Schacht's Paris conversations had been undertaken on his own initiative and without a 'mission from the German Chancellor' to discuss the matters he raised,[58] Hitler had been kept informed and was evidently very pleased with the results. He told the French ambassador that 'he had been keenly interested by the report of his minister and had authorised him to continue in the way he had begun'.[59]

The French can be forgiven for assuming that it was the prospect of a colonial settlement that had provoked Hitler's interest. In his recent proclamation to the Nuremberg rally Hitler had mentioned that Germany could more easily surmount her economic difficulties if she possessed colonies.[60] Moreover, this coincided with the publication by General von Epp of an article in the *Europäische Revue* that argued, along the well-worn lines, in favour of the restitution of Germany's colonial empire. Hitler's statement was thought to reflect the influence of Schacht[61] and the latter later informed the French *chargé d'affaires*, Lamarle, that von Epp's article could not have been published without the author being assured that it corresponded with Hitler's ideas. According to Schacht, 'the settlement of this question was . . . one of the principal elements in the pacification of Europe'.[62]

It would appear, however, that the interest of the German government in Schacht's report was more concerned with the future of France's relations with the Soviet Union.[63] During the Schacht–Blum conversation the question of the Soviet Union arose in connection with the guarantees that Germany would be prepared to give in a European settlement. Schacht stated categorically that Germany could not guarantee the Soviet Union directly, but that she would do so indirectly, which Blum understood 'to mean that Germany would give a guarantee to France and Great Britain not to attack Russia'. Recognising the inconvenience that the Franco–Soviet pact caused Germany, the French premier observed: 'The cure for this state of things was . . . to relieve France of the apprehensions from Germany which had brought about these policies.' In reporting this statement to Hitler, Schacht added a nuance which suggested that if France was assured of pacific German intent toward her she would dispense with the Franco–Soviet pact.[64] It is, therefore, hardly surprising and easily credible that Hitler should have been encouraged by Schacht's efforts to such an extent that he was willing for his minister to go further.

By the time that Blum saw Eden it is evident that the French Prime Minister considered Schacht's overtures to have acquired an 'official' status. Eden, however, was astonished and cautious. If the Germans wished to bring about a European settlement and wished to intrude other matters into it they should do so 'in the course of the confidential diplomatic exchanges' that had taken place regarding the convening of a five power conference. On the other hand, he appreciated that it was a German tendency not to use 'normal methods'. But

> there seemed . . . to be a certain danger in negotiations which started on the basis that our two Governments were willing to discuss Germany's desire for colonial compensation even though that basis were combined with a German intimation of a desire for a European settlement and for an agreement for the reduction and limitation of armaments. It was true that the German attitude as defined by Dr Schacht appeared to constitute a considerable advance, but when accurately defined the German proposals, both in respect of a European settlement and in respect of an arms agreement, might be found to mean a great deal or very little. Even if they only meant a very little, we should have been committed to a discussion with Germany of her desire for satisfaction in the colonial sphere.

This was a situation that Eden found unacceptable. The British attitude in the colonial question was governed by the 'carefully considered' statement he had made in the Commons on 27 July, which meant that he could not agree immediately to the opening of negotiations on the bases proposed by Schacht. Before this could be entertained he would have to consult his Cabinet colleagues.[65] Even then, he later informed Blum, he thought that the British government would not wish to proceed with discussion without 'a more complete and detailed appreciation of the attitude of the German Government towards the problems that . . . [had] . . . to be solved' before a European settlement could be accomplished.[66]

Eden's attitude was fully endorsed by Vansittart. Britain was being asked 'to play the ace of spades the very first trick in order to take the two of clubs'. He was more inclined than most to treat the German claim for colonial restoration sympathetically, but at the present time it was not 'practical politics'. To move in this direction would arouse great hostility in Britain and such a measure could not be contemplated until Britain was sure of 'getting something very real and tangible in return'. It was necessary to wait upon the five power conference materialising, although there was a question mark over the prospects of that. But what was certain was that it would never take place if Britain allowed herself 'to be inveigled into a surreptitious and semi-secret Three Power meeting' to discuss colonies.[67]

Some days later Eden and Halifax discussed the colonial question further with Delbos and Spinasse at Geneva. To Eden's amazement it emerged that the French were indeed more ready to consider colonial compensation than had been anticipated, Delbos indicating that they would contemplate it in exchange for a settlement of the Rhineland question alone. There was, however, general agreement that further progress could not be made until the German proposals were more exactly clarified. Eden and Halifax reiterated that they had no authority for departing from the statement of 27 July, but added: 'Though we had not yet received any communication from London we felt confident that so far as we were concerned the next step should be to ask the German government for some clearer definition of any proposals they might have to make.'[68]

This caused immediate alarm in the Foreign Office where it was considered as an unwelcome advance on Eden's earlier statements.[69] Vansittart thought that to ask for a definition of Germany's proposals was akin to putting 'the cart before the horse!'. He informed Eden:

The Germans themselves always said they hoped the colonial question could be dealt with after a European settlement and Germany's return to the League. The position really is that the Germans have obtained their advantage by the recovery of the demilitarized zone. What we are really after is to get into a conference whereby a substitute Locarno will be concluded without the demilitarized zone, that is the Germans will keep their profit. But it is really going rather far if in spite of their previous professions they now want some further and strong inducement before they come into a conference which is to repair and obliterate the effects of their unilateral action.

The colonial question, therefore, should only be considered after a European settlement.[70]

It is of considerable importance that Vansittart did not act solely on his own initiative in writing to Eden in this way. He had, in fact, sought political endorsement for the views contained in his letter, for it was only sent after consultation with Neville Chamberlain, who was the only senior Cabinet member available at the time. Undoubtedly, Chamberlain accepted the advice of Vansittart without too much question, as did subsequently Eden, much to the chagrin of Sir Alexander Cadogan. Cadogan took the view that in acting as he did Vansittart had regrettably put Eden off the Schacht proposals altogether. For Cadogan, Vansittart's opposition to asking the Germans for a more precise definition of what they would be prepared to contribute was a mistake. He wrote:

Van has urged that we shdn't do this, as it wd. give impression that we were prepared to consider colonial deal. That may be strictly right, but Van does it because he's against discussing things with G.[ermany] on principle. There, I think he's wrong . . . we've left the *whole* initiative to G.[ermany]: we've submitted time and again to faits accomplis: we've never challenged her to formulate reasonable demands.

And he commented one day later:

I'm quite sure that one wants a long spoon in dealing with the Germans, but by resolutely refusing to come to the table, even, we are letting them get all the soup. It can't be said that the policy so far is successful. In fact we haven't got a policy: we merely wait and see what will happen next.[71]

Clearly, from the beginning, Cadogan considered that Vansittart was deliberately letting an opportunity slip by. Neville Chamberlain and opinion within the Treasury were soon to come to the same conclusion.

There, for the moment, the situation remained. On 26 September Blum informed Schacht of the response that his proposals had elicited from Eden and that he anticipated further news from the British government after the Foreign Secretary's return to London. Meanwhile, he hoped that he and Schacht could continue their work for 'lasting reconciliation and peace'.[72] Blum's hopes, however, were shattered by the resolution passed by the Margate

conference of the Conservative Party on 1 October 1936.[73] Speaking
to Eden in Geneva, he stated that he feared that the 'conversations
initiated by Schacht in Paris were not likely to have any sequel', to
which Eden retorted that the resolution might do some good by
demonstrating to the Germans that 'other nations could be stiff
also'. Nonetheless, the British Foreign Secretary promised to raise
the matter of the Schacht proposals with his colleagues when he
returned from his holiday in the south of France, although he did
not suppose that their attitude would differ materially from his. He
was sorry if this was 'too rigid', but it was up to the Germans to
explain what they had to offer towards a European settlement and
the next step lay with them.[74] Eventually, on 14 October 1936, the
Schacht proposals were discussed by the British Cabinet, but
without further issue, which meant that Blum did not receive the
promised considered reply.[75]

For the moment the Foreign Office appeared to have willingly and
successfully stifled any development of the Schacht overtures. They
would not be deflected from their course of attempting to convene a
five power conference through the normal diplomatic channels.
Neverthless, Schacht was nothing if not persistent. The urgency
with which Germany required a colonial settlement was impressed
upon Phipps directly and indirectly by Schacht throughout the
autumn of 1936.[76] Perceptively, Phipps commented:

> It seems clear that Dr Schacht's position is becoming more difficult
> and that in order to retain [the] Chancellor's good will he would
> work for such a colonial settlement now. I doubt however Herr
> Hitler's readiness to accept even this settlement as final apart
> altogether from inherent difficulties of getting the other countries
> concerned to foot the bill.[77]

Moreover, Phipps did not believe that Hitler would be deflected
from the course of expansion in eastern Europe outlined in *Mein
Kampf* by the acquisition of colonies: colonies would only 'accelerate
or at any rate . . . facilitate' the realisation of that objective.[78]

Early in November 1936 Schacht attempted to arouse Phipp's
interest in the colonial question, his failure to do so causing him to
mutter that Britain would one day be 'disagreeably surprised'.[79] Of
more moment, however, was the exchange between the two men at
a British embassy luncheon on 29 October. In his accustomed
manner, Schacht observed that the German people were a '*Volk*

ohne Raum'. Phipps replied that, if this was so, why was it that 'the German Government tried artificially to stimulate the birth-rate by offering premiums for babies, and by other means'.[80] Subsequently, Schacht twisted this comment in an offensive manner in a speech he delivered to the Geographical and Statistical Society at Frankfurt on 9 December. He stated:

> We are a country which possesses on too small an area too great a population, and this fact presses on us like a mountain. When I recently had occasion to discuss this fact in conversation with a foreign diplomatist in Berlin, this friend of mankind . . . gave me the advice that the German nation should reduce its births. This outlook which we meet in Anglo-Saxon circles also in other connexions . . . is in my opinion in contradiction with the most primitive principles of the divine order.

The rest of the speech was devoted to blaming other countries for Germany's difficulties. He argued that the attempt 'to constrict a great people through constant pressure from outside' would only lead inevitably 'to some sort of expansion'. Colonies were the answer to Germany's problems.[81]

Within the Foreign Office there was great indignation over this 'impertinent and mendacious attack on our ambassador'. It was suggested that Ribbentrop should be spoken to 'sharply' about it.[82] Ribbentrop, however, had inconveniently departed for Germany, which left Vansittart fulminating frustratedly about Schacht's 'monstrous performance'.[83] Ashton-Gwatkin was able to afford him some solace by remonstrating with Herr Wienke of the Reichsbank, who promised to see what could be done 'to make amends'.[84] But this was scarcely enough to pacify Vansittart's anger and neither was Eden's complaint to Ribbentrop when he was finally able to make it,[85] for he minuted on 22 December:

> He [Schacht] is a bully & needs a lesson badly indeed. Till he has had it, we had better not talk more of his meeting Sir F. Leith-Ross, for he wd. only be truculent and impossible. If & when he has made honourable amends, he may be in a more chastened & reasonable mood, & the interview might then have a chance of being useful. Otherwise he will only come out of it with a fresh set of grievances & start hitting Sir F. Leith-Ross below the belt too.[86]

Yet, in spite of the considerable annoyance that Schacht provoked in the Foreign Office, it is clear from Vansittart's comments that by the end of 1936 the British were beginning to respond, if only half-heartedly, to Schacht's unceasing representations.[87]

But the general feeling remained that Germany's colonial demands should be resisted until she had shown willing in a five power conference.[88] Neither did the French now seem very anxious to enter into this controversial area. On 24 November the *Paris-Soir* reported M. Moutet, the French minister of colonies, as saying that the question of France surrendering the Cameroons 'did not arise'. Furthermore, the colonial question was 'only a political pawn on the international chessboard', corresponding 'to no serious opinion or serious aspiration of any country'.[89] Generally, it was thought by the British embassy in Paris that there was little interest in the colonial question in France. As for the attitude of the French government, it was reported that:

> it would seem likely . . . that . . . in so far as they may have considered the matter at all . . . they . . . do not contemplate satisfying Germany's colonial hunger otherwise than at some-body else's expense, and their ideas as to who that somebody else should be have presumably not yet been worked out at all clearly.[90]

But that the colonial question was again in the air can be discerned by the fact that the Portuguese were beginning to take a lively interest in official British statements concerning the relevance of the Anglo–Portuguese alliance to Portugal's overseas territories.[91] Moreover, for political reasons, the Portuguese foreign minister, Armindo Monteiro, became Portguese ambassador at London, with Salazar adding the foreign ministry to his other responsibilities, the object of this reshuffle being to improve Anglo–Portuguese relations.[92] No doubt the outbreak of the Spanish Civil War was an important catalyst in this development; but equally important to the Portuguese were matters concerning the colonial question, and early in 1937 Salazar was compelled to scotch rumours that Portugal had granted Germany concessions in Angola.[93]

Whatever the state of French feeling in Paris regarding the colonial question, the French ambassador at Berlin was in no doubt by the end of 1936 that the Germans were vigorously renewing their colonial demands. Schacht's speech at Frankfurt, Ribbentrop's address to the Anglo–German Fellowship and Schacht's article in *Foreign Affairs* all seemed to him indicative of this. He commented:

> In making their trumpets resound right under the walls of the Foreign Office and the White House, they [the Germans] have perhaps recalled that this tactic, employed not long since before Jericho, did not give unsatisfactory results.[94]

But the effect on the Foreign Office was precisely the reverse. At the beginning of 1937 there was considerable discussion of the possibility of undertaking a counter-propaganda campaign in the colonial question.[95] The upshot was that it was decided to approach *The Times* with the suggestion that they might publish an article on the colonial question that would give the British view. These efforts, however, seem only to have inspired a rather lame editorial in *The Times* in the wake of Ribbentrop's speech at the Leipzig Fair.[96]

Nevertheless, despite the strong inclinations of the Foreign Office to redress the balance of colonial propaganda, the possibility of making contact with Schacht was discussed at the end of 1936 and the beginning of 1937, with the result that Sir Frederick Leith-Ross was sent to Germany to listen to Schacht's proposals in more detail. Undoubtedly, Schacht was most relieved. On the last day of 1936 he expressed his desire to François-Poncet for further conversations similar to those he had had the previous August. These could dissipate 'prejudices and mutual suspicions' provided that they were not 'followed, as was the case in August, by long silences and a total breakdown in the exchange of views'.[97] Moreover, he suggested to Joseph E. Davies, the American ambassador to the Soviet Union that, given the British refusal, in contrast with the sympathetic French attitude, to respond to his proposals, President Roosevelt should call a conference in Washington to discuss them.[98]

The reason for British caution in responding to Schacht had lain as much as anything else in the vague nature of his outline of possible German contributions to European peace. As François-Poncet put it:

> It is only a pity that, while the president of the the Reichsbank is prolix in the exposition of German demands, in their justification and in the refutation of the objections that they raise, he is vague and brief regarding the contributions that the Reich could make. What concessions would Germany be disposed to make for the realization of a general, European settlement? Would she agree to

sign a new Locarno, taking account of French undertakings towards Czechoslovakia and Russia? Would she envisage resuming one day the way of the League of Nations? Neither M. Schacht nor M. Hitler have ever spoken on this precisely and explicitly.[99]

Thus when Schacht put out feelers to Sir Frederick Leith-Ross in the autumn of 1936 regarding a meeting between them he was not encouraged. Schacht had in fact been replying to an earlier letter from Leith-Ross which the latter had sent on the occasion of the completion of German repayment of commercial debts under the Anglo–German Payments Agreement, which he had negotiated with Schacht in 1934. In his letter the British official had also expressed the hope that Germany might soon dispense with exchange control and offered to discuss the possibilities with Schacht in London.[100] Schacht, however, did not reply to Leith-Ross until the devaluation of the French franc, on 24 September 1936, together with the tripartite agreement between Britain, the United States and France on currency had been announced.[101] Referring to his declaration of 30 September, he confirmed that he saw no immediate advantage in an adjustment of Germany's currency, but expressed a willingness to co-operate with the three powers over currency questions. Praising the work of Leith-Ross in maintaining good trading relations between Britain and Germany, he stated that there were 'some remainders of the past which . . . should be liquidated in a fair way to open up a peaceful future for Europe'. Being a minister made it difficult for him to come to London, but he wanted to discuss these matters with Leith-Ross and acquaint him with the possibilities he saw 'for peace and prosperity'.[102]

But the Foreign Office did not believe that a meeting at this juncture would be beneficial[103] and Leith-Ross himself, in the light of recent statements made by Goering, was of the same view. If Schacht was invited to London it would be taken as an indication that Britain would be prepared to pay for the devaluation of the French franc and other currencies 'by handing over Colonies and/or credits', both of which were, in the opinion of Leith-Ross, 'unnecessary and undesirable concessions to offer'. Before discussions with the Germans could begin, they had to 'purge themselves of their present diseased mentality'.[104] Within the Treasury there was general agreement with Leith-Ross. Sir Richard Hopkins, the second secretary, thought that the reply to Schacht, later vetted by Vansittart, was correct and Neville Chamberlain minuted: 'The trouble is that . . . [Schacht] . . . mixes up politics with his economics and I never know how to disentangle one from the other.'[105] The important point though is that Leith-Ross and his colleagues arrived at this view in almost total ignorance of what Schacht had proposed in Paris the previous August, even though Vansittart had allegedly discussed this with Chamberlain. The Treasury considered that Schacht was essentially dealing with economic matters and were unaware that Schacht had made political proposals to the French that had later been transmitted to the Foreign Office. When Leith-Ross was belatedly informed of these details he rapidly revised his views on the virtues of a meeting with Schacht, as did his Treasury colleagues.

On 21 December 1936 Mr E. H. Lever, the Secretary of the Prudential Assurance Company and Chairman of the Committee for German Long-term and Medium-term Debts, met Schacht. The Reichsminister stated that he wanted to settle the issue of German indebtedness to Britain in a definite manner, but he did not believe this possible outside a more comprehensive settlement that would also involve political matters. He then proceeded to give an account of his Paris conversations which he felt had failed on account of British obstruction. This was unfortunate because 'the peace of Europe was at stake, and the key to a settlement rested with England'. It seemed to Schacht that Eden was not taking him seriously. He admitted that his own speeches had been strident, but they were for German consumption. If nothing was done the situation in Germany would deteriorate. But if 'some arrangement could be arrived at, the present tendencies in Germany could and would be reversed', and he emphasised that:

> he spoke in this way because the Führer had definitely offered to back him up to 100% in his proposals despite the fact that they would not be popular with the Party. But the Führer was now complaining that Schacht's feelers had raised no response in this country [Britain]. If it was difficult for the British Government to get in touch with him direct, surely they could have sent an answer through the French Government; but as things were he had no opportunity of putting his proposals forward.

During the conversation Schacht intimated that it would be possible to arrange a discreet visit to Britain by him at, for instance, the invitation of the governor of the Bank of England.[106]

Leith-Ross, to whom Lever reported, was inclined at first to think that Schacht was romancing. He was 'such a curious fellow' that it was possible his account was pure invention. At the same time he felt that some consideration ought to be given to inviting him to London to see if he indeed had proposals 'which would help break the present deadlock'. After receiving Eden's account of his conversation with Blum in September, he became more decidedly of this view. He thought that it confirmed, 'in all principal points, the statements which Schacht made to Lever'.[107] Although he appreciated Foreign Office apprehensions regarding the irregular procedures contemplated, he nonetheless considered it 'advisable' to follow up Schacht's approaches. At the end of the day the gulf between Britain and Germany might indeed prove unbridgeable, but if Schacht continued to speak as he did to Lever the details could get into the press and 'provoke considerable criticism of our attitude'.[108]

In an undated minute, Vansittart informed 'Leithers' of the Foreign Office view. Given the attitude of the British government in the colonial and the Conservative Party's Margate resolution, it had been decided not to encourage Schacht to visit London. This might have resulted 'in some tactless pressure from him and a further negative by His Majesty's Government – thereby making matters worse'. Furthermore, it had not been regarded as prudent to allow the question of disarmament to be raised 'at a moment so unfavourable to ourselves'. In addition, Schacht had never presented clear and precise suggestions which were what the British government required. All that was obvious was that colonial satisfaction for Germany was a crucial element in Schacht's concept of a 'comprehensive settlement'. This would not be 'easily reached' and the Foreign Office only wished 'to avoid . . . a meeting which, if fruitless, might increase tension'. There was no reason, however, why Leith-Ross himself should not attempt to elicit from Schacht a more precise statement of what he had in mind, although it had to be recognised that the position of the German minister of economics was now 'precarious'. Vansittart's attitude was endorsed by Eden. Schacht had never proffered 'definite proposals of any kind', and neither had von Neurath or Ribbentrop 'despite frequent promptings given . . . to . . . the latter'. In effect, Britain was being asked to make the concession of saying that she was prepared to discuss the return of colonies without knowing what was 'to be offered in return'. He would, on the other hand, discuss the matter with Leith-

Ross after the Christmas holiday; there was nothing that he would 'like more than a "general settlement", if by any means it could be got'.[109]

Leith-Ross was irritated by the attitude of the Foreign Office. He believed that he had been misled by them in his response to Schacht the previous October, when he had suggested that the 'next step' lay with him [Schacht].[110] Had he been informed of the facts pertaining to Schacht's August initiative he would 'have hesitated to write' in the manner he did. But he had been told that a 'non-committal reply to Schacht' was required, because economic discussions could not be contemplated with Germany 'without getting satisfaction on political questions'. To Leith-Ross it was evident that Schacht had been promoting a political initiative from the start. However, he wrote that 'no effort was made to ascertain whether or not a definite agreement could be worked out on the basis suggested by Schacht'. Both Vansittart and Eden disagreed. It had been impossible to do anything because of the vague and imprecise nature of Schacht's proposals.[111] It was, nevertheless, agreed that Eden, Neville Chamberlain and Leith-Ross should discuss the matter further.[112]

Although the attitude of the Foreign Office remained firmly one of being unable to respond to indefinite suggestions, the feeling began to grow that Blum may not have passed on to Schacht the entirety of Eden's response. On 26 October 1936 Mr Lloyd Thomas, the British *chargé d'affaires* at the Paris embassy, had informed Eden:

> As regards 'the subsequent correspondence with M. Blum', I have it on the assurance of M. Léger [secretary-general at the Quai d'Orsay] that this correspondence was limited to a letter in which M. Blum gave Dr Schacht a faithful account of his conversations with you, and gave it as his opinion that no further progress could be made until you had expressed the views of His Majesty's Government.[113]

Orme Sargent thought that this read 'somewhat suspiciously' in the light of subsequent developments; if Blum had limited his observations to the extent implied by Lloyd Thomas, he had done so 'incorrectly'. He considered that the British government might 'have a very real cause for complaint against Blum'. Phipps, therefore, was asked to ascertain from François-Poncet exactly what Blum had told Schacht and also to offer his opinion as to the likelihood of Hitler having in fact authorised Schacht 'to conduct negotiations covering the whole field of the issues' germane to the conclusion of a general settlement.[114]

François-Poncet was unable to be very illuminating. Schacht had been told that Britain's attitude in the colonial question was governed by Eden's statement of 27 July. The ambassador added that Schacht had understood all along that there could be no question of colonial satisfaction outside a general settlement 'under which Germany would make her contribution by binding assurances in the East, limitation of armaments, return to the League etc.'. Concerning the second part of the Foreign Office enquiry, Phipps was surprisingly optimistic. He had little doubt that if Schacht 'succeeded in initiating negotiations with the French and ourselves on a promising basis, he would be able to get the Führer to continue the discussion'. Germany had embarked on a course of economic autarchy and the Four Year Plan was proving more burdensome than had been anticipated. It was possible that if Schacht could 'indicate a way out . . . the Party [NSDAP] might possibly yield'. Hitler was unable openly to abandon his course, but he might be willing to do so through the agency of a non-Nazi such as Schacht. If Eden wished to start a 'global' negotiation, he saw no objection to Leith-Ross and Schacht meeting, perhaps at Basle.[115]

As a result of Phipps's despatch the view was immediately expressed throughout the Foreign Office that the breakdown in the contact with Schacht was the consequence of the failure of Blum to inform him of the whole of Eden's written reply of 23 September 1936.[116] This reply had contained, in essence, three points. Britain was anxious to promote a general settlement, but her attitude in the colonial question was defined in the statement of 27 July. Secondly, discussions could not go further without 'a more complete and detailed appreciation of the German attitude' towards a European settlement. Finally, the current five power negotiations seemed the most convenient vehicle for the revelation of the German position. Thus, it was argued, Blum had only informed Schacht of the first of these points. Were there to be further contacts with Schacht, it would be better to leave the French out of them. For his part, Eden minuted:

It is very unsatisfactory that my answer was not passed on completely. I do not suppose that it has in fact made any great difference . . . but I should like to put the matter right. How? It is not much use asking M. Delbos to do so. Is this perhaps an argument for Sir F. Leith-Ross seeing Dr Schacht or should Sir E. Phipps tell the latter?[117]

Eventually, both courses were taken.[118]

In reality, Eden and the Foreign Office had very little grounds for justified complaint. No impartial reading of the surviving documentation relating to Eden's contacts with Blum during September and October 1936 can render anything other than the impression that Eden was very discouraging about the Schacht overtures, besides which it had even been argued by Vansittart that it would be undesirable to ask Schacht for detailed proposals![119] It is, of course, true that Eden had implied in his interview with Blum on 20 September that an 'interim' response could be conveyed to Schacht and his written reply of 23 September was styled 'interim and . . . tentative'. The fact, however, cannot be avoided that throughout these exchanges Eden insisted that he could not supply an authoritative answer until he had consulted his Cabinet colleagues. In this the Foreign Secretary showed no urgency at all; in fact, following the relevant Cabinet discussion no letter or other communication was sent to Paris.

Why, therefore, should Blum have communicated to Schacht anything other than he did, namely a record of his conversation with Eden on 20 September and the observation that no further progress could be made until the considered views of the British government were known? Any other action could easily have been repudiated as misrepresenting the views of the British government. If, indeed, Blum can be criticised for not having more fully reported to Schacht the contents of Eden's interim observations, and there is a case, albeit a slender one, for arguing this, Eden and his Foreign Office colleagues can also be criticised for bungling. Certainly, G. H. S. Pinsent, the financial adviser to the Berlin embassy, was of the opinion that the combination of Eden's response to Blum's initial revelation of the Schacht initiative and the letter Leith-Ross sent to Schacht on 15 October 1936 had inevitably been treated by the Reichsminister as a snub. And he thought the Schacht initiative might be 'serious'. Neville Chamberlain was kept fully informed of these matters and there can be little doubt that they assisted him in developing a rather unflattering view of the capabilities of the Foreign Office. Significantly, he minuted on Pinsent's letter: 'I think I shall have to see Sir F. L. Ross and Foreign Sec about this'.[120]

Equally, Blum and Delbos can be excused for having interpreted the British reaction to Schacht's August proposals as a rejection. Delbos was quite explicit about this to the American ambassador at Paris, Bullitt, informing him that Schacht's initiative had not been pursued because the British, who 'had frowned' on the mention of colonies, were opposed. This, however, did not mean that the French government would not continue with their efforts to reach an agreement with Germany and they would do so, if necessary, alone.[121] As Blum later emphasised to Schacht, his interview with Count Welczeck, the German ambassador at Paris, on 18 December 1936, was not to be understood as the termination of the August initiative, added to which he made a conciliatory speech at Lyon on 24 January 1937, in which he had referred to the interdependence of political and economic questions.[122] Moreover, on 23 December 1936, Delbos impressed upon Welczeck the desire of the French to reach a *rapprochement* with Germany, which would be enthusiastically supported by the British and Americans. He told the ambassador that Germany 'should have raw materials, colonies and loans, in return for which the only compensation required . . . was *peace*'. After the termination of the Spanish Civil War, an atmosphere 'conducive to peace' should be created, which would be followed by 'discussion and satisfaction of Germany's wishes and, at the same time, settlement of the Locarno question'. Thereafter, limitation of armaments would be discussed.[123] The French foreign minister was similarly eloquent to Bullitt, speaking of his high hopes that talks with Schacht might lead to the reintegration of Germany into the western economy; Germany would be given a colony in Africa, perhaps the Cameroons, following which all African colonies would be thrown open to consortiums.[124]

François-Poncet himself was infected by the mood of the times, although he reversed the procedures envisaged by Delbos. Returning from Paris in January 1937, he informed Phipps that he had outlined to Blum and Delbos a scheme which they had liked. There should first be limitation of armaments by the powers and measures for humanising war. When these had been agreed, there would be a favourable atmosphere for proceeding towards a general settlement, including a new western pact, 'economic outlets for German trade, currency agreements and finally return of Germany to the League with possible colonial mandate'.[125] The views of the French ambassador were sent to Leith-Ross for comment. Opinion within the Foreign Office was decidedly hostile towards the François-

Poncet scheme.[126] In this Leith-Ross detected a somewhat unhelpful
and curmudgeonly attitude. He agreed that the French ambassador's proposals were 'somewhat vague' and that there were 'serious
dangers in getting involved in discussions with Germany on so
indefinite a basis', but considered that the posture of the Foreign
Office was likely to 'perpetuate the present deadlock'. Fundamentally, the Foreign Office wanted a 'change of heart' and a political
settlement with Germany before moving into the sphere of economic concessions. On the other hand Leith-Ross thought

> that there is something to be said for approaching the negotiations
> from the economic aspect, which is, of course, the aspect with
> which Schacht is mainly concerned. His preoccupations are for
> Germany, but it should be remembered that an improvement of
> the economic situation in Germany would also be very beneficial
> to us and to the rest of the world. Schacht is on strong ground in
> arguing that world trade cannot be put right so long as the
> population of Germany is more or less shut off from world
> markets. Approaching the problem from this angle, it can be
> pointed out that the present political tension is upsetting the
> markets throughout Europe and that a definite relaxation of
> tension and a restoration of confidence is essential before any
> practical programme for economic improvement can be set on
> foot. From this one can try and elicit from Schacht how Germany
> once more can be made into good European.[127]

To his Treasury colleagues Leith-Ross was more blunt. He did not
'altogether like the Foreign Office attitude' which it appeared was
'bound to lead to an impasse'. Neville Chamberlain endorsed this
view. Sir Warren Fisher, the permanent head of the Treasury,
fulminated: 'Whatever the merits or demerits of this rather vague set
of proposals, "the fact is that what is wanted is a complete change of
mind" [a quotation from Vansittart's comments on the François-
Poncet proposals] no less in our own F.O. than in Germany.'[128]
    Meanwhile, despite the growing coolness between the Treasury
and the Foreign Office, the meeting with Eden and Leith-Ross that
Chamberlain had wanted took place on 18 January 1937. Its purpose
was to consider whether or not to give Schacht a chance to amplify
his 'general settlement' proposals. The meeting had before it the
advice of Dr Puhl of the Reichsbank, to the effect that Schacht's
influence on Hitler was increasing,[129] and the record of a convers-

ation between Leith-Ross and M. Monick, the financial attaché to the French embassy in London. Monick had submitted three documents to Leith-Ross. The first emphasised the importance of not letting the initiative pass to Germany and the danger of embarking on separate negotiations with Germany in economic and financial matters. The second suggested that the President of the United States should be approached with a view to making an appeal for peace. The last dealt with raw materials and put forward the idea that, given the urgent need of Germany and other countries for raw materials, the supply of these commodities could be most expeditiously facilitated by the creation of international 'Trading and Financial Companies'.[130] Monick's schemes were dismissed as 'impracticable'. Moreover, it was felt at the meeting of 18 January that the notion of enlisting the support of the United States should not be encouraged. In the discussion, however, of the advantages and disadvantages of arranging a meeting with Schacht, the knowledge that he seemed to have 're-established contact with the French' and that they appeared so desperate to enter into discussions that they might offer imprudent concessions, contributed to a consensus of opinion that 'if there were to be conversations with Schacht, it would be far safer if we [Britain] got control of them from the very beginning, instead of allowing them to be conducted by the French'. Consequently, it was decided that an early meeting should be arranged with the Reich minister of economics.[131]

Leith-Ross was naturally delegated to undertake the task of meeting Schacht. On 19 January Eden instructed him to make no proposals of his own, but rather to listen to what Schacht had to say. The fundamental attitude of the British government was that there would have to be political undertakings and assurances by Germany if Schacht's proposals were to serve as the basis of further discussions. He wrote:

> there must be a definite change of political orientation in Germany, and Germany's undertakings and assurances must not therefore be merely 'eyewash': there must be outward and visible signs of this reorientation.

What this meant, in practice, was that there had to be a new Locarno, an end to autarchy and territorial expansion, good German relations with Czechoslovakia, co-operation in ending the arms race and Germany's return to the League. Nevertheless, Leith-Ross was to be deliberately 'vague' on these matters as it was up to Germany to make the decisive move. On the colonial question, the view put forward in the Commons on 27 July 1936 continued unchanged, but Eden did not think that there would be much harm in 'listening to any ideas that Schacht' might 'put forward'.[132] Leith-Ross was in substantial accord with this approach.[133] But the overriding purpose of Leith-Ross's visit to Germany was to correct the impression, which Eden claimed the French had given, that, whereas the French government was prepared to accept Schacht's bases for discussion, Britain had returned a blank refusal.[134]

The meeting between Schacht and Leith-Ross took place at Badenweiler on 2 February 1937. Prior to the meeting, Schacht informed Pinsent, financial adviser to Britain's Berlin embassy, that:

> If he had had any intimation that His Majesty's Government would welcome a further statement of his ideas he would never have made his Frankfurt speech on December 9th last or published his article in 'Foreign Affairs'.[135]

Clearly, therefore, Schacht's bellicose and crude utterances during the autumn of 1936 can be seen as a desperate attempt on his part to awake Britain to the dangers, as he saw them, and of the possibilities of a solution to them. At Badenweiler, however, Schacht did little more than reiterate what he had told the French the preceding August. Leith-Ross derived the impression that Schacht was mostly responsible for the current obsession with the colonial question in Germany and that the Reichsminister's 'prestige . . . [was] . . . wrapped up with securing satisfaction on the point'. Although Schacht's suggestions had been submitted to Hitler, he did not think that they represented 'definite decisions on the part of the German Government'.They were rather bases for discussion, 'which sensible members' of the German government believed 'that they could get Hitler to adopt and carry through'. Indeed, during their conversation, Leith-Ross asked Schacht point-blank what authority he had for speaking on all the economic and political questions he raised. Schacht replied:

> that on the economic side (including colonies) he had full authority and would guarantee that Hitler would accept his views. On the purely political issues assurances to east and central European states, limitation of armaments, and Germany's

return to the League his position was that he had told Neurath that he would not commit him on political questions. But he had frequently discussed these questions both with Hitler and with Neurath, and what he told me [Leith-Ross] represented their views. If we could meet his demands on economic questions, we could be assured that satisfaction could be obtained for our demands on political questions.[136]

This was hardly what the Foreign Office had been looking for when Leith-Ross had been sent out to Germany. Moreover, Leith-Ross was himself more aware of the difficulties. He told Phipps that it would be hard to get Hitler to accept Britain's political requirements; nonetheless, the position in Europe was so fraught that he thought it best 'to continue the discussions by whatever method' in the hope that a basis of agreement could be achieved.[137]

Despite very considerable doubts within the Foreign Office about dealing with Schacht further,[138] following the failure of the German and Italian governments to respond satisfactorily in the negotiations for a five power conference, Eden raised the whole matter of the Schacht proposals in the Cabinet Foreign Policy Committee on 18 March 1937. By this time the records of Schacht's discussions with the French the previous August had been acquired[139] and they were circulated with the entirety of the relevant correspondence in a massive document comprising a memorandum by Eden and seven annexes. What, in fact, Eden was asking his colleagues to consider was whether or not conversations should take place with Germany regarding a general settlement on the basis of the Schacht proposals. These consisted of three elements. First, Germany would have to have colonies; Schacht had now specifically mentioned Togoland and the Cameroons, which were mostly under French mandate. Secondly, in the economic sphere, Germany wanted a number of concessions such as the reduction of interest on long-term debts, after which relaxation in exchange controls could be contemplated. Finally, in the purely political sphere Germany would be conciliatory in assurances to all European states, arms limitation and her return to the League. Eden pointed out that Schacht's statements regarding Germany's possible contributions in the political field represented 'a complete reversal of German policy'. So far, Hitler had shown no enthusiasm for guaranteeing the states in east and central Europe and he had been discouraging over a western pact. In addition, he had virtually ruled out arms limitation because of the military strength of the USSR. The Foreign Secretary, therefore, concluded that it would be unwise to rely on Schacht's views as they touched political issues.

The central issue for discussion, however, was the colonial question, for as Eden himself indicated, the nature of the reply to Schacht, positive or negative, depended on the willingness of the British government to agree that the colonial issue should form part of the conversations with the German government. If the British government was prepared to proceed on this basis, it had to be understood that 'the colonial question' would 'become the crux of the whole discussion'. Eden argued that it would mean that the colonial question would have been 'officially raised by Germany' and 'accepted' by Britain as the basis of further exchanges. This would be tantamount to a total contradiction of British policy in this matter as outlined in public statements. If it was decided not to take Schacht's overtures further, Eden urged that he should be informed at once. But, if a considered reply was to be sent, he favoured telling him that his proposals were under discussion and that further replies would be transmitted through the normal diplomatic channels. If Britain received satisfactory assurances, the French government could then be consulted with a view to a joint reply to the Schacht proposals. Eden considered the following Anglo–French political conditions essential: a new western pact, German reassurances in treaty form or otherwise to governments in east and central Europe, return of Germany to the League, and an international convention for the limitation of armaments.[140]

The Foreign Policy Committee also had before it for consideration a memorandum by W. Ormsby-Gore, the Colonial Secretary, which strongly opposed any idea of the return of Tanganyika territory on political, strategic and economic grounds. In an annex the views of the Colonial Office were circulated. For that department the moral issue remained paramount. If the problem of colonial retrocession was looked at from the point of view of the indigenous peoples, and not from that of Britain's 'convenience', it was clear that an 'absolute refusal' was inescapable. Would the transfer of a colony prevent a war, it was asked? Was it not possible that such a gesture would merely result in Germany demanding more? There was no guarantee that Germany would be satisfied; Britain, therefore, should refuse Germany's demands. It was argued that this might result in war, but this possibility was dismissed. Germany's rearmament had not proceeded as smoothly as had been anticipated. Furthermore, her food supplies were so low that a refusal to gratify Germany's colonial demands was unlikely to provoke armed conflict. Ormsby-Gore wrote:

> It would no doubt result in a violent fit of sulks, which would not go so far as to imperil the working of the Anglo–German Payments Agreement; but the only 'explosion' which it might precipitate . . . is an internal explosion within the German Government . . . it is not impossible that Dr Schacht might be sacrificed, and that I take to be one of his motives for being particularly anxious to achieve some success in the Colonial sphere.

Germany's problem was an economic one which could not be solved by colonies, but only by a change of economic policy. The Colonial Office felt that they could not recommend any suggestions for a reply other than a negative one. If a refusal weakened the German government, it might make them less bent on war and more amenable to a general agreement.[141]

The discussion in the Foreign Policy Committee was wide-ranging. Halifax wondered if the best course would be to indicate that Britain could not contemplate a discussion of the colonial question 'until British public opinion was convinced that this was the only outstanding question which prevented a full, final and general settlement being reached'. And before this, Britain would have to know precisely what Germany was prepared to offer. Eden agreed with Halifax as to method, but emphasised 'that it would be neither safe nor honest' for Britain to start discussions with Germany without deciding at the outset that she was prepared to make colonial concessions, given the satisfaction of all her desiderata. Addressing himself to this central issue, Neville Chamberlain declared that he was prepared to discuss the return of Togoland and the Cameroons if that was the only obstacle to 'a full, final and general settlement', but he was not prepared for discussion if that represented the initial demand. Eden pointed out that the real difficulty in the way of the Togoland–Cameroons solution was that France would be required to make the major sacrifice and Malcolm MacDonald, the Dominions Secretary, concurred, stressing that Britain would be subjected to great pressure to make an equivalent sacrifice. Ormsby-Gore thought that all the mandatory powers should be first consulted and that the 'insuperable objections' to the transfer of mandates should be put to the French. Eden, however, did not believe that such difficulties existed in practice. He stated that 'there was no reason to believe that the League would not agree to the transfer'.

At this point, Chamberlain pulled the entire discussion together:

he gathered that . . . Eden . . . shared his view that if a full, final and general settlement could be obtained by the return of the Cameroons and Togoland to Germany we should not rule out the possibility of discussions on this basis. He suggested that we might approach the French Government and ask whether in return for a completely satisfactory settlement in other respects they would be prepared to hand over to Germany the Cameroons and Togoland, indicating that if so we ourselves would raise no objection, and would indeed be prepared to go further and to hand over to Germany those parts of her former West African possessions which we now held. We should say that before any conversations with Germany were started we thought that France should be told quite frankly what our position in the matter was, and we therefore gave her in detail our reasons for thinking that there are insuperable objections to handing over to Germany territories now held by us outside the West African area. We could illustrate this by indicating the grave objections to the return to Germany of Tanganyika, and we could point out that South Africa and Australia had already refused to entertain any suggestion for the return to Germany of territories now held by them under mandate. Any discussions would have to be on the basis that there could be no further return of her ex-colonies to Germany beyond the Cameroons and Togoland, and that there must be a clear understanding that this was the last word on the subject. We should also indicate to France that we were prepared to endeavour to meet Germany in matters such as access to raw materials etc. If this course commended itself to the Committee, M. Blum might be asked whether he was prepared to proceed on this basis.

Eden did not think this would appeal to Blum. Malcolm MacDonald asked if there was territory that could be given to France in compensation. Ormsby-Gore, on the other hand, did not want to hand British subjects over to French or German rule. Halifax believed that it would be impossible to keep Germany out of Africa 'indefinitely' without war, or even with war. He opined: 'If it could be done privately he would like to gather all the Powers interested in Africa together and see whether it might not be possible to have some repartition of Africa in which Germany could find a place.' Provided Germany adhered to the terms of the naval agreement, he did not think this would present a strategic threat. Eventually, Eden suggested that Chamberlain's view commanded a majority in the committee and it was agreed in principle that exploratory talks with the French should be started with the object of a joint approach to Berlin. The task of preparing a draft note to the French was entrusted to Eden and Ormsby-Gore.[142]

But the Foreign and Colonial Secretaries were unable to agree and they submitted separate documents. Eden's draft did follow the lines agreed by the Foreign Policy Committee, but it was very heavily concentrated on the colonial question and negative in tone. In a covering note, moreover, he registered his dissatisfaction with these proposals.[143] Ormsby-Gore's draft, by way of contrast, was a blatant attempt to influence the French government against colonial concessions. On moral and strategic grounds it was undesirable.[144] Prior to the next meeting of the Cabinet Foreign Policy Committee, Neville Chamberlain submitted his own memorandum and draft despatch to the French. The Chancellor had been encouraged in this by Leith-Ross, who found the memoranda of Eden and Ormsby-Gore quite unsatisfactory. He told Chamberlain that 'both play straight into the hands of Germany on a major question of tactics: viz: they concentrate entirely on the question of Colonies'. He suggested that Chamberlain circulate a memorandum of his own and submitted a draft, which *mutatis mutandis* was the same as the one ultimately submitted to the committee by the Chancellor.[145]

Chamberlain's main point of criticism was that Eden's and Ormsby-Gore's drafts concentrated on the colonial question to the exclusion of everything else. This he thought an error. It was undoubtedly a 'cardinal point' with Schacht, but to let him 'dictate . . . the direction of the discussions' would allow the initiative to pass to Germany. The international situation was serious and no opportunity of alleviating tension should be allowed to slip. It was 'difficult for a dictator to climb down publicly', but he believed that Hitler's last speech [on 30 January] contained some promising signs and Schacht's overtures, which had been made with Hitler's approval, could not 'be regarded as anything but an invitation to a general discussion'. Chamberlain continued:

Any government which turned down this invitation without at least exploring the possibilities sufficiently to make sure that there was no possible basis of agreement would incur a very heavy responsibility. Even a slight improvement in the international atmosphere may lead gradually to a general 'detente', whereas a policy of drift may lead to a general war. M. Blum, who should be alive to the difficulties of any negotiation with Germany, appears anxious to pursue the conversations as rapidly as possible, and if this is not done we may be sure that the responsibility for failure will be laid at our door.

The main problem with the notes submitted by the Foreign and Colonial Secretaries was that their excessive emphasis on the colonial question effectively put to the fore an issue which was 'the last which should be tackled'. If either of these notes was submitted to the French there was a distinct possibility that the prospect of further discussions would come to an end because of 'Britain's refusal to discuss Colonies'. This was a situation which had to be avoided. Chamberlain urged:

> Our objective should be to set out the political guarantees which we want from Germany as part of any general settlement; and if the discussions have to break down, we want the breakdown to be due to Germany's refusal to accept our reasonable requirements in the political field.

The content of Chamberlain's draft note, therefore, dealt, in the main, with the terms of a joint Anglo–French approach to Germany. Before negotiations could begin the German government would have to agree in principle to certain political conditions: treaties of non-aggression to replace Locarno, German reassurance of the east and central European states, the return of Germany to the League, and an international arms limitation agreement. The German government was also to be informed that if it endorsed these desiderata, the matter of placing the German economic and financial system on a more sound footing could be examined. Chamberlain noted that his proposed communication to the German government did not mention colonies except in so far as no proposals would be excluded from discussion, but as the Germans were bound to raise the issue he urged that Britain and France should establish their attitude in advance. Britain could not cede

Tanganyika under any circumstances. On the other hand, if the French were agreeable, Britain would sanction the retrocession of Togoland and the Cameroons in their entirety. To compensate the French for their larger territorial loss, Britain would give Germany guarantees of freedom of access to colonial raw materials and markets. Clearly, Chamberlain's strategy was to push the colonial question into the background, for if such a contentious issue were to be given a position of prominence, it could easily jeopardise the commencement of general discussions.[146]

Within the Cabinet Foreign Policy Committee it was ultimately agreed that Chamberlain's suggestions should form the basis of an approach to the French government.[147] Thus, on 27 April 1937, a despatch which closely followed Chamberlain's draft was sent to Sir Eric Phipps, now transferred to the Paris embassy, instructing him to outline the British attitude to French ministers.[148] This the ambassador did on 3 May. While, however, the French agreed that Schacht's overtures should continue to be pursued, they proved reluctant to accept the British proposals for a possible colonial settlement. Delbos thought it would be difficult to justify such a scheme 'before the French Parliament, since it would imply that France, who received by no means the lion's share of the German colonies . . . would be called upon to make by far the greater sacrifice'.[149] The French attitude was further defined when Phipps was told by Blum and Delbos that, although the French government favoured resuming conversations when he visited France on 25 May, they were opposed for the present to submitting any 'written communication to the Germans'.[150] The British strategy for developing the Schacht contacts was, therefore, effectively damaged before it had been put into operation.

It is, though, clear that it would never have had any prospect of success. By the beginning of May the British government was reliably informed, as Eden had always feared, that Schacht had no competence in the political field.[151] Moreover, it would appear that Schacht, who François-Poncet now considered to be in irretrievable political decline,[152] had been told by no less a person than Hitler himself to keep away from political topics,[153] which probably accounts for his 'lamb-like' performance when he saw Blum on 28 May.[154] During his conversation with the French Prime Minister Schacht remained uncharacteristically mute as Blum outlined the details of the political settlement that Britain and France would require before entering into negotiations on economic and colonial matters.[155] On his return to Germany, Schacht showed no urgency in reporting the results of his visit to Hitler or von Neurath.[156] His 'initiative' had run its course.[157] As François-Poncet later recalled, regarding the Schacht proposals:

> The reticence of the British government, the French refusal to discuss the colonial problem outside a general, European peace settlement did not allow them to go further. But above all, Dr Schacht himself, after his second visit to Paris, seemed no longer to be supported, if not openly disavowed, by his government.[158]

Following a visit to Berlin in May and June 1937, Leith-Ross was 'pessimistic' and had obviously lost hope.[159]

It is evident that François-Poncet considered the initial tardiness of the British response to have been a major factor in the collapse of the Schacht initiative. This was a view that was widely shared in the Treasury, where dissatisfaction with the Foreign Office performance culminated in August in a note by a Treasury official, Hale, which castigated the 'frigid' attitude of the Foreign Office and argued that a 'fresh start' with Germany was badly needed. Sir Warren Fisher minuted on 19 August: 'I wish that the admirable spirit & sense of Mr Hale's note cd. be infused into the Foreign Office.'[160] It is not unreasonable to assume that the views of Neville Chamberlain, now Prime Minister, were similar and that it had been the Foreign Office's handling of the Schacht affair that was the principle cause of this disenchantment. Numerous studies have recited the fact that on becoming Prime Minister Chamberlain considered the Foreign Office unsatisfactory and to have missed opportunities, but none has ever established what the opportunities were.[161] This has been a strange omission, for most writers are agreed that Chamberlain was meticulous in coming to his conclusions.[162] It is scarcely credible that his view amounted to a mere caprice. The more, therefore, the evidence surrounding the British response to the Schacht overtures is examined, the clearer it becomes that this was the missed opportunity in the mind of the Prime Minister.

In many respects this was unfair. Had discussions ever got off the ground they would eventually have collapsed on the refusal of the German government to have their hands tied in eastern Europe, for German 'abstention from aggression' was the 'political precondition' of the western powers.[163] On the other hand, it is hard to escape the conclusion that the Foreign Office mishandled Schacht's proposals in such a way as to convince the Treasury that they were being irresponsible. Chamberlain was almost certainly misled when Vansittart first informed him of Schacht's suggestions in September 1936; Eden did not transmit the considered views of the British Cabinet to Blum the following October as promised; and, with some justification, Leith-Ross believed he had been deliberately misled and used in order to stifle what he believed was a genuine attempt to bring about *détente*. Still, the British government had committed themselves to the principle that colonial concessions could form part of a general settlement and within a year that commitment was to be expressed clearly and directly to the German government.

8
Chamberlain

In May 1937 Neville Chamberlain became Prime Minister and the colonial question moved rapidly towards the pinnacle of its importance in Anglo–German relations during the inter-war years. This was not the result of design on the part of Chamberlain, although it was to some extent the consequence of his decision to play a more active role in foreign policy than his predecessors[1] and his determination not to let 'pass the critical moment' when it arose.[2] Hence his enthusiasm for Lord Halifax, Lord President of the Council, to accept an invitation from Goering to attend a hunting exhibition in Berlin and to meet Hitler if it could be arranged.[3] As a result of the subsequent Halifax visit to Germany in November 1937 the impression was gained that there could be no satisfactory settlement with Germany that ignored the colonial aspect; some three months later the approach to Hitler mentioned at the beginning of this study was made.[4]

It was not clear, however, at the beginning of Neville Chamberlain's premiership, that events would develop in this way. The ending of the Schacht initiative seemed to have closed down for the moment, if not permanently, the prospect of general discussions with Germany that included the colonial question. At any rate, that is the impression that Chamberlain conveyed to the Prime Ministers of the dominions at the imperial conference of May–June 1937. It seems, in fact, that Chamberlain wanted to tell his Commonwealth colleagues as little as possible about the Schacht proposals and the British reaction, although given the existing speculation on the colonial question it was impossible that the conference should have met without at least touching on the subject. On the day he acceded to the premiership, Chamberlain, against the wishes of Malcolm MacDonald, the Dominions Secretary, suppressed the circulation to the imperial conference of the despatch that had been sent to Sir Eric Phipps on 27 April 1936.[5]

The discussion of the colonial question on 2 June proved, in the circumstances, rather lame. Ormsby-Gore introduced the subject, concluding that

So far as his personal opinion was concerned, he felt that he could not, for the sake of any gesture, treat 5.5 millions of people as a pawn in the game of European diplomacy . . . To transfer them to any Power against their will would be to do a great moral wrong and, in his opinion, any Government in the United Kingdom which attempted to do so would be split internally and could not survive.

Speaking for Australia, R. G. Casey expressed the 'firm determination' of the Commonwealth government not to surrender New Guinea or the British empire mandate for Nauru.[6] The New Zealand Prime Minister, M. J. Savage, observed that 'the position in Western Samoa was that the native Samoans appeared to be definitely opposed to going back under German rule'. Nevertheless, his government did not take the view that the subject of colonial retrocession should be ruled out of a 'general scheme of settlement', provided that suitable safeguards for the indigenous populations could be arranged. He added later that 'New Zealand would regard the interests of the inhabitants as the first and primary consideration'. On the other hand, General Hertzog rehearsed the by now familiar South African line.[7] The Union government would not surrender South-West Africa, but wished to come to some arrangement with the German government by which the latter would 'waive her claim naturally on consideration'. South Africa had so far held back on this pending the conclusion of a general settlement, but she would have to 'initiate such negotiations if nothing were done by the United Kingdom and others with regard to the German claim to colonies'. Concerning the general issue of colonial retrocession, Hertzog argued that Germany could not demand total restoration, but considered that she had a good claim for a 'partial restoration'. He continued:

If any such partial restoration could be carried out without involving the transfer of Tanganyika Territory, he felt this would be in the interests of the Union. But if Germany could be pacified and peace secured for Europe and the world by the restitution of Tanganyika, the Union would not stand in the way if the United Kingdom felt this course was advisable. This was the considered view of himself and his colleagues.[8]

It was, though, clear from the South African Prime Minister's subsequent remarks that the colonial settlement most favoured by the Union government was the return in their entirety of Togoland and the Cameroons. In summing up the meeting, Chamberlain, somewhat deviously, claimed that the British government had not arrived at a decision on the subject, but that if Germany could be satisfied 'at the price of some territory, that would be such a tremendous desideratum that it would be criminal not to take careful pains to examine the possibilities'.[9]

All that had happened at this meeting was that the various Commonwealth governments had stated their positions. This was evidently regarded as unsatisfactory by MacDonald, who prevailed upon Chamberlain to call a meeting of the heads of delegation on 4 June at which the British despatch to Phipps of 27 April 1937 was read to the dominions premiers and details of contacts with Schacht over the preceding six months recounted. Hertzog, who obviously thought that the terms of the draft despatch had been officially communicated to the German government, and who was not disabused,[10] 'suggested that the conditions in the despatch made it rather difficult for the German Government'. This was particularly true of the requirement that the German government, with a view to giving substance to its expressions of peaceful intent, should 'enter into some arrangement with regard to the Soviet Union'. For Hertzog this was a condition that could have been allowed to emerge during negotiations. Eden emphasised that it was the view of the British government that there could be no discussion of the colonial question without assurance that their desiderata in other respects would be met in a general settlement. At the end of the meeting the Australian Treasurer, Casey, asked if there would be a further discussion of the colonial question, as consideration of the matter 'had not been brought to a very fine point'. Chamberlain replied that he did not contemplate further discussion unless something fresh was raised.[11]

In the Foreign Office, the treatment of the colonial question at the imperial conference was regarded as having been most deficient. The dominions premiers had not been fully or properly apprised of the British attitude. Moreover, it was felt that 'it would be a pity to leave . . . them . . . under the impression that the German Government now . . . cared . . . so little for the colonial question that even Dr Schacht confined his recent discussions in Paris to economic and financial points'. To give the dominions the idea that the Germans had put the colonial question into a state of abeyance was 'fundamentally wrong'.[12] Vansittart, now nearing the end of his tenure as permanent under-secretary, was quite blunt about this. He commented:

> Anyone who thinks the colonial question is more than temporarily shelved – with an eye to the Imperial Conference – wd. indeed be naif. The Colonial question is upon us for keeps. Everyone of importance in Germany is too deeply committed now for it to be otherwise. Besides the Germans definitely want & mean eventually to have the colonies back too.[13]

Apparently, however, the discussion of the colonial question did not end quite so abruptly as Chamberlain indicated. The matter was discussed confidentially and privately with Hertzog at a dinner.[14] Still, the records of the imperial conference show that the colonial question was not pressing at this time, at least in the mind of Neville Chamberlain. It had been right to examine what was a topical and controversial issue in broad terms and exchange ideas, but there was no urgency about concerting a 'Commonwealth' approach, assuming that one could have been devised, and, therefore, no need to risk unnecessary complications.[15]

Moreover, by June 1937 the likely results of the League of Nations enquiry into raw materials were known. These amounted to a virtual downright renunciation of the economic basis of the German claim to colonies. The origins of the enquiry went back to Hoare's celebrated speech to the League assembly in September 1935,[16] although since the inception of the League the Italians had been very active in promoting the need for such action prompting Lord Balfour to comment at the League assembly of 1920 that 'the better distribution of sunshine also required consideration'.[17] In the immediate aftermath, however, of the Italian attack on Abyssinia it had been decided not to press the issue.[18] But with the ending of the Abyssinian war and the lifting of sanctions on Italy, arguments in favour of proceeding with a raw materials enquiry were found to be attractive. Ashton-Gwatkin warned that some might hold Britain accountable for 'the destruction of the League'. He wrote: 'If it is desired to correct this interpretation, it might be found advisable to invoke the assistance of the League in an important matter.' In his estimation, an enquiry into the accessibility of raw materials was precisely such an issue; it was in economic matters that the League, 'during the years of its partial eclipse', might prove most useful. He urged the institution of an enquiry without delay and concluded:

'The enquiry is desirable on its own merits. For one thing, it has been suggested by His Majesty's Government, and it should serve to expose a good deal of nonsense which has been current on the subject.' Eden signalled his concurrence with these views.[19]

By early September 1936 the preparation of a resolution was under way for the forthcoming League assembly and the agreement of the French to a League enquiry into raw materials was secured on 2 October. The requirement of M. Bastid, the French minister of commerce, that the colonial aspect of the supply of raw materials should be played down was met in advance, for it had already been decided in London that the scope of any enquiry should be enlarged to encompass sovereign states as well as colonial territories.[20] Still, the dangers of an enquiry were also appreciated. It could easily lead on to the issues of 'territorial possession and control of colonies'. Therein lay the critical importance of strictly defining and limiting the terms of an enquiry 'to *commercial* access to the materials in question'. Even so, it was anticipated that the issue of the 'open door' at least would probably come under consideration.[21]

On 10 October 1936 the League assembly passed a resolution authorising the appointment of a committee, composed of nationals from member and non-member states, to enquire 'into the question of equal commercial access for all nations to certain raw materials'.[22] From the British point of view, the participation of nationals from non-member states was important because it was hoped that the enquiry would be able to identify 'the grievances of those countries which . . . thought . . . that grievances . . . existed'. Thus the association of Germany with the enquiry was regarded as particularly important. Ashton-Gwatkin wrote:

> If Germany will co-operate . . . she will be able to state her grievances; if she refuses, her refusal will be evidence that her grievances in the matter are not so much concerned with commercial access as with territorial possession.[23]

On 26 January 1937 the League council finally appointed a committee but, while the United States and Japan agreed to nominate representatives, the Germans and Italians steadfastly declined to do so. For its part the government of the United States was keen to participate in the enquiry believing that the exercise would secure 'recognition for the necessity of reviving international trade' and subject 'to careful examination various inadequate ideas regarding economic conditions'. On the other hand, the American Secretary of State, Cordell Hull, felt that American involvement would be undesirable 'if there were to be direct discussion of European political problems'.[24]

Three meetings of the committee were held on 8–12 March 1937, 16–25 June 1937 and 1–4 September 1937, with the final report being made public on 8 September 1937.[25] Addressing the committee on 8 March 1937, Sir Frederick Leith-Ross, representing the British government, commented that no country could be completely self-sufficient; the raw materials problem 'could not be settled by any transfer of territory, even if it were decided to transfer whole continents'. Generally, he thought that the production of raw materials was sufficient; the problem lay in acquiring them. Possession of colonial territory did not automatically imply that the possessor could buy more cheaply. Sometimes Britain paid a higher price for raw materials from her dependencies than that which obtained on the world market. The idea of the 'open door' had been advanced, but this could not be considered in isolation of the trade policies pursued by other countries. Finally, he observed that the financial policies of some countries and the creation of synthetic products might possibly damage their ability to acquire raw materials. Significantly, the United States representative, Grady, thought the attitude of Leith-Ross 'negative'; his purpose seemed to be to 'deflate' the issue in the eyes of public opinion.[26] And almost inevitably Leith-Ross's remarks provoked a strong response from the German journal *Völkerbund*, which declined to argue with Leith-Ross's assertion that world production of raw materials was adequate, but pointed out that 'the question at Geneva is . . . not whether the world produces too much or too little raw materials, but whether the sources of raw materials in the world are reasonably distributed'. The views of *Völkerbund* were summed up in the following paragraph:

> The subject under discussion is: In what manner can industrial countries which have difficulty in working and are short of foreign exchange and raw materials have access, without special expenditure of foreign exchange, to the raw materials which they require in order to give employment to their workers and contribute to the general prosperity of the world? To this there is only one reply: colonies.[27]

The League committee had no intention of coming to any such conclusion. As was pointed out in the Cabinet Foreign Policy Committee on 11 June 1937, its findings would be an answer to Germany's colonial demands and, judging by Eden's comment that the only way to save the forthcoming report would be for Leith-Ross to associate himself with a statement in it 'to the effect that a relaxation of the preferential system in Colonial territories . . . would benefit world trade, would tend to meet the complaints of various countries and thereby contribute to the appeasement of the present tension', the answer was not going to be a happy one from the point of view of the German colonial enthusiasts.[28] In the light of Eden's representations, it was eventually decided by the Cabinet Foreign Policy Committee to authorise Leith-Ross to associate himself with the following statement in the report of the League committee:

> As part of the efforts now being made to effect economic and political appeasement and to increase international trade by the lowering of tariff barriers and other obstacles, it would be appropriate for the Colonial Powers, without prejudice to the principle of Colonial Preference, to announce their readiness to enter into discussions with any Powers which may approach them for an abatement of particular preferences in non-self-governing Colonial territories, where these can be shown to place undue restrictions on international trade. The Committee recognise that this offer must be subject to such reservations as may be necessary in regard to revenue considerations.

Leith-Ross was also informed of the British government's willingness to abrogate all 'preferences to the United Kingdom in their Tropical African Colonies', provided that the other colonial powers in Africa made 'some appreciable contribution to the lowering of tariff barriers or preferences in Colonial markets'.[29]

The report of the League committee, when it was finally published, demonstrated that raw materials were produced almost wholly in 'sovereign countries'. Only rubber, tin, palm oil and copra derived mostly from colonies.[30] The essential findings of the committee were summed up in one sentence: 'A calculation, which necessarily can only be a rough one, seems to indicate that, including production both for domestic consumption and for export, the total present production of all commercially important raw materials in all colonial territories is no more than about 3 per cent. of world production, a substantially smaller percentage than is the proportion (12.5 per cent.) of these territories to world population.' Equally, the report indicated the unimportance of colonies to world trade.[31] The committee had found little evidence to show that there were widespread prohibitions and restrictions on the export of raw materials, although it had insufficient details of complaints to determine if real discrimination was being practised. But the depression had hit producing countries harder than those engaged in manufacturing industry; consequently, there should have been no difficulty in industrial countries acquiring raw materials. Furthermore, heavy expenditure on rearmament and the imposition of exchange controls by some states had unquestionably impaired their ability to pay for raw materials. The committee, therefore, recommended that fresh impetus should be given to the establishment of more liberal monetary conditions and action, such as the application of the 'open door' principle in all colonies, should be taken in order to lower trade barriers. The report concluded: 'No doubt certain difficulties in regard to supply exist; but none of them is insuperable . . . the only general and permanent solution of the problem is to be found in a restoration of international exchanges on the widest basis.'[32]

As a result of the League committee's report, Eden decided to amend his proposed speech to the League assembly, in which he had originally intended to put forward the proposal that Britain would be prepared to abolish preferences granted to her in her tropical African dependencies. The League report, however, had illustrated the 'infinitesimal' importance of colonies to world trade; there was, therefore, little point 'in making a gesture as regards the "open door"'.[33] Thus, when Eden addressed the League assembly on 20 September 1937, he announced that, while Britain was prepared to discuss with other governments the 'abatement of particular preferences' in her colonies, where these could 'be shown to place undue restriction on international trade', there could be no modification of the British preferential system, for no modification could 'provide any adequate remedy for the difficulties of those countries which, by maintaining exchange control, find themselves at a disadvantage in obtaining imports of raw materials and other things which they require'.[34] Paul Fauré, speaking for France, was less decorous. He stated:

Some countries fear a scarcity in the event of conflict; let them work for peace. They fear the risk of sanctions – which they can avoid by honouring their signature and accepting the findings of international justice. They complain of the lack of means of payment; they have only to abandon the methods of economic and financial autocracy and those difficulties will disappear.[35]

The German reaction to the League report and subsequent statements was, not unnaturally, petulant.[36]

During the course of the first three months of Chamberlain's premiership, therefore, the importance of the colonial question was at a low ebb. Nevertheless, Chamberlain's determination to inject more urgency into the conduct of British foreign policy provoked a sequence of events that were soon to lead to the issue once more establishing itself in the forefront of British considerations regarding future relations with Germany. In effect, Chamberlain decided to take over the conduct of foreign policy himself.[37] Undoubtedly his strong personality would have made an impact on British foreign policy even had he not quite deliberately decided upon this course, but there were reasons other than autocratic instincts which explain his decision.[38]

Despite much discussion and effort, Britain was no nearer getting Germany into a general settlement. Moreover, the international situation in the summer of 1937 was gloomy. The era of annual *coups de théâtre* on the part of Hitler seemed to be over, but he had done nothing that would have contributed to the establishment of an atmosphere free from tension. Indeed, Germany's diplomatic position had been strengthened. Following their improvement in 1936, Italo–German relations were progressing towards greater intimacy and an anti-comintern pact had been signed by Germany and Japan. And so the nightmare of British policy was unfolding: that of being threatened simultaneously in Europe, the Mediterranean and the Far East.[39] A chiefs of staff memorandum warned:

The intervention of Italy against us would at once impose conflicting demands on our fleet. Our policy must be governed by the principle that no anxieties or risks connected with our interests in the Mediterranean can be allowed to interfere with the despatch of a fleet to the Far East.[40]

Eden had previously pointed out that Hitler had 'from the very first . . . been able to seize and keep the initiative'.[41] If the British government was to succeed in its policy of securing a general settlement, it would have to secure the initiative for itself and to control events meant to set the pace. Animated by the conviction that it was imperative to reach agreement with the dictators and, if possible, divide them, Chamberlain was determined to take advantage of every opportunity that might conduce to that end.

Chamberlain's interest and involvement in foreign policy were not new. Throughout the 1930s his authority in the Cabinet, particularly in this field, grew to such an extent that in March 1935 he could claim: 'I have become a sort of acting P.M. – only without the actual power of the P.M. I have to say "Have you thought" or "What would you say?" when it would be quicker to say "This is what you must do."'[42] In 1933 and 1934 he was, in fact, under consideration as a possible replacement for Sir John Simon, but he declined an informal suggestion.[43] Nevertheless, he was increasingly actively involved in the formulation of British policy, particularly in the immediate aftermath of the Rhineland crisis, even, somewhat immodestly, claiming the entire credit for it. Writing to one of his sisters on 21 March 1936, regarding the negotiations with the Locarno powers, he stated:

> It is true that I have supplied most of the ideas and taken the lead all through but both Edward [Lord Halifax] and Anthony fully played their part and each of them was most helpful. Indeed I don't think any of us could have been spared except poor Ramsay.[44]

Furthermore, Chamberlain was regularly informed by Eden on the international situation.[45] Eden later recalled that he and Chamberlain frequently exchanged views on various matters before the latter became Prime Minister and that there was a strong identity of view between them.[46]

Chamberlain's concern with the establishment of stable international relations in Europe stemmed, of course, from a desire to avoid war, but equally, as Chancellor of the Exchequer, he was concerned with the impact of the international situation on business. In his opinion:

> If we could once get this trouble [the Rhineland crisis] behind us and start Europe on a new basis we should I believe see a rapid expansion in trade for the undertone is firm and enterprise is just waiting for the restoration of confidence to go ahead.[47]

But by July 1936 he was lamenting over 'the foreign situation and the fact that we have no policy'.[48] Undoubtedly it was this concern and apprehension of the Foreign Office's handling of Anglo–German relations, as exemplified in the Schacht initiative, that prompted him in July 1936 and March and April 1937 to exert himself in the Cabinet Foreign Policy Committee and lead it to clear conclusions when the colonial question was under discussion in connection with German policy.[49]

Indeed, on the eve of his premiership, Chamberlain had acquired a position of dominance in the Cabinet that would have been difficult to reverse. This was not yet resented by Eden. He confided to his private secretary, Oliver Harvey: 'Neville Chamberlain had makings of a really great Prime Minister if only his health held out . . . he had a grip of affairs which Stanley Baldwin had never had.'[50] Chamberlain's opinion of Eden was 'less enthusiastic'.[51] The new Prime Minister had been irritated by what he considered to have been Eden's too strident tone in referring to Germany in a Commons speech of 19 January 1937.[52] Moreover, he had been more inclined to pursue the contact with Schacht than Eden.[53] The unflattering portrait of Eden sketched by Hoare in May 1937[54] was almost certainly not endorsed by Chamberlain, but the Prime Minister undoubtely had his reservations. Whereas he was by nature decisive, Eden had shown himself indecisive on a number of occasions and too inclined to submit to the dictates of his officials.[55] The relationship between the two men, however, remained cordial as the warm tribute paid to Eden in Cabinet at the end of July 1937 testifies.[56]

But, his own convictions aside, Chamberlain was given every encouragement to proceed in a forthright manner. Hoare advised him:

Do not let anything irrevocable or badly compromising happen in foreign politics until you are in control. I say this because I am convinced that the F.O. is so much biassed against Germany (and Italy and Japan) that unconsciously and almost continuously they are making impossible any European reconciliation.

I believe myself that when you are Prime Minister, it will be possible greatly to change the European atmosphere. Do, however, make sure that no irreparable harm is done in the immediate future . . . You will only get Germany to play on the basis of full equality – the recent F.O. papers invariably try to undermine this conception by falling back on the idea of Anglo–French agreements.[57]

The crisis in Europe was becoming acute. The Foreign Office was slow and 'sloppy' and 'a foreign secretary left to himself always appeared to be entangled in the web of an intricate department'.[58] The time had come for the Prime Minister to take a hand.

This did not mean that Chamberlain was unaware of the central dangers confronting Britain, or that he had an unrealistic appreciation of the nature of the German and Italian governments. In March 1937 he informed Henry Morgenthau, the United States Secretary of the Treasury:

> The main source of the fears of Europe is to be found in Germany. No other country, not Italy . . . not Russia . . . certainly not France, England or any of the smaller powers, is for the moment credited with any aggressive designs. But the fierce propaganda against other nations . . . the intensity and persistence of German military preparations, together with many acts of the German Government in violation of treaties, cynically justified on the ground that unilateral action was the quickest way of getting what they wanted, have inspired her neighbours with profound uneasiness.[59]

And, after becoming Prime Minister, he wrote to one of his sisters: 'The Germans and Italians are as exasperating as they can be and it is rather difficult to reconcile their professions of friendiship with the incredible insolence and licence of their press.'[60] Yet he believed that 'the double policy of rearmanent and better relations with Germany and Italy will carry us safely through if only the F.O. will play up'.[61]

There were early disappointments. On 29 May 1937 the German pocket battleship *Deutschland* was attacked by Spanish republican aircraft. The German government reacted by withdrawing from the non-intervention committee, which had been set up with the fruitless purpose of leaving the Spanish to themselves while they conducted their civil war. This provided the occasion for Eden to invite the German foreign minister to visit London to discuss Germany's return to the non-intervention committee and generally 'review . . . the international situation', although it seems that the intention to issue such an invitation had been mulled over anterior to the actual attack on the German battleship. The Germans, however, while ostensibly responding favourably to the idea, played hard to get: rather than discussing a settlement of the *Deutschland* incident during the visit, one had to be achieved before it could take place.[62] But eventually a visit was scheduled and Eden expressed his relief to Britain's new ambassador at Berlin, Sir Nevile Henderson, in the following manner:

> I am very glad that the visit has now finally been arranged and I hope that it will lead to useful results. I have always thought that a frank talk would be extremely useful for clearing up any misconceptions which may exist in the German mind, whilst to us it should constitute a valuable opportunity of testing what German intentions really are.[63]

Nevertheless, von Neurath and the German government were resourceful in avoiding this commitment. Following the alleged torpedo attack on the cruiser *Leipzig*, the visit to London was cancelled.[64] In spite of Sir Nevile Henderson's pleadings, Hitler could not be moved to reverse this decision.[65]

The reason for the reluctance on the part of Hitler to let the von Neurath visit proceed was probably involved with the five power conference negotiations and the parallel Schacht initiative that had recently come to its conclusion. The British government in connection with both these matters had repeatedly intimated that there could be no satisfactory outcome of any negotiations for a general settlement that avoided German assurances for the peace of eastern Europe and Hitler was undoubtedly aware of this.[66] Any review of the general situation during a visit by von Neurath to London would inevitably touch on the five power negotiations, still theoretically in progress, and possibly also involve reference to the Schacht overtures. There was, therefore, a risk of exposing too clearly German intentions in eastern Europe, or, and perhaps even worse from Hitler's point of view, the possibility that Germany might be committed to negotiations for a general settlement, which could only lead to the abandonment of his ambitions in eastern Europe, or the rupture of the negotiations at Germany's instance, with Germany incurring the subsequent international odium. All these eventualities would have been inconvenient for the ultimate fulfilment of Hitler's long-term programme.

But even if Hitler was becoming disenchanted with the possibility,[67] he still hankered after the exclusive Anglo–German

understanding that formed the basis of the foreign policy programme he had devised in the 1920s. This becomes clear if one
examines the increasingly amicable dialogue between Britain's new
ambassador at Berlin, Sir Neville Henderson, and Goering that took
place in the summer of 1937. Not only is this dialogue important in
itself, but Eden later turned to it as a means of eliciting the nature of
Germany's grievances and of reassuring the Germans of Britain's
good intentions in the wake of the cancellation of the von Neurath
visit.

Henderson went to work with a will in Berlin. Before he left for
Germany he told Cadogan that he did not 'care what damned
nonsense the F.O. . . . talked . . . he . . . was . . . going to get in
touch with Hitler & Co'. Cadogan thought the ambassador was 'in
the right mood'.[68] On 24 May 1937 Henderson had his first meeting
with Goering, for whom he soon developed 'a real personal liking'.[69]
During this conversation the latter emphasised the importance and
need for Anglo–German co-operation, which would not be detri-
mental to France and which the Führer urgently desired. Goering
also alluded to the perils of allowing Germans to continue to look
upon Britain as 'the enemy in their path'.[70] Eden's response to this
information was to point out that Goering's remark about Britain
being regarded as an enemy in Germany should not have gone
unchallenged, for to allow that would be tantamount to acquiescence in the view that the British government had been following an
anti-German policy. Henderson, therefore, was instructed to obtain
another interview with Goering in which he was to be informed that
the German people were nursing an 'imaginary grievance' and to be
asked for an explanation of the reasons why Britain was regarded as
an enemy in Germany.[71]

Henderson reassured Eden that he had in fact told Goering that to
think of Britain as an enemy was 'as fallacious as it was mischievous', but he was reluctant to meet Goering again until he was
in a position to explain to him the British view of the grievances that
Germans, including Goering on 24 May, invariably listed and which
were outlined in Phipps's despatch of 13 April 1937.[72] Henderson
stated that if he asked Goering to enumerate German grievances he
would be bound to mention all the points that Phipps had made and
would probably be surprised to be asked to do so again. Henderson
added that in conversations he had previously had he had stated
that Germany's grievances were illusory; that the policy of the
British government was one of 'insistence on peace and peaceful

evolution', not obstruction; that French and British security were mutually entwined; that there was no possibility of a settlement with Germany that did not also involve France; that the recognition of Germany's claim to colonies in principle would not necessarily make it any easier to satisfy her in practice; and that Britain would be very willing to discuss raw materials.[73]

By the time that Eden came to reply to Henderson's despatch the von Neurath visit had been cancelled. But the Foreign Secretary still felt that the German attitude should not go unchallenged. He had hoped to discuss the matter of Germany's grievances with von Neurath; now that that was impossible he instructed Henderson to broach the subject with Goering. What was required was an exact definition of the objectives of German policy and a precise statement as to how Britain had obstructed their realisation. Eden thought that during the early stages of the conversation Goering should be reminded that Britain was a League member, pledged to fulfil the covenant. Thus Britain could not contemplate any forcible alteration of the *status quo*, although she would not oppose any changes that were peacefully accomplished. On specific issues, Eden defined the British attitude as follows: the British government would not contemplate forcible change regarding the *Anschluss*; Britain was concerned that the rights of the German minority in Czechoslovakia were respected, but could not 'condone any forcible interference in the affairs of Czechoslovakia'; concerning the Danube basin, Britain could not oppose the co-operation of the states there, but neither would she deny German and Italian economic interests; on Danzig and Memel Germany had furnished no proposals and any changes would have to be negotiated; regarding the east and Communism, the position of the British government was that it could not become party to any ideological bloc directed against the Soviet Union and Britain could not refuse to co-operate with that state if such co-operation was genuinely offered; on the colonial question, the intimations received from Germany, including Goering himself, suggested that this was a secondary issue, but Eden continued:

you might say that you understand the view of H.M. Government and of the French Government to be that the colonial question could not be considered unless and until agreement had been reached in principle on all the other elements which must go to make up a general settlement, and that Dr. Schacht was made aware of this view in Paris last May.

Henderson was to impress upon Goering that all the British government was attempting to do was to 'elucidate Germany's grievances in order that they may . . . try to find a remedy by friendly discussion'.[74]

When Henderson saw Goering on 20 July he read and left with him an *aide-mémoire* asking for a precise definition of Germany's aims and an enumeration of the occasions on which and the manner in which Britain had thwarted Germany.[75] During the course of the subsequent interview Goering proved evasive. Henderson felt that it had not been very productive, which it was not from the British point of view, but the following comments offered by Goering are of some significance:

> His Majesty's Government . . . might preach peaceful evolution and be opposed to possible interference; yet Germany had also the right to live and Austria and the Sudetendeutsche were not vital questions for her as they were for Germany. France might desire to oppose the development of Germany, but there was nothing in Germany's greatness which was contrary to British interests. Germany was willing to recognise British preponderance on the sea which was vital to her. If there was a real Anglo–German understanding, Germany would not even worry about colonies, even if England added to her present Empire. Hitler had indicated in 'Mein Kampf' how earnestly he desired England's friendship. He was bitterly disappointed and resentful of England's unwillingness to reciprocate. It was . . . the bitterest experience of Hitler's life.

Goering also observed that it was difficult for a state to disclose its ultimate ambitions.[76]

As Vansittart predicted, a reply to Henderson's *aide-mémoire* was not forthcoming. Accordingly, Eden instructed Henderson to draw the matter to Goering's attention at the Nuremberg rally.[77] Henderson, who, in characteristic fashion, had decided to attend the rally, a delicate matter, without consulting the Foreign Office, and justified it to Vansittart on the ground that as a consequence one of the days would be devoted to *Arbeit* rather than *Kolonien*,[78] saw Goering at Nuremberg and asked if he was able to reply to his earlier enquiries. The ambassador was told that Germany's grievances could be listed, but that her ultimate aims could not be revealed without Hitler's consent. To this exercise in inscrutability Henderson replied that he would like a response of some kind by October, when he would be going to London. Although he visited Goering shortly thereafter at Rominten on 4 October, where, besides a stag-shoot, he was promised an answer, the latter did little more than reiterate what he had said at Nuremberg, when he had outlined an Anglo–German agreement consisting of two clauses, namely, German recognition of British maritime predominance and British recognition of German primacy in Europe. Replying to Henderson's observation that no Anglo–German agreement would be complete without a colonial settlement, Goering stated that if Britain and Germany reached an understanding, as he defined it, Germany 'would undertake to attempt no solution of the colonial question without consultation and agreement with Great Britain'. In any case, Germany did not want British colonies and 'he hinted that Portugal might be induced to sell hers or part of them to Germany'.[79] It is possible that if the British government had responded to Goering's blandishments an Anglo–German understanding could have been realised. But Goering's proposals ran counter to everything that the British government wanted to attain. The Henderson–Goering dialogue had taken the British government no further in making what they regarded as meaningful contact with Germany. However, the subsequent Halifax visit to Germany, which 'almost certainly' sprang from it, was regarded as more hopeful.[80]

At least until this time it would be true to say that there were no major differences between Chamberlain and Eden as far as policy towards Germany was concerned. Both regarded Vansittart as a distinct impediment in this respect, Sir Alexander Cadogan having been brought back to the Foreign Office from his posting in the Far East, at Eden's wish, as Vansittart's future replacement. For his part, Vansittart could see very little point, by the summer of 1937, in pursuing discussions with Germany, cynically minuting, when he assented to the circulation of the correspondence relating to the Henderson–Goering dialogue to the Cabinet, that he doubted if ministers would perceive how discouraging Goering's attitude really was. It is interesting to note that Eden endorsed this sentiment. While, therefore, Eden and Chamberlain were probably in broad agreement on Germany, in fairness the former was perhaps less hopeful of success.[81] In August 1937, however, the relationship between the two men began to turn sour over the question of Italy. From the time that sanctions, imposed as a result of the Abyssinian war, were lifted there were strong currents in the Cabinet favouring the restoration of Anglo–Italian relations to their former status. This trend was represented, not unnaturally, by Hoare.[82] As Vansittart put it: 'we can never compromise security, or even live safely, with "Dictator Major" [Germany] if we are at lasting loggerheads with "Dictator Minor"'.[83] Despite, however, the conclusion of an Anglo–Italian *Gentlemen's Agreement* in January 1937, relations between the two countries remained tense. So tense in fact that Chamberlain at first thought that better relations with Germany were the means of controlling Mussolini.[84] But 'the way to Berlin was blocked'.[85] Eventually, Italy became the 'obvious target' for reducing Britain's list of potential enemies.[86]

But from the first Eden had very little faith that relations with Italy would ever improve: concessions to the Italians would merely be regarded as weakness. Totally unscrupulous, Mussolini was the 'anti-Christ' and likely 'to incline to whichever side seemed to offer him the greater advantages'.[87] The truth is that Eden's bland public figure concealed a dogmatic, obstinate and irascible temperament. He had been worsted by Mussolini in the Abyssinian crisis and the trauma seems to have blinded him to the realities of the power situation in Europe.[88] For the policy of bringing Germany into a general settlement to have worked at all – undoubtedly it could never have done so given the nature of Hitler's long-term aims and his determination to pursue them – Italy and Germany would have had to have been split and the latter effectively isolated. In other words, the diplomatic trend, which had been running in Germany's favour, would have had to have been reversed. This could only have been accomplished by making concessions to the Italians. Eden, however, would not sup with the devil and to some extent was instrumental in wrecking the last opportunity of bringing Italy back into the Stresa constellation, which would have deprived Hitler of a valuable ally made credible by her successful defiance of the League.[89]

Although the natural reaction of the Italians, after the imposition of League sanctions, was to drift towards Germany, there is strong evidence to suggest that they were still keeping their options open.[90] In July 1937 overtures were made to the British government, following a conciliatory speech by Eden in the Commons. Eden advised against responding too warmly,[91] but Chamberlain, having listened to a translation of a letter from Mussolini during an interview with Count Dino Grandi, the Italian ambassador at London, decided, on the spot, to write a personal letter to Mussolini.[92] This the Prime Minister did without consulting Eden, because he considered the effect of the Foreign Office would be prejudicial rather than catalytic.[93] The incident led to no immediate unpleasantness between Prime Minister and Foreign Secretary. The latter later recalled, somewhat ungenerously, that he had been inclined to forgive this piece of *gaucherie* on the part of a novice in international affairs.[94] It was not possible, though, for Chamberlain to make immediate progress with the Italians, for the Nyon conference took strong measures to counter submarine piracy in the western Mediterranean. This, together with Mussolini's visit to Germany, tended to reinforce the existence of the Axis.[95] But relations between Eden and Chamberlain were now marked by a growing acerbity and there were several stormy sessions between them during the autumn of 1937.[96]

The stormiest was that of 16 November. Ostensibly this related to press reports regarding the forthcoming visit of Lord Halifax to Germany, but almost certainly the pent-up resentments of the previous months, during which the Prime Minister was stealing the limelight in foreign affairs, played their part.[97] It is, however, significant that on that day Eden later minuted his concurrence, against the consensus of Foreign Office opinion, with the view of his deputy, Lord Cranborne, that Britain could not move towards the *de jure* recognition of the Italian conquest of Abyssinia, the *sine qua non* of improved Anglo–Italian relations.[98] It is perhaps claiming too much to state that from this time onwards Eden and Chamberlain were set on a 'collision course', but clearly their relationship had suffered a set-back from which it never fully recovered.[99]

These immediate difficulties were overcome. By December a fragile harmony had been established between Prime Minister and Foreign Secretary as a consequence of the visit of Lord Halifax to Germany. Halifax was initially invited by Goering, in his capacity as Reich game warden, to attend a hunting exhibition in Berlin. This seemed to Halifax to offer an opportunity for the improvement of relations with Germany after the disappointments of the preceding months, a view which was enthusiastically supported by Chamberlain. Eden himself at first was not opposed, although Vansittart demurred. This obstruction caused Chamberlain to comment: 'But really, that FO! I am only waiting my opportunity to stir it up with a long pole.' At the beginning of December 1937 he finally procured Vansittart's removal from the day-to-day running of the Foreign Office by having him elevated to the rank of Chief Diplomatic Adviser.

Clearly, the Prime Minister was determined that Vansittart

should not frustrate the possibility of contact with Goering as, doubtless in Chamberlain's mind, he had previously frustrated the opening with Schacht. Eden, of course, had been agitating for Vansittart's removal ever since he became Foreign Secretary, and Chamberlain considered that the latter's replacement by Sir Alexander Cadogan would have a beneficial effect upon the Foreign Secretary. In this the Prime Minister was a little harsh on Vansittart. Vansittart supported Chamberlain's Italian policy and the basis of British policy towards Germany in the wake of the Halifax visit was in essence that which Vansittart had played a prominent part in devising two years previously. Vansittart, therefore, had some justification in telling Chamberlain that 'he had always been in favour of . . . his policy . . . but had been obstructed by others!' Chamberlain, though, did not believe him.[100]

Objections to the Halifax visit were subsequently raised by Eden when he learnt that Hitler would only receive the British minister at Berchtesgaden, an arrangement he felt redolent of servility if accepted, but he ultimately came round to the view that the visit was 'not necessarily a bad thing'.[101] It was during Halifax's conversation with Hitler that the colonial question was raised by the German Chancellor in such a manner as to suggest that its solution might well assist the realisation of the fundamental and continuing aim of British policy of securing Germany's agreement to a general, European settlement.

Prior to Halifax's departure for Germany the colonial question had been the subject of some controversy in the British press and a propaganda campaign in Germany. At the Nuremberg rally Hitler had raised the colonial question and he did so again during a speech at the harvest thanksgiving festival on the Bückeberg on 3 October 1937. As far as the colonial question was concerned, claimed Hitler, the world had only imbecile comments to make. Some states claimed that colonies were a burden, but they refused to give them up! Worthless colonies, he argued, ought to be restored to their legal owners. It was these remarks that were the cause of the publicity given to the colonial question in succeeding weeks in both Britain and Germany.[102]

The Times carried letters and reports of speeches dealing with the colonial question throughout the last three months of 1937. The balance of opinion, represented by names such as Vernon Bartlett, Gilbert Murray, Lord Noel-Buxton, Arnold Toynbee, W. H. Dawson (inevitably), George Lansbury and Lord Ponsonby, favoured a sympathetic treatment of Germany's claims. Opponents were outnumbered and could only muster Leo Amery and Page Croft as significant names in their cause. Moreover, the former even felt that Page Croft's contribution was not accorded the prominence it deserved.[103] On 28 October 1937 an editorial in *The Times* declared that there was a desire for a peaceful settlement in Britain and that, as the colonial question had assumed a position of primary importance for Germany, the British government could not decline to consider it as part of a general settlement. Moreover, it was argued,

> the recognition that . . . [Germany] . . . was *capax imperii* would be all the more satisfying if such a field could be opened for her by the common action of three or four of the great colonizing powers with contiguous African territories.[104]

The editorial in *The Times* coincided with an intervention by Mussolini in which the Italian dictator lent support to Germany's colonial claims, suggesting that Britain should make a contribution towards the solution of this problem. This provoked a rejoinder from Eden in the Commons on 1 November, in which he pointed out that a state which had made territorial gains in Europe and acquired territory in Africa as a result of the war had championed Germany's claims. He declared: 'We do not admit the right of any Government to call upon us for a contribution when there is no evidence to show that that Government are prepared to make any contribution of their own account.'[105] This statement annoyed Chamberlain. He agreed that Mussolini had been 'insolent', but, he wrote: 'Anthony should never have been provoked into a retort which throws Germany & Italy together in self-defence when our policy is so obviously to try & divide them.'[106]

Mussolini's speech of 28 October also stimulated a surge in colonial agitation in Germany. Eight days later François-Poncet commented that 'colonial propaganda is being increased and is suddenly seized of an ardour that goes beyond what has previously been observed'.[107] Furthermore, rumours began to circulate to the effect that Hitler was going to address the Reichstag with an offer of a general settlement that would include colonial revision.[108] According to von Epp, the man behind the propaganda was Ribbentrop. Through the mediation of Carl von Wiegard of the Hearst press, von Epp sought an interview with an important British person in order to impress upon the British government that the 'recrudescence of press polemics' about colonies was regarded as inconvenient by the German army and that it was considered unreasonable to expect Britain to cede Tanganyika in view of Italy's presence in east Africa. It was von Epp's opinion that the retrocession of Togoland and the Cameroons would be regarded as a 'complete and final settlement of German colonial claims'. According to von Wiegard, von Epp had not vouchsafed this information to Sir Neville Henderson because he did not want Ribbentrop to get wind of it. Von Epp then

> launched into a long tirade against Herr von Ribbentrop, whose reputation he said had sunk to the lowest possible ebb with every member of the German Government except the Führer. Herr von Ribbentrop had been solely responsible for the press agitation about the German colonies. He had excited the Führer and persuaded the latter to give the necessary orders to Goebbels.[109]

In view of Ribbentrop's previous convictions about colonies and the failure of his British mission, which impelled him towards a vehemently anti-British line, his motive was probably straightforward.[110] But what of Hitler's motives? In November 1937, in two despatches, François-Poncet suggested that the colonial question was not necessarily being raised for its own sake, but rather with a view to making gains in eastern Europe. He wrote: 'The colonial claim of the Reich is perhaps only a contrivance, only a tactical means concealing other designs. It is not impossible that Germany dreams or has dreamt of negotiating one day an abandonment of her colonial claims against more substantial concessions . . . in central and eastern Europe.'[111] If François-Poncet was right, this lends powerful support to the colonial 'blackmail' or 'threat' thesis advanced by Professor Hildebrand in the works *Vom Reich zum Weltreich* and *The Foreign Policy of the Third Reich*, for according to this argument the colonial claim was pushed after 1936 with a view to coercing the British into an understanding with Germany the main object of which was the primary acquisition of *Lebensraum* in eastern Europe.

The Halifax visit, therefore, took place in a welter of comment on the colonial question. Moreover, the British government had every reason to suspect that Hitler himself would raise the issue.[112] They were not disappointed. The talks with Hitler left Halifax with the impression that there could be no satisfactory *rapprochement* between Britain and Germany unless the colonial question was settled. Halifax told Hitler that while Britain was not pledged to maintain the *status quo* in eastern Europe in perpetuity, change would have to be realised by peaceful means. Hitler alluded to the colonial question. It was the only issue between Britain and Germany; he hoped that the problem could be examined and an agreeable solution found. Halifax replied that a colonial agreement could only be effected in the context of a general settlement, 'which would give our people a prospect of real understanding and relief of the present tension'. Concluding his personal record of the talks, Halifax commented:

> While I think he [Hitler] wants to be on friendly terms with us, he is not going to be in any hurry to consider the question of League of Nations return – regards disarmament as pretty hopeless, and, in short, feels himself to be in a strong position and is not going to run after us. He did not give me the impression of being at all likely to want to go to war with us over colonies, but, no doubt, if he cannot be met on this issue, good relations, under which I suppose we might exert a good deal of influence . . . would remain impossible.

He urged further exploration of the possibility of a colonial settlement 'with the idea of using it as a lever upon which to pursue a policy of real assurance in Europe . . . to try for the . . . bargain of a colonial settlement at the price of Hitler being a good European.'[113]

Chamberlain was very satisfied with the Halifax visit: contact had been made and a picture of the German attitude obtained.[114] Colonies had obviously assumed a greater importance for the Germans but, Chamberlain felt, Britain should be prepared to facilitate the return of Germany to colonial activity if that was required to secure an agreement. Already a scheme was evolving in his mind that would require a general readjustment of the map of Africa rather than a straightforward retrocession of Germany's colonies, which was essential in view of the predetermined attitude of the government that Tanganyika could not be returned. He informed his sister:

> I have no doubt that Portugal would strongly object to parting with any territory but it is worth seeing whether in a Conference of African Powers we could not arrive at such adjustments as

would satisfy the Germans compensating the Powers which surrendered territories by money or territory elsewhere.[115]

But the issue could only be considered in a general settlement and nothing could be done without the prior consent of the French or without a German *quid pro quo*. Eden also evinced satisfaction with the results of Halifax's activities in Germany.[116]

At the end of November 1937 consultations took place with the French when Chautemps and Delbos, the French Prime Minister and foreign minister respectively, came to London. There was a large measure of agreement on a number of points: Germany would have to rejoin the League, there would have to be a renegotiated western pact, and a pledge of German pacific intent in eastern Europe. In other words, the Anglo–French desiderata developed since the remilitarisation of the Rhineland still stood. Moreover, there was more agreement on the colonial question than had been anticipated. The French ministers proved surprisingly complaisant, remarking that the French government was more 'progressive' in its attitude towards Germany's colonial claims than the French electorate. During the conversations Chamberlain broached the problem of Tanganyika, suggesting that Germany might be given a mandate of Belgian and Portuguese territory in west Africa, Belgium and Portugal being compensated by cash or territory elsewhere. Nevertheless, it was recognised that there could be no consideration of the German colonial claim 'in isolation' from other problems, a point which was registered in the official communiqué at the end of the Anglo–French talks. The communiqué announced that a 'preliminary examination' of the colonial question had taken place.[117] When Chamberlain informed the Commons of this significant new departure in policy he was amazed by the lack of reaction. He informed his sister: 'I can read this communiqué and not a dog barks. That has taken me over the French hurdle and over the first British hurdle without losing a stirrup.'[118]

On 1 December the Cabinet reviewed the situation created by the Halifax visit and the Anglo–French talks. On the colonial question the Prime Minister made it clear that there could be no satisfaction for Germany unless she made what was tantamount to a positive approach towards peace; it was not a question that could stand by itself. Summing up, Eden said that the Anglo–French talks had been useful. They had put at rest rumours of divergence between Britain and France on policy over the colonial question; he was convinced that France was anxious 'to induce the Germans to come to terms'. Generally, 'the conversations had enabled us [Britain] to take an indispensable first step in the direction of some dealings with Germany over colonies, and the views of the two Governments had proved to be identical'.[119]

If the Commons was proving to be unexpectedly docile at the prospect of colonial concession to Germany, the same could not be said of Britain's oldest ally, Portugal. From the moment that Mussolini and *The Times* pronounced on the colonial question on 28 October 1937 the Portuguese, fearing a threat to their colonial domain, had pursued developments in this matter most attentively.[120] By the time that Lord Halifax arrived in Berlin, Veiga Simões, the Portuguese ambassador at Berlin, had learnt from Sir Nevile Henderson that when Halifax saw Hitler the colonial question was likely to be discussed.[121] The day following the Berchtesgaden conversation Simões reported to Lisbon that this indeed had been so, but that 'the Chancellor always put the question on the legal basis of the restitution of the old colonies'. On the other hand, the ambassador's high-ranking informant stressed that this formula could 'be substituted by a proposal that comes from other quarters'.[122]

Following the Anglo–French conversations the Portuguese ambassador at London, Armindo Monteiro, obtained an interview with Eden at which he impressed upon the Foreign Secretary that it was in Britain's interests to maintain Portugal's overseas possessions intact. The Lobito to Beira rail link was, he argued, a second Mediterranean.[123] According to Eden's account of this conversation, Monteiro 'made no attempt to conceal the horror with which he regarded' the prospect of Germany returning to Africa. The ambassador stated: 'Today Africa is at peace. Nobody wants Germany back. No native anywhere wishes for such an event, nor does any white man. If Germany goes back to Africa you may gain peace in Europe, but you will destroy peace in Africa.' To reassure Monteiro, Eden pointed out that Hitler had not mentioned 'the cession of any Portuguese territory', although he, of course, omitted to inform the ambassador that Chamberlain had and that he [Eden] had made no demur.[124] This was not good enough for the secretary-general of the Portuguese foreign ministry, who called in the British *chargé d'affaires*, Bateman, and gave him a dressing-down. Recalling the pre-war Anglo–German accords regarding Portuguese territory, he stated that Portugal was now a different nation and 'would surrender nothing in the matter of colonies'.[125] Sir Walford Selby's first duty on taking up his ambassadorship at Lisbon was to make an earnest reassurance in this matter, which Eden himself reinforced on 20 December 1937 when he told the Commons that the 'pre-war proposals are dead and that His Majesty's Government have no intention of endeavouring to revive them'.[126]

Complications of this sort could easily have been avoided. Halifax himself had hinted in his report on his conversation with Hitler that the latter would probably have willingly sacrificed Germany's colonial claims for a free hand in Europe.[127] And this indeed was, in reality, the only sort of colonial deal with the German government that the British government could have contemplated with success at this time. Had the British ministers recognised this fact with sufficient clarity, they could have spared themselves the embarrassments and trouble of the coming months. While the offer of an understanding with Britain, on German terms, still probably remained intact, Hitler was now less inclined to see it as the precondition of the accomplishment of the European phase of his programme. What appeared to him as British weakness over the Abyssinian crisis, the Spanish Civil War and events in the Far East, convinced him that he could carry out the realisation of his aims in central and eastern Europe without armed intervention on the part of Britain.[128] Indeed the Schacht talks and the negotiations over the five power conference were probably also instrumental in causing Hitler to conclude that, although the western powers might not like the idea of German expansion in eastern Europe, there existed 'a desperate reluctance on their part to go to war to prevent it'.[129] In view of the failure of the understanding with Britain to materialise and increasing doubts as to its imperative necessity, therefore,

> Hitler was from the autumn of 1937 on a sort of 'middle course' . . . The idea of the alliance with Great Britain which he had long advocated with dogmatic rigidity he had to give up out of necessity . . . The unchanged aim, continental expansion, was no longer striven for in union with England, but without England.[130]

At the famous meeting in the Reich Chancellery on 5 November 1937 Hitler observed that Germany 'had to reckon with two hate-inspired antagonists, Britain and France, to whom a German colossus in the center of Europe was a thorn in the flesh'. However, he clearly felt that the British empire was in a state of decline and beset by internal difficulties that would inhibit Britain intervening in the fulfilment of Germany's aim of acquiring *Lebensraum*. This would have to be achieved by force by 1943–5, after which Germany's military position would be comparatively weaker. Thus, that Britain was filled with hate did not necessarily betoken serious opposition. Furthermore, once Germany had completed her European expansion the time would have arrived for 'serious discussion of the return of colonies . . . which . . . could only be considered at a moment when Britain was in difficulties and the German Reich armed and strong'. During his discourse, Hitler also looked at more immediate possibilities, namely, 'the annexation of Czechoslovakia and Austria'. The circumstances in which he thought that Germany could take such action are not of immediate relevance to this study, but what is of importance is that he considered that Britain and France had probably 'tacitly written off the Czechs' and that he anticipated early developments.[131] If Hitler had concluded by the autumn of 1937 that the alliance or understanding with Britain was not within his grasp,[132] he evidently was not dissuaded from proceeding towards the realisation of his programme and now contemplated the first moves.

However, despite his references to Britain, it is unlikely that he had given up completely on his concept of an alliance with Britain,[133] and it is even possible, if the suggestions that Goering made to Henderson during the summer of 1937 had any firm approval,[134] that he would have been agreeable to a temporary renunciation of Germany's ultimate overseas aim to achieve it. It was, however, well known in Berlin that Britain was opposed to the essential condition that the German government laid on such an alliance, namely, freedom of action in Europe,[135] which probably explains why the Germans had wanted to sabotage the Halifax visit.[136] Hitler had no intention of settling the colonial question in a general settlement, or even discussing such arrangements. His course was set.

That this was the case was rapidly conveyed to Eden when he outlined to Ribbentrop the results of the Anglo–French conversations. To Eden's comment that Britain and France would require a *quid pro quo* in exchange for colonial satisfaction, which he defined as 'an increased sense of international security and enhanced prospects of the preservation of peace', the German ambassador replied that the colonial question was an issue based upon justice and that Germany would regret its linkage with other matters that might make it difficult to solve. Ribbentrop even later suggested to von

Neurath that the German press should emphasise that the colonial question was not subject to bargaining.[137] The German attitude in Berlin was equally discouraging. When Sir Nevile Henderson asked von Neurath what Hitler expected to come of the Halifax visit, he received the reply 'not much'.[138] Undaunted, Henderson found a way out. He suggested that the Germans should be told: 'We are prepared to do this and that as regards colonies. Are you prepared to come and discuss the question in London, it being understood, though not necessarily stated, that we shall expect you to put something in the pot?' But Eden pointed out that it had clearly to be understood that a *quid pro quo* was required and that it could not be 'left as a mere matter of tacit understanding'.[139] It was unlikely, Eden thought, that the idea of a general settlement would commend itself to the Germans, for it was the converse of the bilateral Anglo–German arrangement that they desired. Still, he felt that the importance that the British government attached to the concept should be conveyed to the Germans.[140] In all the circumstances, it did not require much perception on the part of William Strang when he minuted on 10 December: 'I fear it is vain to hope that colonies would solve the question of peace and war in Europe.'[141]

But the convictions of the Prime Minister were not shaken. Indeed, they were strengthened. Sir Thomas Inskip, the Minister for Coordination of Defence, warned of the dangers to the British economy that too rapid rearmament and too lavish expenditure on it would entail. As British participation in any war against a major power was likely to result in a long drawn-out war of attrition, Britain would be well advised to enter this type of conflict with her economic resources intact.[142] These were arguments that strongly appealed to Chamberlain.[143] Furthermore, the chiefs of staff emphasised that Britain's forces were still insufficiently developed to meet her global commitments. Although Britain's forces would probably act as a deterrent to Germany, the nub of the problem was that a war with Germany would in all probability extend to a war with Italy as well. Thus anything that the government could do to reduce potential enemies would be welcome.[144] Inskip's arguments were approved by the Cabinet on 22 December and the figure of approximately £1500 million over a five year period, which had been allocated for defence spending, was adhered to. During this Cabinet meeting, however, Halifax observed that the limitations being imposed on defence spending placed a heavy burden on diplomacy; he urged that in this situation Britain ought to do her best 'to get on good terms with Germany'. Eden commented that it would be necessary first of all to ascertain with the French what could be done in connection with colonies. Chamberlain agreed. He thought that 'no further move could be made with Germany until after further explorations' and he announced his intentions of studying the problem during the recess 'with a view to a Meeting of the Committee on Foreign Policy in the New Year'.[145]

When the Foreign Policy Committee met on 24 January 1938 the revived animus in the relationship between Eden and Chamberlain was evident. Usually unrevealing about the attitudes of ministers towards one another, the minutes of the Foreign Policy Committee on this occasion leave little doubt that a pronounced degree of hostility now existed. The two men had, in fact, quarrelled over Anglo–American relations quite bitterly. The President of the United States had suggested earlier in the month that he should address the diplomatic corps in Washington on his readiness 'to take a series of steps hopefully leading to international agreement on the fundamentals of world peace, including arms limitation, equal access to raw materials, and the rights and obligation of neutrals and belligerents in times of war'.[146] In effect, Chamberlain turned down this proposal as an immediate contribution to peace. He later recorded in his diary:

> I was in a dilemma. The plan appeared to me fantastic & likely to excite the derision of Germany and Italy. They might even use it to postpone conversations with us & if we were associated with it they would see in it another attempt on the part of the democratic bloc to put the dictators in the wrong.[147]

Chamberlain, therefore, at a time when negotiations with the dictators seemed to be promising results, did not want to damage them by open encouragement of a bizarre scheme. Thus Chamberlain replied to Roosevelt that he would prefer it if the President postponed his initiative pending the outcome of Britain's efforts with the dictators.[148] Eden, who had taken a short leave, was not consulted about any of this and he was furious.[149] He was convinced that the Roosevelt initiative marked a step forward. Taken together with the Anglo–American naval conversations that had recently been held in London, he thought it augured well for meaningful Anglo–American relations in the future.[150] Ultimately, he prevailed upon Chamberlain to inform Roosevelt that he welcomed his suggestions and would do his 'best to contribute to' their 'success', but by then it was too late. Doubtless Eden's triumph was a real success for his point of view, but it was a Pyrrhic victory. The crisis placed a further strain on his relationship with the Prime Minister, from which it never recovered. Had the American initiative not been secret Eden would probably have resigned then.[151]

The Foreign Policy Committee had been convened on 24 January to determine future action concerning Germany. Chamberlain had given this much thought. Early in the new year the Prime Minister had had the benefit of the personal advice of Sir Nevile Henderson, who was gratified to learn that the government shared his conviction that the colonial question could not be evaded if there was to be 'any solid progress towards appeasement and stability'. Henderson explained to Halifax:

All I mean is that, in my opinion, the lines of a colonial settlement in principle (i.e. something more than a vague offer to discuss the question of Colonies) is an essential preliminary to asking Hitler whether and what Germany is prepared to contribute to world peace and stability.[152]

Chamberlain had clearly been encouraged and Halifax found that he was quite determined to prosecute his policy with vigour.[153] On 23 January the Prime Minister informed his sister of his new scheme which seemed 'to open up a hopeful prospect'.[154]

At the Foreign Policy Committee Chamberlain amplified his scheme. He began by outlining a new approach to Germany, in which the colonial question had been placed 'in the forefront'. But this, he added, in no way implied a change of policy. The colonial question could not be settled 'independently of . . . other issues' and 'the examination of the colonial question could only be undertaken as a part and parcel of a general settlement'. Nevertheless, as colonies were the only obstacle in the way of better Anglo–German relations the matter had to be faced. In order to meet the objections which other countries would offer to a revival of German colonialism, Chamberlain proposed the institution of a new colonial regime in Africa south of the Sahara and north of South Africa and the Rhodesias. In this region there would be some colonial redistribution, so that Germany could be accommodated,[155] and all governments in the area would be compelled to subscribe to a uniform set of principles governing colonial administration, most of which were already enshrined in the mandates system. Fundamentally, Chamberlain's aim was to stimulate German interest in a general settlement by offering to negotiate in principle the prior settlement of the colonial question. Sir Samuel Hoare was the only member of the committee to offer reasoned objections to this plan. Eden confined himself to captious remarks. There was not, he claimed, sufficient stress on the link between a colonial settlement and a general settlement. It is, however, clear from the record of the meeting that there was. For Eden's particular satisfaction, Chamberlain repeated his earlier remarks on this point.[156] On 3 February a further meeting of the Foreign Policy Committee, which was attended by Sir Nevile Henderson, decided to go ahead with this approach to Germany, although the ambassador warned that the German government would not be 'greatly thrilled' by Chamberlain's proposals.[157] Definitive instructions were supplied to Henderson by Eden on 12 February, but the former was told not to make any approach until he received further instructions from London.[158]

Fully confident of his plan by the end of January,[159] Chamberlain's enthusiasm received a set-back with von Neurath's dismissal and replacement by Ribbentrop.[160] It was not, therefore, until this and other governmental changes had fully taken effect in Berlin that Henderson finally saw Hitler. Moreover, by that time there had also been a significant governmental change in Britain. Eden had resigned over the question of negotiations with Italy. His frangible temperament and the accumulated resentments of the preceding months, as the Prime Minister had increasingly taken upon himself the primary decision-making role in foreign policy, had ultimately compelled his departure. The issues on which Chamberlain and Eden parted were not as clear-cut as they appeared at the time and subsequently. Undoubtedly, Eden was more temperamentally antipathetic towards dictatorship than the Prime Minister, but it would be wrong to deduce from this that his reluctance to treat with Mussolini, as a matter of principle, extended to a similar reluctance to treat with Hitler. Eden might well have had fears of a specious nature that Chamberlain was going 'to throw colonies away as a sop apart from any general settlement', but it can readily be assumed that if Oliver Harvey believed that 'negotiations can only do good provided we insist on a general settlement', Eden's own views were similar.[161] Eden resigned on the relatively minor issues of Anglo–American and Anglo–Italian relations and 'not some great question of principle'.[162]

Lord Halifax succeeded to the foreign secretaryship and it became possible for Chamberlain to proceed with his Italian policy without obstruction. On 16 April 1938 an Anglo–Italian agreement was concluded. Britain promised to accord *de jure* recognition of the Italian conquest of Abyssinia and Italy accepted the British scheme for the Italian withdrawal of 'volunteers' from Spain, British ratification of the agreement being contingent on the implementation of this scheme. The initiative concerning Germany was predictably less successful, despite all the preparation.

On 1 March Henderson called upon Ribbentrop and requested an early meeting with Hitler in order to acquaint the Führer with a message from the British Prime Minister dealing with colonies. The ambassador, however, insisted that 'the British Government would have to obtain some *quid pro quo*, since, in return for its concessions, it must offer the British people something in the way of security for European peace'. It was explained by Henderson that he had been instructed to ascertain what Germany could contribute towards this end. Ribbentrop, in typical fashion, replied that the German colonies were the subject of a 'legal claim' and could not become a 'bargaining point'.[163] Nevertheless, it was arranged that Henderson should see Hitler on 3 March. It is, though, in the circumstances, understandable that he was disinclined towards optimism.[164]

The French, Belgians and Italians were to be generally informed of the Hitler–Henderson interview as it took place, but perhaps the most interesting British communication with a foreign government was that with the Portuguese. No doubt anxious to avoid an altercation similar to that which accompanied the Halifax visit and the subsequent Anglo–French talks, the Foreign Office instructed Sir Walford Selby early in the morning of 3 March to inform the secretary-general of the Portuguese foreign ministry that, while the British ambassador at Berlin would be seeing Hitler with a view to resuming the negotiations started by Lord Halifax the preceding November, which would deal with colonies along with central Europe and disarmament, there was no question of reviving the pre-war Anglo–German accords respecting Portugal's colonies. The new Foreign Secretary would stand by his predecessor's Commons statement of the previous December. It was also emphasised that 'the negotiations with Germany that concerned the colonial issue would not be carried out to the detriment of any nation', although it is clear that they would have been.[165]

But there were to be no such negotiations. From the British point of view the Hitler–Henderson interview of 3 March was a complete disaster. During the conversation, the term *general settlement* was avoided, out of deference to German hostility to it, but Henderson clearly implied that it was this that was regarded as desirable by the British government. Was it not possible, he asked, for Germany to take steps to 'inspire confidence in Austria and Czechoslovakia?' What would Germany think of the prohibition of aerial bombardment and the limitation of bombing aircraft? Finally Sir Nevile Henderson unveiled the colonial offer and

> put to the Chancellor the questions whether Germany – (1) was ready in principle to take part in a new colonial regime as outlined in the English proposal, and – (2) what contribution she was ready to make for general order and security in Europe.

Hitler, as soon as Henderson finished, was animated with rage. He would not tolerate any interference with his right 'to secure fair and honourable treatment for the Austro- and Sudeten Germans' and he could only consider arms limitation once the risk of Germany having to fight a war in central Europe had been eliminated. As for the colonial question, he stated:

> Instead of creating a complicated new system, why not solve the colonial question in the simplest and most natural way by giving back the former German colonies? He, the Chancellor, must nevertheless openly admit here that he did not consider the colonial question ripe for solution since Paris and London had set themselves too strongly and too definitely against a return. For this reason he did not want to press the question. They could easily wait four, six, eight or ten years. Perhaps by that time there would be a change of heart in Paris and London and they would see that the best solution was to give back to Germany that which by purchase and treaty was her rightful property.

Hitler promised a written reply on the colonial proposals, but Henderson drew the conclusion that the Führer had rejected a colonial settlement because he did not want to tie his hands thereby in central Europe.[166] It was not, therefore, and at least for the present, colonies that interested him.[167]

Veiga Simões, the well-informed Portuguese ambassador at Berlin, was able to afford his government some reassurance. In his opinion, this latest British attempt at a general settlement would come to nothing. On the colonial question, he wrote that 'as Germany will be asked for vast concessions in European policy, everything indicates that an accord will not be arrived at in the matter'.[168] In this he was fully correct.

Hitler's derisory treatment of the British colonial offer and the *Anschluss* that followed some days later effectively killed off the colonial question in Anglo–German relations for good. They also killed off the last opportunity of Britain making progress towards a general settlement. Henderson commented: 'All the work of the past 11 months has crashed to the ground!' Halifax replied: 'we must certainly admit that our constructive efforts have suffered a pretty severe set-back'. [169] Chamberlain's determined attempt to seize the initiative had come to nought.

9

The Van Zeeland Report

While the colonial question was frequently presented on the German side as an economic issue, the British government, in its deliberations on the subject and in its suggestions of March 1938, never gave serious credence to such claims. For the British government the German colonial grievance was essentially a political and psychological issue as various departmental, League and private investigations had shown, or were to show.[1] However, it was impossible to keep the colonial question and the related issue of access to raw materials out of public and international debate on economic and trade matters during the 1930s, as was the case with the enquiry of the Belgian Prime Minister Van Zeeland and his report of 1938. The Van Zeeland report is worth examining in some detail because it and its British reception are indicators of the kind of wider European settlement that the British government had in mind as far as its economic content was concerned. It also merits attention because it was considered important at the time and because those scholars who have specialised in *economic appeasement* in recent years have tended to ignore the issue altogether, or make only fleeting reference to it. Moreover, it once again illustrates the formidable influence that Leith-Ross had on affairs at this time.

The Van Zeeland enquiry had it origins in the tripartite currency declaration of 25 September 1936, also known as the tripartite stabilisation agreement. One of the principal purposes of the ill-fated world economic conference of 1933 had been to encourage a revival in international trade through agreement on exchange rates. This, however, was the issue on which the entire proceeding collapsed. The United States would not agree even to a temporary stabilisation of the dollar against sterling for the purposes of the conference, and so it ended abruptly and in total failure.[2] This led not unnaturally to bitterness in Britain where it was felt that Roosevelt had behaved treacherously; thereafter, the British 'acted . . . peculiarly about stabilization', to quote the American Secretary of the Treasury, 1933–1945, Henry Morgenthau.[3] By the following year Colonel House was complaining to one State Department

241

official that both Stanley Baldwin and Neville Chamberlain were 'distinctly unfriendly' towards the United States. Furthermore, the same official reported the British ambassador, Sir Ronald Lindsay, as having said that 'the British Government was not in the least interested in playing ball with . . . [the USA] . . . partly because they had made up their minds that the United States Government was a hopeless proposition to play ball with'.[4]

Still, despite mutual mistrust and misunderstanding, there was a fundamental community of interest between Britain and the United States in international economic matters. Both governments regretted the drift to autarchy in Europe, desiring to replace it with freer international trading conditions. An increase in world trade, it was held, would end the depression; the end of the depression would signal a rise in prosperity in the industrialised world; and prosperity would reduce domestic friction, leading ultimately to a relaxation in international tension and the institution of a regime of global peace. The key to success though was the proper 'reintegration of Germany into the world economy'.[5] From 1933 until 1944 Cordell Hull, a man of deep Wilsonian convictions, occupied the position of Secretary of State in Washington. He put the emphasis on 'more and freer trade' in the belief that 'the way to a successful foreign policy lay in liberal trade agreements' based upon the principle of reciprocity.[6] One of his most cherished aspirations was to persuade the British to support his programme of trade agreements by the conclusion of an Anglo–American trade treaty, which he anticipated would disrupt the British imperial preference system set up at Ottawa in 1932 and lead to the reintroduction of a liberal, international trading regime.[7] The British, on the other hand, while not unsympathetic to an Anglo–American trade treaty in principle, were reluctant to conclude one at the expense of imperial preference as long as the Americans insisted upon maintaining a high tariff wall. As Ashton-Gwatkin commented:

> if the United States would contemplate a change of commercial policy comparable to our own repeal of the corn laws, then 'the removal of trade barriers' might really mean something; as it is it means very little, and her most liberal tariffs do not even meet our most severe protection.[8]

Nevertheless, in 1936 it did prove possible for the British to remove one of their preconditions to the conclusion of a trade treaty with the

United States, namely, currency stabilisation, still outstanding since the world economic conference.[9]

The opportunity for an agreement on currency exchanges was provided by the weakness of the French franc. By the middle of 1935 it was becoming clear to American experts that the French would soon have to abandon the gold standard and devalue the franc. This could set in train a process of competitive devaluation which Henry Morgenthau, who favoured currency stabilisation,[10] wished to avoid because of the disorder it would entail. He perceived, however, that Franco–American co-operation in currency matters might persuade the British to come round to '*de facto* stabilisation'. Thus during May and June 1935 Morgenthau provided assistance to the French through the Stabilization Fund in order to support the franc.[11] This, however, could only delay the inevitable; it could not prevent it. The election of the popular front government in France in 1936 provided the final strain and the weakness of the franc in the wake of the Rhineland crisis encouraged the British, who since 1931 had managed sterling in terms of the franc and its gold base, to think in terms of monetary co-operation. In May 1936 Morgenthau was made aware of this after he had approached the British government; he learnt also of the desire of the British to maintain the current rate of exchange between the dollar and sterling. Cordell Hull was most gratified. He informed the Secretary of the Treasury: 'I congratulate you on the most important diplomatic step that has been taken . . . It touches the trade agreement programme; it touches everything.'[12]

During the summer of 1936 discussions took place between the British and Americans concerning France and the franc, but the reluctance of the French to formally abandon the gold standard and the disinclination of the British to appear to be forcing them off it caused progress to be slow until heavy French gold losses at the end of August turned the situation. Thus on 25 September the devaluation of the franc by 25–34.35 per cent was announced in Washington, London and Paris and, *mutatis mutandis*, similar statements were issued by the three governments affirming their desire to maintain equilibrium in the money markets and their hopes for a relaxation 'of the present system of quotas and exchange controls with a view to their abolition'. The dollar and sterling were to exchange at about $5.00.[13]

Morgenthau was ecstatic about this achievement. Prior to its realisation he wrote:

If this goes through I think it is the greatest move taken for peace in the world since the World War . . . It may be the turning point for again resuming rational thinking in Europe. It may be just the thing to bring reason back to these perfectly mad people. Let's hope so . . . After all, we are the only three liberal governments left . . . And the beauty of the thing is – there are no signatures. It is good faith. We have confidence in each other, and I would ten times rather shake hands than have all the signatures in the world. Signatures haven't been worth much.[14]

In retrospect some authorities in this field have been less enthusiastic and even dismissive of the importance of the tripartite currency declaration.[15] While it is true that the declaration, as Morgenthau observed, committed no government and while the British continued to remain opposed to formal stabilisation of sterling and currency management, preferring to aspire to the ultimate reinstatement of the international gold standard and the free exchange of gold,[16] it nevertheless did, as Kindleberger has observed, constitute 'a significant step in rebuilding the international economic system'.[17] The Americans, influenced by the views of Schacht, contemplated during the winter of 1936 and 1937 making further progress on the bases propounded by the German minister of economics; in the spring of 1937 Norman Davis was sent to London to ascertain the views of the British government regarding the Schacht initiative.[18] The British, meanwhile, had already begun the process of building upon the tripartite currency declaration through the good offices of the Belgian Prime Minister, Paul Van Zeeland. Given the balance of payments deficit of £18 million at the end of 1936, there were strong reasons why the British government should want to encourage an enquiry into the possibilities of liberalising trade. In addition, one of the reasons why they later found the Schacht proposals attractive was that they promised advances in precisely this direction.

Immediately after the announcement of the tripartite currency declaration it had been suggested by the French that Van Zeeland be asked to undertake some preparatory groundwork with a view to ascertaining the attitudes of the various interested powers on the measures necessary to give effect to the policy outlined in the declaration. At the end of November 1936, Sir Frederick Leith-Ross put precisely this suggestion to the Belgian premier. Van Zeeland replied on 21 January 1937. If invited he was prepared to prepare a 'plan for the demobilisation of trade barriers'. To set this in train he suggested that a Belgian banker, M. Frère, should tour the principal European countries and perhaps the United States. The view of the Foreign Office was that it had been initially hoped to ascertain through Van Zeeland what contribution the Germans could make towards the improvement of international trading conditions. This now seemed superfluous as it was anticipated that a direct answer would be obtained from Dr Schacht when he met Leith-Ross.[19] Orme Sargent had, for his part, considered the Van Zeeland idea dead and viewed its 'resurrection' as 'embarrassing'. Nothing could be done until Leith-Ross had seen Schacht, or the nature of Hitler's forthcoming speech had been analysed. Furthermore, there was the matter of the Anglo–French loan discussions which might be a more convenient forum for discussing the relaxation of French quotas than an enquiry by Van Zeeland. For Leith-Ross this was undoubtedly yet a further example of the obstructionism and unreasonableness of the Foreign Office. On 30 January he informed Sargent:

> I do not agree that it is too late to try and give effect to the Three Power currency declaration. Our position is as stated by the Chancellor [Neville Chamberlain] . . . that though no actual negotiations are taking place we continue to keep in constant contact with the other governments concerned and will take every opportunity of promoting the policy set out in the agreement.

He thought, therefore, that there was still much to commend Van Zeeland undertaking some preparatory investigations.[20] Within the Foreign Office Ashton-Gwatkin supported Leith-Ross as did the Board of Trade and the Chancellor of the Exchequer. Eventually, the Foreign Office had to give way, and on 11 February 1937 Leith-Ross informed Van Zeeland of the British government's acceptance of the latter's willingness to undertake an enquiry and its agreement that M. Frère should carry out the primary work.[21]

At an early stage the Americans were advised of Van Zeeland's offer to conduct an enquiry, although Lindsay was instructed to make it clear to the United States government that the problems likely to obstruct progress were 'very great'.[22] Just how great was revealed when Leith-Ross informed the French that their earlier suggestions concerning Van Zeeland had been acted upon. In a private letter to M. Jacques Rueff of the French ministry of economics, Leith-Ross stated:

I hope that M. Spinasse . . . has not lost his former interest in the abolition of quotas. It seems to me that if international action is taken in this matter, the attitude adopted by the French Government is of decisive importance. Moreover, I believe that it is becoming every day more evident that the relaxation of your quotas is in the interests not only of international trade but of France herself . . . I hope therefore that some action will be taken and that M. Spinasse's discouraging reference to 'economic weapons' does not close the door.

On the other hand, Leith-Ross was optimistic that conditions in Europe were auspicious for a mission such as that envisaged by Van Zeeland: he thought that Schacht 'would probably be ready to take "luxury" goods if he' could 'get better export outlets'.[23] In the event the French agreed to associate themselves with the British, at the beginning of April 1937, in formally inviting Van Zeeland to undertake an enquiry into the possibilities of dismantling economic nationalism.[24]

As was earlier suggested, it was immediately decided that M. Frère should survey opinion in European capitals while Van Zeeland himself would take soundings in Washington.[25] At the start of his tour Frère visited London, where he had a conversation with Leith-Ross. As he had earlier intimated to M. Rueff, the latter indicated the importance of the French doing something about relaxing their quotas, especially in respect of countries operating exchange control systems. The current French position was that they would not relax their quotas in favour of such states, but Leith-Ross saw little prospect of bringing about the abolition of exchange control unless states employing such measures 'obtained outlets for their exports, which were largely manufactured goods'. Frère observed that it was likely that the Germans would raise the question of raw materials, to which Leith-Ross replied that in his opinion that was not a 'real' issue. The Germans wanted export markets and there was a chance that at this juncture they would be met. Frère, he thought, would be well-advised to 'avoid discussing colonial and political questions'.[26]

This advice, especially when dealing with Schacht, was easier to offer than to act upon. During the course of April 1937 Schacht visited Brussels where, apart from launching an absurd attack on the United Kingdom in which he alleged that British policy was largely the cause of the current 'extraordinary mentality' in

Germany,[27] he entertained Van Zeeland to a repetition of the views he had conveyed to Leith-Ross the previous February. Schacht stressed Germany's desire for economic co-operation, but he considered it to be contingent upon a prior political settlement, which presumably meant that Germany would acquire colonies. The colonial obsession was challenged by Van Zeeland. Discussing this matter with Eden in Brussels, the British Foreign Secretary endorsed the Belgian's attitude on this point. There was little that Germany could gain economically from colonial territory in Africa that it would be possible to return to her; he thought the open-door ideal to be a far better possibility for Germany in Africa. Van Zeeland, however, was not despondent regarding the prospects for international co-operation in economic matters. Economic circumstances in both Germany and Italy were poor and this fact, coupled 'with the rearmament and consequently increased authority of Great Britain in Europe, were conducive to a greater appreciation of the value of international collaboration'.[28]

It was also the American view that the prospects were good at this time for improved international economic relations. Speaking to Lord Cranborne, the under-secretary of state for foreign affairs, Norman Davis emphasised that it appeared that the Germans were 'moderating their views' and inclined towards a general settlement. The French were also becoming more accessible to reason. Cranborne, however, pointed out that in the sphere of economic appeasement it would be impossible for Britain to do much without the conclusion of a political agreement in advance. Davis explained that he was anxious to find out if there was a way that negotiations could be started for a political settlement. President Roosevelt was keen to become involved in such a settlement, 'but very reluctant to do so unless the moment was opportune'. It was thought by Cranborne that Germany could start the process and if so that would provide an opportunity for the American President to intervene; in his view, 'the key to the whole problem lay in the hands of the United States themselves'. It would be of 'overwhelming importance' if the views of the United States were vigorously publicised. But Davis objected that the United States could not become involved politically: 'They might, however, make an approach to Europe by way of some economic agreement. He said that one could get away with murder under the name of economic appeasement in the United States today.' The American representative urged the speedy conclusion of an Anglo–American trade agreement, the preliminary exchanges having already begun.[29]

While in London, Davis also saw Eden and Chamberlain. To the former he intimated that while the United States wanted to co-operate in bringing about 'economic rehabilitation and disarma-ment', it would be necessary first for Britain to put herself fully behind any such efforts. Eden stated that the time had not yet come for such developments. On 29 April Chamberlain made it plain to Davis that while Britain was still investigating the Schacht proposals and had not dismissed appeasement, there would have to be substantial agreement at least in principle on political matters before moving on to economic issues. Furthermore, he did not think it would be possible for Britain to discuss disarmament until British rearmament was more complete. Both Eden and Chamberlain, however, were keen on the prosecution of the Anglo–American trade talks, although the complications presented by the Ottawa agreements and imperial preference would involve difficulties and delay. Still, the purpose of Davis's mission, to persuade the British to prime an international effort for peace, had failed.[30] At the beginning of his sojourn in London Davis had revealed to the French minister of economics, M. Spinasse, impatience with the British attitude over the colonial question and disappointment concerning their position on the trade agreement. He was, there-fore, no happier at the end. Significantly, Davis exhibited an interest in the Van Zeeland enquiry, which was now to enter its crucial phase.[31]

Towards the end of May Frère had completed the first stage of his European tour having visited Berlin, The Hague, Paris, Berne and Rome. Accordingly he briefed Leith-Ross on his impressions so far. In Berlin he had found Schacht clamant on the colonial question, although he now demanded a 99 year lease on colonial territory rather than the transfer of territory. In return he promised German commitment to freer international trade, the ultimate removal of quotas and the ending of exchange control. Goering, on the other hand, disputed the emphasis placed by Schacht on the colonial question. For his part, he thought that if private property held abroad could be guaranteed in time of war, the German government would be able to encourage its citizens to invest overseas, and he implied that were the League to abolish Article 16 of the convenant that might bring about relaxation in the German Four Year Plan. Frère's 'impression was that Germany was not in extreme economic difficulties; the shortage of raw materials had not yet developed to the point where a crisis was imminent, and consequently Dr Schacht was trying to sell his co-operation at a price.' More importantly, both Schacht and Goering 'seemed much clearer about what they wanted than what they had to offer'.

In Paris Frère found a commitment to the renunciation of the quota system in the 'framework of a general international agreement', but there was strong pressure from industrialists and the unions for increased protection. The minister of commerce, M. Bastid, felt that many of France's difficulties were due to British imperial preference. Frère's discussions in Paris had been heavily marked by emphasis on 'Monetary security' and the need for 'general stabilisation of currencies'. In both the Netherlands and Switzerland Frère found a strong desire for economic co-operation in an international form. He had also been well received in Italy where there was a strong desire for a currency stabilisation; as part of such an agreement, the Italians wanted to secure support for the lira. Ciano told Frère that Italy was prepared 'to come into any effective scheme, but not an inadequately prepared international conference'. Asking Leith-Ross and his associates what Britain was prepared to contribute, Frère was told that Britain at this stage could offer little more than the hope that she would not have to increase tariffs. At the end of this meeting Frère emphasised that three points had emerged from his discussions: first, an unprepared conference was regarded as undesirable; secondly, British imperial preferences were held to be particularly damaging to international trade; thirdly, there was a need for currency stabilisation.[32]

The British government were well aware of the sort of criticisms that had been directed at them concerning trade policy. On 4 May 1937 an interdepartmental committee on trade policy had been constituted on the initiative of Neville Chamberlain. Its report, presented on 6 June, asserted that British protection and imperial preference had adversely affected trade with foreign countries. Germany, Italy and Japan would all denounce Britain as the principal cause of their difficulties. Moreover, while Britain wanted to co-operate with France and the United States in matters affecting trade, both complained about Britain's protectionism. The committee thought that Britain was well able to defend her record of 'keeping open the channels of trade', but the problem was that the United Kingdom, along with the USA and France, was one of the world's three great creditor states and any practice on her part of economic nationalism, or imposition of 'restrictive policies', was bound to attract adverse comment and criticism. Now that it was established, it would be very difficult to break imperial preference.

The committee, however, suggested that in addition to impressing upon the dominions 'the importance of consenting to those modifications of their preferential rights now required in the interests of an Anglo–American Agreement', the British government should indicate its readiness to make equivalent sacrifices in any agreements that the dominions were able to conclude with the United States or other nations. On quotas it was recommended that the government should be prepared to abolish the quantitative regulation of bacon imports. With regard to tariffs it was suggested that the UK import duties advisory committee should only in very special circumstances endorse further duties and that there should be a review of all tariffs. The demand for the application of the 'open-door' principle in the colonies was considered undesirable because of the threat of cheap Japanese manufactured goods. Nevertheless, it was argued that it would be necessary to modify preferences in the colonies, not because it would do much good, but because it was thought that 'it would have a good psychological effect in Europe and America' and because Britain had sponsored the raw materials enquiry at Geneva. In other words, colonial preferences should be altered because others thought, however misguidedly, that such action would be beneficial. On Germany, the committee felt that that country should be pressed to return to normal trading practices, which to a large extent was the nub of the problem.[33]

During June Van Zeeland made his visit to the United States. Speaking at a dinner given in his honour by the council for foreign relations in New York, Van Zeeland publicly argued the case for the importance of his enquiry. He stated:

> All these rumours and threats of war are far from constituting an insurmountable barrier to closer economic relations and are, to my mind, a further reason to act, and to act swiftly. Delay at this moment is against the interest of peace.

Referring to the economic difficulties with which certain of the leading nations were faced he warned:

> Should these difficulties become more acute, they might – who knows? – create an internal situation so strained that recourse to

war would appear as the lesser of two evils, or as a last desperate card to play.

He was, therefore, gratified at the support that his ideas for improving world economic conditions had received in the United States.[34] On his return to Brussels Van Zeeland expressed himself well satisfied with his American trip. He felt that Cordell Hull had already contributed much to the dismantling of barriers to trade and was impressed by 'America's readiness to support every effort to maintain the peace of the world'. World peace and the resumption of world trade were, he thought, the twin foundations of the future.[35] Van Zeeland was, in fact, very much more optimistic with regard to genuine American collaboration than the British. He considered 'Roosevelt was both ready and anxious to promote action which would help to restore peaceful conditions in Europe and . . . that he would be quite ready to include financial aid if a definite plan promoting real results could be put forward'.[36]

In London it was hoped that Van Zeeland would circulate fairly soon his conclusions resulting from the travels of Frère and himself. The Belgian Prime Minister, however, wanted further semi-official exchanges with the governments concerned. It was, he believed, possible that the Americans would become involved if the other countries accepted the need to promote the maintenance of peace by international co-operation, the progressive removal of hindrances to international exchanges of all kinds, the 'abolition or attenuation' of 'discriminatory systems', and the return to 'complete equality' in economic agreements. Both Leith-Ross and Neville Chamberlain were disappointed by this turn of events. They had understood that Van Zeeland would issue a statement of principles without further enquiry, but if Van Zeeland wanted more discussion and another meeting with Leith-Ross it was felt that he could not be refused.[37] Leith-Ross, however, was unavailable for such a meeting until October. This was found inconvenient by Van Zeeland because political developments in Belgium were likely to have forced him from office by then.[38] Leith-Ross, though, now asked him not to be in too much of a hurry. Van Zeeland eventually agreed to present a report which would be discussed by a committee of four (Van Zeeland himself, and representatives from Britain, France and the United States), which could then widen the discussion by inviting the participation of representatives from other states. According to Leith-Ross, 'the question of creating a permanent body can be reserved till we see how things develop'.[39] Clearly, it was hoped that something of substance would emerge from these labours.

When Leith-Ross finally visited Brussels he did not meet Van Zeeland, who had gone into retreat in order to prepare his report, but spoke to Frère and the secretary-general of the Belgian foreign ministry, Langenhove. According to the Belgians the issue of exchange control was the most problematic and the draft report would recommend ways in which this might be abolished. It was in Van Zeeland's mind to communicate the report first to the governments of Britain, France and the United States and to ask them to send representatives to Brussels where representatives of the states practising exchange control would also be invited to discuss their difficulties. This procedure was not liked in the Foreign Office, where it was thought the German and Italian governments would take offence at it. Rather it was felt that the final report should be transmitted simultaneously to all the governments concerned. In essence the Foreign Office argued in favour of first receiving the report and then deciding upon procedure.[40] This in the end was what happened.

At the end of November 1937 Leith-Ross finally saw Van Zeeland and was simultaneously favoured with a copy of the draft of his report.[41] It was not, however, finally published until 26 January 1938. The report opened by stating that the autarchic policies pursued by various nations in the wake of the depression could do nothing other than lower the standard of living in those countries. Only the fostering of international trade could ensure prosperity within national frontiers. An underlying assumption of the report was that such views would be shared almost universally by contemporary statesmen. The report, however, in its preliminary remarks, highlighted a major difficulty in that while there was support for these views in many quarters, when it came to discussing practical details there was 'a very marked reserve'. In dealing with obstacles to trade, tariffs were first touched upon. It was not considered that these were a major impediment in the way of increased trade, but it was recommended that governments should not increase or expand tariffs and should undertake a gradual reduction in duties. Bilateral commercial treaties incorporating the most-favoured-nation clause were adjudged 'one of the most efficacious methods for reducing tariff barriers'. Indirect protection could also best be eliminated by bilateral agreements. Quotas were severely condemned by the report. They should be phased out over a period of time so as not to provoke undue dislocation, but in the meantime it was hoped that agreement could be reached not to impose further quotas or tighten those already in existence.

One of the most serious obstacles to trade though was found to be exchange control and 'clearing' systems. The re-establishment of the gold standard, even in a much altered form, was regarded as the ideal solution, but that was for the future. The report, therefore, advocated as an interim measure the revision and extension of the tripartite currency declaration. States currently employing exchange control practices would in the first instance agree to the stabilisation of their currencies; to protect them in the period of transition a central fund of the Bank for International Settlements would be created and contributed to by participating nations 'to support the exchange of any of the participants in the scheme who might temporarily find difficulty in maintaining the external value of their currency at the agreed level'.[42]

Although Leith-Ross had wished to avoid the colonial question being discussed in the report, it had not proved possible to ignore it altogether. It featured in its final section which dealt with issues that were not considered direct impediments to trade, but which, nevertheless, hindered 'the smooth flow of commercial relations between nations'. It was acknowledged that some governments perceived their main economic problem to be the unequal distribution of raw materials, or rather the unequal distribution of territories containing them. For these governments the best solution was the redistribution of colonial territory. The report, however, did not endorse such a step, but rather indicated a number of possibilities that had been variously suggested. It was possible that the mandates system could be revised by removing the 'national element' and making it 'completely international, both from the economic and political point of view'. In colonies proper, the open-door system as practised in the Congo basin could be extended to them all. In cases where this was not possible 'privileged companies' could be established 'whose activities would be strictly limited to the economic sphere and whose capital would be divided internationally in such a way as to offer real guarantees of impartiality'. Concerning raw materials, the report observed:

a most interesting proposal has been formulated tending to the supply of colonial goods in exchange for industrial products. An agreement would be concluded between a colony and an industrial State, and colonial goods supplied would be carried to an account and paid for by the execution in return of important public works – bridges, railways, ports, &c. The immediate finance would be provided by the metropolitan State.

The report concluded by calling for the conclusion of a pact of economic collaboration, the first step towards which would be a meeting between representatives of the United States, Britain, France, Germany and Italy to thrash out a number of important questions.[43]

Even before its publication difficulties in the way of making progress on the basis of the work done by the Belgian Prime Minister began to manifest themselves. As has already been mentioned, Leith-Ross had seen a draft of the report at the end of the previous November. He told Van Zeeland that he was favourable to much contained in it, but the suggestion of a central fund administered by the Bank for International Settlements to assist states which were abandoning exchange control provoked difficulties. There were large issues involved and Britain's attitude would be very much contingent upon American co-operation. On the section in the report dealing with colonies and raw materials Leith-Ross observed that there was not much to commend the idea of 'privileged' or chartered companies. Furthermore, he did not think that British industrialists would be very enamoured of 'barter arrangements for Colonial public works'. Replying to the comments of Leith-Ross, Van Zeeland admitted that there was not really a raw materials problem, but he had felt it essential to make some reference to the subject.

> He thought that if Germany really wished to deal with the problem on economic lines, some advantage could be obtained from Chartered Companies, and Belgium was ready to make barter arrangements for the Congo, e.g. to build railways which they couldn't afford in exchange for bananas which they couldn't otherwise sell.[44]

Still, Leith-Ross was impressed with the report; he understood that Van Zeeland would see the French and Germans privately before the report was published.

In the Foreign Office Ashton-Gwatkin was enthusiastic. As he pointed out, the objective of the recommendations contained in the report was to bring Germany and Italy into the framework of the tripartite currency declaration. The crucial point, though, was to get Germany in. Technically Germany could come in and there were elements in Germany that would welcome such a development economically. But in political terms it would mean a retreat from autarchy. He commented:

> If we require from Germany a manifest sign, e.g., in return for colonies, that she will work for European peace, there can be no more practical sign, or more sensitive touchstone than economic cooperation and modification of self-sufficiency.
>
> It is at the centre of any possible future development of peace with Germany . . . and very closely connected with the colonial question; and should be studied in this relation here, at home; and internationally.[45]

Germany's willingness, or lack of it, to co-operate in matters pertaining to the international economy would, therefore, prove her sincerity in responding to attempts at political appeasement.

Ashton-Gwatkin was, at this time, very keen on developing the colonial question in such a way as to promote international collaboration in economic matters. At the end of November 1937 Mr Eastwood of the Colonial Office sent to the Foreign Office a purely private and personal commentary objecting to the transfer of colonial territory to Germany, but suggesting simultaneously a scheme based upon the Berlin Act of 1885 and the mandates system that would give 'renewed reality and increased content to the ideals of international co-operation for the wellbeing and peaceful development not only of the mandated territories but of the whole of tropical Africa'. What Eastwood proposed was the creation of an international commission that would supervise development in tropical Africa. The commission would be composed of representatives from all the colonial powers, plus two or three from non-colonial states. It would have a right of inspection, it would be able to undertake major public works, it could encourage development through large companies and should prepare the ground for an ultimate customs union. There would be no change in the current administrative complexion of the continent. Eastwood stated:

> The primary object of the scheme would be to convince public opinion in this country and elsewhere that failure to satisfy

Germany was not due to selfish causes. It is not pretended that the scheme would go any distance towards satisfying Germany, and if it were adopted the Powers should go ahead with it irrespective of Germany's reaction to it.[46]

In a minute of 6 December Ashton-Gwatkin observed that he feared that Germany was going to obtain the 'transfer of a colonial area in full sovereignty'. This he thought a retrograde step in comparison with Eastwood's enlightened approach. His proposal would not be welcomed in Germany, where it would be regarded as 'dodging', but he saw a future for it in the anticipated signature of the Anglo–American trade agreement in 1938. Roosevelt should then be ready to take joint action with Britain for the maintenance of peace and Britain ought to have a programme already prepared. One of the main elements would have to relate to colonies and Eastwood's proposals would serve well. Ashton-Gwatkin felt that such ideas presented by Britain alone would doom them, but they 'might come from President Roosevelt'.[47]

But American opinion was not overwhelmingly enthusiastic about acting on the Van Zeeland report. Cordell Hull liked the report's 'general tone', but thought that there would be more benefit in an enunciation of the 'principles of international co-operation', such as those adumbrated in the various speeches he had given. He also intimated

> that the United States Trade Agreement policy is the most useful method of making progress, since the reduction of tariff barriers spreads as new agreements . . . are made. He suggested that other countries which had hitherto participated in such negoti-ations should be urged to proceed in this direction, i.e. by bilateral negotiations, without delay. He was anxious that countries should not wait for the comprehensive solution, which might be a distant one, but that they should do what they can, by individual and bilateral efforts, to reduce barriers when and as opportunity occurs.

Hull generally thought that the report glossed too easily over 'economic disequilibria' such as rearmament and, ominously, he considered that the central fund proposal would create problems in the United States.[48] This was not very encouraging. Nor was the news from France following the publication of the report. There was considerable interest in its contents, but scepticism as to its practicality at that time. Monick, the financial attaché at the French embassy in London, told Leith-Ross that he was not impressed by it, finding it something of a jumble, but he agreed that the British and French governments could not just drop the report. On the other hand, he was apprehensive of the situation in France which he thought might end in the imposition of exchange control![49]

Nevertheless, Neville Chamberlain was determined, if he could, to make progress on the foundations laid by Van Zeeland. On 1 February he stated in the Commons that the report would be treated as an 'urgent matter'.[50] At a Cabinet meeting the following day he proposed that Van Zeeland should now be asked to visit Washington, Berlin and Rome for further discussions. He admitted, however, that 'nations were not at present in a receptive spirit' and that this was an obstacle. But, he continued, 'If we could obtain a more conciliatory atmosphere the prospects of some arrangement would be more satisfactory.' Interestingly, Neville Chamberlain had previously outlined to Leith-Ross in some depth his reservations regarding the Van Zeeland report. Given Germany's present mood, it was, he thought, likely that Germany would consider the recommendations in it 'as a favour asked from her rather than offered to her'; she would, therefore, contemplate further demands as the price of her acceptance. He then stated:

> I regard a scheme of this kind as the sort of plan which may some day be practicable and which may then give us something like a solution of the economic difficulties of Europe. But I think it will have to wait until the general political settlement is at least in sight. We should then be working in an atmosphere of goodwill in which every country would be looking for ways of helping instead of examining every new proposal to find the nigger in the woodpile. In such an atmosphere even the U.S.A. might be disposed to lend a hand without provoking the virulent hostility of Congress.
>
> I disagree with some who think you can solve political difficulties by removing economic thorns from the flesh. Politics in international affairs govern actions at the expense of economics, and often of reason.

This clearly indicates the primacy of political appeasement in Chamberlain's foreign policy calculations although, of course, economic considerations were a powerful stimulant to the need for international political agreement. Chamberlain might well have echoed Roosevelt's criticism of Cordell Hull's reciprocal trade treaties as a means of securing peace – they were 'just too goddamned slow'.[51] At the Cabinet meeting of 2 February the Prime Minister had intimated that one of the better responses to the Van Zeeland report had come from Germany.[52] It was, however, Germany and the attitude and actions of its Führer that ultimately turned the report into an irrelevance.

Even before Hitler's speech of 20 February 1938 it was believed in the Foreign Office that Germany had recently been moving more and more in a direction of economic isolation, which boded ill for any efforts towards international economic collaboration.[53] This impression was confirmed by Hitler's denunciation of international plans and his observation that it was 'a joke of history' that 'those very countries which are themselves suffering from depressions . . . consider it necessary to criticise us and give us good advice'. Foreign states had contributed nothing whatever to Germany's very successful economic salvation. Moreover, Germany would not bargain away her just colonial claim in exchange for credits.[54] The following day Leith-Ross commented:

> It seems to me that the passages in Hitler's speech on economic subjects – and particularly the statement that he could not deal with international plans which are uncertain and lack clarity – show that there is little prospect of any cordial response from Germany at the present time to the Van Zeeland proposals. Indeed, Hitler's statements are so definite that he wants Colonies, but is not prepared to offer anything in return, that it seems to me doubtful whether anything can come of the further tour . . . suggested for Van Zeeland.[55]

On the eve of the *Anschluss*, Ashton-Gwatkin, in a Foreign Office memorandum, highlighted the gulf that separated the democracies and the dictatorships by showing that in almost every particular German economic policy was tending in the opposite direction to that recommended by Van Zeeland. Whereas Van Zeeland wanted to modify autarchy, the Germans wanted to intensify it; whereas Van Zeeland wanted to abolish exchange control, the Germans wanted to maintain it; whereas Van Zeeland wanted to expand the open, international economy, Germany wanted to extend its closed area into central and south-eastern Europe.[56] Writing in the *Political Quarterly*, Hugh Gaitskell, the future leader of the Labour Party, was more blunt. He argued that in both Germany and Italy political considerations had primacy over economic ones. It was not the purpose of state control of the economy in these countries to increase their national income, but rather 'to prepare . . . for war'. Autarchy had been introduced and synthetic raw materials were being manufactured 'not because they cannot be obtained from abroad, nor even because of crazy Nazi economic theory, but because of the fear of blockade in a future war'.[57] The prospects for Van Zeeland were therefore decidedly bleak.

The *Anschluss* of March 1938 made them bleaker still. Ashton-Gwatkin was inclined to put a favourable gloss on this – the customs barrier between Austria and Germany had at least been removed! And he advocated a resumption by Van Zeeland of his work. Leith-Ross, however, dismissed this suggestion out of hand. The *Anschluss* had stunned the world and the government would be 'bitterly attacked' if it attempted to make progress in the current circumstances. He did not believe that the Van Zeeland report should be abandoned completely, but that further action should be suspended pending more favourable circumstances.[58] In the context of the mounting Czech crisis, this was not an immediate prospect. On 13 July 1938 the Cabinet decided that for the time being no useful purpose could be served by pursuing the Van Zeeland proposals.[59]

Following the Munich conference it was very much hoped by Neville Chamberlain that the right conditions had been created for the settlement with Germany of outstanding political and economic issues.[60] Accordingly, there was brief consideration of a resumption of Van Zeeland's mission in October and November 1938. Van Zeeland, on a visit to London, saw Leith-Ross and opined that the time was now ripe for an initiative to reduce trade barriers to 'be launched with real hope of success'. The United States, he believed, would collaborate; in France the situation was becoming so difficult that he considered French co-operation inevitable. He did, however, admit that Germany was a problem. That country 'was concentrating all her energies on war preparations under a regime of control of that of war-time'. It was probable that she would not participate, but he thought there was something to be said for proceeding without her. Leith-Ross disagreed with the Belgian's analysis. He thought the posture of the United States in respect of tariffs discouraging and the French he considered had not carried out all their assurances in the tripartite currency declaration. But Germany was the crucial issue. Without her 'nothing could really be done'. He realised the force of Van Zeeland's comments regarding German rearmament, but his impression was 'that there were some indications that she [Germany] might be willing to take part in international discussions if definite and concrete proposals could be found'.[61]

Within the Foreign Office Ashton-Gwatkin was much more optimistic. He believed that now Germany had solved the problem of central Europe on her terms, there was a distinct possibility that a 'fresh start' could be made in the direction of international economic collaboration. He thought contact with Goering the key to success and the colonial question a central element in any deal. He wrote:

I think the economic sphere . . . is much the best for dealing with the colonial question and that the return of colonies should be part of an economic settlement rather than a political one (though I don't want to over-emphasize the distinction since it is not a very real one). But I have always thought that the return of Germany to the Western economy would be a more real counter-weight to the return of colonies to Germany than a necessarily uncertain agreement regarding armaments; also that the return of a colony to a relatively free area would be very much less objectionable than a return of a colony to the present German currency system.

The idea of 'privileged' or chartered companies in colonial territory also appealed. Ashton-Gwatkin doubted if Van Zeeland was any longer the right person to conduct such negotiations, but he was happy for him to continue if the Germans were satisfied with him.[62]

The sort of proposals that Leith-Ross had in mind for encouraging German economic collaboration seem to be those he presented to a German economic delegation in London on 19 October. He suggested a scheme of reciprocal trade whereby the need of Balkan countries to acquire the foreign exchange necessary to buy British and colonial goods could be satisfied. If the western powers were to provide Germany with up to 25 per cent more foreign exchange to purchase Balkan produce, the Balkan states could use that exchange to buy British and colonial goods and thus stimulate world trade. These proposals have been seen as part of a British attempt to create a European economic bloc to counter American competition, but this overlooks the fact that the first question Leith-Ross asked the

German delegation was, what did they think of the Van Zeeland scheme? Disappointingly he was told that while the German government was naturally in favour of international economic co-operation, the Van Zeeland proposals were not as a whole regarded in Germany as 'a suitable basis for discussion', although some of the Belgian's suggestions did perhaps merit some consideration. Leith-Ross was, however, assured that his suggestions would be transmitted to Berlin for consideration. It seems, therefore, more likely that Leith-Ross had mentioned the 'ever growing strength of the economy of the United States' in order to attract the Germans to the virtues of economic co-operation generally, rather than as an anti-American move.[63]

Indeed hostility towards America on the part of Chamberlain and Leith-Ross has probably been overplayed. Despite the difficulties, Chamberlain had been keen to see the completion of an Anglo–American trade agreement from the moment he became Prime Minister;[64] in the weeks following the Munich conference this ambition was realised. In the end the British had to concede more to the American point of view than they wanted but, as Halifax commented, the political importance of the treaty now exceeded 'trade and economic considerations', for any major rift between Britain and the United States could only encourage the Japanese and Germans to be more difficult than ever.[65] Thus on 17 November 1938 the Anglo–American trade agreement was signed on the 'old Lincoln table' in the East Room of the White House.[66] It may well be that Chamberlain feared that the United States would adopt the role of *tertius gaudens* in any Anglo–German conflict, but not to the point at which he became so rationally and morally bereft that he would do any deal with the Germans to avoid such an eventuality. Moreover, as Corbin, the French ambassador in London, observed it was best not to make too much of Anglo–American differences, which, given time, usually disappeared, and it was certainly inadvisable to try to exploit them.[67]

When Leith-Ross again saw Rüter, the head of the German economic delegation, he was told that it had not been possible to obtain a reaction from Berlin regarding his proposals. Rüter, who apparently saw Leith-Ross on instructions to spin out 'matters as far as possible', claimed in his record of the conversation that Leith-Ross made no further mention of a conference of economic experts of the four great European powers, although Leith-Ross's record mentions that Rüter approved the idea of continuing economic discussions, mentioning Van Zeeland as the best intermediary. It is, however, clear that Leith-Ross was becoming despondent and disenchanted, emphasising to Rüter 'a certain disappointment felt in Great Britain that, in spite of repeated British advances, there was in Germany apparently still no great readiness to build upon the basis of the Munich Agreement'.[68]

His worst fears were confirmed by a conversation with a prominent German banker, Dr Otto Jeidels, who had been very close to those in Germany responsible for the Four Year Plan, and who was about to take up a post in the United States. Jeidels informed Leith-Ross:

> We ought to realise that Nazi Germany was definitely an aggressive power. Hitler himself aimed at being a Napoleon and whatever he said he wanted war. Of course, he wanted it to be a little war, like the one against Czechoslovakia alone. He was as hard as stone; we could expect no fairness and no generosity from him. He would take anything he could get and give nothing in exchange.

Relaying this to Sir Horace Wilson, Leith-Ross advised:

> By all means let us cultivate his [Hitler's] acquaintance but don't count on him, and above all don't imagine that we can gain his real friendship; if we do there will be bitter disappointments in store. And meanwhile, the stronger we can make ourselves the better will be the chances of peace for Europe.[69]

The Foreign Office had from the moment Van Zeeland exhibited his willingness to resume his work been generally lukewarm.[70] The *Kristallnacht* pogrom and the atmosphere emanating from Germany finally killed off any prospect of further development along this line. Significantly, the briefing for the Prime Minister and Foreign Secretary for the Anglo–French talks at the end of November suggested that there was no further point in taking up the threads of the Van Zeeland report.[71]

The Van Zeeland report was ultimately to have a relevance for the future rather than the present. It served as a precursor of the kind of international economic co-operation established after 1945. Still, it is an indicator of the sort of international settlement that the British wished to promote in the 1930s, even if it was overwhelmed by the events of 1938 and 1939. Political and economic aspects were very closely intertwined and, thus, almost inevitably, despite the deprecations of Leith-Ross, the colonial question was involved. An examination of the Van Zeeland enquiry and report shows just how great the gulf was that existed between Nazi Germany and the democracies. Essentially the latter wished to promote international co-operation; the former wished to pursue the international competition of the *Völkerwanderung*. Finally, although the enquiry was undertaken by a Belgian, it is clear that the British were the driving force behind it from the beginning. While, therefore, mistrust of the United States played a significant part in the decision of Neville Chamberlain to reject Roosevelt's peace initiative of January 1938, which among other things aimed at a considerable measure of economic appeasement, it is also worth noting that, in addition to British efforts at appeasement which it was held the President's scheme would cut across, the British were pursuing their own scheme of economic appeasement which possibly would have suffered adversely by untimely intervention from the other side of the Atlantic. The role played by Sir Frederick Leith-Ross in this was substantial and he emerges as a very considerable figure in the formulation of British policy in the years 1937 and 1938.

Various economic and financial contacts with the Germans were maintained in the months succeeding Munich, but it is perhaps wise not to read too much into them. The hope of ultimate success was limited, for as Leith-Ross informed Berkeley Gage in July 1939:

> My main criticism is that the policy which Chamberlain tried to carry through has been made impossible by Hitler's actions after Munich, and it is in Germany the change of leadership seems necessary. As no German seems to be competent for the job, they might offer it to Schuschnigg or Benesch [sic]![72]

10
Conclusion

In the months succeeding the *Anschluss* Hitler's plans moved rapidly towards their denouement and the colonial question never again verged upon the point of becoming practical politics, as the British government concentrated upon patching up Europe as crisis succeeded crisis. For the British government to have raised the colonial question it would have been necessary for them to have held the initiative. This they did not. The initiative was firmly with Hitler. He was total master of his fate and that of Europe. Fixed upon his predetermined course, there was no possibility of his showing himself responsive to the normal give and take of international affairs. His mind was closed to compromise. Perceiving that the colonial question could be traded for nothing desired by them, the British government refused to allow it to enter the sphere of practical politics, although there were clearly occasions when it verged upon doing so, particularly in the immediate aftermath of the Munich conference when hopes of further appeasement were temporarily high.

On 10 March 1938 Leo Amery wrote to Lord Halifax, recommending to him Taylor's recently published *Germany's First Bid for Colonies*. He stated:

> There are a certain number of people who might acquiesce in the cession of Togoland and a bit of the Cameroons by France and ourselves in return for an absolute black and white pledge to leave Austria and Czechoslovakia in peace. But I think you will find the country practically unanimous in repudiating any idea of handing over Colonies to Germany as a mere 'peace offering', alias Danegeld.[1]

Amery need not have worried, at least for the immediate future. On 30 March Sir Nevile Henderson told Halifax that he had not mentioned the colonial question to anybody since his interview with Hitler on 3 March, and that he did not propose to do so. If he was taxed on the subject he intended saying that he was 'waiting for the promised written reply while adding that after Germany's last display of jungle law . . . [he found] . . . it difficult to believe that His Majesty's Government would be in the mood to think about colonies'.[2] Halifax thought that the written reply should not even be mentioned for, in his opinion, 'the prospect of any action of the kind we were contemplating in the colonial sphere has necessarily receded under the influence of recent events'.[3] This position was, in effect, stated publicly by the Prime Minister in the Commons on 16 March.[4] Later Halifax once again reassured the Portuguese ambassador that Britain was not going to negotiate over the Portuguese colonies.[5] In fact, there is nothing whatever to suggest that the British government, and particularly Lord Halifax, were, in the immediate pre-Munich period, still contemplating any kind of colonial deal.[6] For his part, Sir Nevile Henderson was very despondent about the prospects of any kind of *rapprochement*. He informed Leith-Ross: 'the Germans are impossible people. All foreigners are impossible: its a matter of degree but the Germans are worse than most – in their present uplift.' He was tired of his post, finding it 'unsatisfactory & disheartening'.[7]

Nevertheless, it was in the period from the *Anschluss* onwards that public anxiety in Britain and the empire was most manifest regarding the possibility of colonial retrocession.[8] And it was undoubtedly the impact of the Munich settlement that did most to stimulate such fears. At the Berchtesgaden meeting Hitler mentioned that colonies were still a German requirement, although they were not the subject of a 'bellicose demand'.[9] Again at the Godesberg meeting Hitler informed Chamberlain that Germany would bring up the colonial question, to which the latter replied that 'after the solution of the Czech crisis he had in mind further and greater problems'.[10] Subsequently, Chamberlain revealed in the Commons that the colonial question had been mentioned during his visits to Germany.[11] During the month following the Munich conference the German ambassador, von Dirksen, confidently reported back to Berlin the continued readiness of Chamberlain and the British government to consider colonial satisfaction for Germany, although as part of the policy of *détente* they felt they had inaugurated at Munich.

It should also be noted, however, that Dirksen's observations were not the result of conversations with 'official personages'.[12] Nonetheless, it is quite apparent that in the post-Munich review of policy that took place in the Foreign Office the colonial question remained an important element in the discussion. Strang was prepared to trade colonial concessions for British naval superiority, or German neutrality in certain instances. Ashton-Gwatkin wanted to offer colonial satisfaction to Germany in exchange for her co-operation in economic matters. The resulting consensus was contained in another memorandum by Strang in which he suggested the revamping of the approach to Germany that had been undertaken the previous March. Once France, Belgium, Portugal and Britain had agreed upon the scale of the colonial concessions that could be offered, 'he favoured dealing with Germany through the medium of an international conference'.[13] Naturally, these ruminations took place in private, but the fact of the matter was that the issue had featured once more during a major European crisis and the fact was well known throughout the British empire.

In east Africa the *Tanganyika League* was formed under the chairmanship of Major F. W. Cavendish-Bentinck with the objective of opposing the cession of the mandate.[14] Soon, a branch of this organisation was formed in Salisbury, Southern Rhodesia, where hostility towards colonial retrocession was also strong.[15] The fears of British settlers in Africa may well have been exaggerated, but they were real enough. Colonel Charles Ponsonby, MP, a member of the Joint East Africa Board, reporting on a recent visit to Tanganyika, informed the Colonial Secretary, Malcolm MacDonald:

> all over the country, at . . . Tanga, Moshi and Arusha and Dar es Salaam, when I was alone with British or Indians the subject [of colonial retrocession] always came up as the anxiety for a definite statement was almost pathetic.
>
> You will realise that all business commitments are restricted and no one wishes to venture any new capital in Tanganyika. Responsible Indians in Dar es Salaam, three or four of them members of the Legislative Council, told me privately that if they approached their banks for financial help, for instance for buying a plantation, the doubt as to the Mandate was always given as a reason for a refusal. I should be doing you a disservice if I did not emphasize the great apprehension of British and Indians lest the return of the Territory should form part of the discussion with Germany, and it is hardly necessary to point out that a state of uncertainty is a great deterrent to a young country both from the political and economic point of view.[16]

Similarly, Humphrey Leggett, chairman of the British East Africa Corporation Ltd., transmitted to MacDonald an extract from the report of the branch manager at Dar es Salaam which made gloomy reading. The report stated:

> The Mandate question is undoubtedly having an effect on the bazaars at the present moment, and dealers are scared about the placing of forward business. The situation has not yet reached a stage where dealers can make use of it for declining to meet their commitments, but there would undoubtedly be great difficulty should the Home Government show serious signs of giving way to the German threatened demands.

It was also recounted that one German was refusing to pay rent on the ground that the mandate would be in Germany's possession within six months.[17]

Unrest in Tanganyika found expression in mass meetings such as that at the Lupa goldfields and a meeting at Arusha where it was declared that the transfer of the territory would be resisted by force.[18] African opinion was equally eloquent in opposing the return of German administration.[19] Moreover, concern and disquiet were no less evident in neighbouring Kenya.[20] An attempt was made to mollify this anxiety when Neville Chamberlain replied in the Commons to a question on 14 November 1938. Asked if Britain contemplated transferring Tanganyika or any other part of Africa to another power, the Prime Minister replied 'No, Sir'.[21] Malcolm MacDonald immediately informed the governors of Britain's African colonies and possessions that Chamberlain's answer was to be interpreted as meaning that the government did not have in contemplation the transfer of any territory under British administration.[22] The following day Chamberlain explained to the Cabinet that his answer had been intended to indicate that there could be no colonial concessions outside a general settlement. Furthermore, as 'such a settlement was, he believed, clearly impossible in existing circumstances . . . it followed that there could be no question of a return of Colonies to Germany'.[23]

Thus the decision to foreclose with regard to colonial concessions was not taken merely in the light of public opinion and the knowledge that for Germany this was not a pressing issue.[24] It was taken because the *Kristallnacht* pogrom and the various statements, public and private, made by Hitler in the post-Munich weeks made it apparent that Germany could not be contained within any rational international system.[25] There was a further dimension. Whereas British policy during 1936, 1937 and most of 1938 had been formulated in the context of an intelligence picture, exacerbated by the employment of 'worst case' scenarios, that over emphasised and exaggerated German strengths in rearmament, towards the end of 1938 a more realistic picture began to emerge that highlighted German economic weaknesses in the overall strategic picture. Inevitably this injected a much needed self-confidence into the government in its dealings with Germany.[26]

MacDonald's explanation of Chamberlain's Commons reply of 14 November, which the colonial governors were allowed to use as they thought fit, did nothing much to calm apprehensions in Africa as a whole. Nigeria now emerged as the focus for speculation. The governor of that colony, Sir Bernard Bourdillon, clearly regarded the sort of statements so far authorised concerning British policy in the colonial question to be insufficient to assuage the anxieties of those who doubted the intentions of the British government.[27] In a personal and secret letter to Malcolm MacDonald he elaborated on his problems. It seemed to him that while he had been authorised to make statements denying current consideration of colonial transfer, it was not impossible that such transfer could be considered and effected in the future. Bourdillon did not wish to concern himself with the Cameroons or the fitness or otherwise of the Germans to engage in colonial administration, but, in his view, 'to hand over to . . . [Germany] . . . Nigeria proper, or any portion of it, would be an act of treachery which would hammer the last nail into the coffin of the African's faith in us'. British administration in Nigeria, the governor argued, had been a real success, based, as it was, on democratic principles, and 'to hand it over to Germany would be to undo all that we have done for the people, and to blacken our name all over Africa'.[28] With the agreement of Lord Halifax and Chamberlain, the governor was subsequently authorised to state that the British government had 'no intention of considering the transfer of Nigeria from British administration'.[29] MacDonald hoped that this would put a stop to rumours and bring the troubles of the governor to an end.[30]

On 7 December MacDonald was provided with an opportunity of further defining the attitude of the government over the whole range of the colonial question when the Labour MP Philip Noel-

Baker, tabled a motion in the Commons calling for there to be no redistribution of colonies or mandated territory without the consent of the inhabitants and the extension of the mandates system to all colonial territories in any 'general peace settlement'. The statement made by MacDonald in the debate on this motion was subjected in advance to the approval of the Prime Minister and foreign secretary.[31] It was, in the circumstances, a fairly categorical assertion that the colonial question was, as far as the British government was concerned, no longer a live issue. MacDonald stated:

I do not believe that there is to-day any section of opinion in this country that is disposed to hand over to any other country the care of any of the territories or peoples for whose government we are responsible either as a colonial or as a mandatory power. That view has been expressed this afternoon in every part of the House, and it is a view which is shared by His Majesty's Government. We are not discussing this matter; it is not now an issue in practical politics.[32]

The Colonial Secretary's words were greeted in the German press with a chorus of execration.[33]

The British government, therefore, had no intention of allowing the colonial question to become a serious issue. Indeed, everything was done to ensure that controversy surrounding the matter was kept to a minimum. The Portuguese, who, as one might have anticipated, had observed a nascent colonial dimension in the Munich crisis and had hurriedly sought reassurance from the British government,[34] complained that Lord Beaverbrook was about to start a campaign in the *Daily Express* which would favour 'the amalgamation of Portuguese, French and Belgian colonial possessions in Central Africa into a kind of commercial company, the majority of the shares in which should be in the hands of Germany'. The Foreign Office was unable to obtain confirmation of this story, but Halifax asked Sir Samuel Hoare to make enquiries. He wondered whether it would not be worthwhile to give Lord Beaverbrook a timely word of warning, and thus avert the launching of any such campaign.[35] Apparently, Lord Beaverbrook had no such designs. Even so, the action of Halifax clearly illustrates the negative attitude of the government in the colonial question at this time.[36]

When Oswald Pirow toured Europe in the months immediately following the Munich conference with the purpose of mediating between Britain and Germany, the British government, despite speculation in the press, refused to use his good offices to expedite a solution of the colonial question. Chamberlain even declined to accord Pirow semi-official status during his visit to Berlin.[37] Although Sir George Mounsey of the Foreign Office's western department offered a personal opinion to the Portuguese ambassador, Monteiro, 'that Germany was a great power with the indisputable right to colonies',[38] there is no evidence to show that the British government had any intention of making a serious colonial offer to Germany through Pirow. On the contrary, the kind of Anglo–German deal that Pirow had in his mind when he went to Berlin was fair treatment for the Jews in exchange for a free hand for Germany in eastern Europe.[39] In his talks with Hitler and Ribbentrop the colonial question did come up for discussion, but largely it would seem on German initiative and then only to indicate that it was a matter that could wait five or six years for a solution. It is, however, evident from the German record that what Pirow wanted to talk about was the Jewish problem.[40] This, therefore, probably explains his reticence on the colonial question when he discussed his European tour with the Portuguese *chargé d'affaires* in Pretoria on his return to South Africa, rather than lack of success in his talks with the Germans over their claims to South-West Africa.[41]

Nevertheless, while the colonial question might once more have receded into the background, colonial concessions to Germany remained a distinct possibility, within the general context of British policy, contingent on German good behaviour. For example, in February 1939 Chamberlain informed Sir Nevile Henderson that after the termination of the Spanish Civil War, the improvement of Franco–Italian relations and the commencement of disarmament talks, 'the atmosphere' might 'have so improved . . . that we might begin to think of colonial discussions'.[42] This, however, was a mere aspiration, not a plan for instant action. Halifax could see no sense in the immediate future of colonial discussions[43] and Henderson himself thought it best 'to keep the colonial question at a long arms length at present'.[44] Indeed this whole episode should be seen in the context of the temporary euphoria stimulated by Hitler's Reichstag speech of 30 January 1939 which, contrary to expectations, proved moderate in tone and in which he stated that Germany must 'trade or die'. Taken in conjunction with Germany's decision two days previously to enter into a coal agreement with Britain, this seemed to indicate an inclination on the part of Hitler to pursue a course of conduct in foreign policy that could be understood by British politicians. During February and March various economic contacts took place, but the German disruption of Czechoslovakia brought progress to an end and an iciness entered into Anglo–German relations.[45]

Some historians still argue that Chamberlain persisted in foolishness after Munich, and more particularly after Prague, by continuing to attempt 'to buy off Hitler'.[46] There is some justification for this criticism for the period after March 1939. But all hypothetical discussions about a settlement with Germany at this time should be seen also in the context of Britain's policy of guaranteeing the states of eastern Europe and of the British government's reluctance to countenance German expansion in that region by force, despite suggestions from the Foreign Office that Britain should acquiesce in such developments as a means of diverting Germany from colonial expansion overseas.[47] It was, in fact, quite natural that Chamberlain should attempt to broaden the discussion with Germany after the Munich conference, because that, after all, was what Munich was fundamentally about. The removal of Germany's, at least plausible, grievance regarding Czechoslovakia was intended to clear the ground in order to grapple with much wider political and economic issues. When Hitler's public utterances made it clear that progress was impossible and the *Kristallnacht* opened the curtain a little on the wickedness within Germany, Chamberlain withdrew. Significantly, the Van Zeeland report was virtually abandoned and the government adopted a more definitely negative attitude on the colonial question. Chamberlain still hoped, of course, that war could be avoided and with good reason. In 1939 it was clear that war could irreparably damage the empire and probable that the 'material costs of victory . . . would be almost indistinguishable from those of defeat'.[48] But ultimately it was evident that peace was only to be had on Hitler's terms and, despite the risk, no Briton was going to pay such a price.

On the eve of war the colonial question surfaced once more, although this time unofficially, in the notorious contacts that took place in July 1939 between Dr Wohltat, on the one hand, and Sir Horace Wilson and Robert Hudson, under-secretary at the Department of Overseas Trade, on the other. Wilson's comportment in this episode seems to have been beyond reproach, but Hudson appears to have been attempting some sort of personal and spectacular enterprise. While 'acting on his own initiative' and 'playing a solitary and dangerous hand', Hudson unfolded to Wohltat wide-ranging plans for economic appeasement that included a colonial scheme. These he later leaked to the press. But the measure of support that these ideas received from the British government is revealed in the fury with which Neville Chamberlain greeted the news of his minister's indiscretion and in his comments to his sister. According to the Prime Minister it would be premature to open negotiations with the Germans as 'they had not yet given up the use of force'.[49]

Curiously, as the British thought less and less of colonial concessions, the Germans contemplated more and more the overseas empire they were going to acquire and began planning for it.[50] But, given the vast scope of Hitler's programme and its essential repugnance to British interests, the realisation of German overseas ambitions now depended upon success in war against Britain. There was one brief moment in May 1940 when even Churchill briefly contemplated peace with Germany that would have involved a colonial settlement, but this was little more than a fleeting consideration at a particularly low point during the war.[51] For the British, colonial concessions had always had as their objective the prevention of war, the regeneration of Germany and her return to more liberal economic and trading methods. Sir Nevile Henderson, who had not always represented the attitude of the British government as accurately as he ought to have done, clearly implied this when, responding to Hitler's suggestion during the last days of peace that Britain might make an immediate colonial offer to Germany as evidence of her good intentions, he stated that his government would discuss this matter in an atmosphere of goodwill, but not one of malevolence.[52] From the British point of view, if Germany was bent on the use of force to secure her aims, there was little point in the further pursuit of colonial concessions.

British policy towards Germany in the 1930s was a response to a last German bid for colonies at two levels. Hitler's primary aim, the acquisition of *Lebensraum*, was in his mind the German equivalent of British overseas expansion; his references to the Ukraine as Germany's India illustrate this point quite clearly. Although this was only the first stage in his programme for world supremacy, it was the part to which his entire regime was devoted and which was ultimately and mercifully frustrated. But it was to this that the British government was reacting throughout the 1930s, although only gradually and hazily did they become aware of it. Hitler obviously could not be too explicit about such an aim because of the inconvenient resistance it would have provoked. He hoped, however, to make the British generally acquiescent regarding Germany's foreign policy aims by initially not pressing her colonial demands. Again he could not be too explicit or categorical about renouncing Germany's colonial claims because that would have offended many of the conservative colonial enthusiasts, who by the 1930s were essentially part of the Nazi coalition. Thus professions of any kind of colonial renunciation were simply not believed in London. Moreover, the colonial activists in Germany were as clamant as ever and had not been renounced.

In addition, the official programme of the Nazi party stated that Germany desired colonies. Imperialists themselves, the British understood this to be a natural aspiration. In their general reaction to recrudescent Germany, therefore, they were inclined to be sympathetic to Germany's colonial demands provided that such a gesture would bring Germany into normal relations with the rest of Europe. Such inclinations were intensified once Hitler began to push the colonial question himself in the belief that such action would coerce the British into granting him a free hand in eastern Europe. On the other hand, British willingness to meet Germany's colonial demands was intended precisely to curb forcible German expansion in that region. During the 1930s the British were responding to what was in effect tactical use of the colonial question by Germany, but it now seems certain that after Hitler had achieved his European goals he intended that Germany should in addition become a conventional colonial power. This aim was, however, contingent upon success in achieved *Lebensraum* in the Ukraine, which could only be acquired by conquest and which Britain could not endorse. Whatever might be said about the intrinsic lack of morality involved in the concept of colonial or mandatory transfer[53] and however much Britain had been forced in this direction by economic and military weakness, there was incorporated in Britain's preparedness to readmit Germany to the ranks of the colonial powers a real element of co-operative internationalism. It was a far cry from the Darwinian, competitive imperialism represented by Hitler and his regime.

Notes and References

1. Introduction

1. *Documents on German Foreign Policy*, (hereinafter cited as *DGFP*), (London, 1948 –), series D, vol. I, No. 138, Von Neurath to Sir N. Henderson, 4.3.1938, and *Public Record Office*, (hereinafter cited as *PRO*), Premier 1/247, Sir N. Henderson to Lord Halifax, 5.3.1938.
2. A. J. Crozier, 'Prelude to Munich: British Foreign Policy and Germany, 1935–8', *European Studies Review*, 1976.
3. *Documents on British Foreign Policy*, (hereinafter cited as *DBFP*), (London, 1946 –), third series, vol. I, appendix I, Sir N. Henderson to Lord Halifax, 30.3.1938 and Lord Halifax to Sir N. Henderson, 4.4.1938.
4. The most extensive account contained in a non-official published work of the offer and of the interview between Sir Nevile Henderson, the British ambassador at Berlin, and Hitler of 3 March 1938 is to be found in Sir Nevile Henderson's *Failure of a Mission*, (London, 1940), pp. 114–8. The published diaries of the two Foreign Office officials, Sir Alexander Cadogan and Oliver Harvey, give some details, but provide very little of the background to the offer, see D. Dilks (ed.), *The Diary of Sir Alexander Cadogan, 1938–1945*, (London, 1971), pp. 40–58, and J. Harvey (ed.), *The Diplomatic Diaries of Oliver Harvey*, (London, 1970), pp. 17–21, 61–2, and 78–109. Some books summarily dismiss the colonial question, such as A. J. P. Taylor, *The Origins of the Second World War*, (London, 1964), pp. 139–40. Others such as M. Gilbert and R. Gott, *The Appeasers*, (London, 1967), pp. 80–101, seize upon the issue as evidence of the cravenness of Chamberlain's foreign policy. The colonial question is given some treatment in I. Colvin, *The Chamberlain Cabinet*, (London, 1971), pp. 36–7, 39–40, 42–3, 53–4, 87–8, and 90; K. Middlemas, *The Diplomacy of Illusion*, (London, 1972), pp. 110–4, 138–98, 141–3, and 148–56; A. Adamthwaite, *France and the Coming of the Second World War*, (London, 1977), pp. 53–6, 67–8, 80 and 296–7; R. Ovendale, *'Appeasement' and the English Speaking World*, (Cardiff, 1975), pp. 34–5, 38, 47–8, 53, and 95–6; G. L. Weinberg, *The Foreign Policy of Hitler's Germany: Diplomatic Revolution in Europe 1933–36*, (Chicago and London, 1970), pp. 276–81, and *The Foreign Policy of Hitler's Germany: Starting World War II 1937–1939*, Chicago and London, 1980), pp. 52–14.
5. Lord Duncan-Sandys to A. J. Crozier, 8.4.1982.
6. D. J. Morgan, *The Origins of British Aid Policy*, (London, 1980), pp. 14–5.
7. *Daily Telegraph*, 5.5.1972.
8. Several files in the Colonial Office records remain closed. See, for example, *PRO*–CO 323/1510/6656/5 and CO/847/17/47128/2. The latter

contains correspondence between Neville Chamberlain and the South African Prime Minister, Hertzog, regarding the colonial question in January 1939 and an important despatch from the British High Commissioner in South Africa, Sir W. H. Clark. More frustrating is the fact that some of the Colonial Office material appears to have been lost and is listed as 'missing at the time of transfer' – see ibid., CO 323/1510/665/1.

9. Economic appeasement has in recent years been the subject of some penetrating researches, particularly by Germans. See B.-J. Wendt, *Economic Appeasement: Handel und Finanz in der britischen Deutschland-Politik, 1933–1939*, (Dusseldorf, 1971); B.-J. Wendt, 'Grossbritannien – Demokratie auf dem Prüfstand: Appeasement als Strategie des Status Quo,' in E. Forndran, F. Golchewski and D. Riesenburger (eds), *Innen–und Aussenpolitik unter nationalsozialistischer Bedrohung*, (Opladen, 1977); B.-J. Wendt, '"Economic Appeasement" – A Crisis Strategy', in W. J. Mommsen and L. Kettenacker (eds), *The Fascist Challenge and the Policy of Appeasement* (London, 1983); G. Schmidt, *England in der Krise. Grundlagen und Grundzüge der britischen Appeasement-Politik, 1930–1937*, (Wiesbaden, 1981); G. Schmidt, 'The Domestic Background to British Appeasement Policy', in Mommsen and Kettenacker, op. cit.; P. Kennedy, 'The Logic of Appeasement', in *The Times Literary Supplement*, 28.5.1982; C. A. MacDonald, 'Economic Appeasement and the German "Moderates", 1937–1939', in *Past and Present*, 56 (1972); and Gilbert and Gott, op. cit., pp. 189–232.

10. A. J. Crozier, 'Imperial Decline and the Colonial Question in Anglo–German Relations 1919–1939', *European Studies Review*, XI (1981).

11. It would be wrong to suggest that the colonial question in the post-war era has been totally neglected. The following works have examined it at considerable length, although the function of the colonial question in the formulation of British foreign policy has not yet been treated by any of them in the light of the currently available evidence: W. W. Schmokel, *Dream of Empire*, (New Haven, 1964); K. Hildebrand, *Vom Reich zum Weltreich*, Munich 1969; Gilbert and Gott, op. cit., pp. 80–101; *Dez Anos de Política Externa, 1936–1947. A naçao portuguesa e a segunda querra mundial*, hereinafter cited as DAPE), (Lisbon 1961–), vols. I and II. *O rearmamento do Exercito no quadro polítco da Aliança Luso–Britanica, 1936–1939*: and R. W. Logan, *The African Mandates in World Politics*, (Washington, 1948).

12. See P. Gifford and W. R. Louis (eds), *Britain and Germany in Africa*, (Yale, 1967); R. Robinson, J. Gallagher and A. Denny, *Africa and the Victorians*, (London, 1961); W. O. Henderson, *Studies in German Colonial History*, (London, 1962); A. J. P. Taylor, *Germany's First Bid for Colonies* (London, 1938); M. E. Townsend, *Origins of Modern German Colonialism, 1871–1885* (New York, 1920); M. E. Townsend, *The Rise and Fall of Germany's Colonial Empire, 1884–1918* (New York, 1930); and W. R. Louis, *Great Britain and Germany's Lost Colonies* (London, 1967).

13. Controversy still surrounds Bismarck's motives. For example, the view has been advanced by H. A. Turner, jnr., in 'Bismarck's Imperialist Venture: Anti-British in Origin?' in Gifford and Louis, op.

cit., p. 50 that 'Bismarck was not primarily motivated by any of the ulterior motives imputed to him . . . he simply changed his mind and decided that there must be overseas possessions . . . He acted, that is, only in order to avert what he feared might be the damaging effects of not doing so'. See also H.-U. Wehler, 'Bismarck's Imperialism 1862–1890', in *Past and Present*, 48 (1970) and his *Bismarck und der Imperialismus* (Cologne/Berlin, 1969). For P. Kennedy's commentary on Wehler see 'German Colonial Expansion. Has the "Manipulated Social Imperialism" been ante-dated?' in *Past and Present*, 54 (1972).

14. Louis, *Lost Colonies*, pp. 25–27.
15. For a discussion of these negotiations see P. H. S. Hatton, 'Harcourt and Solf: the Search for an Anglo–German Understanding through Africa, 1912–1914', *European Studies Review*, I (1971); R. Langhorne, 'Anglo–German Negotiations Concerning the Future of the Portuguese Colonies, 1911–1914', *The Historical Review*, XVI (1973); and J. O. Vincent-Smith, 'The Anglo–German Negotiations over the Portuguese Colonies in Africa, 1911–1914', *The Historical Review*, XVII (1974).
16. Louis, *Lost Colonies*, pp. 31–32, and Woodruff D. Smith, *The German Colonial Empire* (Chapel Hill, 1978), pp. 183–220. Much has been done in recent years to rehabilitate the image of German colonial administration. A balanced view of its successes and failures can be found in R. Oliver and G. Matthew (eds), *History of East Africa*, vol. I (London, 1963); V. Harlow, E. M. Chilver and A. Smith (eds), *History of East Africa*, vol. II (London, 1965); L. H. Gann and P. Duignan (eds), *Colonialism in Africa*, vol. I (London, 1969); Gifford and Louis, op. cit.; I. Goldblatt, *History of South-West Africa* (Cape Town, 1971); W. R. Louis, *Ruanda–Urundi, 1884–1919* (London, 1963); H. Bley *South-West Africa under German Rule* (London, 1971); Henderson, op. cit.; and Smith, op. cit.
17. Louis, *Lost Colonies*, p. 36, and Henderson, op. cit., p. 97.
18. F. Fischer *Griff nach der Weltmacht*, (Dusseldorf, 1961), pp. 90–95.
19. Smith, op. cit., pp. 224–32.
20. Henderson, op. cit., pp. 96–112.
21. Goldblatt, op. cit., pp. 202–5, and Louis, *Lost Colonies*, pp. 50–54.
22. W. O. Henderson, 'German East Africa, 1884–1918', in Harlow, Chilver and Smith, op. cit., p. 156.
23. Ibid., p. 159.
24. See, for example, C. M. Andrew and A. S. Kanya-Forstner, 'The French Colonial Party and French Colonial War Aims, 1914–1918', *The Historical Journal*, XVII (1974).
25. L. S. Amery, *My Political Life*, vol. II *War and Peace* (London, 1953), p. 161; J. Nevakivi, *Britain, France and the Arab Middle-East, 1914–1920* (London, 1969), p. 17; C. M. Andrew and A. S. Kanya-Forstner, *France Overseas: The Great War and the Climax of French Imperialism* (London, 1981), p. 70.
26. H. R. Winkler, *The League of Nations Movement in Great Britain 1914–1918* (New Brunswick, 1952), p. 200.
27. Louis, *Lost Colonies*, p. 86. On Brailsford see the important new study, F. M. Leventhal, *The Last Dissenter: H. N. Brailsford and his World*

(London, 1985). Norman Angell was fundamentally in favour of empire and preached the virtues of interdependence and federation over those of independence and nationalism. See L. Bisceglia, *Norman Angell and Liberal Internationalism in Britain, 1931–1935* (New York and London, 1982), pp. 64–5. See also J. A. Hobson, *Imperialism* (London, 1901), pp. 101, 113–4 and 137; H. N. Brailsford, *The War of Steel and Gold* (London, 1915), pp. 326–8, and pp. 333–7; L. W. Martin, *Peace Without Victory* (New Haven 1958), pp. 7 and 77; and H. G. Wells, *A Reasonable Man's Peace* (London, 1917). Wells thought an equitable colonial arrangement essential to a secure peace.

28. Winkler, op. cit., p. 200.
29. Ibid., p. 206
30. On the connections between Wilson and the British radicals, see Martin, op. cit. pp. 18–19, 80–81, 85–86, 114–20 and 121–5.
31. Ibid., pp. 19 and 91.
32. Rudolf von Albertini, 'Die USA und die Kolonialfrage (1917–1945), *Vierteljahrshefte für Zeitgeschichte*, XIII (1965).
33. H. Duncan Hall, *Mandates, Dependencies and Trusteeship*, (London, 1948), p. 112.
34. M. Swartz, *The Union of Democratic Control in British Politics during the First World War*, pp. 193, 196–8 and 201.
35. D. Lloyd George, *War Memoirs of David Lloyd George*, vol. II (London, 1938), p. 1515. See also *PRO–CAB 23/5, Minutes of War Cabinet*, 3.5.1918.
36. V. H. Rothwell, *British War Aims and Peace Diplomacy* (London, 1971), Appendix I.
37. Louis, *Lost Colonies*, pp. 97–100. See also Cd. 8306, *German Atrocities and Breaches of the Rules of War in Africa* (1916); Cd. 8371. *Papers Relating to Certain Trials and Executions of Natives in South-West Africa* (1916); Cd. 9146, *Report on the Natives of South-West Africa and their Treatment by Germany* (1918); and Cd. 9210, *Correspondence relating to the Wishes of the Natives of the German Colonies as to their Future Government* (1918).
38. *PRO–CAB 29/1/3*, Memorandum by J. C. Smuts, *The German Colonies at the Peace Conference*, 11.7.1918.
39. Andrew and Kanya-Forstner, *France Overseas*, pp. 97–99.
40. *Foreign Relations of the United States*, (hereinafter cited as *FRUS*), *The Paris Peace Conference, 1919* (Washington, 1942–1947), vol. I, House to Wilson, 30.10.1918, p. 407.
41. *PRO – CAB 23/42, Minutes of Imperial War Cabinet*, 20.12.1918, and S. Roskill, *Hankey*, vol. II (London, 1972), p. 37.
42. Ibid., pp. 378.
43. *PRO – CAB 23/42 Minutes of Imperial War Cabinet*, 20.12.1918.
44. Louis, *Lost Colonies*, p. 117–160.
45. *PRO – FO 371/9425/W8425/70/98*, R. H. Campbell to Sir Eyre Crowe, 24.10.1923.
46. A. Bullock, *Germany's Colonial Demands* (London, 1939), pp. 38–39. Cf. the views of Colonel House in 1920 in N. G. Levin, *Woodrow Wilson and World Politics* (New York, 1968), pp. 245–6. With hindsight it is, however, possible to see in the mandates system something more than

hypocrisy and paternalism. In focusing attention on colonies and the issues of independence and self-determination it created the atmosphere in which decolonisation became possible. See D. Armstrong, *The Rise of the International Organisation* (London, 1982), pp. 40–41.

47. Cf. the terms of the mandate for South-West Africa.
48. *FRUS, Peace Conference*, vol. IV, *Notes of a Meeting held at the Grand Hotel Trianon, Versailles*, 7.5.1919, pp. 506–9. The British empire as a whole was also to hold Nauru in the Pacific as a 'C' mandate.
49. V. R. Berghahn, *Germany and the Approach of War in 1914* (London, 1973), pp. 38–40.
50. R. Lansing, *War Memoirs* (Indianapolis, 1935), p. 197.
51. Logan, op. cit., p. 9.
52. Ibid., pp. 9–11.
53. A reference to the provisions of the Congo Basin treaties.
54. Logan, op. cit., pp. 12–13.
55. *FRUS, Peace Conference*, vol. VI, *Proposals of the German Government for the Establishment of a League of Nations*, 9.5.1919, pp. 772–3.
56. Ibid., Brockdorff-Rantzau to Clemenceau, *Observations of the German Delegation on the Conditions of Peace*, 29.5.1919, pp. 797–8 and 841–4. See also ibid., Brockdorff-Ranzau to Clemenceau, *Statement of the Financial Commission of the German Delegation*, 29.5.1919, p. 906.
57. Ibid., Clemenceau to Brockdorff-Rantzau, *Reply of the Allied and Associated Powers to the Observations of the German Delegation on the Conditions of Peace*, 16.6.1919, pp. 932 and 951–4.
58. Ibid., Bauer to Clemenceau, 21.6.1919, pp. 609–11.
59. Schmokel, op. cit., pp. 1–2 and 14–15.
60. Hildebrand, *Weltreich*, pp. 79–83.
61. Although the colonial revisionists in the 1920s were often influential people, the colonial movement had a fatal weakness: 'There was no younger generation of leaders, or followers with a truly spontaneous interest in the colonies. By and large it is true that "nobody talked of colonial questions in Germany in the post-war years, except for direct participants".' Maria Holtsch, *Die ehemaligen deutschen Südseekolonien im Wandel seit dem Weltkreig*, (diss. Marburg, 1934), p. 79. Quoted in Schmokel, op. cit., p. 10.
62. Ibid., pp. 1 and 15.
63. Mary E. Townsend. 'The Contemporary Colonial Movement in Germany', *The Political Science Quarterly*, March 1928.
64. *PRO* – FO 371/12146/C6180/1323/18, J. Addison to O. Sargent, 15.7.1927.
65. Schmokel, op. cit., pp. 2–7.
66. Ibid., pp. 10–14.
67. *PRO* – FO 371/4766/C4283/154/18, Report presented by Paul Hymans on 5.8.1920 and later adopted by the League Council.
68. Ibid., 4768/C12585/154/18, German memorandum addressed to the secretary-general of the League of Nations. Undated, but communicated to League members on 22.11.1920. See also minutes by S. P. Waterlow and Sir Eyre Crowe, 2.12.1920.
69. F. S. Joelson, *Germany's Claims to Colonies* (London, 1939), p. 65.

70. M. Howard, *The Continental Commitment* (London, 1974), p. 72.
71. *House of Commons Debates*, Fifth Series, (hereinafter cited as *H. of C. V*), vol. 118, col. 1035; vol. 132, cols. 2411–2; and vol. 157, col. 185.
72. J. L. Garvin, *The Economic Foundations of Peace* (London, 1919), pp. 1, 260–1 and 266–7.
73. N. Angell, *The Fruits of Victory* (London, 1921) pp. 87–88, and *W. H. Dawson Papers*, (hereinafter cited as *WHD*), University of Birmingham Library, 1074, N. Angell to W. H. Dawson, 9.12.1929.
74. For a fuller discussion of Dawson and his views see below, pp. 45–7.
75. *WHD*, 1890, W. H. Dawson to J. C. Smuts, 20.2.1921.
76. See, for example, *WHD*, 519, Dr. Paul Rohrbach to W. H. Dawson, 2.12.1920.
77. Ibid., 509, Record of a conversation between W. H. Dawson and Friedrich Sthamer, 19.8.1920.
78. It was Amery who was responsible for the creation of the Dominions Office.
79. See A. J. Crozier, 'The Colonial Question in Stresemann's Locarno Policy', *The International History Review*, 1982; A. J. Crozier, 'Friedrich von der Ropp and Unofficial Anglo–German Contacts in the Locarno Era', Unpublished paper; A. J. Crozier, 'Imperial Decline'; and *Sir Henry Page Croft Papers*, (hereinafter cited as *CRFT*), 1/2, L. S. Amery to Sir Henry Page Croft, 4.7.1925.
80. Archives of the *Ministère des Affaires Étrangères*, (hereinafter cited as *MAE*), 1F/SDN/545, *Note sur les revendications coloniales allemandes*, probably October 1926. See also ibid., M. Herbette to M. Hymans, 29.9.1924. M. Hymans to M. Herbette, 28.10.1924, M. de Margerie to M. Herriot, 8.11.1924, M. de Margerie to M. Herriot, 2.3.1925, M. Perrier to M. Briand, 26.9.1925; ibid., 546, M. Perrier to M. Briand. 24.12.1925. M. Herbette to M. Briand, 9.3.1926; and *PRO–FO 371/10756.C16692.2994/18*, Lord Crewe to Sir A. Chamberlain, 21.12.1925. The end of the First World War ushered in a period of colonial enthusiasm in France and the French were not going to surrender their gains lightly – see Andrew and Kanya-Forstner, *France Overseas*, p. 209ff. During the inter-war years, however, the French were most preoccupied with Italian colonial claims – see A. J. Crozier, 'Philippe Berthelot and the Rome Agreements of January 1935', *The Historical Journal*, 1983.
81. The Germans feared that the realisation of 'closer union' in east Africa would destroy the distinctive status of Tanganyika and end in its annexation. This would effectively preclude its reacquisition by Germany. 'Closer union' was, in fact, shelved by the British government in 1932 following a report by a joint select committee of both houses of parliament, but the permanent mandates commission which had followed these developments attentively was on the whole inclined to take a doubtful view of the British proposals. At its twenty-third session in 1933 it passed a resolution which took note of Britain's decision not to effect in east Africa a political or constitutional union which would endanger the existence of Tanganyika 'as a distinct entity in international law' and stated that any such political union could not

be carried out while the mandate was in force. On the German objections, see *WHD*, 1022, Heinrich Schnee to W. H. Dawson, 15.2.1929; and *PRO* – FO 371.13615/C290/43/18, Sir H. Rumbold to Sir A. Chamberlain, 1.2.1929, ibid., 14948/W91266/10/98, German aide memoire, 4.9.1930 and ibid., 15225/C2093/929/18, W. H. Dawson to R. G. Leigh, 25.3.1931. See also B. T. G. Chidzero, *Tanganyika and International Trusteeship* (London, 1961), p. 61ff.
82. *PRO* – FO 371/12908/C3474/1069/18, Sir R. Lindsay to Sir A. Chamberlain, 3.5.1928.
83. Ibid., Minute by M. H. Huxley, 11.5.1928.
84. See A. J. Crozier, 'Imperial Decline'.

2. British and German Attitudes in 1933

1. The empire was not for all British politicians and officials the sacred institution it was for others. See R. F. Holland, *Britain and the Commonwealth Alliance 1918–1939* (London, 1981), pp. 208–9.
2. *PRO* – CAB 24/227, Memorandum by Sir R. Vansittart, *The British Position in Relation to European Policy*, 1.1.1932.
3. Ibid., 221, Memorandum by Sir R. Vansittart, *An Aspect of International Relations in 1931*, 14.5.1931.
4. The *Cecil Papers*, (hereinafter cited as *VCP*), Add. Mss., 51082, Note of a Conversation with Sir John Simon and Lord Hutchison of Montrose, 14.6.1934.
5. See W. N. Medlicott, *Britain and Germany: the Search for Agreement 1930– 1937* (London, 1968).
6. J. Harvey (ed.), *The Diplomatic Diaries of Oliver Harvey* (London, 1970), p. 222.
7. A. Wolfers, *Britain and France between the Two Wars* (New York, 1940), p. 202.
8. M. Gilbert, *The Roots of Appeasement* (London, 1966), p. 50.
9. D. Lloyd George, *Peace Treaties* vol. I, pp. 404–14. The attitude of Lloyd George towards the Treaty of Versailles and his advocacy of good Anglo–German relations caused him to be highly regarded by Hitler. See A. Hitler, *Hitler's Table Talk* (London, 1973), p. 657.
10. For the French response to the *Fontainebleau Memorandum* see D. Lloyd George *Peace Treaties*, vol. I, pp. 416–20.
11. W. N. Medlicott, *British Foreign Policy since Versailles* (London, 1968), p. 2.
12. Leventhal, op. cit., pp. 157–8.
13. H. N. Brailsford, *After the Peace* (London, 1920), pp. 21, 22–3, 30, 39, 82 and 173.
14. W. H. Dawson, 'Germany After the War', *The Contemporary Review*, March 1917.
15. W. H. Dawson, 'How Germany Makes Peace', *The Nineteenth Century and After*, March 1918.
16. *WHD*, 388, W. H. Dawson to W. Wray Skilbeck, 29.9.1918. and W. H.

Dawson, 'The Fifth Year of the War', *The Contemporary Review*, August 1918.

17. W. H. Dawson, 'The Liabilities of the Peace', *The Fortnightly Review*, July 1919.

18. W. H. Dawson, 'The League and the Peace', *The Fortnightly Review*, September 1919.

19. *WHD*, 425, Lady Wester Wemyss to W. H. Dawson, 6.3.1919, and 444, Lady Wester Wemyss to W. H. Dawson, 29.6.1919. There is strong evidence in the Dawson papers to suggest that he had a pronounced tendency towards anti-Semitism. See *WHD*, 535, Lady Wester Wemyss to W. H. Dawson, 16.2.1921, and ibid., 1606, G. P. Gooch to W. H. Dawson, 19.1.1936.

20. *WHD*, 559, W. H. Dawson to D. Lloyd George, 10.5.1921.

21. W. H. Dawson, 'Can France and Germany be Reconciled?', *The Fortnightly Review*, July 1922.

22. D. C. Watt, *Personalities and Policies* (Notre Dame, 1965) pp. 1–15.

23. Cmd. 4827, *Statement Relating to Defence issued in connexion with the House of Commons Debate on 11th March 1935*, p. 2. Quoted in Wolfers, op. cit., p. 206.

24. Garvin, op. cit., pp. 152–3.

25. Ibid., pp. 257–8.

26. Ibid., pp. 258–9.

27. Angell, *Fruits*, p. 54.

28. A. J. P. Taylor, *The Trouble Makers* (London, 1957), p. 158. Keynes's views were later challenged by E. Mantoux, *The Carthaginian Peace* (London, 1946). More recently they have been challenged by Lord Balogh – see *The Times Literary Supplement*, 10.10.1975.

29. J. M. Keynes, *The Economic Consequences of the Peace* (London, 1919), pp. 14 and 102.

30. Taylor, *Trouble Makers*, p. 158.

31. Gilbert, op. cit., p. 64.

32. Wolfers, op. cit., p. 203.

33. Ibid., p. 207.

34. Gilbert, op. cit., pp. 122–3.

35. PRO – CAB 24/225, Memorandum by O. Sargent and F. Ashton-Gwatkin, *Changing Conditions in British Foreign Policy, with reference to the Disarmament Conference, a possible Reparations Conference and other contingent Problems*, 26.11.1931.

36. Memorandum by Sir R. Vansittart, 11.1.1932, loc.cit. Not even Sir Austen Chamberlain was able to escape the prevailing anti-French mood, See *MAE/Z/ITALIE/CARTON* 1110, M. P. Berthelot to M. J. Paul-Boncour, 1.9.1932.

37. Memorandum by Sir R. Vansittart, 14.5.1931, loc.cit.

38. *Thomas Jones Papers*, National Library of Wales, Aberystwyth, Class S, Vol. I, No. 134, T. Jones to A. Flexner, 22.2.1936.

39. A. Eden, *Facing the Dictators* (London, 1962), p. 323.

40. PRO – FO 800/285, *Sir John Simon Papers*, (hereinafter cited as *JSP*), Sir V. Wellesley to Sir J. Simon, 23.12.1931.

41. Ibid., 287/*JSP*, J. Ramsay MacDonald to Sir J. Simon, September 1932.

42. *Documents Diplomatiques Français* (hereinafter cites as *DDF*), (Paris, 1964–), series 1, vol. I, No. 235, J. Ramsay MacDonald to M. E. Herriot 10.10.1932.
43. *PRO* – FO 800/286/*JSP*, J. Ramsay MacDonald to Sir J. Simon, 31.5.1932.
44. M. Cowling, *The Impact of Hitler* (London, 1975), pp. 74–5.
45. *PRO* – CAB 23/76, *Cabinet Minutes*, 26.7.1933.
46. Zara S. Steiner, *Britain and the Origins of the First World War* (London, 1977), pp. 44–5.
47. *PRO* – FO 800/285/*JSP, NOTE as regards ANGLO–GERMAN RELATIONS*, Sir Walford Selby, 6.12.1931. Sir Maurice Hankey later wrote of Selby: 'Nice fellow. I don't always agree with him, but do generally. He is very pro-French and anti-German.' – the *Lord Hankey Papers*, (hereinafter cited as *HNKY*), 3/42. Sir M. Hankey to H. Hankey, 28.3.1936.
48. *PRO* – FO 800/285/*JSP*, Minute by O. Sargent, 9.12.1931.
49. Ibid., 287/*JSP*, Sir W. Selby to Sir J. Simon, 10.10.1932.
50. *VCP*, Add. Mss., 51080, S. Baldwin to Lord R. Cecil, 12.3.1933. On 17 May 1933 Simon informed the Cabinet that current German policy was 'definitely disquieting'. The German government was 'giving State sanction and encouragement to an attitude of mind, as well as to various forms of military training, which could end in only one way'. See *PRO* – CAB 23/76.
51. A. Hillgrüber, *Germany and the Two World Wars* (London, 1981), pp. 59–60.
52. Below, pp. 216–31.
53. Cowling, op. cit., p. 105.
54. Gilbert, op. cit., pp. 154–5.
55. Cowling, op. cit., p. 148.
56. Ibid., p. 105.
57. Cf. K. Middlemas, *The Diplomacy of Illusion: The British Government and Germany, 1937–39* (London, 1972).
58. As late as January 1938 Eden still thought 'that an agreement with' Hitler 'might have a chance of a reasonable life especially if Hitler's own position were engaged'. *PRO* – Premier 1/276, A. Eden to N. Chamberlain, 9.1.1938. Quoted in Cowling, op. cit p. 143. Eden was, of course, reflecting widely held assumptions. See Leventhal, op. cit., p. 233, and Biscelgia, op. cit., pp. 217–8.
59. *PRO* – FO/800/286./*JSP*, R. Boothby to Sir J. Simon, 18.1.1932.
60. Ibid., FO 800/309, *Lord Halifax Papers*, (hereinafter cited as *LHP*), Lord Halifax to Lord Runciman, 6.9.1938. Quoted in Cowling, op. cit., p. 177.
61. Hillgrüber, *Two World Wars*, p. 54.
62. G. Fleming, *Hitler und die Endlösung* (Wiesbaden and Munich, 1982), pp. 30–1.
63. A. Bullock, *Hitler: A Study in Tyranny* (London, 1952).
64. H. Trevor-Roper 'Hitlers Kriegsziele', *Vierteljahrshefte für Zeitgeschichte*, VIII (1960).
65. A. Hillgrüber, 'England's Place in Hitler's Plans for World Dominion',

Journal of Contemporary History, IX (1974).

66. M. Michaelis, 'World Power Status or World Dominion', *The Historical Journal*, XV (1972).

67. See Gunter Moltman, 'Weltherrschaftsideen Hitlers', in O. Bruner and D. Gerhard (eds), *Europa und Ubersee. Festschrift für Egmont Zechlin* (Hamburg, 1961), pp. 197–240; A. Hillgrüber, *Hitlers Strategie: Politik und Kriegführung 1940–41* (Frankfurt, 1965): A. Hillgrüber, *Two World Wars*; K. Hildebrand, *Weltreich*; K. Hildebrand, *The Foreign Policy of the Third Reich* (London, 1973); and J. Henke, *England in Hitlers politischem Kalkul 1935–1939* (Boppard am Rhein, 1973). It would, however, be misleading to suggest that all Hitler's contemporaries were incapable of arriving at the same conclusions without the benefits of post-war German scholarship. For example, one of them wrote in 1937: 'Hitler, according to his own statement, believes in a continental policy and at the same time defends the Pan–German programme of world-conquest. His policy does not in any sense involve a renunciation of world power, but it proposes to reach the goal by indirect stages because this will make success more certain.' S. Erckner, *Hitler's Conspiracy Against Peace* (London, 1937), p. 170.

68. Hillgrüber, art. cit.

69. A. Hitler, *Hitler's Secret Book* (New York, 1961).

70. Hillgrüber, *Two World Wars*, p. 49. Not all historians, however, accept this view uncritically. See the review by A. J. Nicholls of W. Michalka, *Ribbentrop und die deutsche Weltpolitik 1933–1940: Aussenpolitische Konzeptionen und Entsheidigungsprozesses im Dritten Reich*, in *History*, IXIX (1984). See also I. Kershaw, *The Nazi Dictatorship: Problems and Perspectives of Interpretation* (London, 1985), pp. 106–129, for a discussion of the recent literature on Nazi foreign policy.

71. A. Hitler, *Mein Kampf* (London, 1969), p. 597.

72. Hillgrüber, *Two World Wars*, p. 50.

73. Hildebrand, *Weltreich*, p. 72.

74. Ibid., pp. 73–4. A recent writer on Hitler and his anti-Semitism argues that elimination of world Jewry was Hitler's fundamental motive from the beginning. See Fleming, op. cit., pp. 22, 26–7 and 29–30. For a discussion of the 'intentionalist' versus 'structuralist' debate on the extermination of the Jews, see Kershaw, op. cit., pp. 85–105. See also J. P. Stern, *Hitler, the Führer and the People* (London, 1975), pp. 198–224.

75. Hitler, *Mein Kampf*, p. 60.

76. Hildebrand, *Weltreich*, pp. 750–7.

77. Ibid., p. 73, and Hitler, *Mein Kampf*, p. 617.

78. Ibid., pp. 140–1.

79. Ibid., pp. 126 and 212–3. These anti-urban concepts were common currency amongst the European radical right. The Portuguese dictator, Salazar, for example, told a British diplomat in July 1941 that 'he looked on the Americans as a barbaric people, illuminated not by God but by electric light'. See *PRO* – FO 371/26795/C7570/41/36.

80. Hitler, *Hitler's Secret Book*, p. 23.

81. Hitler, *Table Talk*, p. 619.

82. Ibid., p. 16.

83. Hitler, *Mein Kampf*, pp. 559–61.
84. Hitler, *Secret Book*, p. 72.
85. Hitler, *Mein Kampf*, p. 561.
86. Ibid., p. 126. Until now the prevailing orthodoxy has been that Hitler intended to conquer the necessary territory by *Blitzkrieg* tactics, for which Germany was armed in 'width' rather than 'depth'. This meant minimal expenditure on armaments appropriate to 'Germany's limited economic resources'. See K. Hildebrand, *The Third Reich* (London, 1984), pp. 43, 48, 57, 63 and 132–3, and A. S. Milward, *The German Economy at War* (London, 1965), pp. 1–27 and *War, Economy and Society* (London, 1977), Chapters 1–3. British intelligence came to the same kind of conclusions about Germany's military preparations during the years 1936–8. See W. K. Wark, *The Ultimate Enemy: British Intelligence and Nazi Germany 1933–1939* (London, 1985), pp. 93–100. It has, however, recently been argued that Germany in fact did prepare for war 'in depth' from the beginning and that Hitler anticipated a long and global war. See R. J. Overy, 'Hitler's War and the German Economy: A Reinterpretation', *Economic History Review*, 35 (1982). Also see Overy's *Goering. 'The Iron Man'* (London, 1984), pp. 82–6.
87. Hitler, *Secret Book*, pp. 13–4.
88. Hitler, *Mein Kampf*, p. 587.
89. Hitler, *Secret Book*, pp. 70–1. See also A. Hitler, *Hitlers Politisches Testament: Die Bormann Diktate vom Februar und April 1945* Hamburg, 1981), pp. 54–5: 'For continental peoples [Hitler stated] it seems to me necessary that they extend themselves only when the connection with the motherland is secure.'
90. Hitler, *Mein Kampf*. p. 128.
91. Ibid., p. 129.
92. Hitler, *Secret Book*, p. 151.
93. Hitler, *Mein Kampf*, pp. 598–9.
94. Hillgrüber, art. cit.
95. Hitler, *Secret Book*, p. 145. By the end of the first year of the German onslaught on the Soviet Union, Hitler thought that the German colonies in the Ukraine would be showing results within ten years. See Hitler, *Table Talk*, p. 625.
96. Hitler, *Politisches Testament*, p. 64. See also Hitler, *Table Talk*, pp. 92–3.
97. Hitler's resolve in this respect would be undoubtedly have been encouraged by Arnold J. Toynbee, who told him in February 1936: 'In a duel between Germany and Russia . . . we expect that Germany would be the winner. Indeed, we expect her victory to be so decisive that it would enable her to annex the Ukraine and the Urals, with their vast agricultural and mineral resources. In that event Germany would shoot up to the stature of a super-power of the scale of the United States; and then we, Germany's western neighbours, would be dwarfed and overshadowed by this vastly expanded Third German Reich. We might then find ourselves at its mercy.' Quoted in Hillgrüber, *Two World Wars*, pp. 60–1.
98. Hitler, *Secret Book*, pp. 157–8.
99. Hillgrüber, *Two World Wars*, p. 53. On Hitler's attitude towards Italy

see Weinberg, *Diplomatic Revolution*, pp. 16–8.
100. Hitler, *Mein Kampf*, pp. 607–8.
101. Hitler, *Table Talk*, pp. 186–7.
102. Hitler, *Politisches Testament*, pp. 78–9.
103. Hitler, *Mein Kampf*, p. 72.
104. Ibid., p. 588.
105. Ibid., p. 571. See also Hitler, *Table Talk*, p. 74.
106. Hillgrüber, *Two World Wars*, p. 69.
107. Hitler, *Table Talk*, pp. 32–5.
108. Ibid., p. 74. Erckner commented in 1937: 'In fact, a continental policy, in Hitler's view, may be the best foundation for securing colonies in the future.' Erckner, op. cit., p. 168. Moreover, in October 1938, the Portuguese ambassador at London, Armindo Monteiro, told Lord Halifax that he 'had studied *Mein Kampf* and could not forget that Herr Hitler had there professed a policy, after European questions were settled, of asserting the colonial claims for Germany'. *PRO* – FO 371/21;681/C12051/184/18, Lord Halifax to Sir W. Selby, 6.10.1938.
109. Hitler, *Table Talk*, p. 361.
110. Hitler, *Mein Kampf*, p. 629.
111. Hillgrüber, *Two World Wars*, p. 51.
112. Hitler, *Secret Book*, p. 156.
113. Hitler, *Table Talk*, p. 50. Before America's entry into the Second World War, Hitler argued that the only reason why the United States was favourably disposed towards Britain's resistance to Germany was the fact it brought 'the moment nearer when she will inherit her [Britain's] inheritance'. Ibid., p. 26.
114. Hitler, *Secret Book*, p. 106–7.
115. Hitler, *Table Talk*, p. 50.
116. Hildebrand, *Foreign Policy*, p. 21. See also Hitler, *Table Talk*, p. 26: 'I shall no longer be there to see it, but I rejoice on behalf of the German people at the idea that one day we will see England and Germany marching together against America.' During the 1920s Hitler recognised that the United States would pose a threat to Germany's world pre-eminence, but during the following decade concluded that the threat was not as great as he feared initially. Miscegenation in the United States had, he felt, weakened the nordic element there to the advantage of Germany in the coming struggle. See Weinberg, *Diplomatic Revolution*, pp. 21–2, and the same author's 'Hitler's Image of the United States', in the *American Historical Review*, 69, (1964).
117. Hildebrand, *Foreign Policy*, pp. 21–2.
118. Hillgrüber, *Two World Wars*, p. 55.
119. Cowling, op. cit., p. 294.
120. Dilks, *Cadogan*, p. 161.
121. Evidence of Hitler's plans was finally presented to the English speaking world with the publication of Hermann Rauschning's *Hitler Speaks* (London, 1939). In this book Rauschning, the former Nazi leader in Danzig, recounted conversations he had had with Hitler which illustrated the global scope of the latter's ambitions – see particularly p. 119 ff. Professor Hildebrand, however, takes the view

that Rauschning's evidence is unreliable. He quotes Goering as stating, while in captivity in Nuremberg: 'I have only seen Herr Rauschning once and can scarcely remember him. It is impossible that he should have met the Führer frequently without my knowing it. And then, can one believe that the Führer would have disclosed his most secret thought to every provincial politician who ran after him? That is indeed laughable.' Hildebrand believes that the somewhat inaccurate recollections of Rauschning are best treated as perceptive, but at times contradictory, analyses and warnings written from the conservative viewpoint. Hildebrand, *Weltreich*, pp. 453–4.

3. The Colonial Question and the Reaction to Hitler

1. Cowling, op. cit., p. 65, and *PRO – CAB* 23/75, *Cabinet Minutes*, 19.1.1933.
2. E. W. Bennett, *German Rearmament and the West* (Princeton, 1979), p. 91.
3. Ibid., pp. 232–3.
4. *PRO – CAB* 23/75, *Cabinet Minutes*, 1.3.1933.
5. Ibid., CAB/24/239, Memorandum by Sir John Simon, *The Crisis in Europe*, 28.2.1933.
6. *VCP*, ADD., Mss., 51084, Lord R. Cecil to Lord E. Irwin, 27.3.1933. Ramsay MacDonald had informed on acquaintance before leaving for Geneva that he was going there in order to give the disarmament conference a 'decent burial'.
7. A. J. Toynbee, *Survey of International Affairs 1933* (London, 1934), pp. 251–7.
8. *PRO – CAB* 23/75, *Cabinet Minutes*, 10.5.1933.
9. Ibid., 76. *Cabinet Minutes*, 10.5.1933.
10. *DBFP*, second series, vol. v, No. 127, A. Cadogan to A.W.A. Leeper, 10.5.1933. Enclosed a memorandum by Brigadier A. C. Temperley, *Germany and Disarmament*. Brigadier Temperley was the head of the war office section of the British delegation to the disarmament conference.
11. *PRO – CAB* 24/241, Memorandum by Sir John Simon, 16.5.1933.
12. Ibid., CAB 23/76, *Cabinet Minutes*, 17.10.1933.
13. S. Heald and J. Wheeler-Bennett (eds), *Documents on International Affairs 1933* (London, 1934), pp. 196–208.
14. Weinberg, *Diplomatic Revolution*, p. 162.
15. *DBFP*, second series, vol. v, No. 406, *Record of a Conversation at the British Embassy (Paris)*, 22.9.1933.
16. Toynbee, *Survey 1933*, pp. 293–4 and 296.
17. *PRO – CAB* 23/76, *Cabinet Minutes*, 26.7.1933.
18. Ibid., CAB 24/241, Memorandum by Sir John Simon, 14.7.1933.
19. Ibid., 23, *Record by Sir John Simon of a Conversation with von Neurath*, 30.9.1933.
20. Ibid., 241, Memorandum by Sir R. Vansittart, 14.7.1933.
21. Toynbee, *Survey 1933*, pp. 302–4, and *DGFP*, series C, vol. I, No. 499,

Minutes of the Conferences of Ministers on 13 and 14.10.1933.

22. In this sense Lord Cecil and Lloyd George had some basis for their argument that the British draft disarmament convention should have been presented before Hitler came to power. See the *Lloyd George Papers*, (hereinafter cited as *LGP*). G/4/1, D. Lloyd George to Lord R. Cecil, 25.4.1934, and Lord R. Cecil to Lord E. Irwin, 27.3.1933, loc. cit.

23. *PRO – CAB 24/243*, Memorandum by Sir John Simon, *Material for deciding British Policy in view of Germany's withdrawal from the Disarmament Conference*, 2.10.1933, and CAB 23/77, *Cabinet Minutes*, 23.10.1933.

24. Sir Samuel Hoare later wrote of Simon: 'good in Cabinet as long as he did not have to give a lead'. The *Templewood Papers*, (hereinafter cited as *TP*), X/5.

25. D. Lloyd George to Lord R. Cecil, 25.4.1934, loc. cit.; *LGP*, G/4/1, Lord R. Cecil to D. Lloyd George, 27.4.1934; and Lord R. Cecil to Lord E. Irwin, 27.3.1933, loc. cit.

26. *HNKY*, 1/7, Diary 4.3.1934, and the *Neville Chamberlain Papers*, (hereinafter cited as *NCP*), 2/23a, Diary Jan. 1934.

27. Wark, op. cit., pp. 76–7, 228–9.

28. *PRO – CAB 23/77, Cabinet Minutes*, 6.11.1933.

29. Ibid., CAB 24/248, Memorandum by Sir John Simon, 9.3.1934, and CAB 23/78, *Cabinet Minutes*, 14.3.1934.

30. The *Sir Eric Phipps Papers*, (hereinafter cited as *PHPP*), 3/3, Sir M. Hankey to Sir E. Phipps, 24.11.1933.

31. *PRO – CAB 24/248*, Memorandum by Sir John Simon, 21.3.1934.

32. N. H. Gibbs, *Rearmament Policy* (London, 1976), pp. 87–99; Middlemas, op. cit., pp. 32–4; N. Rose, *Vansittart: Study of a Diplomat* (London, 1978), pp. 124–7; and J. F. Naylor, *A Man and an Institution: Sir Maurice Hankey, the Cabinet Secretariat and the Custody of Cabinet Secrecy* (Cambridge, 1984), pp. 238–9.

33. *PRO – CAB 23/80, Cabinet Minutes*, 21.11.1934.

34. Ibid., CAB 24/251, *Report of Cabinet Committee on German Rearmament*, 23.11.1934.

35. Ibid., CAB 23/80, *Cabinet Minutes*, 26.11.1934.

36. Ibid., CAB 24/251, Appendix, *Memorandum by Sir John Simon*, 29.11.1934.

37. Ibid., *Report of Cabinet Committee on German Re-armament*, 11.12.1934, and ibid., CAB 23/80, *Cabinet Minutes*, 2.12.1934.

38. British preparations for the Anglo–French talks can be followed in *PRO – CAB 24/251, Report of Cabinet Committee on German Re-armament*, 18.12.1934; ibid., *Resumé of Talks at the Quai d'Orsay*, 22.12.1934; ibid., 253, *Memorandum by Sir John Simon*, 9.1.1935; ibid., *Instructions for Representatives at the Anglo–French Conversations*, 24.1.1935; ibid., CAB 23/80, *Cabinet Minutes*, 19.12.1934; and ibid., 81, *Cabinet Minutes*, 9, and 14.1.1935. For the French lack of preparation see L. Noël, *Les illusions de Stresa* (Paris, 1975), p. 47 and J. B. Duroselle, *La Décadence 1932–1937* (Paris, 1979), p. 144.

39. *PRO – FO 800/280/JSP*, Sir G. Clerk to Sir J. Simon, 18.1.1935.

40. Ibid., CAB 24/253, *French Proposals for an Agreement on Air Attack*, 1.2.1935.

288 *Notes and References*

41. *HNKY*, 1/7, Diary 10.2.1935 and 24.2.1935. On 20 February Hankey, who was bitterly opposed to the air pact proposals, lunched with Simon. The latter was trying to get Hankey's support for his retention of the foreign secretaryship in a Cabinet reconstruction. Hankey wrote: 'I don't feel inclined to support him after this terrible gaffe of the Pact, though I have to admit that he has done a good deal for the fighting services.' See also Naylor, *A Man and and Institution*, pp. 241–2.
42. *PRO* – CAB 24/253, Note by Sir John Simon, 1.2.1935, and ibid., CAB 23/81, *Cabinet Minutes*, 2.2.1935.
43. A. J. Toynbee, *Survey of International Affairs 1935* (London, 1936) vol. I, pp. 122–3.
44. Weinberg, *Diplomatic Revolution*, p. 205.
45. *PRO* – CAB 23/81, *Cabinet Minutes*, 30.1.1935. See Naylor, *A Man and an Institution*, p. 240.
46. *PHPP*, 3/3, Sir M. Hankey to Sir E. Phipps, 8.3.1935.
47. *PRO* – CAB 23/81, *Cabinet Minutes*, 25/2/1935; K. Middlemas and J. Barnes, *Baldwin: A Biography* (London, 1969), pp. 795–6; and *Statement Relating to Defence*, loc. cit.
48. Weinberg relates the postponement rather to Hitler's desire to announce German rearmament in the air at the beginning of March. Weinberg, *Diplomatic Revolution*, p. 205, fn. 119. See also *PRO* – CAB 23/81, *Cabinet Minutes*, 6.3.1935.
49. Weinberg, *Diplomatic Revolution*, p. 205.
50. *PRO* – CAB 23/81, *Cabinet Minutes*, 13.3.1935, and CAB 24/254. Note by Sir John Simon, 17.3.1935.
51. Ibid., CAB 23/78, *Cabinet Minutes*, 25.9.1934, 31.1.1934, 7.2.1934 and 14.2.1934, and ibid., 79, *Cabinet Minutes*, 25.9.1934.
52. Logan, op. cit., p. 64.
53. *PRO* – CAB 23/77, *Cabinet Minutes*, 5.9.1933.
54. Ibid., 78, *Cabinet Minutes*, 19.3.1934.
55. Interestingly, there was in France at the beginning of the 1930s a school of thought mainly associated with Albert Sarraut, colonial minister 1920 to 1924 and Prime Minister briefly during 1933, that favoured Germany's return to colonial activity. This was largely founded in the fear that all colonial unrest was inspired by Communism. Sarraut believed that 'the solution . . . was a Holy Alliance of imperial powers to combat communist subversion'. What he proposed, therefore, was 'co-operation with Germany and Italy in "the *mise en valeur* of the immense African continent"'. Andrew and Kanya-Forstner, *France Overseas*, p. 249. See also an article by Sarraut in the weekly *Marianne* of 17.5.1933 and Duroselle, op. cit., pp. 65–6. At a meeting of the German government's economic policy committee of 24 April 1933, Hitler stated that 'he had no obligations to sounding out France concerning joint colonial activity'. See *DGFP*, series C, vol. I, No. 182.
56. *MAE*, Z/ITALIE/CARTON 1110, M. Dampierre to M. Herriot, 2.8.1932.
57. Toynbee, *Survey 1933*, pp. 207–8.
58. *PRO* – CAB 23/75, *Cabinet Minutes*, 22.3.1933. MacDonald and Simon

had gone to Rome at the invitation of Mussolini, but the visit itself had received substantial promptings from the Foreign Office. Bennett, op. cit., pp. 371–2.

59. Ibid., pp. 371–2.
60. Heald and Wheeler-Bennett, *Documents 1933*, pp. 240–8.
61. *Cabinet Minutes*, 22.3.1933, loc. cit. The *Echo de Paris* of 23.3.1933 carried an article which stated in a footnote: 'Sir John Simon has insisted upon removing from the text . . . the phrase which mentioned common action among the four powers in the colonial field.' A Foreign Office minute of 1.4.1933 confirmed that this was so. *PRO* – FO 371/ 17419/W3581/2294/36.
62. *H. of C. V*, vol. 274, col. 834.
63. Toynbee, *Survey 1933*, p. 219.
64. See A. J. Crozier, 'Imperial Decline'.
65. *PRO* – FO 371/16730/C5431/411/18, *Memorandum Regarding the Possibility that Dr. Schacht may raise the Colonial Question at the Monetary and Economic Conference*, 15.6.1933, by M. H. Huxley. The immediate reaction of the Colonial Office was very much to the effect of wanting to let sleeping dogs lie, Mr. Green of that department informing Huxley that the Colonial Office 'while not disagreeing with anything in the draft [memorandum]. took the line that the less we thought and talked *about* this subject the better, since it had finally been settled years ago'. Ibid., Minute by M. H. Huxley, 15.6.1933. Schacht did indeed raise the possibility of advancing Germany's colonial claims at the world economic conference at a meeting of the German government's economic policy committee on 24 April 1933, loc. cit., and the *New York Times* of 18.6.1933 revealed that during his Washington talks of the previous April the *Reichsbank* president had made hints in this direction. Logan, op. cit., p. 66.
66. *PRO* – FO 371/16730/C5578/411/18, W. D. Wilkinson (Cabinet office) to F. Ashton-Gwatkin, 21.6.1933.
67. Ibid., C5582/411/18, Sir H. Rumbold to Sir J. Simon, 21.6.1933.
68. Ibid., C5653/411/18, Sir H. Rumbold to Sir J. Simon, 22.6.1933.
69. *DGFP*, series C, vol. I, No. 331, Memorandum by State Secretary von Bülow, 22.6.1933.
70. Schmokel, op. cit., pp. 87–8 and *PRO* – FO 371/16730/C5652/411/18, W. Strang to Sir J. Simon, 20.6.1933.
71. Ibid., Karl Radek in *Izvestiya* argued that Britain was in some way implicated in a long term capitalist onslaught on the USSR. 'There is no doubt', he wrote, 'that such plans are being worked out by fascist cliques in Germany together with the most frantic of the English diehard cliques.' Ibid., C5582/411/18, *Notes on the German Delegation to the Economic Conference*, 21.6.1933, by Duncan Sandys. See also *DGFP*, series C, vol. I, No. 335, *Minutes of Conference of Ministers*, 23.6.1933; No. 336, Hugenberg to von Neurath, 24.6.1933; and No. 338, *Minutes of Conference of Ministers*, 27.6.1933.
72. *PRO* – FO 371/16731/C6269/411/18, G. L. M. Clauson to O. Sargeant, 6.7.1933; Minute by J. V. Perowne, 13.7.1933; and R. Wigram to G. L. M. Clauson, 14.7.1933.
73. *The Times*, 19.6.1933.

74. Hildebrand, *Weltreich*, pp. 301–14.
75. The number of occasions on which Hitler spoke publicly and did not mention colonies is more significant than the number of times he mentioned them. Ibid., p. 453, fn. 34.
76. Schmokel, op. cit., p. 89.
77. Hildebrand, *Weltreich*, p. 458.
78. Ibid., p. 456.
79. *PRO* – FO 371/16730/C4392/411/18, Sir H. Rumbold to Sir J. Simon, 10.5.1933.
80. *Daily Mail*, 19.10.1933.
81. Hildebrand, *Weltreich*, p. 458.
82. *Daily Mail*, 21.3.1934.
83. *PRO* – FO 371/17702/C1873/27/18, Minute by R. Wigram, 24.3.1934; Minute by Sir R. Vansittart, 26.3.1934; and Minute by Sir J. Simon, 2.5.1934. Anthony Eden was also opposed to a parliamentary question. Stiffness 'might be criticised by the Vernon Bartlett's of this world' and the Germans be correspondingly encouraged. Ibid., Minute by A. Eden, 27.3.1934.
84. Hildebrand, *Weltreich*, pp. 462–3. Hitler undoubtedly knew that colonies were a costly luxury because Captain V. A. Cazalet had said so in the House of Commons on 18 May 1934. *H. of C. V*, vol. 229, col. 2091. See also *PRO* – FO 371/17704/C67124/22/18, Sir E. Phipps to Sir J. Simon, 11.9.1934.
85. Hildebrand, *Weltreich*, p. 463. In September 1934, Hitler told one British visitor: 'He wanted to see a solid basis for European peace . . . Germany and England had enjoyed 500 years of peace . . . if he could do anything to lay the foundations for another 500 years of peace between the 2 nations he would consider it the greatest act of statesmanship.' *VCP*, Add. Mss. 51083, *Memorandum by J. Weigall of an Interview with Hitler, September 1934*.
86. *PRO* – FO 371/17704/C8759/27/18, Sir E. Phipps to Sir J. Simon, 16.12.1934. Rothermere evidently considered that a Socialist government would soon be in office in Britain and would be more likely to take a detached view of Germany's colonial claims. Phipps disagreed after which he 'joined the ladies, leaving our host [Ribbentrop] to continue his interpreter's task in a corner of the drawing room in more private and comfortable surroundings, and in an idyllic and unruffled atmosphere of complete Anglo–German misunderstanding'.
87. Hildebrand, *Weltreich*, p. 463.
88. *PRO* – FO 371/16731/C7766/411/18. Minute by J. V. Perowne, 5.9.1933, and Wing-Commander Herries (air ministry) to the Foreign Office, 29.8.1933).
89. Hildebrand, *Weltreich*, pp. 459 and 461–2.
90. *PRO* – FO 371/16731/C8136/411/18, Berlin chancery to central department, 5.9.1933; C11006/411/18, Sir E. Phipps to Sir J. Simon, 8.12.1933; 17703/C3194/27/18, B. C. Newton to Sir J. Simon, 10.5.1934; and 18819/C627/21/18, Sir E. Phipps to Sir J. Simon, 23.1.1935.
91. Ibid., 17703/C2731/27/18, Sir E. Phipps to Sir J. Simon. 26.4.1934.
92. Ibid., C4364/27/18, Sir E. Phipps to Sir J. Simon, 20.6.1934.

93. Ibid., C5468/27/18 Sir E. Phipps to Sir J. Simon, 8.8.1934.
94. *DGFP*, series C, vol. I, No. 142, *Minutes of Conference of Ministers*, 7.4.1933. Von Neurath stated that the colonial question would have to remain in the sphere of propaganda for the moment. This coincided with Hitler's aim, although from the Weimar revisionist stance rather than from that of Hitler. Hildebrand, *Weltreich*, p. 455.
95. This stated: 'We demand land and territory (colonies) for the nourishment of our people and for settling our superfluous population.'
96. *PRO* – FO 371/16731/C11006/411/18, Minute by A. R. Dew, 18.12.1933.
97. Ibid., CAB 23/79, *Cabinet Minutes*, 30.5.1934. Nonetheless, Cunliffe-Lister did feel compelled to state in the House of Commons on 20.12.1933 that Tanganyika would not be surrendered and that such action had never been contemplated by the government. *H. of C. V*, vol. 284, cols 1278–9.
98. *PRO* – FO 371/17703/C4364/27/18, Minute by J. V. Perowne, 11.7.1934.
99. Ibid., 18819/C627/21/18, Minute by A. R. Dew, 24.1.1935.
100. Above, p. 43, and A. J. Crozier, 'Stresemann's Locarno Policy'.
101. In spite of Hitler's desire to play down the colonial issue, this assertion had the weight of fact behind it as Schmokel's graph illustrates. Schmokel, op. cit., p. 42.
102. The disclaimers which always accompanied Hitler's avowels of colonial disinterest, by him or through others, and which were always intended for internal political consumption, clearly had the same impact on Vansittart.
103. *PRO* – CAB 24/248 Memorandum by Sir R. Vansittart, *The Future of Germany*, 7.4.1934. See also *DBFP*, second series, vol. VI, appendix III.
104. Above pp. 70–81.
105. The two had previously met when Lugard was Governor of Hong Kong and Voretzsch the German Consul-General there.
106. Chartered companies could not be established in mandates because the administering power was not sovereign. *PRO* – FO 371/17704/C7481/27/18, E. B. Boyd (colonial office) to H. J. Seymour, 5.11.1934.
107. Ibid., Minute by J. V. Perowne, 14.11.1934.
108. Ibid., C8789/27/18, *Record of an Inter-Departmental Conference*, 19.12.1934; 18819/C11/21/18, Sir J. Shuckburgh to Dr I. F. Voretzsch, 31.12.1934; C1030/21/18, Sir P.Cunliffe-Lister to the Governors of African Colonies 4.2.1935.
109. Ibid., C1487/21/18, Dr I. F. Voretzsch to Sir J. Shuckburgh, 7.2.1935.
110. Ibid., Sir J. Shuckburgh to J. V. Perowne, 22.2.1935.
111. Ibid., J. V. Perowne to Sir J. Shuckburgh, 7.3.1935, the Voretzsch affair can also be followed in ibid., CO 323/1282/31479/1.
112. Ibid., FO 37116744/C10295/2293/18, S. C. Wyatt to Sir F. G. A. Butler, 21.11.1933.
113. Ibid., 18819/C1822/21/18, Memorandum by S. C. Wyatt, *The Former German Colonies*, 3.3.1935.
114. Ibid., *Notes of an Interview in Berlin with Dr. Weigelt*, n.d.
115. Ibid., undated Minute by J. V. Perowne.
116. Logan, op. cit., p. 65.
117. Below p. 169.

118. Logan, op. cit., p. 71.
119. *PRO* – FO 371/18819/C144/21/187, Sir E. Phipps to Sir J. Simon, 4.1.1935.
120. Ibid., Minute by Sir R. Vansittart, 8.1.1935.
121. Ibid., Minute by Sir R. Vansittart, 8.1.1935; O. Sargent to Sir R. Vansittart, 24.1.1935; Minute by Sir R. Vansittart, 24.1.1935; and O. Sargent to Sir E. Phipps, 24.1.1935.
122. Ibid., C678/21/18, Sir E. Phipps to Sir J. Simon, 26.1.1935, and Minute by C. J. Norton, 28.1.1935.
123. Ibid., C1738/21/18, Minute by Sir R. Vansittart, 14.3.1935 and C1487/21/18, Minute by Sir R. Vansittart, 1.3.1935.
124. Ibid., C2112/21/18, Sir E. Phipps to Sir J. Simon, 15.3.1935.
125. Ibid., Minute by J. V. Perowne, 18.3.1935.
126. Ibid., C144/21/18, Minute by Sir R. Vansittart, 8.1.1935.

4. German Irredentism in Africa

1. J. C. Fest, *Hitler* (London, 1977), pp. 543–4.
2. *PRO* – FO 371/17301/W2595/1828/17, Acting Vice-Consul Howell to Consul General Cusden, 8.2.1933, and W3074/1828/17, Colonial Office to Foreign Office, 20.3.1933.
3. The immediate impact on the British community was discernible at an early stage, particularly amongst businessmen. See correspondence in *PRO* – CO 691/130/5089.
4. Ibid., 130/5089, Sir G. S. Symes to Sir P. Cunliffe-Lister 1.9.1933. See also *Tanganyika Standard*, 14.8.1933.
5. *East Africa*, 14.12.1933.
6. *PRO* – CO 691/130/5089, Sir J. Sandeman Allen to Sir P. Cunliffe-Lister, 10.10.1933. See also *Tanganyika Standard*, 9.10.1933.
7. Ibid., FO 371/17703/C3194/27/18, B. C. Newton to Sir J. Simon, 14.5.1934, and Hildebrand, *Weltreich*, p. 276.
8. W. Schoenfeld, *Geraubtes Land*, (n.p.n.d.).
9. *PRO* – CO 691/136/25089, P. E. Mitchell (deputy governor Tanganyika Territory) to Sir P. Cunliffe-Lister, 9.5.1934.
10. Ibid., Sir H. MacMichael to Sir P. Cunliffe-Lister, 9.4.1934.
11. Ibid., 142/42022, Sir H. MacMichael to Sir P. Cunliffe-Lister, 23.1.1935. Ernst Troost had come to Tanganyika in 1926 and settled at Moshi. He owned a farm and was also a plantation manager for the Usagara Company. In April 1934 he returned to Germany for instruction at the NSDAP training school at Altona, re-entering the mandate the following October.
12. *East African Standard*, 10.2.1934.
13. *PRO* – CO 691/136/25089, Sir H. MacMichael to Sir P. Cunliffe-Lister, 9.4.1934, and Sir P. Cunliffe-Lister to Sir H. MacMichael, 16.4.1934.
14. *PRO* – CO 691/136/25089, Sir H. MacMichael to Sir P. Cunliffe-Lister, 14.6.1934, and *Tanganyika Standard*, 26.5.1934.
15. *PRO* – CO 691/136/25089, Sir H. MacMichael to Sir P. Cunliffe-Lister, 5.9.1934.

16. Ibid., Sir H. MacMichael to Sir P. Cunliffe-Lister, 17.10.1934. On South-West Africa see below pp. 151–71.
17. Sir H. MacMichael to Sir P. Cunliffe-Lister, 14.6.1934, loc. cit.
18. *PRO* – CO 691/136/25089, Sir P. Cunliffe-Lister to Sir H. MacMichael, 5.11.1934.
19. Ibid., Sir H. MacMichael to Sir P. Cunliffe-Lister, 21.11.1934.
20. Ibid., Sir H. MacMichael to Sir P. Cunliffe-Lister, 6.11.1934.
21. Ibid., FO 371/17702/C1021/27/18, Sir E. Phipps to Sir J. Simon, 8.2.1934; 17703/C5784/27/18, Sir H. MacMichael to Sir P. Cunliffe-Lister, 25.7.1934; 18819/C405/21/18, Sir H. MacMichael to Sir P. Cunliffe-Lister, 30.11.1934.
22. Ibid., C1432/21/18, J. A. Calder (Colonial Office) to Sir R. Vansittart, 21.2.1935.
23. Ibid., Minute by J. V. Perowne, 23.2.1935.
24. Judge of disputes of honour.
25. Schoenfeld was evidently upset by the Ward Price/Hitler interview, in which the latter referred to colonies as a luxury. See above, p. 108, and *PRO* – FO 371/18820/C3034/21/18, Circular by E. Troost, 13.12.1934.
26. Ibid., CO 691/142/42022, Sir H. MacMichael to Sir P. Cunliffe-Lister, 23.1.1935. See also *Morning Post*, 15.1.1935.
27. *PRO* – CO 691/142/42022, Sir P. Cunliffe-Lister to Sir H. MacMichael, 2.3.1935.
28. Ibid, FO 371/18820/C3034/21/18, Sir H. MacMichael to Sir P. Cunliffe-Lister, 21.3.1935, and CO 691/142/42022, G. F. Sayers to M. Mac-Donald, 27.7.1935.
29. Ibid., FO 371/18821/C7059/21/18, *Extract from the Tanganyika Territory Intelligence Report for the half year ended* 30.6.1935.
30. Ibid., 19926/C2522/97/18, Sir H. MacMichael to J. H. Thomas, 25.3.1936, and J. H. Thomas to Sir H. MacMichael, 3.4.1936.
31. See, for example, ibid., CO 691/142/42022, A. de V. Leigh (Secretary of the London Chamber of Commerce) to J. Ramsay MacDonald, 23.5.1935.
32. Ibid., 147/42022/2, H. S. L. Grenfall (chairman East African Goldfields Limited) to Sir J. L. Maffey, 6.4.1936; A. M. Landauer (Landauer & Co.) to J. H. Thomas, 23.4.1936; R. B. Harvey (secretary of the Joint East Africa Board) to J. H. Thomas, 11.5.1936; and A. de V. Leigh to S. Baldwin, 21.5.1936.
33. *Tanganyika Standard*, 2.5.1936; *PRO* – CO 691/147/42022, R. Nicholson (Secretary of the Royal African Society) to E. B. Boyd, 23.6.1936; ibid., 323/1510/6656, Anonymous letter, March 1937; and ibid., 691/147/42022/2, Bishop of Massai to W. Ormsby-Gore, 25.6.1937.
34. Ibid., 42022, Sir H. MacMichael to J. H. Thomas, 22.4.1936.
35. Ibid., 153/42022, Sir H. MacMichael to W. Ormsby-Gore, 13.3.1937.
36. Ibid., D. M. Kennedy to W. Ormsby-Gore, 19.8.1937.
37. Ibid., E. B. Boyd to Sir R. Vansittart, 4.10.1937; W. Strang to Sir C. Parkinson, 21.10.1937; O. Harvey to E. B. Boyd, 21.10.1937; D. M. Kennedy to W. Ormsby-Gore, 20.10.1937; G. M. B. Ingram to Sir C. Parkinson, 11.11.1937; and W. C. Bottomley to Sir H. MacMichael, 26.11.1937.

38. Sir H. MacMichael to W. Ormsby-Gore, 13.3.1937, loc. cit.
39. *PRO* – CO 691/136/25089, G. Pilcher (secretary of the Royal Empire Society) to Sir P. Cunliffe-Lister, 3.1.1934.
40. *Morning Post*, 6.6.1934.
41. P. E. Mitchell to Sir P. Cunliffe-Lister, 9.5.1934, loc. cit.
42. *PRO* – FO 371/17703/C4061/27/18, Minute by A. R. Dew, 28.6.1934.
43. Ibid., C4307/27/18, Sir H. MacMichael to Sir P. Cunliffe-Lister, 31.5.1934.
44. Ibid., Sir H. MacMichael to Sir P. Cunliffe-Lister, 6.6.1934.
45. Ibid., C5588/27/18, Mr Rowe Dutton (Treasury) to G. L. M. Clauson (Colonial Office), 14.7.1934.
46. Ibid., C5636/27/18, J. W. Golsby (Department of Overseas Trade) to Sir J. L. Maffey (Colonial Office), 8.8.1934.
47. Ibid., 17704/C5957/27/18, Memorandum, by J. V. Perowne, *German Settlers in Tanganyika*, 8.8.1934.
48. Ibid., Minute by J. V. Perowne, 8.8.1934.
49. Ibid., FO 371/17704/C5957/27/18, Minute by Sir R. Vansittart, 9.8.1934.
50. Ibid., CO 691/136/25089, Sir H. MacMichael to Sir P. Cunliffe-Lister, 25.7.1934.
51. Ibid., FO 371/17704/C5957/27/18, Minute by J. V. Perowne, 22.8.1934.
52. Ibid., Minutes by C. W. Baxter and W. E. Beckett, 2.8.1934 and 29.8.1934; ibid., C. W. Baxter to Sir J. L. Maffey, 6.9.1934; Sir H. MacMichael to Sir P. Cunliffe-Lister, 6.11.1934, loc. cit; and *PRO* – FO 371/18819/C21/21/18, Minute by J. V. Perowne, 8.1.1935.
53. Ibid., CO 691/136/25089, Sir P. Cunliffe-Lister to Sir H. MacMichael, 1.1.1935; ibid., FO 371/18819/C583/21/18, Minutes by J. V. Perowne, 19.2.1935, O. Sargent, 20.2.1935, and Sir R. Vansittart, 21.2.1935.
54. Below pp. 180–81.
55. *Rand Daily Mail*, 26.1.1933.
56. A. J. Toynbee, *Survey of International Affairs 1920–1923* (London, 1925), p. 398, and I. Goldblatt, *History of South-West Africa* (Cape Town, 1971), pp. 219–21.
57. Ibid.
58. *PRO* – FO 371/16731/C6935/411/18, Memorandum by Colonel Venning, *The German Problem in South-West Africa*, n.d. See also J. H. Hofmeyr, 'Germany's Colonial Claims: A South African View', *Foreign Affairs*, July 1939.
59. Goldblatt, op. cit., pp. 214 and 219–21.
60. Ibid., and cf. A. J. Toynbee, *Survey of International Affairs 1929* (London, 1930), pp. 243–4.
61. Ibid., pp. 245–6.
62. Ibid.
63. Ibid., pp. 250–1.
64. Ibid., pp. 245–6.
65. Goldblatt, op. cit., pp. 229–32.
66. Toynbee, *Survey 1929*, p. 245.
67. *The Times*, 7.8.1933; Goldblatt, op. cit, pp. 229–32; and Toynbee, *Survey 1929*, pp. 245–6.
68. Venning Memorandum, loc. cit., and *PRO* – FO 371/16731/C6935/411/

18, Sir H. J. Stanley to Sir E. Harding, 15.6.1933.

69. *Cape Argus*, 27.7.1933; *Cape Times*, 28.7.1933; *Rand Daily Mail*, 26.7.1933, 27.7.1933, 29.7.1933, 3.8.1933, 4.8.1933, 12.8.1933 and 18.8.1933; and the *Star*, 1.8.1933, 2.8.1933, and 11.8.1933.
70. *Cape Times*, 31.7.1933.
71. *The Times*, 12.8.1933.
72. *PRO* – FO 371/16731/C8203/411/18, P. Liesching to J. H. Thomas, 6.8.1933.
73. B. Bunting, *The Rise of the South African Reich* (London, 1964), pp. 44 and 54 ff.; *Rand Daily Mail*, 26.8.1933, 28.8.1933, 4.11.1933 and 7.11.1933; *The Star* 1.11.1933; and *PRO* – FO 371/16731/C10257/411/18, P. Liesching to J. H. Thomas, 30.10.1933, and C10667/411/18, P. Liesching to J. H. Thomas, 8.11.1933.
74. Ibid., 18819/C2166/21/18, Sir W. H. Clark to J. H. Thomas, 4.2.1935.
75. P. Liesching to J. H. Thomas, 6.8.1933, loc. cit.
76. Sir W. H. Clark to J. H. Thomas, 4.2.1935, loc. cit.; *Rand Daily Mail*, 2.11.1933; and *Johannesburg Sunday Times*, 22.10.1933.
77. B. Bennett, *Hitler Over Africa* (London, 1939), p. 179.
78. *Rand Daily Mail*, 2.11.1933.
79. Ibid., 30.11.1933, and *Cape Argus*, 7.12.1933.
80. Goldblatt, op. cit., pp. 220–32.
81. *Rand Daily Mail*, 10.11.1933.
82. *Cape Times*, 27.1.1934.
83. *Cape Argus*, 30.4.1934.
84. *Cape Times*, 16.4.1934.
85. Bennett, op. cit., pp. 158–9.
86. Ibid., pp. 162–4.
87. *Cape Times*, 5.4.1934.
88. Ibid., 16.5.1934.
89. Ibid.
90. Ibid., 15.5.1934, 19.5.1934 and 21.5.1934
91. Bennett, op. cit., pp. 168–9.
92. *Johannesburg Sunday Times*, 8.7.1934.
93. *Rand Daily Mail*, 13.7.1934 and 14.7.1934, and *Johannesburg Sunday Times*, 15.7.1934.
94. *Rand Daily Mail*, 10.10.1934, 12.10,1934, 2.11.1934, and the *Star*, 30.10.1934. See also 'South Africa: Nationalism, Nazism and Neighbourliness', *Round Table*, March 1935. In Bennett's view the only result of the ban was to drive the Nazis underground, Bennett, op. cit., pp. 20–1.
95. *PRO* – FO 371/18819/C1606/21/18, Memorandum by P. Liesching, 10.1.1935.
96. *Johannesburg Sunday Times*, 30.9.1934.
97. *Rand Daily Mail*, 2.11.1935, and Goldblatt, op. cit., pp.   229–32.
98. *PRO* – FO 371/17704/C8734/27/18. Sir H. J. Stanley to J. H. Thomas, 27.11.1934.
99. *Rand Daily Mail*, 30.11.1934. See also *Round Table*, March 1935, art. cit.
100. *Cape Times*, 19.1.1935.
101. Goldblatt, op. cit., pp. 233–4.

102. Below pp. 248–49.
103. *PRO* – CAB 24/268, Memorandum by Malcolm MacDonald 26.2.1937. See also ibid., FO 371/20718/C209/37/18, *Declaration of the Administration of South West Africa*; ibid., 20719/C1512/37/18, Draft memorandum by Malcolm MacDonald; ibid., 19930/C8372/97/18, Record of a conversation between Malcolm MacDonald and Mr C. Te Water, 16.11.1936; ibid., CO 323/1398/6656, Malcolm MacDonald to E. B. Boyd, 17.11.1936; and Hofmeyr, art. cit.
104. *PRO* – FO 371/20721/C3638/37/18, E. Wiehl to H. D. J. Bodenstein, 31.10.1936; ibid., 19930/C8925/97/18, Sir E. Phipps to A. Eden, 14.12.1936; and ibid., C9215/97/18, Sir E. Phipps to A. Eden, 26.12.1936.
105. Ibid., 20720/C3385/37/18, Sir W. H. Clark to M. MacDonald, 7.4.1937, and C3166/37/18, Mr. C. Te Water to M. MacDonald, 15.4.1937, and Mr C. Te Water to MacDonald, 16.4.1937. See also ibid., C2727/37/18, A. Eden to Sir E. Phipps, 9.4.1937.
106. Ibid., CO 323/1511/6656,R. W. Spraggett to Director of Naval Intelligence, 9.10.1937.
107. Bennett, op. cit., pp. 100–2.
108. *PRO* – FO 371/17704/C6415/27/18, Sir H. J. Stanley to J. H. Thomas, 22.8.1934.
109. *Cape Times*, 1.2.1935.
110. Ibid., 2.2.1935, and *PRO* – FO 371/18819/C2166/21/18, Sir W. H. Clark to J. H. Thomas, 4.2.1935 and H. D. J. Bodenstein to South African Editors, 22.8.1934.
111. Ibid., 18820/C2822/21/18, Sir W. H. Clark to Sir E. Harding, 8.3.1935.
112. Ibid., 16731/C6935/411/18, Minute by O. Sargent, 24.8.1933.
113. Ibid., 17704/C8621/27/18, Sir H. J. Stanley to J. H. Thomas, 12.11. 1934.
114. Joelson, op. cit., p. 254.
115. *PRO* – FO 371/18819/C660/21/18, Sir W. H. Clark to J. H. Thomas, 21.1.1935.
116. *Cape Argus*, 18.1.1935.
117. *PRO* – FO 371/18819/C660/21/18, Sir W. H. Clark to J. H. Thomas, 23.1.1935.
118. Ibid., C240/21/18, Minute by J. V. Perowne, 11.1.1935. Sir John Simon also now asked the Dominions Office to furnish him with details of German activities in all mandates held by the governments of dominions for use should the German government elect to raise the colonial question in the near future. See ibid., CO 323/1343/6656, C. W. Baxter to the Dominions Office, 16.1.1935.
119. Ibid., FO 371/18819/C660/21/18, Minute by Sir R. Vansittart, 5.2.1935.
120. Ibid., C1273/21/18, Berlin Chancery to the Central Department, 12.2.1935. In March 1935 the British High Commissioner in South Africa, Sir W. H. Clark, established that the Union government, despite the statements of ministers, had made no formal pronouncement of its view of Germany and the colonial question. It soon, however, became clear that Pirow was not a solitary voice in the belief that Germany should receive colonial satisfaction. See ibid., 18820/C3123/21/18, Sir W. H. Clark to Sir H. Batterbee, 14.3.1935; ibid.,

C4054/21/18, British Library of Information, New York, to the Foreign Office, n.d.; ibid., 19929/C7785/97/18, Sir W. H. Clark to, M. Mac-Donald, 18.9.1936; ibid., 19926/C3400/97/18, M. E. Antrobus to Sir H. Batterbee, 3.4.1936; ibid., 19925/C1447/97/18, A. Eden to Sir E. Phipps, 5.3.1936; Hofmeyr, art. cit.; O. Pirow, *James Barry Munnick Hertzog*, (London, 1958), p. 223; *PRO* – FO 371/18819/C2166/21/18, Sir W. H. Clark to J. H. Thomas, 4.2.1935; and ibid., 19926/C3018/97/18, Sir W. H. Clark to M. MacDonald,. 10.3.1936.
121. Ibid., 18819/C1273/21/18, Minute by J. V. Perowne, 26.2.1935.
122. Ibid., C1738/21/18, Memorandum by J. V. Perowne, *Germany's Colonial Aspirations*, 4.3.1935.
123. Ibid., Minute by Sir R. Vansittart, 14.3.1935.
124. Ibid., C1487/21/18, Minute by Sir R. Vansittart, 2.3.1935.

5. The Colonial Question and a General Settlement

1. *PRO* – FO 371/18820/C4762/21/18, Memorandum by J. V. Perowne, 11.2.1935.
2. Ibid., 18819/C1033/21/18, Sir H. F. Batterbee to Sir G. Mounsey, 5.2.1935.
3. Ibid., 18820/C4762/21/18, Undated Minute by Sir J. Simon, presumably early February 1935.
4. Ibid., Minute by R. Wigram, 12.2.1935.
5. Ibid.,C4763/21/18, Memorandum by R. Wigram, 22.2.1935.
6. Ibid., 18819/C1738/21/18, Minute by R. Wigram, 6.3.1935. See also Minute by R. Wigram 6.3.1935 in ibid., 18820/C4764/21/18.
7. Ibid., 18819/C1738/21/18, Minute by Sir R. Vansittart, 14.3.1935.
8. Ibid., 18820/4765/21/18, Memorandum by Sir H. F. Batterbee, 11.3.1935; Minute by R. Wigram, 11.3.1935; Minute by O. Sargent, 12.3.1935; and Minute by Sir R. Vansittart, 12.3.1935. See also ibid., CO 323/1343/6656, Minute by Sir H. F. Batterbee.
9. Ibid., FO 371/18819/C1994/21/18, Sir J. Sandeman Allen to Sir J. Simon, 11.3.1935; ibid., 18820/C2990/21/18, Sir J. Sandeman Allen to Sir J. Simon, 2.4.1935; ibid., C4767/21/18, Minutes by J. V. Perowne, 24.4.1935, O. Sargent, 24.4.1935, Sir R. Vansittart, 25.4.1935 and H. J. Seymour, 16.5.1935; ibid., CO 323/1343/6656, Minute by Sir H. F. Batterbee, 26.4.1935; and ibid., FO 371/18820/21/18, Minute by J. V. Perowne, 13.6.1935.
10. Ibid., CAB 23/81, *Cabinet Minutes*, 20.3.1935.
11. Ibid., appendix, *Note Delivered by H. M. Ambassador Berlin to the German Government*, 18.3.1935.
12. *DBFP*, second series, vol.XII, No. 527, Sir E. Phipps to Sir J. Simon, 5.3.1935.
13. Ibid., No. 504, Sir E. Phipps to Sir J. Simon, 23.2.1935.
14. Ibid., No. 530, Sir R. Vansittart to Sir E. Phipps, 5.3.1935.
15. Ibid., No. 511, Sir E. Phipps to Sir J. Simon, 27.2.1935.
16. Above, pp. 119–120.

17. *DGFP*, series C, vol. III, No. 544, H. Schacht to Hitler, 19.3.1935, and No. 549, H. Schnee to Hitler, 20.3.1935.
18. There must be some doubt about this interpretation as it is not clear whether or not von Epp's copy was submitted before or after the Simon talks – see ibid., No. 544, fn. 3, p. 1027. There was, however, little urgency in this because Schacht had made it clear in his statement that he was simultaneously informing the Chancellor of his views.
19. Hildebrand, *Weltreich*, pp. 464–5.
20. Quite why Simon and Eden should have been so astonished by this revelation is not clear – see ibid., p. 469 – that they were credulous – see Taylor, *Origins*, p. 18. – is understandable. British estimates of Germany's air strength had been hinting in this direction for some time – see Memorandum by Sir. J. Simon, 29.11.1935, loc. cit., and *DBFP*, second series, vol. XII, No. 516, *Memorandum on present state of the German air force*, 28.2.1935. See also Wark, op. cit., pp. 40–5. At the end of 1934 the RAF expansion scheme A was accelerated because of alarming intelligence reports in respect of the *Luftwaffe*. Eventually, however, it was correctly concluded in London that Hitler's parity claim had been an exaggeration. It is also worth noting that this whole episode stimulated greater spending on British intelligence. See C. Andrew, *Secret Service: The Making of the British Intelligence Community* (London, 1985), p. 377.
21. According to Hitler's interpreter, Schmidt, Hitler accompanied all references to the colonial question with the statement: 'Germany has for the moment no colonial demands to bring forward.' See Hildebrand, *Weltreich*, pp. 467–8. See also *PRO* – FO 800/290/*JSP*, Sir John Simon to King George V, 27.3.1935. Simon informed the King that he took a 'very firm line . . . and held out no hope that Germany's aspirations could be satisfied by dismembering the Empire or transferring mandates'.
22. Ibid., CAB 24/254, *Notes of Anglo–German Conversations, held at the Chancellor's Palace, Berlin, on March 25 and 26,. 1935*. See also ibid., CAB 23/81 and *DGFP*, series C, vol. III, No. 555.
23. *NCP*, 2/23a, Diary, 2.4.1935.
24. *PRO* – FO 800/290/*JSP*, Sir J. Simon to Sir E. Phipps, 5.4.1935.
25. Ibid., Sir E. Phipps to Sir J. Simon, 11.4.1935.
26. *DGFP*, series C, vol. III, No. 564, Circular of the Foreign Minister, 29.3.1935.
27. Ibid., No. 358, Unsigned Memorandum, and *DBFP*, second series, vol. XII, No. 215, Sir J. Simon to Sir E. Phipps, 26.11.1934, No. 221, Sir E. Phipps to Sir J. Simon, 27.11.1934, and No. 230, Sir E. Phipps to Sir J. Simon, 28.11.1934.
28. *Notes of Anglo–German Conversations 25 and 26 March, 1935*, loc. cit.
29. *DBFP*, second series, vol. XII, No. 722, *Notes of Anglo–French–Italian Conversations, held at the Palazzo Borromeo, Isola Bella, Stresa, from April 11 to 14, 1935*.
30. *PRO*–CAB 23/81, *Cabinet Minutes*, 8.4.1935. See also ibid., CAB 24/254, Memorandum by Sir John Simon, 4.4.1935. Cecil thought 'the meeting at Stresa is most unfortunate'. According to him, 'it would be regarded by the Germans as a threat in consequence of their unreasonable . . .

attitude at Berlin'. Baldwin thought that there was 'a good deal' in what Cecil said. *VCP*, Add. Mss., 51080, Lord R. Cecil to S. Baldwin, 29.3.1935, and S. Baldwin to Lord R. Cecil, 2.4.1935.

31. *PRO–FO 371/18732/A3190/22/45*, Minute by R. L. Craigie, 29.3.1935, and Minutes by R. Wigram and O. Sargent, 1.4.1935; ibid., 18733/ A4679/22/45, Minute by P. H. Gore-Booth, 23.5.1935; *DGFP*, series C, vol. IV, pp. 171–9 and *PRO–FO 371/18734/A5302/22/45*, Memorandum by P. H. Gore-Booth, 12.6.1935; *DBFP*, second series, vol. XIII, No. 348, *Notes of the seventh meeting between representatives of the United Kingdom and Germany, June 18, 1935*: and Eva H. Haraszti, *Treaty-Breakers of Realpolitiker. The Anglo–German Naval Agreement of June 1935* (Boppard am Rhein, 1974), passim.

32. *PRO–FO 371/18735/A5987/22/45*, Memorandum by Sir S. Hoare, 1.7.1935. See also ibid., FO 800/295, *Sir Samuel Hoare Papers*, (hereinafter cited as *SHP*), Record of a Conversation with the French Ambassador, 13.6.1935.

33. Ibid., CAB 23/82, *Cabinet Minutes*, 19.6.1935.

34. Ibid., 81, *Cabinet Minutes*, 1.5.1935, 22.5.1935, 29.5.1935 and 5.6.1935; Ibid., CAB 24/255, Report of a Cabinet Committee, 3.6.1935; ibid., CAB 23/82, *Cabinet Minutes*, 19.6.1935; ibid., CAB 24/255, Memorandum by Sir S. Hoare and Sir P. Cunliffe-Lister, 21.6.1935, and Memorandum by Sir S. Hoare, 24.6.1935; ibid., CAB 23/82, *Cabinet Minutes*, 26.6.1935; ibid., CAB 24/255, Memorandum by Sir S. Hoare on the Air Pact and on Air Limitation Agreement, 2.7.1935, – see also *DBFP*, second series, vol. XIII, No. 389; ibid., No. 409, Sir G. Clerk to Sir S. Hoare, 10.7.1935, and *PRO–FO 371/18851/C7698/55/18*, Memorandum by R. Wigram, 15.11.1935; and *DBFP*, second series, vol. XIII, Sir G. Clerk to Sir S. Hoare, 29.7.1935.

35. Ibid., No. 447, Sir S. Hoare to Mr. Newton, 1.8.1935.

36. Memorandum by R. Wigram, 15.11.1935, loc. cit.

37. *PRO–CAB 23/82*, *Cabinet Minutes*, 4.12.1935.

38. *DGFP*, series C, vol. IV, No. 252, von Neurath to von Bulow, 7.8.1935.

39. *PRO–CAB 24/257*, Note by Sir S. Hoare, 4.12.1935.

40. *The Times*, 27.3.1935 and 1.4.1935.

41. *H. of C. V*, vol. 300, col. 977. See also *PRO–CAB 23/81, Cabinet Minutes*, 8.4.1935, and ibid., FO 371/18820/C3071/21/18, Minute by Sir R. Vansittart.

42. *H. of C. V*, vol. 300, cols. 986–7.

43. Ibid., vol. 301, cols. 595–7.

44. Ibid., vol. 301, cols. 686–7.

45. *House of Lords Debates*, Fifth Series, (hereinafter cited as *H. of L. V*), vol. 96, cols. 746–50.

46. *DGFP*, series C, vol. IV, No. 27, von Hoesch to von Neurath, 12.4.1935.

47. *The Times*, 2.5.1935.

48. *PRO–FO 371/18820/C4434/21/18*, Sir E. Phipps to Sir J. Simon, 29.5.1935.

49. Ibid., C4407/21/18, Sir E. Phipps to Sir J. Simon, 31.5.1935.

50. Ibid., C2595/21/18, *Memorandum regarding German Colonial Aspirations*, 29.6.1935, by J. V. Perowne.

51. Ibid., 18821/C5142/21/18, *Memorandum respecting Germany and the*

Portuguese Colonial Empire, 29.6.1935, by J. V. Perowne. See also ibid., C5144/21/18.

52. Ibid., 18820/C2595/21/18, Minute by J. V. Perowne, 29.3.1935.
53. Ibid., Minute by R. Wigram, 26.7.1935.
54. Ibid., 18821/C4873/21/18, Minute by Sir R. Vansittart, 26.7.1935.
55. Ibid., C5142/21/18, Minute by Sir R. Vansittart, 2.8.1935.
56. Ibid., 18820/C2595/21/18, Minute by Sir R. Vansittart, 4.8.1935.
57. Ibid., Minute by Sir S. Hoare, 8.8.1935.
58. Ibid., 18821/C5142/21/18, Minute by Sir S. Hoare, 14.8.1935.
59. *MAE*, SDN/549, P. Laval to L. Rollin, 27.8.1935.
60. *PRO*–FO 371/19692/W7711/7711/98, A. Loveday (Director of the Financial Section and Intelligence Service of the League Secretariat 1931–9) to F. P. Walters, 27.8.1935.
61. Ibid., Minutes by F. Ashton-Gwatkin, 4.9.1935, Lord Cranborne, 4.9.1935, Sir G. Mounsey, 4.9.1935, and Sir R. Vansittart to Sir S. Hoare, 4.9.1935.
62. Ibid., W8079/7711/98, Note by Sir W. Runciman, n.d.
63. *NCP*, 18/1/932, Neville Chamberlain to Hilda Chamberlain, 7.9.1935.
64. *PRO*–FO 800/295/*SHP*, F. Ashton-Gwatkin to Sir S. Hoare, 7.9.1935.
65. Ibid., FO 371/18822/C8522/21/18, Sir Samuel Hoare's speech to the League Assembly, 11.9.1935. See also Neville Chamberlain to Hilda Chamberlain, 7.9.1935, loc. cit.
66. Joelson, op. cit., pp. 257–8.
67. *The Times*, 19.9.1935 and 20.9.1935.
68. *The Economist*, 26.10.1935.
69. Ibid., 16.11.1935.
70. *The Times*, 13.1.1936 and 14.1.1936.
71. *H. of C. V*, vol. 305, cols. 31, 55–6, 72, 78, 113, and 125–6.
72. Ibid., vol. 307, cols. 81, 329–30 and 335.
73. *PRO*–CAB 24/259, *Report by an Interdepartmental Committee on the distribution and accessibility of Colonial raw materials*, 17.1.1936. See also ibid., FO 371/19692/W8217/7711/98, Minute by F. Ashton-Gwatkin, 13.9.1935.
74. Ibid., W8867/7711/18, Minutes by Sir R. Vansittart, 7.10.1935, Sir S. Hoare, 7.10.1935, and F. Ashton-Gwatkin to G. L. M. Clauson, 9.10.1935.
75. Ibid., W9558/7711/18, F. Ashton-Gwatkin to G. L. M. Clauson, 7.11.1935.
76. Ibid., Minute by O. Sargent, 8.11.1935.
77. J. T. Shotwell was Professor of History, Columbia University, New York, 1908–42. Actively involved in international affairs throughout his life, he published widely on the subject.
78. *PRO*–FO 371/19692/W10033/7711/98, Memorandum by Sir S. Hoare, 19.11.1935.
79. Ibid., Minutes by Gladwyn Jebb, 21.11.1935, R. Wigram, 22.11.1935, L. Collier, 27.11.1935, and F. Ashton-Gwatkin, 18.11.1935.
80. Ibid., Minute by Sir R. Vansittart, n.d.
81. Ibid., Minutes by H. J. Seymour and F. Ashton-Gwatkin, 6.12.1935.
82. Ibid., Minutes by Sir G. Mounsey, 9.12.1935, O. Sargent, 13.12.1935,

V. Wellesley, 16.12.1935, Lord Stanhope, n.d. and Sir R. Vannsittart, 31.12.1935.

83. Ibid., Minute by A. Eden, 3.1.1936.
84. *Report by an Interdepartmental Committee on the distribution and accessibility of Colonial raw materials*, 17.1.1936, loc. cit. See also *PRO*–CAB 24/ 259, Note by Eden, 17.1.1936, and CAB 23/83, *Cabinet Minutes*, 29.1.1936.
85. *H. of C. V*, vol. 308, cols. 244–5.
86. Ibid., cols. 246–60. In the course of these exchanges both Churchill and Amery pointed out the erroneous interpretation which Lloyd George put on the origins of the mandates.
87. *PRO*–FO 371/19925/C802/97/18, Sir E. Phipps to A. Eden, 8.2.1936, and C854/97/18, Sir E. Phipps to A. Eden, 11.2.1936.
88. Ibid., 19728/W8292/1718/36, Acting Consul-General Nias (Loanda) to Sir S. Hoare, 23.8.1935, and W7632/1718/36, K. T. Gurney, Chargé d'Affaires at Lisbon, to Sir S. Hoare, 24.8.1935; and ibid., 19925/C1749/ 97/18 and 20512/W771/762/18, A. Eden to Sir C. Wingfield, 22.1.1936.
89. Ibid., W1326/895/36, A. Eden to Sir C. Wingfield, 11.2.1936.
90. Ibid., C838/97/18, Sir E. Ovey to A. Eden, 11.2.1936 and A. Eden to Sir E. Ovey, 13.2.1936.
91. Ibid., CAB 23/83, *Cabinet Minutes*, 12.2.1936.
92. *H. of C. V*, vol. 308, cols. 933–4.
93. *Cabinet Minutes*, 12.2.1936, loc. cit.
94. *PRO*–FO 371/19925/C838/97/18, Minute by J. V. Perowne, 12.2.1936.
95. Ibid., C978/97/18, Minute by R. Wigram, 12.2.1936.
96. Joelson, op. cit., pp. 295–60.
97. *PRO*–FO 371/20513/W2222/933/36, Sir C. Wingfield to A. Eden, 6.3.1936.
98. Above pp. 50–53.
99. *PRO*–FO 371/18821/C6286/21/18, B. C. Newton to Sir S. Hoare, 30.8.1935 and Minute by Sir R. Vansittart, 6.9.1935; ibid., C6576/21/18, B. C. Newton to Sir S. Hoare, 29.8.1935, and Minute by J. V. Perowne, 24.9.1935.
100. *Morning Post*, 28.10.1935, and 15.11.1935, and *News Chronicle*, 15.11.1935.
101. *PRO*–FO 371/18822/C8522/21/18, Sir E. Phipps to Sir S. Hoare, 10.10.1935, and ibid., 18821/C7493/635/18, Sir E. Phipps to Sir S. Hoare, 8.11.1935.
102. Ibid., 18821/C7921/21/21/18, Sir E. Phipps to Sir S. Hoare, 27.11.1935.
103. Ibid., C8047/21/18, Sir E. Phipps to Sir S. Hoare, 5.12.1935.
104. Ibid., C8266/55/18, Sir E. Phipps to Sir S. Hoare, 13.12.1935. See also *DBFP*, second series, vol. xv, No. 383, Sir E. Phipps to Sir S. Hoare, 16.12.1935.
105. *PRO*–FO 371/18821/C8421/21/18, Sir E. Phipps to A. Eden, 21.12.1935, and Minute by A. Eden, 31.12.1935. See also ibid., 18860/C7515/134/18, Sir E. Phipps to Sir S. Hoare, 7.11.1935. At the end of 1935 the Foreign Office was again favoured with the views of Voretzsch on the colonial question and those of Baron von Stumm. See ibid., 19924/C276/97/18, Lord Lugard to Lord Plymouth, 31.11.1935, and 18821/C8328/21/18,

Memorandum by R. Wigram, 11.11.1935.
106. Ibid., 18860/C7515/21/18, Sir R. Vansittart to Lord Clive Wigram, 7.11.1935.
107. Ibid., 18851/C8039/55/18, Sir G. Clerk to Sir R. Vansittart, 14.11.1935. See also ibid., C7813/55/18, Sir E. Phipps to Sir S. Hoare, 22.11.1935; C7762/55/18, Sir E. Phipps to Sir S. Hoare, 21.11.1935.
108. Ibid., C7752/55/18, Memorandum by O. Sargent and R. Wigram, 21.11.1935, *Britain, France and Germany*.
109. Ibid., 18851/C7752/55/18 Note by Mr. Ashton-Gwatkin on Germany's economic position. n.d.
110. *DBFP*, second series, vol. XV, appendix I, Comments by L. Collier, 22.11.1935.
111. Ibid, Comments by Sir R. Vansittart, 1.12.1935, and Minute by Sir S. Hoare, 3.12.1935.
112. *PRO–FO* 371/18860/C8198/134/18, Sir E. Phipps to Sir S. Hoare, 10.12.1935, and Minutes by R. Wigram, 12.12.1935, and Orme Sargent, 15.12.1935. Sir M. Hankey was very opposed to the retrocession of mandates. *HNKY*, 5/5, Sir E. Phipps to Sir M. Hankey, 30.12.1935, and Sir M. Hankey to Sir E. Phipps, 2.1.1936.
113. See *DBFP*, second series, vol. V, No. 492; vol. VI, No. 241; vol. XII, Nos. 361 and 700; vol. XIII, Nos. 204. 327, 500 and 518; and vol. XV, Nos. 213, 383 and 404.
114. Ibid., No. 460, Memorandum by A. Eden, 17.1.1936, *The German Danger*. See also *PRO–CAB* 24/259.
115. Ibid., CAB 23/83, *Cabinet Minutes*, 29.1.1936.
116. Ibid., *Cabinet Minutes*, 5.2.1936. See also ibid., FO 381/19879/C587/92/ 62, Record of a conversation between A. Eden and M. van Zeeland, 29.1.1936.
117. *DBFP*, second series, vol. XV, appendix IV, *Memorandum by Messrs. F. T. A. Ashton-Gwatkin and H. M. G. Jebb respecting German 'expansions'*. 31.1.1936. The Colonial Office was not very happy about these conclusions. See *PRO–CO* 323/1398/6656, Minutes by Mr. Lee, 25.1.1936, Mr. Vernon, 27.1.1936, and G. L. M. Clauson, 31.1.1936; FO 371/19885/C987/4/18, G. L. M. Clauson to H. M. G. Jebb, 15.12.1936; and FO 371/19925/C663/97/18, W. Ormsby-Gore to A. Eden, 30.1.1936.
118. *PRO–CAB* 24/260, Memorandum by Sir R. Vansittart, 3.2.1936, *Britain, France and Germany*.
119. Ibid., Memorandum by A. Eden, 11.2.1936.
120. *DBFP*, second series, vol. XV, No. 522, *Foreign Office Memorandum on terms of a working arrangement with Germany*, 15.2.1936. Eden had already tacitly written off the demilitarised zone, although he hoped to trade it off as a concession. See ibid., No. 521, *Memorandum by Mr. Eden on the Rhineland Demilitarised Zone*, 14.2.1936, and *PRO–FO* 371/19885/ C979/4/18, Foreign Office Minute, 3.2.1936.
121. *DBFP*, second series, vol. XV, p. 643.
122. *PRO–CAB* 27/599G.(36), *Meeting of Cabinet Committee on Germany*, 17.2.1936. Neville Chamberlain informed his sister in December 1935: 'reports from Germany though always accompanied by pacific assur-

ances are yet far from reassuring'. *NCP*, 18/1/941, Neville Chamberlain to Ida Chamberlain, 8.12.1936.
123. *PRO*–CAB 23/83, *Cabinet Minutes*, 5.3.1936, and *DBFP*, second series, vol. XVI, No. 29, A. Eden to Sir E. Phipps, 6.3.1936.
124. *DGFP*, series C, vol. IV, Nos. 485, 506, 525, 564, 575 and 579.
125. *PRO*–CAB 24/261, Memorandum by A. Eden, 8.3.1936.
126. Foreign Office Minute, 3.2.1936, loc. cit. and D. Carlton, *Anthony Eden* (London, 1981), pp. 77–8.

6. The Plymouth Report

1. *PRO*–CAB 23/83, *Cabinet Minutes*, 5.3.1936.
2. Hildebrand, *Foreign Policy*, p. 35. The picture of Italo–German relations during 1935–6 is now rather more complicated than at first appeared. For a summary see A. Cassels, 'Switching Partners: Italy in A. J. P. Taylor's Origins of the Second World War', in G. Martel (ed.), *The Origins of the Second World War Reconsidered: The A. J. P. Taylor Debate after Twenty-Five Years* (London, 1986). p. 81.
3. *PRO*–FO 371/18821/C6576/21/18, D. St. Clair Gainer to B. C. Newton, 27.8.1935, and ibid., C6286/21/18, B. C. Newton to Sir S. Hoare, 30.8.1935. See also G. K. Johannsen and H. K. Kraft, *Germany's Colonial Problem* (London, 1937), p. 37.
4. Above, p. 240, fn. 124, and S. Heald and J. Wheeler-Bennett (eds), *Documents on International Affairs, 1936* (London, 1937), pp. 41–5.
5. Ibid., pp. 127–33.
6. Ibid., pp. 183–94.
7. N. H. Baynes, *Hitler's Speeches* (London, 1942), vol. II, p. 1271ff.
8. *PRO*–FO 371/18821/C8521/21/18, A. Hitler to Lord Rothermere, 20.12.1935. See also ibid., 19925/C924/97/18, Sir E. Phipps to A. Eden, 12.2.1936.
9. Baynes, op. cit., vol. II, pp. 1258–9, and *Daily Mail*, 27.1.1936.
10. *PRO*–FO 371/19925/C685/97/18, Mr Ferguson (Treasury) to O. Harvey, 27.1.1936.
11. Schmokel, op. cit., pp. 25–6.
12. Hidlebrand, *Weltreich*, p. 349.
13. Ibid., pp. 348 and 349–53, and Schmokel, op. cit., pp. 20–1.
14. Hildebrand, *Weltreich*, p. 351.
15. Schmokel, op. cit., pp. 21–5.
16. Ibid., pp. 27–8.
17. W. Michalka, *Ribbentrop und die deutsche Weltpolitik, 1933–1940* (Munich, 1980), pp. 30–9; Hildebrand, *Weltreich*, pp. 357–8; G. A. Craig, 'The German Foreign Office from Neurath to Ribbentrop', in G. A. Craig and F. Gilbert (eds), *The Diplomats*, vol. II, pp. 421–2; and see Phipps's assessment of Ribbentrop's rise in *PRO*–FO 800/275, *The Orme Sargent Papers*, Sir E. Phipps to O. Sargent. 7.3.1934.
18. Hildebrand, *Weltreich*, p. 360.
19. Michalka, op. cit., p. 139.

20. Hildebrand, *Weltreich*, p. 359.
21. Above, pp. 108–109.
22. Michalka, op. cit., p. 144.
23. Hildebrand, *Foreign Policy*, p. 40, and *Weltreich*, pp. 359–61.
24. Hildebrand, *Foreign Policy*, p. 39. On 3 July 1935, Ribbentrop informed the *Auslandsorganisation*: 'In future the conduct of all colonial policy is my responsibility.' Hildebrand, *Weltreich*, p. 361.
25. Ibid., pp. 874–80.
26. Schmokel, op. cit., pp. 28–30, and Hildebrand, *Weltreich*, pp. 880–1.
27. Schmokel, op. cit., pp. 30–1.
28. Ibid., pp. 34–6.
29. Ibid., p. 42.
30. Johannsen and Kraft, op. cit., pp. 28 and 31.
31. Ibid., p. 57.
32. F. Ritter von Epp, 'The Claim to Colonies', *Journal of the Royal African Society*, January, 1937.
33. Michalka, op. cit., p. 141.
34. H. Schacht, 'Germany's Colonial Demands', *Foreign Affairs*, January 1937.
35. Schmokel, op. cit., p. 56.
36. Johannsen and Kraft, op. cit., p. 43.
37. Ibid., p. 40.
38. Von Epp, art. cit.
39. Schmokel, op. cit., pp. 49–50.
40. Hildebrand, *Foreign Policy*, p. 18, and *Weltreich*, p. 314ff.
41. Schmokel, op. cit., p. 51.
42. *DGFP*, series C, vol. IV, No. 151, von Hoesch to von Neurath, 13.6.1935.
43. *DBFP*, second series, vol. XIII, No. 356, Memorandum by Sir R. Vansittart, 19.6.1935. See also *TP*, VIII/1, Lipski Diary, 15.7.1935. Lipski, the Polish ambassador at Berlin, recorded that Hitler had been annoyed by Hoare's speech in the Commons of 11 July 1935 – *H. of C. V*, vol. 304, cols. 509–24 – in which the British Foreign Secretary had appealed to Hitler to agree to an eastern pact. Lipski observed: 'the German Government would not give way to Britain who was using the air pact as a trump card'.
44. Hildebrand, *Foreign Policy*, p. 39.
45. *DBFP*, second series, vol. XV, No. 383, Sir E. Phipps to Sir S. Hoare, 16.12.1935; *DGFP*, series C, vol. IV, No. 460, *Minutes of Conference of Ministers held at the Reich Chancellery*, 13.12.1935; and *TP*, VIII/1, Lipski Diary, 18.12.1935.
46. Hildebrand, *Weltreich*, p. 475. Weinberg disagrees with this interpretation on the basis that there is not enough evidence to support it, 'at least for the mid-1930s'. Weinberg, *Diplomatic Revolution*, p. 278.
47. Hildebrand, *Weltreich*, p. 476.
48. Hildebrand, *Foreign Policy*, p. 47.
49. Hildebrand, *Weltreich*, p. 897. See also *PRO*–FO 371/20718/C404/37/18, Sir G. Clerk to A. Eden, 15.1.1937.
50. Ibid., Premier 1/247, A. Eden to S. Baldwin, 8.3.1936.

51. Ibid., CAB 27/626/F.P.(36)4, *Report of the Plymouth Committee on the transfer of a Colonial Mandate or Mandates to Germany*, 9.6.1936, and ibid., CAB 16/145/CMG 1.
52. Ibid., CAB 16/145, *Plymouth Committee Minutes*, 19.3.1936.
53. Ibid., *Plymouth Committee Minutes*, 30.3.1936.
54. It was also felt that colonial generosity would be a prelude to demands for further concessions. Mussolini at this time was evidently of a similar opinion. He told Duncan-Sandys on 17 April 1936 that, while Italy would be a 'satisfied' power once the Abyssinian adventure was over, 'Germany . . . would not become a "Have" at any payable price. Her appetite was insatiable, and he thought that this country [Britain] would be very unwise to commence the hopeless task of satisfying it by handing over colonies. This . . . would only be the beginning of an endless process of extortion and absorption.' See ibid., FO 371/J3234/ 841. I am very grateful to an anonymous American scholar for having brought my attention to this piece of information.
55. Ibid., CAB 16/145/CMG 23, Foreign Office Note, 'Possible Courses of Action', 2.4.1936.
56. Ibid., *Plymouth Committee Minutes*, 3.4.1936.
57. Ibid., CMG 7, Colonial Office Note, 'Moral Considerations', 25.3.1936.
58. Ibid., CMG 26, Colonial Office Note, 3.4.1936.
59. Ibid., CMG 18, Colonial Office Note, 'Special Considerations: Political and Administrative', 27.3.1936.
60. Cf. Cowling, op. cit., p. 162.
61. *PRO*–CAB 16/145/CMG 8, Combined Admiralty, War Office and Air Ministry Memorandum, 'General Strategic Considerations'. n.d.
62. Ibid., *Plymouth Committee Minues*, 3.4.1936.
63. Ibid., CAB 16/146/CMG 33, Colonial Office Note, 'The Possibility of Granting a Large Concession in Africa to a German Company', 8.4.1936.
64. Ibid., CMG 44, Colonial Office Note, 'Proposed International Development Company', 20.4.1936.
65. Ibid., FO 371/19926/C2496/97/18, O. Sargent to Sir E. Phipps, 25.3.1936, and C2497/97/18, Sir E. Phipps to O. Sargent, 28.3.1936.
66. *Plymouth Report*, loc. cit. On the economic aspects of the report see also *PRO*–FO 371/19925/C1419/97/18, *Memorandum respecting the Economics of a German Colony*, 4.3.1935, by G. H. S. Pinsent (Financial Adviser to the Berlin embassy); ibid., 2267/97/18, Memorandum by Sir R. Cahill, Commercial Counsellor to the Paris embassy; and *PHPP*, 5/6, Memorandum by G. H. S. Pinsent, *Germany's Economic Difficulties: An Imaginery Conversation between an Englishman and a German*, 6.11.1936.
67. *PRO*–FO 371/19927/C4275/97/18, Minute by C. W. Baxter, 27.5.1936.
68. Ibid., Minute by F. Ashton-Gwatkin, 17.6.1936.
69. Above, pp. 229–30.
70. *DBFP*, second series, vol. XVI, p. xi, and below, pp. 303–304.
71. *PRO*–FO 371/19927/C4275/97/18, Minute by Sir R. Vansittart, 22.6.1936.
72. Ibid., Marginal comment by Vansittart on Ashton-Gwatkin's Minute of 17.6.1936.

73. Ibid., Marginal comment by Vansittart on C. W. Baxter's Minute of 27.5.1936.
74. Ibid., Minute by A. Eden, 24.6.1936. See also ibid., Minute by Lord Cranborne, 27.6.1936; ibid., 19928/C5185/97/18, Minute by R. Wigram, 23.6.1936; and ibid., 19927/C5027/97/18, Memorandum by R. Wigram, 7.6.1936.
75. Ibid., Minute by Sir R. Vansittart, 24.6.1936.
76. Ibid., Minute by F. Ashton-Gwatkin, 23.6.1936.
77. Ibid., CAB 27/626/F.P.(36)4, appendix, *Draft Minutes of 280th Meeting of CID, 10.7.1936*, and ibid., F.P.(36), Sir M. Hankey to S. Baldwin, 8.7.1936.
78. Above, p. 244.
79. *DBFP*, second series, vol. XVI, No. 115, *Record of a conversation between the Chancellor of the Exchequer and M. Flandin*, 16.3.1936. See also *NCP*, 2/23a, Diary, 15.3.1936.
80. *PRO*–CAB 27/622/F.P.(36), *Foreign Policy Committee Minutes*, 21.7.1936. Eden's mind had been considerably more open the previous January and February when he had been prepared to contemplate the colonial satisfaction of Germany in west Africa. See *DBFP*, second series, vol. XVI, p. 797.
81. *PRO*–CAB 27/626/F.P.(36)7, Draft Statement on the Colonial Question, 21.7.1936.
82. Essentially the reconstruction of Locarno, below, pp. 303–304.
83. Memorandum by Wigram, 7.6.1936, loc. cit.
84. Below, pp. 303–304.
85. *PRO*–CAB 27/622/F.P.(36), *Foreign Policy Committee Minutes*, 27.7.1936. See also *TP*, IX/3. Hoare, under the heading, 'Irresponsibility of Foreign Office', wrote of Eden's performance: 'Anthony Eden's proposal that we should give a definite refusal about German colonies. Discussion at Foreign Office. Committee and immediately dropped and altered without any protests from him into the July statement in the House of Commons.'
86. *H. of C. V*, vol. 315, cols. 1131–2. Cf. Middlemas, *Illusion*, p. 111.
87. L. S. Amery, *The Unforgiving Years* (London, 1955), p. 246.
88. *H. of C. V*, vol. 310, col. 2415. See also FO 371/19926/C2757/97/18. Dealing with the preparation of Baldwin's answer, Orme Sargent wrote that, as the German memorandum of 31 March contained references to colonial equality of rights and that as Eden had declared in the Commons on 3 April 1936 that the British government was going to give the German memorandum careful study, it was no longer possible for the government to declare that it was not considering the colonial question. Duncan Sandys was by this time active in soliciting information about the colonial question, particularly from the Conservative and Unionist Central Office – see ibid., CO 323/1398/6656/4, P. Cohen to E. B. Boyd, 27.3.1936, and E. B. Boyd to P. Cohen, 7.5.1936.
89. Amery, *Unforgiving Years*, p. 249.
90. *H. of C. V*, vol. 310, cols. 2480–4, 2499 and 2503.
91. Ibid., cols. 2556–8. See also *NCP*, 18/1/956. Neville Chamberlain to Ida Chamberlain, 13.4.1936: 'Austen took me to task for what I said about

mandated territories. But if he didnt [sic] want to give the Germans any encouragement he should not have insisted upon a clear statement of the Governments views. It was really impossible to declare that in no circumstances and at no time would we ever consider the surrender of our mandate over any territory that we hold now. No one would have believed me if I had made such a declaration and in any case it would certainly have caused embarrassment to some Govt in the future & would probably have had to be repudiated. I dont believe myself that we could purchase peace and a lasting settlement by handing over Tanganyika to the Germans, but if I did I would not hesitate for a moment to do so. It would be of no more value to them than it is to us.'

92. *H. of C. V*, vol. 310, cols. 2750–1.
93. Ibid., vol. 311. cols. 81–104 and 119–20.
94. Ibid., cols. 309 and 522–4.
95. Amery, *Unforgiving Years*, p. 248.
96. *PRO*–Premier 1/190, Resolution of the Imperial Affairs Committee.
97. Ibid., T. L. Davies to S. Baldwin, 13.5.1936.
98. Ibid., E. B. Boyd to E. B. B. Speed, 15.5.1936.
99. Amery had some justification. On 6 April 1936, Phipps informed the Foreign Office that remarks allegedly attributable to Lord Stanhope at a Conservative Party meeting, in which he said that he was ready to discuss Germany's colonial equality of rights and had mentioned Tanganyika, had been noted in Germany. Similarly, the German embassy in London was reported as being gratified by Neville Chamberlain's statement in the Commons. See ibid., FO 371/19926/C2720/97/18, Sir E. Phipps to A. Eden, 6.4.1936, and minute by V. Lawford, 9.4.1936. See also *Evening Standard*, 3.4.1936.
100. *PRO*–Premier 1/190, Statement by L. S. Amery, n.d.
101. Ibid., T. L. Davies to O. S. Cleverly, 20.5.1936.
102. Amery, *Unforgiving Years*, p. 248.
103. *PRO*–CAB 24/262, Record of a conversation with O. Pirow, 9.6.1936.
104. Ibid., FO 371/19927/C4611/97/18, Memorandum by A. Eden, 25.6.1936.
105. *The Times*, 10.7.1936.
106. Presumably Lord Rothermere. See *PRO*–Premier 1/247, Record of a conversation between A. Eden and Sir Stuart Campbell, 19.6.1936.
107. Ibid., FO 371/19928/C5265/97/18, M. E. Antrobus to M. MacDonald, 15.7.1936. See also *Rand Daily Mail*, 14.7.1936; *Daily Mail*, 14.7.1936; and *Morning Post*, 15.7.1936.
108. *PRO*–FO 371/19928/C5934/97/18, M. E. Antrobus to M. MacDonald, 17.7.1936. See also J. C. Smuts to Sir M. Hankey, 17.7.1936, in *HNKY*, 4/28.
109. *PRO*–CAB 23/85, *Cabinet Minutes*, 16.7.1936.
110. *H. of C. V*, vol. 314, col. 2233. See also *PRO*–FO 371/19928/C5418/97/18.
111. Amery, *Unforgiving Years*, p. 248.
112. Gilbert and Gott, op. cit., p. 90.
113. *H. of C. V*, vol. 315, cols. 1176–8, 1939–48, and 1954–63.
114. *PRO*–FO 371/19926/C2947/97/18, Minute by Sir R. Vansittart, 9.4.1936;

ibid., 19927/C2947/97/18, Sir N. H. H. Charles to A. Eden, 10.6.1936; ibid., 19925/C2255/97/18, Sir N. H. H. Charles to C. W. Baxter, 23.3.1936; ibid., C4363/97/18, Sir C. Wingfield to A. Eden, 11.6.1936; ibid., 20512/W2977/895/36; and ibid., 19926/C3292/97/18, Sir G. Clerk to A. Eden, 29.4.1936. Not all opinion abroad was hostile to the German colonial claims. The Belgian journal, *Vingtième Siecle*, 13.8.1937, for example accused mandatory powers of hypocrisy in claiming that Germany could buy raw materials. It was also wrong of them to argue that they could not return colonies on the grounds that they held them under the League. The League could revoke mandates and colonial redistribution was not impossible.

115. *PRO–FO* 371/19926/C3095/97/18, G. Whiskard to M. MacDonald, 31.3.1936. See also correspondence contained in ibid., CO 353/1510/6656 and CO 691/147/42022/2 and the *Gold Coast Spectator*, 6.3.1937.
116. *The Times*, 6.8.1936.
117. *PRO–FO* 371/19928/C5829/97/18 and CO 691/147/42022/4.
118. M. E. Townsend, 'The German Colonies and the Third Reich', *The Political Science Quarterly*, June 1938.
119. See, for example, *WHD*, 1065, W. H. Dawson to A. Ponsonby and J. R. MacDonald, 13.11.1929.
120. Space precludes a full examination of this issue. Dawson's role can be followed in: *PRO–FO* 371/15225/C2093/929/18, W. H. Dawson to R. G. Leigh, 25.3.1931, and *WHD*, 1022, 1140, 1144, 1147, 1195, 1206 and 1262.
121. W. H. Dawson, 'The Urgency of Treaty Revision', *The Contemporary Review*, July 1933.
122. W. H. Dawson, 'Hitler's Challenge', *The Nineteenth Century and After*, April 1936.
123. *WHD*, 1346, H. Schnee to W. H. Dawson, 10.5.1934, and ibid., 1349, G. Murray to W. H. Dawson, 18.5.1934.
124. Ibid., 1545, Sir R. Beazley to W. H. Dawson, 16.3.1936, and Baynes, op. cit., vol. II, p. 1344.
125. *WHD*, 1675 and 1676, W. H. Dawson and Sir R. Beazley to S. Baldwin, 14.4.1937. See also Phipps's account of a lecture given by Sir R. Beazley to the Anglo–German Society at the University of Berlin, 28.1.1937, in *PRO–FO* 371/20719/C1035/37/18, Sir E. Phipps to A. Eden, 30.1.1937.
126. Baynes, op. cit., vol. II, p. 1328.
127. *The Times*, 12.9.1936, 15.9.1936, 29.9.1936, 1.10.1936, 3.10.1936, 5.10.1936, 9.10.1936, 12.10.1936, and 14.10.1936.
128. *PRO–FO* 371/19930/C7875/97/18, Sir E. Phipps to A. Eden, 4.11.1936.
129. *The Times*, 4.11.1936.
130. Ibid., 17.11.1936.
131. *World Review*, March 1937.
132. Ibid., April 1937.
133. *WHD*, 1569, H. Schnee to W. H. Dawson, 8.5.1936.
134. Ibid., 1503, Ada Schnee to W. H. Dawson, n.d.
135. Ibid., F. von Lindequist to W. H. Dawson, 14.3.1937. Ribbentrop's estimate of the position in Britain was much more optimistic. See *DGFP*, series C, vol. V, No. 520, Note by Ribbentrop, 28.8.1936.

136. Lord Londonderry, *Ourselves and Germany* (London, 1938), pp. 85, 100, 105–6, 147–8, and 152. Commenting on this book generally, Hoare wrote: 'Even if the future is obscure, it is none the less wise and useful to set out the main features of the problem. I have read enough of your book to realise that it will greatly help the British public to assess the real position.' See *TP*, X/3, Sir S. Hoare to Lord Londonderry, 4.4.1938.
137. Londonderry, op. cit., pp. 29–30.
138. Ibid., p. 133.
139. *LGP*, G/12/4, Lord Londonderry to D. Lloyd George, 18.9.1936. The colonial question was hardly touched upon when Lloyd George and Hitler met on 4 and 5.9.1936. Hitler mentioned colonies, but Lloyd George 'did not avail himself of this opportunity to express any view'. While in Germany, however, Lloyd George warned Hesse that 'it would be premature to raise the colonial question' and he 'made a very wry face' when Hesse stated that Germany would not be satisfied with access to raw materials and wanted rather colonial redistribution. *PRO*–FO 371/19929/C7221/97/18, Sir E. Phipps to A. Eden, 13.10.1936. See also *PHPP*, 3/3, Sir M. Hankey to Sir E. Phipps, 29.9.1936 and 15.10.1936. Hankey informed the ambassador: 'I gave you my views about what our line should be, namely, to make quite clear that if they are tiresome about the colonies we shall do what otherwise we do not want to do, and join the encirclement of Germany.' T. P. Conwell-Evans, who acted as Lloyd George's interpreter, was himself a strong supporter of Germany's colonial claims. See T. P. Conwell-Evans, 'Between Berlin and London', *The Nineteenth Century and After*, January 1936. Lloyd George was very impressed with Hitler, informing Ribbentrop that 'the greatest admiration' he had had for Germany's 'wonderful Fuhrer' before his visit had been 'deepened and intensified'. *LGP*, G/19/6, D. Lloyd George to von Ribbentrop, 21.9.1936.
140. Londonderry, op. cit., pp. 173–5.
141. J. R. M. Butler, *Lord Lothian* (London, 1960), pp. 197 and 337.
142. Ibid., p. 215.
143. *PRO*–FO 371/19906/C4184/4/18, Lord Lothian to A. Eden, 3.6.1936.
144. *LGP*, G/12/5, Lord Lothian to D. Lloyd George, 14.7.1936.
145. Butler, op. cit., p. 216.
146. Ibid., pp. 337–53. See also *PRO*–FO 800/268, *Sir Nevile Henderson Papers*, (hereinafter cited as *NHP*), Lord Lothian to Sir Nevile Henderson, 10.5.1937.
147. Joelson, op. cit., passim.
148. L. S. Amery, 'The Problem of Cession of the Mandated Territories', *International Affairs*, January 1937.
149. L. S. Amery, *The German Colonial Claim* (London, 1939).
150. Ibid., p. 137.
151. Ibid., p. 155.
152. Ibid., pp. 175–86. See also an article by Amery in the *Evening Standard*, 6.7.1936.
153. A. Bullock. *Germany's Colonial Demands* (London, 1939), pp. 91–7.
154. E. M. Ritchie, *The Unfinished War* (London, 1940), p. 227. Both Bullock

and Ritchie made it clear that the Allies' justification for depriving Germany of her colonies had been overdone. This was tacitly recognised in the Foreign and Colonial Offices by 1936, but it was also tacitly recognised that it would be imprudent for the British government to declare this. See *PRO*–FO 371/19927/C3937/97/18, Memorandum by C. W. Baxter, May, 1936, *German Colonial Guilt*, and ibid., C. Eastwood to C. W. Baxter, 28.5.1936. Harold Nicolson thought it had been a mistake in 1919 not to annex the colonies: 'Instead of basing our rights on military victory . . . we based them upon a moral comment which was both ungenerous and untrue'. See H. Nicolson, 'The Colonial Problem', *International Affairs*, January 1938. See also Ritchie, op. cit., pp. 319 and 337.

155. G. Roberts, *The Nazi Claim to Colonies* (London, 1939). pp. 26–7.
156. F. Borkenau, *The New German Empire*, (London, 1939), p. 13.
157. Ibid., pp. 178–9.
158. Nicolson, art. cit.
159. *Morning Post*, 25.6.1936, and *News Chronicle*, 25.6.1936. Sir Henry Page Croft was infuriated by the *News Chronicle's* coverage of this meeting. He felt that the newspaper had misrepresented Hoare's speech at Geneva the previous September by implying that the former foreign secretary had advocated an examination of the problem of colonial distribution. See *CRFT*, 1/3, Sir Henry Page Croft to G. Barry, 26.6.1936, and ibid., 1/14, Sir S. Hoare to Sir Henry Page Croft, 3.7.1936.
160. *The Times*, 2.10.1936; Joelson, op. cit., pp. 269–70 and 280; Amery, *Unforgiving Years*, p. 248; and Gilbert and Gott, op. cit., p. 90.
161. A. J. Crozier, 'Stresemann's Locarno Policy'.
162. *WHD*, 1195, Lord Lugard to W. H. Dawson, 11.1.1932.
163. Lord Lugard, 'The Basis of the Claim for Colonies', *International Affairs*, January 1936. Lugard dismissed the German economic argument completely, as he had done in *The Times* – see above, p. 207. He was subsequently supported from across the Atlantic by Ida Greaves, 'A Modern Colonial Fallacy', *Foreign Affairs*, July 1936. The shallowness of the German economic arguments was also revealed in C. K. Leith, 'Mineral Resources and Peace', *Foreign Affairs*, April 1938, and B. S. Keeling, 'Colonies: The Economic Case Examined', *The Contemporary Review*, February 1937.
164. N. Bentwich, 'Colonies and Mandates', *The Contemporary Review*, January 1936. See also Lord Marley, 'The Empire as an Economic Unit', *The Political Quarterly*, October 1938. The advocacy of the extension of the mandates system to all colonies did not necessarily imply international administration of mandated territories as was advocated by Sir John Maynard, 'The Answer to Germany', *The Political Quarterly*, July 1939.
165. 'The Future of Colonial Trusteeship', *Round Table*, September 1934.
166. 'Colonial Raw Materials', *Round Table*, March 1936.
167. 'From Agadir to Nuremberg', *Round Table*, December 1936.
168. 'The Empire and World Trade', *Round Table*, June 1937.
169. L. Barnes, *The Duty of Empire* (London, 1935), pp. 112–3.

170. Ibid., p. 47.
171. N. Angell, *The Defence of Empire* (London, 1938), p. 20. Angell was fundamentally in favour of the international administration of mandates and before the advent of Hitler favoured bringing Germany back into such a system with 'a large share in administration'. *WHD*, 1074, N. Angell to W. H. Dawson, 9.12.1929.
172. Barnes, op. cit., pp. 100 and 112–3. See also L. Barnes, 'The Empire as a Sacred Trust', *The Political Quarterly*, October 1938.
173. Angell, *Defence*, pp. 28–9.
174. *H. of C. V*, vol. 310, cols. 1506–7, and vol. 315, cols. 1948–52.
175. Labour Party Pamphlet, *The Demand for Colonial Territories and Equality of Opportunity* (London, 1936), pp. 12–3, 24–7, 30–3, 41–4 and 46–9.

7. Schacht

1. *CRFT*, 1/18, Duncan-Sandys to Sir H. Page Croft, 2.10.1936.
2. See *DBFP*, second series, vol. XVI, No. 8, *Memorandum by Mr. Eden on Germany and the Locarno Treaty*, 8.3.1936; ibid., No. 65, Sir E. Phipps to A. Eden, 11.3.1936; *PRO*–CAB 23/83, *Cabinet Minutes*, 11.3.1936; and J. T. Emmerson, *The Rhineland Crisis 7 March 1936: A Study in Multilateral Diplomacy* (London, 1977), p. 130ff.
3. Weinberg, *Diplomatic Revolution*, p. 274, fn. 46.
4. *DBFP*, second series, vol. XVII, No. 389, *British Memorandum*, 19.11.1936. Von Neurath could find no basis for further negotiations in this memorandum. See *Akten zur Deutschen Auswärtigen Politik, 1918–1945*, (hereinafter cited as *ADAP*), (Göttingen, 1971–), series C, vol. VI, No. 49, *Aufzeichnung des Reichsministers des Auswärtigen Freiherr von Neurath*, 23.11.1936.
5. *PRO*–CAB 27/626/F.P.(36)6, *Memorandum on the proposed meeting of Locarno Powers*, 13.7.1936.
6. *PRO*–FO 371/20706/C989/1/18, Sir E. Phipps to A. Eden, 4.2.1937, and C1638/1/18, A. Eden to Sir E. Phipps, 26.2.1937.
7. Hildebrand, *Foreign Policy*, p. 46.
8. Weinberg, *Diplomatic Revolution*, pp. 274–5. Ribbentrop was not very popular in Britain from the beginning of his ambassadorship. See *PHPP*, 3/3, Sir M. Hankey to Sir E. Phipps, 29.9.1936 and 9.10.1936.
9. *The Times*, 16.12.1936.
10. Below, pp. 373–379.
11. *PRO*–FO 371/20706/C1185/1/18, Lord Halifax to Sir E. Phipps, 11.2.1937. See also *ADAP*, series C, vol. VI, No. 201, von Ribbentrop to von Neurath and Hitler, 14.2.1937.
12. *PRO*–FO 371/20719/C2081/37/18, Note be Eden, 16.3.1937.
13. *DBFP*, second series, vol. XVII, No. 350, Sir E. Phipps to A. Eden, 4.11.1936.
14. Ibid., No. 300, Sir E. Phipps to A. Eden, 19.10.1936.
15. See the correspondence contained in *PRO*–FO 371/19929/C7774/97/1.
16. *DBFP*, second series, vol. XVII, appendix II, Memorandum by Sir R. Vansittart, *The World Situation and British Rearmament*, 31.12.1936.

17. Ibid., appendix I, *Account by Sir R. Vansittart of a visit to Germany in August 1936*, 10.9.1936. Sir Alexander Cadogan who had been brought back from China to the Foreign Office as Vansittart's putative replacement, commented in his diary: 'Read Van's account of his Berlin visit. Awful stuff, quite unreadable in his typical style. If he has any ideas or impressions, why can't he put them down straight on paper instead of dancing literary hornpipes.' *The Papers of Sir Alexander Cadogan*, (hereinafter cited as *ACAD*), 1/4, DIARY, 11.9.1936. On the attempt to remove Vansittart see *DBFP*, second series, vol. XV, No. 437, A. Eden to King George V, 8.1.1936, and *ACAD*, 1/5, Diary, 14.10.1936. Cadogan evidently knew nothing of the reasons that were behind his return to the Foreign Office until told by Lancelot Oliphant.

18. Memorandum by Sir R. Vansittart, *The World Situation and British Rearmament*, 31.12.1936, loc. cit. Sir M. Hankey found this memorandum 'depressing'. He thought that 'the deterrents to war operating on Germany', such as 'their food position, internal difficulties, vulnerability of the Ruhr', were greater than Vansittart estimated, but he too was 'anxious' and felt that Britain needed to hasten her rearmament. He told Vansittart that it was 'an appalling reflection on our past foreign policy that we have lost our old friends, Japan and Italy, cannot get on terms with Germany, and have as our only friend a France half rotted with discontent and communism'. *HNKY*, 3/42, Sir M. Hankey to H. Hankey, 28.3.1936.

19. *PRO*–CAB 23/87, *Cabinet Minutes*, 13.1.1937. Eden also thought that Germany's economic situation would perhaps make her pliable, affording for Britain 'one more chance, perhaps a final one of coming to terms with Germany'. *DBFP*, second series, vol. XVII, No. 350, Minute by A. Eden, 16.11.1936. For further discussion of Britain and the German 'moderates', see C. A. MacDonald, 'Economic Appeasement and the German "Moderates": An Introductory Essay', *Past and Present*, 1972.

20. H. Schacht, *Account Settled* (London, 1949), pp., 92–5 and 290–3.

21. Michalka, op. cit., pp. 192–7.

22. *DGFP*, series C, vol. III, No. 544, Schacht to Hitler, 19.3.1935.

23. *DDF*, series 2, vol. I, No. 251, M. François-Poncet to M. Flandin, 28.2.1936. The text of a speech delivered by Schacht at Bremen was confiscated by the Gestapo.

24. Weinberg, *Diplomatic Revolution*, p. 280.

25. H. Schacht, *My First Seventy-Six Years* (London, 1955), p. 366, and Overy, *Goering*, p. 40.

26. Ibid.

27. A. E. Simpson, *Hjalmar Schacht in Perspective* (The Hague, 1969), p. 99.

28. Overy, *Goering*, pp. 40–3.

29. Simpson, op. cit., p. 146.

30. Overy, *Goering*, pp. 45–6.

31. *DDF*, series 2, vol. I, No. 253, M. François-Poncet to M. Flandin, 29.2.1936.

32. Ibid., No. 411, M. François-Poncet to M. Flandin, 12.3.1936, and No. 413, M. Berthelot to M. Baumgartner, 12.3.1936.

33. *PRO*–FO 371/19927/C3906/97/18, Minute by O. Sargent, 3.6.1936.
34. J. Tusa and A. Tusa, *The Nuremberg Trial* (London, 1983), pp. 42, 128, 149.
35. Ibid., pp. 337–41.
36. *PRO*–T 188/288, Note by Sir F. Leith-Ross of a Conversation with Sir T. Barnes, 3.12.1945.
37. Ibid., Per Jacobsen to Sir F. Leith-Ross, 15.2.1939.
38. Note by Sir F. Leith-Ross of a Conversation with Sir T. Barnes, 3.12.1945, loc. cit.
39. *PRO*–T 188/169, Note by Sir F. Leith-Ross on Dr. Schacht, 20.9.1937.
40. Ibid., T 188/288, Note by Sir F. Leith-Ross on Dr. Schacht, 3.12.1945.
41. Ibid., FO 371/19927/C3906/97/18, Minute by R. Wigram, 29.5.1936.
42. A. J. Crozier, 'Imperial Decline', art. cit.
43. *PRO*–FO 371/19926/C2518/97/18, Sir E. Phipps to Sir R. Vansittart, 25.3.1936.
44. Ibid., 19927/C3906/97/18, A. L. Kennedy to Sir E. Phipps, 25.5.1936.
45. Ibid., Sir E. Phipps to A. Eden, 26.5.1936, Minute by O. Sargent, 3.6.1936, Minute by Sir R. Vansittart, 28.5.1936, and Minute by G. Jebb, 21.7.1936.
46. Ibid., 19928/C6228/97/18, Dr. Gie to Dr. Bodenstein, 20.7.1936.
47. Ibid., C6435/97/18, B. C. Newton to A. Eden, 11.9.1936. W. E. Dodd, the United States ambassador at Berlin, also reported on Schacht's optimism following his visit to Berlin – see C. A. MacDonald, *The United States, Britain and Appeasement, 1936–1939* (London, 1981), pp. 5–6.
48. Ibid., T 172/1801, Sir S. Hoare to Neville Chamberlain, 18.11.1935, and FO 371/19928/C6435/97/18, Minute by Sir R. Vansittart, 16.9.1936. The board of trade was very much in favour of a meeting between Schacht and Leith-Ross. See T 188/168, W. B. Brown to Sir F. Leith-Ross, 28.8.1936.
49. Ibid., CAB 24/264, B. C. Newton to A. Eden, 15.9.1936.
50. Ibid., FO 371/19928/C6636/97/18, A. Eden to Sir R. Vansittart, 20.9.1936.
51. *DDF*, series 2, vol. III, No. 196, M. François-Poncet to M. Delbos, 24.8.1936.
52. Ibid., No. 63, M. François-Poncet to M. Delbos, 3.8.1936.
53. Ibid., p. 309, fn. 1.
54. *PRO*–CAB 27/626/F.P.(36)18, Annex E, *Record by Schacht of Conversation with French Ministers*, 26.8.1936, and *Procès-Verbal of Talks with Schacht*, 28.8.1936.
55. *DDF*, series 2, vol. III, No. 213, *Compte Rendu*, by M. Blum, 28.8.1936. See also J. Colton, *Leon Blum: Humanist in Politics* (Cambridge and London, 1966), pp. 214–5.
56. *PRO*–CAB 27/626/F.P.(36)18, Annex E, M. Blum to H. Schacht, 9.9.1936.
57. A. Eden to Sir R. Vansittart, 20.9.1936, loc. cit.
58. Ibid. See also *DDF*, series 2, vol. III, No. 229, M. François-Poncet to M. Delbos, 2.9.1936, and No. 213.
59. Ibid., No. 334, M. François-Poncet to M. Blum, 10.10.1936.

60. Baynes, op. cit., vol. II, p. 1328.
61. *DDF*, series 2, vol. III, No. 244, M. Lamarle to M. Delbos, 10.9.1936.
62. Ibid., No. 255, M. Lamarle to M. Delbos, 15.9.1936.
63. Ibid., No. 235, M. Lamarle to M. Delbos, 7.9.1936.
64. A. Eden to Sir R. Vansittart, 20.9.1936, loc. cit. See also *PRO*–CAB 27/ 626/F.P.(36)18, Annex E, *Record by Schacht of conversation with M. Blum, 28.8.1936*.
65. A. Eden to Sir R. Vansittart, 20.9.1936, loc. cit.
66. *PRO*–FO 371/19928/C6637/97/18, A. Eden to Sir R. Vansittart, 20.9.1936. Eden's written reply to Blum, via Delbos, was sent on 23.9.1936 – see ibid., CAB 27/626/F.P.(36)18, Annex A, A. Eden to M. Delbos, 23.9.1936. See also *DGFP*, series C, vol. V, No. 574, Schacht to Dieckhoff, 6.10.1936, and *PRO*–FO 371/19928/C6638/97/18, A. Eden to Sir R. Vansittart, 21.9.1936.
67. Ibid., C6637/97/18, Sir R. Vansittart to A. Eden, 21.9.1936.
68. Ibid., C6639/97/18, A. Eden to Sir R. Vansittart, 23.9.1936.
69. Ibid., Minute by R. Wigram, 23.9.1936.
70. Ibid., Sir R. Vansittart to A. Eden, 23.9.1936.
71. *ACAD*, 1/5, Diary 24.9.1936 and 25.9.1936.
72. Schacht to Dieckhoff, 6.10.1936, loc. cit., and *DDF*, series 2, vol. V, p. 710, fn. 1.
73. Above, p. 285.
74. *PRO*–FO 371/19929/C6904/97/18, A. Eden to Sir R. Vansittart, 2.10.1936, and C7159/97/18, Minute by A. Eden, 10.10.1936.
75. Ibid., CAB 23/85, *Cabinet Minutes*, 14.10.1936.
76. *PRO*–FO 371/19929/C7411/97/18, Sir E. Phipps to A. Eden, 19.10.1936, and C7461/97/18, Sir E. Phipps to A. Eden, 20.10.1936.
77. Ibid., C7412/97/18, Sir E. Phipps to A. Eden, 19.10.1936.
78. Ibid., C7500/97/18, Sir E. Phipps to A. Eden, 22.10.1936.
79. Ibid., 19930/C7894/97/18, Sir E. Phipps to A. Eden, 5.11.1936.
80. Ibid., C8801/97/18, Sir E. Phipps to A. Eden, 9.12.1936.
81. Ibid., C8869/97/18, Sir E. Phipps to A. Eden, 10.12.1936.
82. Ibid., C8801/97/18, Undated minute by Sir R. Vansittart.
83. Ibid., C8869/97/18, Minute by Sir R. Vansittart, 17.12.1936, and Minute by F. Ashton-Gwatkin, 14.12.1936.
84. Ibid., C8977/97/18, Minute by F. Ashton-Gwatkin, 15.12.1936.
85. Ibid., C9063/97/18, A. Eden to Sir E. Phipps, 19.12.1936.
86. Ibid., C8977/97/18, Minute by Sir R. Vansittart, 22.12.1936.
87. It is of some interest that Baron von Stumm was again active in presenting Germany's colonial demands at this time. See *PRO*–FO/ 19929/C7565/97/18, Baron von Stumm to Sir R. Vansittart, 21.10.1936.
88. For a French estimate of the general negative attitude in Britain towards Germany's colonial demands see *DDF*, series 2, vol. IV, No. 117, M. Corbin to M. Delbos, 8.12.1936.
89. *PRO*–FO 371/19930/C8402/97/18, Sir G. Clerk to A. Eden, 24.11.1936; C8495/97/18, Sir G. Clerk to A. Eden, 26.11.1936; and C8700/97/18, J. V. Perowne to R. Wigram, 3.12.1936.
90. Ibid., C9172/97/18, Lloyd Thomas to A. Eden, 23.12.1936.
91. *DAPE*, vol. I, No. 2, Calheiros to Monteiro, 13.11.1936, and No. 5, Calheiros to Salazar, 17.12.1936.

92. *PRO*–FO 371/20512/W17156/762/36, Monteiro to Sir C. Wingfield, 26.11.1936, and Sir C. Wingfield to Eden, 27.11.1936. See also *DAPE*, vol. I, No. 1, Monteiro to Sir C. Wingfield, and No. 9, Monteiro to Salazar, 14.1.1937.

93. See the correspondence in *PRO*–FO 371/20718 and 20719. See also *DAPE*, vol. I, No. 10, Monteiro to Salazar, 3.2.1937, and *Daily Telegraph*, 30.1.1937.

94. *DDF*, series 2, vol. IV, No. 187, M. François-Poncet to M. Delbos, 21.12.1936.

95. See the correspondence in *PRO*–FO 371/20718 and *ACAD*, 1/5, Diary, 16.12.1936.

96. *PRO* – FO 371/20719/C1591/37/18. Memorandum by O. Sargent, February 1937, and Minutes by C. W. Baxter, W. Strang and O. Sargent, 18.2.1937. See also *The Times*, 3.3.1937.

97. *DDF*, series 2, vol. IV, No. 230, M. François-Poncet to M. Delbos, 31.12.1936.

98. Logan, op. cit., pp. 117–8, and MacDonald, *United States, Britain and Appeasement*, p. 12.

99. François-Poncet to M. Delbos, 21.12.1936, loc. cit.

100. *PRO* – T 188/168, Note by Sir F. Leith-Ross, 5.10.1936.

101. The tripartite agreement was designed 'to avoid as far as possible currency disturbances and to maintain orderly conditions in the Exchange Market'. Sir F. Leith-Ross, *Money Talks* (London, 1968), p. 228.

102. *PRO* – T 188/168, Schacht to Sir F. Leith-Ross, 1.10.1936.

103. Ibid., Sir. R. Vansittart to Sir. F. Leith-Ross, 8.10.1936.

104. Leith-Ross op. cit., pp. 234–6, and *PRO* – CAB 27/626/F.P.(36)18, Annex B, Schacht to Sir F. Leith-Ross, 1.10.1936, and Sir F. Leith-Ross to Schacht, 15.10.1936. Schacht was very disappointed by the negative response. Pinsent of the Berlin embassy favoured a meeting. See ibid., T 188/168, G. H. S. Pinsent to Sir F. Leith-Ross, 19.10.1936.

105. Ibid., T188/168, Minutes by Sir R. Hopkins, 5.10.1936, Neville Chamberlain, 5.10.1936.

106. Ibid., FO 371/20718/C156/37/18, *Note of a Conversation with Mr. Lever on 23rd December, 1936*, by Sir F. Leith-Ross. See also T 188/168, Sir F. Leith-Ross to Sir R. Hopkins, 24.12.1936.

107. In a marginal comment Eden noted that he disagreed.

108. *PRO* – FO 371/20718/C156/37/18, Sir F. Leith-Ross to Sir R. Vansittart, 23.12.1936, and Sir F. Leith-Ross to Sir R. Vansittart, 24.12.1936.

109. Ibid., Sir R. Vansittart to Sir F. Leith-Ross, 26.12.1936, and A. Eden to Sir R. Vansittart, n.d. Sir Alexander Cadogan, who as early as 16 December 1936 was favouring a meeting between Leith-Ross and Schacht, undoubtedly had his worst fears confirmed by these comments. See *ACAD*, 1/5, Diary, 16.12.1936.

110. Sir F. Leith-Ross to Schacht, 15.10.1936, loc. cit.

111. *PRO* – FO 371/20718/C156/37/18, Sir F. Leith-Ross to Sir R. Vansittart, 28.12.1936.

112. Ibid., Minutes by Sir R. Vansittart, 29.12.1936, and A. Eden, 30.12.1936.

113. Ibid., CAB 27/626/F.P.(38)18, Annex A, Lloyd Thomas to A. Eden,

26.10.1936. Leger disliked the sort of Discussion that Blum and Delbos had got themselves into with Schacht. The latter was trying to get France to commit herself without committing Germany.
114. Ibid., FO 371/20718/C156/37/18, O. Sargent to Sir E. Phipps, 7.1.1937.
115. Ibid., C369/37/18, Sir E. Phipps to O. Sargent, 11.1.1937.
116. A. Eden to M. Delbos, 23.9.1936, loc. cit.
117. *PRO* – FO 371/20718/C369/37/18, Minute by A. Eden, 18.1.1937.
118. Ibid., O Sargent to Sir E. Phipps, 19.1.1937.
119. Above, pp. 322–23.
120. See the correspondence contained in *PRO* – CAB 27/626/F.P.(36)18, *Cabinet Minutes*, 14.10.1936, loc. cit., and *PRO* – FO 371/20718/C156/37/18, A. Eden to Sir R. Vansittart, n.d. For Pinsent's letter see ibid., T. 188/168, G. H. S. Pinsent to Sir F. Leith-Ross, 13.1.1937, and Minute by Neville Chamberlain, 13.12.1937.
121. A. P. Adamthwaite, *France and the Coming of the Second World War* (London, 1977), p. 54.
122. *DDF*, series 2, vol. v, No. 470, *Compte Rendu*, by Blum, 28.5.1937; *ADAP*, series C, vol. vi, No. 99, Welczeck to von Neurath, 17.12.1936, and No. 93, *Aufzeichnung des Vortragenden Legationsrat von Rintelen*, 16.12.1936; and *PRO* – FO 371/20705/C569/1/18, Sir G. Clerk to A. Eden, 24.1.1937.
123. *DGFP*, series C, vol. iii, No. 164., Welczeck to von Neurath, 24.12.1936.
124. Schmokel, op. cit., pp. 100–1.
125. *PRO* – FO 371/20705/C424/1/18, Sir E. Phipps to A. Eden, 18.1.1937. See also *ADAP*, series C, vol. vi, No. 123, L. W. Goering to Sabath, 4.1.1937. On French contacts with the Germans during the winter of 1936 to 1937, see, Weinberg, *Starting World War*, pp. 90–1, and Dreifort, op. cit., pp. 167–9.
126. On 25 January Vansittart informed Eden: 'It seems to me that this is another of these half-baked schemes which the French are so busy producing at this time, and against which we will have to be particularly on our guard.' *PRO* – T 188/169, Sir R. Vansittart to A. Eden 25.1.1937. See also ibid., Note by C. W. Baxter, 19.1.1937, and O. Sargent to Sir F. Leith-Ross, 25.1.1937.
127. Ibid., Sir F. Leith-Ross to O. Sargent, 26.1.1937.
128. Ibid., Sir F. Leith-Ross to Sir R. Hopkins, 26.1.1937; Minute by Neville Chamberlain, 27.1.1937, and Minute by Sir W. Fisher, 26.1.1937.
129. *DBFP*, second series, vol. xviii, No. 60, Sir F. Leith-Ross to Gladwyn Jebb, 12.1.1937.
130. Ibid., No. 76, Sir F. Leith-Ross to Sir A. Cadogan, 16.1.1937.
131. *PRO* – FO 371/20705/C475/5/1/18, Minute by O. Sargent, 18.1.1937. Cadogan was delighted with this outcome and hoped that there would be a fresh start. He wrote: 'Van . . . has taken it very well. I thought he'd be angry. Is he simply rudderless and wanting a lead? Maybe.' *ACAD*, 1/6, Diary, 20.1.1936. Neville Chamberlain was similarly delighted that Leith-Ross was going to Germany and took the credit for it himself. He informed his sister: 'Generally speaking Europe seems a little less uneasy and I can't help thinking that the precarious

internal situation of Germany is imposing a certain restraining influence on Hitler. I have got a little scheme on hand for establishing contact with Schacht which may – or may not – lead further in the same direction.' *NCP*, 18/1/991, Neville Chamberlain to Ida Chamberlain, 16.1.1937.

132. *PRO* – FO 371/20705/C475/1/18, A. Eden to Sir F. Leith-Ross, 19.1.1937.
133. Ibid., C630/1/18, Sir F. Leith-Ross to O. Sargent, 26.1.1937.
134. Ibid., CAB 27/626/F.P.(36)18, Memorandum by A. Eden, 15.3.1937.
135. Ibid., FO 371/20718/C619/37/18, Sir E. Phipps to A. Eden, 25.1.1937.
136. Ibid., CAB 27/626/F.P.(36)18, Annex D, Sir F. Leith-Ross to Neville Chamberlain, 4.2.1937, and *Note by Sir F. Leith-Ross of Conversation with Dr. Schacht on 2.2.1937*. See also *ACAD*, 1/6, Diary, 4.2.1937, and *PHPP*, II, 2/1, Sir. F. Leith-Ross to Sir E. Phipps, 4.2.1937. The Badenweiler talks created some resentment in France. Delbos told Bullitt that Leith-Ross's expression of regret that the August meetings had not been pursued 'was of course a typical British remark because the truth is that the British government was furious with us for having the conversations with Schacht . . . the British could pretend to desire Franco–German reconciliation but would continue to follow their old policy of keeping France and Germany hostile'. Adamthwaite, op. cit., pp. 54–5.
137. *PRO* – T 188/169, Sir F. Leith-Ross to Sir E. Phipps, 4.2.1937, and Sir F. Leith-Ross to Neville Chamberlain, 4.2.1937.
138. Ibid., Sir E. Phipps to Sir F. Leith-Ross, 5.3.1937; W. Strang to Sir F. Leith-Ross, 5.3.1937. Eden did not like Leith-Ross's letter to Schacht of 3 March 1937, in which the latter was assured that the issues raised between them were still under consideration. See ibid., T 172/1801, Sir F. Leith-Ross to Schacht, 3.3.1937, and T. 188/169, Sir F. Leith-Ross to Neville Chamberlain, 4.3.1937. Leith-Ross had already vented his frustration in a letter to Chamberlain in which he stated that he saw no difference between what Schacht told Blum and what the Reichsminister had told him. What struck him most significantly was 'the different attitude adopted by Blum and by our Foreign Office to any such discussion with Germany. Schacht's proposals had been discarded with very little consideration'. He lamented: 'a month has now passed since I saw Dr. Schacht and I am disappointed that so little has been done to clear our minds'. Leith-Ross was clearly disappointed by the role of Vansittart in all this. Chamberlain was in agreement with these views and expressed a determination to see Eden at an early stage. See ibid., Sir F. Leith-Ross to Neville Chamberlain, 1.3.1937 and Minute by Neville Chamberlain, 2.3.1937.
139. Ibid., CAB 27/626/F.P.(36)18, Annex E, Sir G. Clerk to Sir R. Vansittart, 24.2.1937.
140. Ibid., Memorandum by A. Eden, 15.3.1937.
141. Ibid., F. P.(36)19, Memorandum by W. Ormsby-Gore, 16.3.1937. See also the Foreign Office minutes in ibid., FO 371/20720/C2302/37/18.
142. Ibid.,CAB 27/622/F.P.(36), *Foreign Policy Committee Minutes*, 18.3.1937.
143. Ibid.,CAB 27/626/F.P.(36)20, Memorandum by A. Eden, 22.3.1937.
144. Ibid., F.P.(36)22, Memorandum by W. Ormsby-Gore, 22.3.1937.

145. Ibid., T 188/169, Sir F. Leith-Ross to Neville Chamberlain, 30.3.1937. See also T 172/1801, Sir W. Fisher to Neville Chamberlain, 31.3.1937. Fisher was very much in agreement with Leith-Ross's proposed line, as was Sir H. Wilson. Fisher wanted one further contact with Schacht 'before the re-introduction of the formal diplomatic' procedures which have hitherto been so barren (& mischievous)'.
146. Ibid., CAB 27/626/F.P.(36)23, Memorandum by Neville Chamberlain, 2.4.1937.
147. *Foreign Policy Committee Minutes*, 6.4.1937, loc. cit.
148. *PRO* – FO371/20735/C3260/270/18, A. Eden to Sir E. Phipps, 27.4.1937.
149. Ibid., Sir E. Phipps to A. Eden, 4.5.1937.
150. Ibid., Sir E. Phipps to A. Eden, 10.5.1937.
151. Weinberg, *Starting World War*, p. 77.
152. Schmokel, op. cit., p. 102.
153. Weinberg, *Starting World War*, p. 92.
154. *PRO* – FO 371/20721/C4135/37/18, Sir E. Phipps to A. Eden, 31.5.1937.
155. *DDF*, series 2, vol. v, No. 470, *Compte Rendu*, by Blum, 28.5.1937.
156. *PRO* – FO 371/20708/C4068/1/18, Sir N. Henderson to A. Eden, 5.6.1937. See also *DGFP*, series D, vol. I, Nos. 71 and 72.
157. Schacht, however, still tried to encourage the Americans, who had shown an interest in his schemes, to support his ideas. *PRO* – CO 323/1510/6656, G. Campbell to Sir R. Lindsay, 19.7.1937. See also Mac-Donald, *United States, Britain and Appeasement*, pp. 1–33.
158. *MAE*/1F/SDN/547, M. François-Poncet to M. Delbos, 5.11.1937.
159. *PRO* – T 188/169, Sir F. Leith-Ross to Sir W. Fisher, 30.6.1937; Sir F. Leith-Ross to Neville Chamberlain, 26.5.1937; and Note by Sir F. Leith-Ross on Schacht, 20.9.1937.
160. Ibid., T 172/1801, Memorandum by E. Hale, 10.8.1937, and Minute by Sir W. Fisher, 19.8.1937.
161. The latest work to treat Chamberlain's view of the Foreign Office in this way is L. W. Fuchser, *Neville Chamberlain and Appeasement: A Study in the Politics of History* (New York/London, 1982), p. 90.
162. D. Dilks, *Neville Chamberlain: Pioneering and Reform, 1869–1929* (London, 1984), pp. 326–7, 408–9 and 412–9.
163. Weinberg, *Starting World War*, .p. 93.

8. Chamberlain

1. This was partly because Chamberlain felt that Eden needed to be stiffened, 'for [he wrote] with all his virtues Anthony does want guidance and support and they are not forthcoming from the F.O.'. *NCP*, 18/1/1024, Neville Chamberlain to Ida Chamberlain, 16.10.1937.
2. Ibid., 1015, Neville Chamberlain to Ida Chamberlain, 18.8.1937.
3. Ibid., 1027, Neville Chamberlain to Hilda Chamberlain, 6.11.1937.
4. Above, p. 4.
5. R. Tamchina, 'The Imperial Conference of 1937', *Institute of Commonwealth Studies, London, Postgraduate Seminar Papers*, 13.1.1972.
6. *PRO* – CAB 32/29E(37)15.

7. Above, pp. 164–71.
8. At the beginning of the imperial conference Hetzog accused the British of adopting an attitude of 'cold repellent indifference' towards Germany. Pirow, op. cit., pp. 223–4.
9. *PRO* – CAB 32/128/E.(P.D.)(37), *Imperial Conference Minutes*, 2.6.1937, and *ACAD*, 1/6, Diary, 4.6.1937.
10. Tamchina, op. cit., and *PRO* – FO 371/20721/C4135/37/18, Minute by O. Sargent, 8.6. 1937.
11. Ibid., CAB 32/128/E. (P.D.)(37), *Imperial Conference Minutes*, 4.6.1937.
12. Minute by O. Sargent, 8.6. 1937, loc. cit.
13. *PRO* – FO 371/20721/C4135/37/18, Minute by R. Vansittart, 9.6.1937.
14. Ibid., Minute by A. Eden, 9.6.1937. Eden was invited by an official to favour the Foreign Office with a record of what transpired at the dinner party, but he did not oblige. See ibid., Minute, 19.6.1937, (name illegible). On the other hand, Chamberlain was more forthcoming with Cadogan, informing him that Hertzog 'had been given to understand (by his contacts) that Germans wd. accept a money payment in respect of S.W. Africa. Thus if a small slice of W. Africa cd. satisfy their pride, an arrangement might be made,' *ACAD*, 1/6, Diary, 17.6.1937. For a discussion of the colonial question at the imperial conference of 1937 see also R. Ovendale, *'Appeasement' and the English Speaking World* (Cardiff, 1975), pp. 47–8.
15. This is not to say that it was assumed that the colonial question would disappear, but the British government had good information that the issue was being soft-pedalled in Germany. *PRO* – FO 371/20735/C3555/270/18, A. Eden to Sir N. Henderson, 13.5.1937, and 20721/C4432/37/18, Sir N. Henderson to A. Eden,. 14.6.1937, See also ibid., 20735/C3793/270/18, Sir N. Henderson to A. Eden, 25.5.1937.
16. Above, p. 205.
17. *PRO* – FO 371/20483/W1932/195/18, Minute by E. H. Carr, 12.2.1936, and Memorandum by H. Godwin, 29.2.1936.
18. Ibid., W195/195/98, Undated minute by Gladwyn Jebb. See also ibid., 20472/W1274/79/98, Minute by Sir R. Vansittart, 4.2.1936.
19. Ibid., 20483/W60785/195/98, Minutes by F. Ashton-Gwatkin, 22.6.1936, and A. Eden, 24.6.1936.
20. Ibid., W10990/195/98, *Note of an Interdepartmental Meeting at the Board of Trade*, 9.9.1936, and W12874/195/98, F. Ashton-Gwatkin to A. Eden, 2.10.1936.
21. Ibid., W13001/195/98, F. Ashton-Gwatkin to A. Eden, 29.9.1936.
22. S. Heald and J. Wheeler-Bennett (eds), *Documents on International Affairs 1937* (London, 1938), pp. 773–4.
23. F. Ashton-Gwatkin to A. Eden, 29.9.1936, loc. cit.
24. *PRO* – FO 371/20718/C1282/37/18, Foreign Office Note, *Raw Materials*, 9.2.1937, and *FRUS*, 1936, vol. I, Cordell Hull to Moore, 14.12.1936, pp. 481–2, and Moore to Gilbert, 15.12.1936, p. 482.
25. Heald and Wheeler-Bennett, *Documents 1937*, pp. 773–4.
26. *PRO* – FO 371/20722/C5558/37/18, and *FRUS*, 1937, vol. I, Gilbert to Hull, 13.3.1937, p. 812, and Grady to Hull, 3.4.1937, pp. 813–4.
27. *Völkerbund*, May/June 1937. This edition was given over entirely to the

problem 'Colonies and Raw Materials'.
28. Ibid., CAB 27/622/F.P,(36), *Foreign Policy Committee Minutes*, 11.6.1937. See also ibid., CAB 27/626/F.P.(36)34 and 34A, *Report of the Inter-departmental Committee on Trade Policy*, 16.6.1937.
29. Ibid., CAB 27/622/F.P.(36), *Foreign Policy Committee Minutes*, 16.6.1937. See also ibid., T188/169, *Note by Sir F. Leith-Ross on Geneva/Berlin Discussions, June 1937*. The Americans ultimately thought that the British had demonstrated a liberal attitude. Reporting to Hull, Consul Gilbert at Geneva stated that Leith-Ross had been as accommodating as possible regarding the Japanese viewpoint. It was Gilbert's view that the Report of the League enquiry into raw materials would 'furnish very real moral support to our policies'. *FRUS*, 1937, vol. I, Gilbert to Hull, 26.6.1937, pp. 817–8.
30. The study produced by the *Royal Institute of International Affairs, The Colonial Problem* (London, 1937), came to the same conclusion. See p. 62. See also P. Orts, 'The Claim for Colonies: A Belgian View', *International Affairs*, March 1937.
31. Colonies on average accounted for under 10 per cent of the world's imports and exports.
32. Heald and Wheeler-Bennett, *Documents 1937*, pp. 774–95.
33. *PRO*–CAB 23/89, *Cabinet Minutes*, 8.9.1937. See also ibid., CAB 24/271, Memoranda by Eden 3.9.1937 and 9.9.1937.
34. Heald and Wheeler-Bennett, *Documents 1937*, pp. 245–7. *Round Table* later commented on the very limited nature of the British offer. See 'Colonies, Tariffs and Quotas', *Round Table*, December 1937.
35. Joelson, op. cit., p. 278.
36. *PRO* – FO 371/20722/C6686/37/18, Sir G. Ogilvie Forbes to A. Eden, 24.9.1937.
37. I. Colvin, *The Chamberlain Cabinet* (London, 1971), p. 46, and Lord Templewood, *Nine Troubled Years* (London, 1954), p. 258.
38. Amery, *Unforgiving Years*, p. 255.
39. J. Joll, 'The Decline of Europe', *International Affairs*, November, 1970.
40. Dilks, *Cadogan*, p. 30.
41. Memorandum by A. Eden, *The German Danger*, 17.1.1936, loc. cit.
42. Middlemas, *Illusion*, p. 51.
43. Ibid., p. 48, and *NCP*, 2/23a, Diary, 11.12.1934.
44. Ibid., 18/1/952, Neville Chamberlain to Hilda Chamberlain, 21.3.1936, and ibid., 951, Neville Chamberlain to Ida Chamberlain, 14.3.1936.
45. Ibid., 955, Neville Chamberlain to Hilda Chamberlain, 4.4.1936.
46. Lord Avon, *Facing the Dictators* (London, 1962), p. 445.
47. Neville Chamberlain to Hilda Chamberlain, 21.3.1936, loc. cit.
48. *NCP*, 2/23a, Diary, 11.7.1936.
49. Above, pp. 265–68 and 339–53.
50. J. Harvey (ed.), *The Diplomatic Diaries of Oliver Harvey* (London, 1970), pp. 33–4.
51. Carlton, op. cit., p. 100.
52. *NCP*, 18/1/992, Neville Chamberlain to Hilda Chamberlain, 30.1.1937, and *HNKY*, 3/42, Sir M. Hankey to R. Hankey, 31.1.1937.
53. *TP*, IX/3.

54. Ibid., X/5, HO7: 'Eden. Not impressive in Cabinet. Jealous of interference. epitome of F.A. superiority. Press dep. of F.O. running him. Too much in hands of a clique. Jealous of Van (behaved very badly to him. Paris embassy – peerage). Very receptive to flattery, particularly from the left . . . able in H. of C. Eden always too sensitive to his surroundings e.g. at Geneva.' Hoare later commented that Eden was good in debate, but never had any 'deep notes'. See ibid., HO11. For Eden's relations with the press department of the Foreign Office see P. M. Taylor, *The Projection of Britain: British Overseas Publicity and Propaganda, 1919–1939* (Cambridge, 1981), pp. 41–2.
55. For instance, the way in which he readily accepted Vansittart's advice in the early stages of the Schacht affair, above, p. 323. There was also the way in which Neville Chamberlain had given the lead in winding up the sanctions that had been imposed on Italy. *PRO* – CAB 23/84, *Cabinet Minutes*, 27 and 29.5.1936; *NCP*, 18/1/965, Neville Chamberlain to Hilda Chamberlain, 14.6.1936; and K. Feiling, *Life of Neville Chamberlain* (London, 1946), pp. 295–7.
56. *PRO* – CAB 23/89, *Cabinet Minutes*, 28.7.1937.
57. *TP*, IX/2, Sir S. Hoare to N. Chamberlain, 17.3.1937.
58. Templewood, op. cit., p. 259, and *HNKY*, 3/43, Sir M. Hankey to R. Hankey, 1.3.1938.
59. I. Colvin, *Vansittart in Office* (London, 1965), pp. 141–2.
60. *NCP*, 18/1/1010, Neville Chamberlain to Hilda Chamberlain, 4.7.1937.
61. Ibid., 1014, Neville Chamberlain to Hilda Chamberlain, 1.8.1937.
62. *PRO* – CAB 23/88, *Cabinet Minutes*, 17.6.1937, and *DGFP*, series D. vol. III, The State Secretary to the Legation in Hungary, 12.6.1937.
63. *PRO* – FO 800/268, *Sir Nevile Henderson Papers*, (hereinafter cited as *NHP*), A. Eden to Sir N. Henderson, 18.6.1937, quoted in Weinberg, *Starting World War*, p. 100, fn. 13.
64. Ibid., pp. 100–1, and *DGFP*, series D, vol. III, No. 346, Circular by Mackensen, 21.6.1937.
65. Sir N. Henderson, *Failure of a Mission* (London, 1940), pp. 68–9.
66. Above, pp. 303–56.
67. *PRO* – FO 800/268 *NHP*, Lord Lothian to Sir N. Henderson, 21.5.1937.
68. *ACAD*, 1/6, Diary, 24.4.1937. Henderson's enthusiasm for the job rather overcame him. He was soon committing appalling indiscretions. *PRO* – FO 371/20736/C5377/270/18, Sir N. Henderson to Sir O. Sargent, 20.7.1937, and Minute by Sir R. Vansittart, 30.7.1937; and ibid., FO 800/268/*NHP*, Sir N. Henderson to Mr . Maxwell Garnett, 14.7.1937. There is further evidence of Henderson's weakness as an ambassador in ibid., FO 371/20737/C8293/270/18.
69. Henderson, op. cit., p. 80.
70. *PRO* – CAB 24/271, *Memorandum by A. Eden circulating correspondence with Sir N. Henderson*, 30.7.1937, Sir N. Henderson to A. Eden, 25.5.1937.
71. Ibid., A Eden to Sir N. Henderson. 4.6.1937.
72. *DBFP*,second series, vol. XVIII, No. 399, Sir E. Phipps to A. Eden, 13.4.1937.
73. *Memorandum by A. Eden circulating correspondence with Sir N. Henderson,*

30.7.1937, loc. cit., Sir N. Henderson to A. Eden, 8.6.1937.

74. Ibid., A. Eden to Sir N. Henderson, 15.7.1937. On the matters that Eden proposed to raise with von Neurath, see *PRO* – FO 371/20749/ C5200/3976/18, *Preparations for a visit of Baron von Neurath to London*, and the summary contained in Weinberg, *Starting World War*, pp. 103–4.

75. *PRO* – FO 371/20736/C5314/270/18, Minute by Sir R. Vansittart, 26.7.1937.

76. *Memorandum by A. Eden circulating correspondence with Sir N. Henderson*, loc. cit., Sir N. Henderson, to A. Eden, 20.7.1937.

77. *PRO* – FO 371/20736/C5314/270/18, A. Eden to Sir N. Henderson, 8.9.1937.

78. Ibid., 800/268/*NHP*, Sir R. Vansittart to Sir N. Henderson, 8.6.1937, and Sir N. Henderson to Sir R. Vansittart, 9.9.1937.

79. Ibid., CAB 24/271, *Memorandum on Anglo–German Relations by A. Eden circulating a despatch from Sir N. Henderson*, 23.9.1937, Sir N. Henderson to A. Eden, 12.9.1937) ibid., FO 371/20736/C7027/270/18, Sir N. Henderson to A. Eden, 10.10.1937; and Henderson, op. cit., pp. 91–2. Henderson's reports of his conversations at Nuremberg and Rominten provoked further dissatisfaction in the Foreign Office with his performance. See *PRO* – FO 371/20736/C7027/270/18, Minutes by Sir O. Sargent, 19.10.1937, Sir R. Vansittart, 20.10.1937, W. Strang, 11.11.1937, and *Draft Instructions for Sir N. Henderson*, October 1937. See also *ACAD*, 1/6, Diary, 20.10.1937.

80. Weinberg, *Starting World War*, p. 113.

81. Roy Douglas, 'Chamberlain and Eden, 1937–38', *Journal of Contemporary History*, 1978, and *PRO* – FO 371/20736/C5314/270/18, Undated Minute by Sir R. Vansittart and Minute by A. Eden, 27.7.1937.

82. Ibid., CAB 23/86, *Cabinet Minutes*, 4.11.1936. That the Hoare-Laval pact had proved abortive was not enthusiastically supported by all. See *TP*, IX/1, Sarita Vansittart to Sir S. Hoare, 9.6.1936, Sir R. Vansittart to Sir. S. Hoare, 10.6.1936, and ibid., Lord Hardinge to Sir S. Hoare,. 6.6.1936; and ibid., X/3, Lord Tyrrell to Sir S. Hoare, 26.4.1938.

83. *The Vansittart Papers*, (hereinafter cited as *VNST*), 1/14, Memorandum by Sir R. Vansittart, *The Future of Anglo–Italian Relations and of the League of Nations*, 21.5.1936. Hankey, who had been strongly opposed to sanctions, was an enthusiastic supporter of better relations with Italy and, it is argued, was Chamberlain's main inspiration in this respect. See Naylor, *A Man and an Institution*, p. 245, and D. T. Rotunda, *The Rome Embassy of Sir Eric Drummond, the 16th Earl of Perth, 1933–1939* (London Ph.D., 1972), pp. 318–20 and 363–4, and P. M. Taylor, op. cit., pp. 34–5.

84. *PRO* – CAB 23/88, *Cabinet Minutes*, 7.6.1937; ibid., CAB 23/89, *Cabinet Minutes*, 14.7.1937; and *NCP*, 18/1/1010, Neville Chamberlain to Ida Chamberlain, 4.7.1937.

85. Ibid., 2/24a, Diary, 19.2.1938.

86. *HNKY*, 3/43, Sir M. Hankey to R. Hankey, 1.3.1938.

87. Avon, op. cit., p. 421, and Harvey, op. cit. pp 65–6.

88. Sir M. Hankey to R. Hankey, 1.3.1938, loc. cit.

89. Italy, for example, was regarded as of cardinal importance in

maintaining the independence of Austria. Following the *Anschluss*, Chamberlain wrote, with perhaps some justice: 'It is tragic to think that very possibly this might have been prevented if I had had Halifax at the F.O. instead of Anthony at the time I wrote my letter to Mussolini.' *NCP*, 18/1/1041, Neville Chamberlain to Hilda Chamberlain, 13.3.1938.

90. Avon, op. cit., p. 423, and Rotunda, op. cit., pp. 368–9.
91. Carlton, op. cit., pp. 107–8.
92. Douglas, art. cit.; Avon, op. cit., pp. 450–3; and *NCP*, 18/1/1041, Neville Chamberlain to Hilda Chamberlain, 1.8.1937. Curiously, the idea of this sort of approach seems to have come from Eden – see Carlton, op. cit., p. 107.
93. *NCP*, 2/24a, Diary, 19.2.1938.
94. Avon, op. cit., pp. 452–3.
95. Count Ciano, *Diary 1937–1938* (London, 1952) Entries for 2.9.1937, 11.9.1937, 13.9.1937 and 21.9.1937; E. Wiskermann, *The Rome–Berlin Axis* (London, 1966), p. 107; and *NCP*, 18/1/1021, Neville Chamberlain to Ida Chamberlain, 19.9.1937.
96. Harvey, op. cit., pp. 47, 55–6, 57–8 and 60–1.
97. On Eden's vanity see Carlton, op. cit., p. 108, and *HNKY*, 3/42, Sir M. Hankey to R. Hankey, 21.11.1937.
98. Carlton, op. cit., pp. 113–4. On the importance of *de jure* recognition see *PRO* – FO 800/328/*LHP*, Neville Chamberlain to Lord Halifax, 7.8.1937, and ibid., CAB 23/89, *Cabinet Minutes*, 8.9.1937.
99. Douglas, art. cit and Carlton, op. cit., p. 114.
100. Ibid., pp. 111–2; *PHPP*, 3/3, Sir M. Hankey to Sir E. Phipps, 11.1.1938; *VNST*, 4/1, The formal reasons for the decision to create a new post; Douglas, art. cit.; Weinberg, *Starting World War*, p. 129; *HNKY*, 3/42, Sir M. Hankey to R. Hankey, 21.11.1937, and Sir M. Hankey to Sir E. Phipps, 26.11.1937; *NCP*, 18/1/1031, Neville Chamberlain to Ida Chamberlain, 12.12.1937, and ibid., 1032, Neville Chamberlain to Hilda Chamberlain, 17.12.1937.
101. Avon, op. cit., p. 510, and Harvey, op. cit., pp. 59–61.
102. Baynes, op. cit. vol. II, pp. 1356–60 and 1364–5; Joelson, op. cit., pp. 273, 277, 278, and 280; *DGFP*, series D, vol. VII, appendix III, D, (iii), Weizsäcker to Hassell, 22.10.1937.
103. *The Times*, 7, 8, 9, 11, 13, 16, 18, 19, 20, 21, 22, 23, 25, 26, 27, 30.10.1937; 1, 2, 3, 6, 9, 10, 12, 13, 19, 23, 25, 27.11.1937; and 3, 4, 7, 8.12.1937. See also *MAE*, 1F/SDN/547, M. Corbin to M. Delbos, 9.10.1937, 14.10.1937, 28.10.1937, 1.11.1937 and 4.11.1937.
104. *The Times*, 28.10.1937.
105. Ibid., 29.10.1937, and *H. of C. V*, vol. 322, col 579.
106. *NCP*, 18/1/1027, Neville Chamberlain to Hilda Chamberlain, 6.11.1937.
107. *MAE*, 1F/SDN/547, M. François-Poncet to M. Delbos, 5.11.1937.
108. *PRO* – FO 371/20722/C7506/37/18, Sir G. Ogilvie Forbes to A. Eden, 1.11.1937, and ibid., CAB 23/90A, *Cabinet Minutes*, 3.11.1937.
109. Ibid., FO 371/20723/C7895/37/18, O. Harvey to F. R. Hoyer, 12.11.1937. Enclosed a memorandum by Charles Peake.

110. Above pp. 246–7. See also *DGFP*, series D, vol. I, No. 93, Memorandum by Ribbetrop, 2.1.1938.
111. *MAE*,. 1F/SDN/547, M. François-Poncet to M. Delbos, 5.11.1937 and 25.11.1937.
112. *PRO* – FO 371/27023/C7679/37/18, N. Law to Sir. O. Sargent, 3.11.1937, and Weinberg, *Starting World War*, p. 115.
113. *PRO* – CAB 27/626/F.P.(36)39, *Account by Lord Halifax of his Visit to Germany*, 26.11.1937.
114. *NCP*, 18/1/1029, Neville Chamberlain to Hilda Chamberlain 21.11.1937; 1030 Neville Chamberlain to Ida Chamberlain 26.11.1937, *PRO* – FO 800/268/*NHP*, Lord Halifax to Sir N. Henderson, 24.11.1937; and *HNKY*, 5/5, Sir M. Hankey to Sir E. Phipps, 26.11.1937.
115. *NHP*, 18/1/1030, Neville Chamberlain to Ida Chamberlain, 26.11.1937.
116. *PRO* – CAB 23/90A, *Cabinet Minutes*, 24.11.1937, Feiling, op. cit., pp. 332–3, and Harvey, op. cit., Entry for 23.11.1937.
117. *PRO* – CAB 27/626/F.P.(36)40, *Record of an Anglo–French Conversation, held at No. 10 Downing Street on November 29 and 30, 1937*, 6.12.1937.
118. *NCP*, 18/1/1030, Neville Chamberlain to Ida Chamberlain, 5.12.1937. Reaction in the Commons was not totally mute, but though Amery and Page Croft schemed it did not come to much. *CRFT*, 1/2, L. S. Amery to Sir H. Page Croft, 5.12.1938, and *H. of C. V*, vol. 329, cols. 2043–4, 2235–6, and vol. 330, cols. 1793–1806 and 1859–60. Interestingly, Winston Churchill indicated he would not now oppose a colonial agreement in a general settlement. Ibid., cols. 1834–5. See also *CRFT*, 1/7, Sir H. Page Croft to Neville Chamberlain, 13.12.1937.
119. *PRO* – CAB 23/90A, *Cabinet Meeting*, 1.12.1937.
120. *DAPE*, vol. I, No. 109, Salazar to Monteiro, 29.10.1937; No. 113, Salazar to Monteiro, 31.10.1937; No. 118, Monteiro to Salazar, 3.11.1937.
121. Ibid., No. 137, Veiga Simões to Salazar, 17.11.1937.
122. Ibid., No. 138, Veiga Simões to Salazar, 20.11.1937.
123. Ibid., No. 160, Monteiro to Salazar, 3.12.1937.
124. *PRO* – FO 371/20723/C8295/37/18, A. Eden to Mr Bateman, 2.12.1937.
125. *DAPE*, vol. I, No. 176, Monteiro to Salazar, 16.12.1937.
126. Ibid., No. 177, Salazar to Monteiro, 18.12.1937; No. 181, Monteiro to Salazar, 21.12.1937; and *H. of C. V*, vol. 330, cols. 1880–1. Monteiro doubted if such statements could be relied upon. See *DAPE*, vol. I, No. 191, Monteiro to Salazar, 30.12.1937.
127. *Account by Lord Halifax of his Visit to Germany*, 26.11.1937, loc. cit.
128. Hillgrüber, 'Hitler's Plans', art. cit.
129. Weinberg, *Starting World War* p. 94.
130. Henke, op. cit., p. 104.
131. *DGFP*, series D, vol. I, No. 19, Memorandum, 10.11.1937.
132. Henke, op. cit., p. 99.
133. Hildebrand, *Foreign Policy*, p. 52.
134. Above, pp. 387–92.
135. *DGFP*, series D. vol. I, No. 15, Mackensen to Leitner, 31.10;.1937.
136. Weinberg, *Starting World War*, p. 116.
137. *DGFP*, series D. vol. I, No. 50, Ribbentrop to von Neurath, 2.12.1937,

and No. 51, Ribbentrop to von Neurath, 2.12.1937. See also *PRO* – FO 371/20737/C8280/270/18, A. Eden to Sir N. Henderson, 1.12.1937.
138. Ibid., C8315/270/18, Sir N. Henderson to A. Eden, 1.12.1937.
139. Ibid., C8634/270/18, Sir N. Henderson to A. Eden, 2.12.1937, and A. Eden to Sir N. Henserson, 17.12.1937. Halifax seems to have favoured Henderson's approach – ibid., FO 800/268/*NHP*, Lord Halifax to Sir N. Henderson, 9.12.1937.
140. Ibid., FO 371/20737/C8466/270/18, A. Eden to Sir N. Henderson, 17.12.1937.
141. Ibid., 20723/C7896/37/18, Minute by W. Strang, 10.12.1937.
142. Ibid.,CAB 24/273, Memorandum by Sir T. Inskip, *Interim Report on Defence Expenditure in Future Years*, 15.12.1937.
143. D. C. Watt, op. cit., pp. 100–16.
144. *PRO* – CAB 24/273, chiefs of staff memorandum, *A Comparison of the Strength of Britain with that of Certain Other nations as at January 1938*, 3.12.1937.
145. *PRO* – CAB 23/90A, *Cabinet Minutes*, 22.12.1937. On the Treasury and the financial limits imposed on defence spending see R. P. Shay, Jnr., *British Rearmament in the Thirties: Politics and Profits* (Princeton, 1977), pp. 159–96, and G. C. Peden, *British Rearmament and the Treasury: 1932–1939*, (Edinburgh, 1979) pp. 60–105.
146. D. Reynolds, *The Creation of the Anglo–American Alliance 1931–41: A Study in Competitive Co-operation* (London, 1981) p. 19.
147. *NCP*, 2/24a, Diary, 19.2.1938.
148. Reynolds, op. cit., p. 20.
149. Dilks, *Cadogan*, p. 37.
150. L. Pratt, 'Anglo–American Naval Conversations on the Far-East', *International Affairs*, 1971.
151. Avon. op. cit., p. 564, and Templewood, op. cit., pp. 258–9.
152. *PRO* – FO 800/269/*NHP*, Sir N. Henderson to Lord Halifax, 10.1.1938.
153. Ibid., Lord Halifax to Sir N. Henderson, 14.1.1938.
154. *NCP*, 18/1/1036, Neville Chamberlain to Ida Chamberlain, 23.1.1938.
155. The territories Chamberlain had in mind seem to have comprised, fundamentally, Togoland and the Cameroons with parts of Nigeria and French Equatorial Africa attached. The problem of Tanganyika was to be solved by offering Germany a colony composed of adjacent portions of the Belgian Congo and Portuguese Angola. The Belgians would be compensated by keeping their mandate for Ruanda–Urundi – a straight swap – while the Portuguese would receive southern Anglola. If necessary Britain would have made further territorial concessions to France in order to equalise the sacrifice. For detailed comments on Chamberlain's scheme see the memorandum, contained in *PRO* – Premier 1/247, and Weinberg, *Starting World War*, pp. 131–2.
156. Ibid., CAB 27/623, *Foreign Policy Committee Minutes*, 24.1.1938.
157. Ibid., 3.2.1938. See also ibid., FO 371/21678/C508/184/18, A. Eden to Sir N. Henderson, 25.1.1938, and C522/184/18, Sir N. Henderson to A. Eden, 26.1.1938.
158. Ibid., Premier 1/247, A. Eden to Sir N. Henderson, 12.2.1938. The

details of this approach were carefully guarded from the French. See ibid., CO 323/1598/6656/Part 1, British Delegation at Geneva to the Foreign Office, 28.1.1938.

159. *NCP*, 18/1/1037, Neville Chamberlain to Ida Chamberlain, 30.1.1938.
160. Ibid., 1038, Neville Chamberlain to Hilda Chamberlain, 6.2.1938.
161. Harvey, op. cit., pp. 82–6.
162. G. McDermott, *The Eden Legacy* (London, 1969), p. 52; *PRO* – CAB 23/92,*Cabinet Minutes*, 19.2.1938. On Eden's resignation see also *TP*, X/3, *A Record of Events connected with Anthony Eden's Resignation 19th–20th February, 1938*, by Lord Halifax; *HNKY*, 3/43, Sir M. Hankey to R. Hankey, 1.3.1938; *PHPP*, 3/3, Sir M. Hankey to Sir E. Phipps, 21.2.1938; *NCP* 2/24a, Diary, 19.2.1938; and Carlton, op. cit. pp. 129–30 for Malcolm MacDonald's testimony that Eden's state of health and mental exhaustion might have been the root cause of his resignation.
163. *DGFP*, series D, vol. I, No. 131, Memorandum by Ribbentrop, 1.3.1938.
164. *PRO* – FO 800/313/LHP, Sir N. Henderson to Lord Halifax, 2.3.1938.
165. *DAPE*, vol. I, No. 234, *Record of a Conversation between Senhor Teixeira de Sampaio and Sir Walford Selby*, 3.3.1938. The Foreign Office did all it could at this time to play down the public discussion of the colonial question. At its request the BBC cancelled a debate on the subject that it had scheduled to broadcast. See *PRO* – FO 371/21679/C1477/184/18, and C1523/184/18, Lord Halifax to Sir Henderson, 4.3.1938.
166. *PRO* – Premier 1/247, Sir N. Henderson to Lord Halifax, 5.3.1938, and Sir N. Henderson to Lord Halifax, 5.3.1938.
167. Henderson, op. cit., pp. 115–6.
168. *DAPE*, vol. I, No. 235, Veiga Simões to Salazar, 4.3.1938.
169. *PRO* – FO 800/269/NHP, Sir N. Henderson to Lord Halifax, 16.3.1938, and Lord Halifax to Sir N. Henderson, 19.3.1938.

9. The Van Zeeland Report

1. Above, pp. 241–90 and see for example the Royal Institute of International Affairs, *Germany's Claim to Colonies* (London, 1939).
2. P. M. H. Bell, *The Origins of the Second World War in Europe* (London, 1986), p. 133. See also Toynbee, *Survey, 1933*, p. 79.
3. R. N. Kottman, *Reciprocity and the North Atlantic Triangle, 1932–1938*. (New York, 1968), p. 44.
4. A. A. Offner, *American Appeasement: United States Foreign Policy and Germany 1933–1938* (Cambridge, Mass., 1969), p. 106.
5. MacDonald, *United States, Britain and Appeasement*, pp. 13 and 16.
6. Offner, op. cit., pp. 56, 63, 67.
7. MacDonald, *United States, Britain and Appeasement*, p. 12, and Reynolds, op. cit., p. 27.
8. MacDonald, *United States, Britain and Appeasement*, p. 21–2.
9. Kottman, op. cit., p. 123, and Leith-Ross, op. cit., p. 170.
10. J. M. Blum, *From the Morgenthau Diaries: Years of Crisis, 1928–1938* (Boston, 1959), p. 131.

11. Ibid., pp. 134–8.
12. Ibid., pp. 138–4.
13. Ibid., pp. 145–9 and 159–173. For the text of the Tripartite Currency Declaration see A. J. Toynbee, *Survey of International Affairs, 1936* (London, 1937), pp. 175–6. Chamberlain refused to make a formal agreement about holding the £ at the $5.00 mark. See D. C. Watt, *Succeeding John Bull: America in Britain's Place 1900–1975* (Cambridge, 1984), p. 86.
14. Blum, *Morgenthau*, p. 171.
15. A. Sauvy, *Histoire économique de la France entre les deux guerres*, vol. II (Paris, 1967), p. 224.
16. C. P. Kindleberger, *The World in Depression 1929–1939* (London, 1973), p. 258, and Toynbee, *Survey, 1936*, pp. 177–9.
17. Kindleberger, op. cit., p. 252.
18. MacDonald, *The United States, Britain and Appeasement*, pp. 1–15.
19. Above, pp. 341–4.
20. *PRO* – FO 371/20699/C629/71/62, Sir F. Leith-Ross to O. Sargent, 26.1.1937; Minute by C. W. Baxter, 26.1.1937; Minute by O. Sargent, 27.1.1937; O. Sargent to Sir F. Leith-Ross, 28.1.1937; and Sir F. Leith-Ross to O. Sargent, 30.1.1937.
21. Ibid., C847/71/62, Minutes of 28.1.1937 and 6.2.1937; Minute by F. Ashton-Gwatkin, 3.2.1937; and O. Sargent to Sir F. Leith-Ross, 10.2.1937; ibid., C1280/71/62, Sir F. Leith-Ross to M. van Zeeland, 11.2.1937.
22. Ibid., W. Strang to Sir R. Lindsay, 23.1.1937.
23. Ibid., Sir F. Leith-Ross to M. J. Rueff, 17.2.1937.
24. Ibid., C2065/71/62, Sir G. Clerk to A. Eden, 15.3.1937, and see also M. Suetens, 'The Van Zeeland Report', *The Contemporary Review*, March 1938, and H. Gaitskell, 'The Politics of Economic Appeasement', *The Political Quarterly*, April 1938.
25. *PRO* – FO 371/20682/C2982/2640/4, Sir N. Charles to A. Eden, 19.4.1937.
26. Ibid., 20699/C2808/71/62, *Record of a Conversation between Sir F. Leith-Ross and M. Frère, 10.4.1937*, by F. Ashton-Gwatkin, 10.4.1937.
27. Ibid., 20700/C2871/71/62, Sir N. Charles to A. Eden, 15.4.1937.
28. Ibid., 20720/C3243/37/18, Memorandum by A. Eden of a Conversation with M. van Zeeland, 26.4.1937. See also ibid., CAB 23/88, *Cabinet Minutes*, 28.4.1937.
29. Ibid., FO 371/20700/C3148/71/62, *Record by Lord Cranborne of a Conversation with N. Davis*, 20.4.1937, and Kottman, op. cit., pp. 139–143.
30. MacDonald, *United States, Britain and Appeasement*, pp. 25–6.
31. *DDF*, series 2, vol. V, M. Corbin to M. Léger, 11.4.1937.
32. *PRO* – CAB 24/270, Memorandum by A. Eden, *M. Frère's Mission*, 9.6.1937.
33. Ibid., FO 371/20699/C6064/71/62, *Report of an Interdepartmental Committee on Trade*, 7.6.1937.
34. A. Toynbee, *Survey of International Affairs, 1937*, vol. I, (London, 1938), p. 76.
35. *PRO* – FO 371/20700/C4944/71/62, Sir N. Charles to A. Eden, 7.7.1937.

36. Ibid., 20699/C5791/71/62, Sir F. Leith-Ross to J. R. C. Helmore, n.d.
37. Ibid., C5295/71/62, Draft Communication to British, American and French Governments by M. P. Van Zeeland, n.d.; Memorandum by Sir F. Leith-Ross, n.d.; Note handed to M. Frère, 16.7.1937.
38. The Rexist opposition in Belgium accused Van Zeeland of irregularities while working with the *Banque Nationale*, which led to him amassing a fortune. The irregularities were apparently trifling by British standards, but sufficient to force him from office on 25 October 1937. See ibid., 20678/C6434/6756/7375/145/4.
39. Sir F. Leith-Ross to J. R. C. Helmore, n.d., loc. cit.
40. *PRO* – FO 371/20699/C7189/71/62, Memorandum by Sir F. Leith-Ross, 15.10.1937, and O. Sargent to Sir F. Leith-Ross, 23.10.1937.
41. Ibid., C8240/71/62, Note by Sir F. Leith-Ross of a Conversation with M. van Zeeland, 28.11.1937.
42. Toynbee, *Survey, 1937*, vol. I, p. 91.
43. Cmnd. 5648, *Report by M. van Zeeland to the Governments of the United Kingdom and France on the Possibility of Obtaining a General Reduction of the Obstacles to International Trade*, 26.1.1938.
44. Note by Sir F. Leith-Ross of a Conversation with M. van Zeeland, 28.11.1927, loc. cit. See also the *Financial News*, 10.1.1938.
45. *PRO* – FO 371/20699/C8240/71/62, Minute by F. Ashton-Gwatkin, 1.12.1937. See also ibid., 21624/C756/63/62, Note by F. Ashton-Gwatkin, 28.1.1938.
46. Ibid., 20724/C8419/37/18, C. Eastwood to C. W. Baxter, 30.11.1937.
47. Ibid., Minute by F. Ashton-Gwatkin, 6.12.1937. C. W. Baxter of the Foreign Office's central department saw little prospect of Germany being atteacted to the colonial sections of the Van Zeeland report, or of Britain being able to act on them. Ibid., 21661/C1500/62/18, Memorandum by C. W. Baxter, 17.2.1938.
48. Ibid., 21623/C288/63/62, Conversation between Mr Butterworth of the United States embassy and Sir F. Leith-Ross, 12.1.1938. See also ibid., 21624/C918/63/72, Sir R. Lindsay to A. Eden, 2.2.1938; C1044/63/62, A. Eden to Sir R. Lindsay, 12.2.1938; and C1371/63/62, Sir R. Lindsay to Lord Halifax, 26.2.1938.
49. Ibid., 21623/C625/63/62, Sir E. Phipps to A. Eden, 31.1.1938; 21624/C696/63/62, Sir E. Phipps to A. Eden, 31.1.1938; and C722/63/62, *French Reaction to the Van Zeeland Report*, by Sir F. Leith-Ross, 2.2.1938.
50. Toynbee, *Survey, 1937*, vol. I, p. 96.
51. *PRO* – FO 371/21624/C756/63/62, *Cabinet Minutes*, 2.2.1938. See also C487/63/62, Notes of a Conversation between Neville Chamberlain and M. van Zeeland; Leith-Ross, op. cit., p. 247; and Lloyd C. Gardner, 'Isolation and Appeasement: An American View of Taylor's Origins', in G. Martel (ed.), *The Origins of the Second World War Reconsidered: the A. J. P. Taylor Debate after Twenty-five Years* (London. 1986). p. 219.
52. German commercial and banking opinion was favourable. See *PRO* – FO 371/21624/C1331/63/62, G. Pinsent to Sir F. Leith-Ross, 22.2.1938, and 21625/C1707/63/62, G. Pinsent to F. Ashton-Gwatkin, 1.3.1938. These circles did not, however, possess political power.

53. *PRO* – FO 371/21624/C1272/63/62, Memorandum by C. W. Baxter, 17.2.1938.
54. N. H. Baynes, op. cit., vol. I, p. 950 ff., and vol. II, pp. 1376 ff.
55. *PRO* – FO 371/21624/C1273/63/62, Sir F. Leith-Ross to F. Ashton-Gwatkin, 21.2.1938.
56. Ibid., C1563/63/62, Foreign Office memorandum by F. Ashton-Gwatkin, 8.3.1938.
57. Gaitskell, art. cit.
58. *PRO* – FO 371/21625/C2871/63/62, Minute by F. Ashton-Gwatkin, 6.4.1938, and Minute by Sir F. Leith-Ross, 7.4.1938.
59. Ibid., Lord Halifax to Sir E. Phipps, 14.4.1938; ibid., C3340/63/62, Sir E. Phipps to Lord Halifax, 22.4.1938; ibid., C5336/63/62, Sir R. Lindsay to Lord Halifax, 2.6.1938; ibid., C6618/63/62, Sir R. Clive to Lord Halifax, 1.7.1938; and ibid., C7039/63/62, *Cabinet Minutes*, 13.7.1938.
60. MacDonald, *United States, Britain and Appeasement*, p. 108.
61. *PRO* – FO 371/21626/C12605/63/62, Note by Sir F. Leith-Ross of a Conversation with M. van Zeeland, 18.10.1938.
62. Ibid., Note by F. Ashton-Gwatkin, 3.11.1938.
63. *DGFP*, series D, vol. IV, No. 257, von Dirksen to Ribbentrop, 19.10.1938. For the assertion that the Leith-Ross scheme was designed to create a four power economic bloc to deal with American competition see Wendt, *Economic Appeasement*, p. 526.
64. Reynolds, op. cit., pp. 17–8.
65. MacDonald, *United States, Britain and Appeasement*, p. 111.
66. Kottman, op. cit., p. 265.
67. Corbin to Léger, 11.4.1937, loc. cit.
68. *DGFP*, series D, vol. IV, No. 267, Minute by Rüter, 10.11.1938, and *PRO* – FO 371/21626/C13950G/63/62, Note by Sir F. Leith-Ross of a Conversation with Herr Rüter, 11.11.1938.
69. Ibid., Sir F. Leith-Ross to Sir H. Wilson, 11.11.1938.
70. See ibid., C12657/13498/13854/63/62.
71. Ibid., C14452/63/62.
72. Ibid., T 188/288, Sir F. Leith-Ross to Berkeley Gage, 19.7.1939.

10. Conclusion

1. *PRO* – FO 371/800/328/*LHP*, L. S. Amery to Lord Halifax, 10.3.1938.
2. Ibid., 269/*NHP*, Sir N. Henderson to Lord Halifax, 30.3.1938.
3. Ibid., Lord Halifax to Sir N. Henderson, 4.4.1938.
4. *H. of C. V*, vol. 333, col. 411.
5. *DAPE*, vol. I, No. 331, Monteiro to Salazar, 27.7.1938.
6. Cf. Cowling, op. cit., p. 276. The references cited by Cowling – *PRO* – CAB 23/93, *Cabinet Minutes*, 18.5.1938 and 25.5.1938, and CAB 24/277, Foreign Office Memorandum entitled, *British Influence in Central and South Eastern Europe*, 24.5.1938 – do not lend any substance to the claim he advances.
7. Ibid., T. 188/288, Sir Nevile Henderson to Sir F. Leith-Ross, 8.6.1938.
8. *PRO* – CO 323/1599/6656/11, 12, 15. The contents of these files have

---

been destroyed under statute, but the extensive lists of letters from the general public regarding the colonial question remain extant.

9. *DBFP*, third series, vol. II, No. 896, *Conversation between Mr. Chamberlain and A. Hitler*, 15.9.1938.
10. DGFP, series D. vol. II, No. 583, *Memorandum on a Conversation between A. Hitler and Mr. Chamberlain*, 23.9.1938.
11. *H. of C. V*, vol. 339, col. 22.
12. DGFP, series D. vol. IV, No. 251, Dirksen to Weizsäcker, 10.10.1938, and No. 260, Dirksen to Ribbentrop, 31.10.1938.
13. D. Lammers, 'From Whitehall after Munich', *The Historical Journal*, XVI, 1973.
14. *PRO* – CO 323/1598/6656/Part 2, Earl of Erroll to the Marquess of Dufferin and Ava, 21.10.1938. See also Joelson, op. cit., pp. 300–1.
15. *The Rhodesia Herald*, 4.11.1938, 8.11.1938, 10.11.1938, 12.11.1938, 29.11.1938, and 30.11.1938. See also the *Bulawayo Chronicle*, 9.11.1938.
16. *PRO* – CO 323/1599/6656/13, Colonel C. Ponsonby to M. MacDonald, 2.11.1938.
17. Ibid., H. Leggett to M. MacDonald, 3.11.1938.
18. Ibid., 1598/6656/Part 2, Sir M. A. Young to M. MacDonald, 11.11.1938. See also *East African Standard*, 1.11.1938, and *Tanganyika Standard*, 29.10.1938 and 31.10.1938.
19. *PRO* – CO 323/1598/6656/Part 2, Daniel Odindo to M. MacDonald, 10.11.1938.
20. Ibid., A. M. Wade to M. MacDonald, 12.11.1938, and ibid., Part 3, Sir R. Brooker-Popham to M. MacDonald, 10.11.1938.
21. *H. of C. V*, vol. 341, col. 492.
22. *PRO* – CO 323/1598/6656/Part 2, M. MacDonald to the Governors of Nigeria, the Gold Coast, Gambia, Sierra Leone, Kenya, Uganda, Nyasaland and Northern Rhodesia, 15.11.1938. See also ibid., Premier 1/247, M. MacDonald to Sir M. A. Young, 15.11 1938.
23. Morgan, op. cit., pp. 19–22.
24. Lammers, art. cit.
25. Bell, op. cit., p. 246.
26. Wark, op. cit., pp. 173–4, 180–7 and 211–40.
27. *PRO* – Premier 1/247, M. MacDonald to Sir B. Bourdillon, 21.11.1938; Sir B. Bourdillon to M. MacDonald, 21.11.1938; and Sir B. Bourdillon, 27.11.1938.
28. Ibid., Sir B. Bourdillon to M. MacDonald, 22.11.1938.
29. Ibid., M. Macdonald to Neville Chamberlain, 26.11.1938, and M. MacDonald to Sir B. Bourdillon, 27.11.1938.
30. Ibid., M. MacDonald to Sir B. Bourdillon, 6.12.1938.
31. Ibid., M. MacDonald to Neville Chamberlain, 6.12.1938; Sir H. Wilson to Neville Chamberlain, 6.12.1938; and Minute by Neville Chamberlain, 6.12.1938.
32. *H. of C. V*, vol. 342, cols. 1199–1261. See also *PRO* – CO 323/1598/6656/Part 2, Malcolm MacDonald to all Governors of African Colonies, 7.12.1938.
33. Ibid., Part 3, Sir G. Ogilvie Forbes to Lord Halifax, 9.12.1938.
34. Ibid., FO 371/21681/C12051/184/18, Lord Halifax to Sir W. Selby,

6.12.1938; ibid., 21684/15064/184/18, Foreign Office memorandum, 18.11.1938; and ibid., 22594/W14180/146/36, Sir W. Selby to Lord Halifax, 17.10.1936.
35. *TP*, X/3, Lord Halifax to Sir S. Hoare, 11.10.1938.
36. Ibid., Sir S. Hoare to Lord Halifax, 18.10.1938.
37. D. C. Watt, 'South African Attempts to Mediate between Britain and Germany', K. Bourne and D. C. Watt (eds), *Studies in International History* (London, 196), p. 419.
38. *DAPE*, vol. II, No. 420, Monteiro to Salazar, 19.10.1938.
39. Bourne and Watt, op. cit., pp. 419–22.
40. *DGFP*, series D, vol. IV, No. 270, Memorandum by Ribbentrop, 18.11.1938, and No. 271, Memorandum by Hewel, 24.11.1938.
41. *DAPE*, vol. II, No. 511, Fonseca to Salazar, 29.11.1938.
42. *PRO* – FO 800/315/*LHP*, Neville Chamberlain to Sir N. Henderson, 19.2.1939.
43. Ibid., Lord Halifax to Sir N. Henderson, 20.2.1939.
44. Ibid., Sir N. Henderson to Lord Halifax, 23.2.1939, and Sir N. Henderson to Neville Chamberlain, 23.2.1939.
45. Baynes, op. cit., vol. II, pp. 1567–8; P. Einzig, *Appeasement* (London, 1942), pp. 112–5 and 117–20; Wendt, *Economic Appeasement*, pp. 582–6; and C. A. MacDonald, 'Economic Appeasement and the German "Moderates" 1937–1939', *Past and Present*, 1972.
46. See P. Kennedy, 'Appeasement', in G. Martel (ed.), op. cit., p. 156.
47. Lammers, art. cit. The official in question was Gladwyn Jebb.
48. Ibid.
49. S. Aster, *1939: The Making of the Second World War* (London, 1973), pp. 243–51; Gilbert and Gott, op. cit., pp. 213–29; *DGFP*, series D, vol. VI, No. 716, Memorandum by H. Wohltat, 24.7.1939; *DBFP*, third series, vol. VI, No. 354, Memorandum by Sir H. Wilson, 19.7.1939, and No. 370, Memorandum by R. Hudson, 20.7.1939.
50. G. L. Weinberg, 'German Colonial Plans and Policies 1938–1942', W. Besson and F. H. von Gaertringen (eds), *Geschichte und Gegenwartsbewusstsein* (Göttingen, 1963); Schmokel, op. cit., p. 143 ff.; and Hildebrand, *Weltreich*, p. 594 ff.
51. Reynolds, op. cit., p. 104, and *PRO* – CAB 65/13, *War Cabinet Minutes*, 27.5.1940. Colonial concessions also featured in correspondence between Lord Noel-Buxton and Lloyd George regarding a compromise peace with Germany. See *LGP*, G//15/11, Lord Noel Buxton to D. Lloyd George, 25.7.1940, 5.4.1941 and 17.4.1941. See also P. Addison, 'Lloyd George and Compromise Peace in the Second World War', A. J. P. Taylor (ed.), *Lloyd George: Twelve Essays* (London, 1971).
52. *DBFP*, third series, vol. VII, No. 472, Sir N. Henderson to Lord Halifax, 29.8.1939, and No. 501, Sir N. Henderson to Lord Halifax, 29.8.1939.
53. The notion of solving Europe's problems by extra-European territorial adjustments and transfers was still acceptable in many quarters during the inter-war years. See A. J. Crozier, 'Philippe Berthelot and the Rome Agreements of January 1935', *The Historical Journal* (XXVI), 1983.

Bibliography

1. Unpublished Primary Sources

(a) Public Record Office
Premier 1   Prime Ministerial Papers
CAB 16   Ad Hoc Sub-Committees of Enquiry
CAB 21   Registered Files
CAB 23   Cabinet Minutes
CAB 24   Cabinet Papers
CAB 27   Cabinet Committee Minutes and Papers
CAB 29   Preparations for Peace and the Peace Conference
CAB 32   Imperial Conferences
FO 371   Foreign Office Political Files
FO 800   The Papers of Sir Austen Chamberlain
FO 800   The Papers of Lord Halifax
FO 800   The Papers of Sir Nevile Henderson
FO 800   The Papers of Sir Samuel Hoare
FO 800   The Papers of Sir Orme Sargent
FO 800   The Papers of Sir John Simon
CO 323   Colonial Office General Correspondence
CO 691   Colonial Office Tanganyika Correspondence
T 172   Various Treasury Papers
T 188   The Papers of Sir Frederick Leith-Ross

(b) The British Museum:
The Papers of Viscount Cecil

(c) The Beaverbrook Library, House of Lords Record Office:
The Papers of D. Lloyd George

(d) University of Birmingham Library:
The Papers of Neville Chamberlain
The Papers of W. H. Dawson

(e) Churchill College, Cambridge:
The Papers of Sir Alexander Cadogan
The Papers of Lord Hankey
The Papers of Sir H. Page Croft
The Papers of Sir E. Phipps
The Papers of Lord Vansittart

(f) University of Cambridge Library:
The Papers of Viscount Templewood

(g) The National Library of Wales, Aberystwyth:
The Papers of Thomas Jones

(h) Ministère des Affaires Étrangères:
Diplomatic Archives

2. Published Primary Sources

Akten zur Deutschen Auswärtigen Politik (Bonn, 1949–).
Dez Anos de Política Externa, 1936–1947. A Nação Portuguesa e a Segunda Guerra Mundial, Part 1, vols. I and II, (Lisbon, 1961–).
Documents Diplomatiques Français (Paris, 1964–).
Documents on British Foreign Policy (London, 1946–).
Documents on German Foreign Policy (London, 1951–).
Foreign Relations of the United States: The Paris Peace Conference (Washington, 1942–7).
Cd. 8306, *German Atrocities and Breaches of the Rules of War in Africa* (1916).
Cd. 8371, *Papers Relating to Certain Trials and Executions of Natives in South-West Africa* (1916).
Cd. 9146, *Report on the Natives of South-West Africa and their Treatment by Germany* (1918).
Cd. 9210, *Correspondence relating to the Wishes of the Natives of the German Colonies as to their Future Government* (1918).
Cmd. 4827, *Statement Relating to Defence issues in connexion with the House of Commons Debate on 11th March, 1935* (1935).
Cmd. 5648, *Report by M. van Zeeland to the Governments of the United Kingdom and France on the Possibility of Obtaining a General Reduction of the Obstacles to International Trade.*
House of Commons Debates, Fifth Series.
S. Heald and J. Wheeler-Bennett (eds), *Documents on International Affairs* (London, 1931–).

3. Newspapers and Periodicals

Cape Argus
Cape Times
Daily Mail
Daily Telegraph
East Africa
East African Standard
Evening Standard
Johannesburg Sunday Times
Morning Post
News Chronicle
Rand Daily Mail
Tanganyika Standard
The Economist
The Nation
The Star
The Times
World Review

4. Memoirs, Biographies and Contemporary Literature

P. Aloisi, *Journal, 25 juillet 1932–14 juin 1935* (Paris, 1957).
L. S. Amery, *My Political Life: War and Peace* (London, 1953).
L. S. Amery, *My Political Life: The Unforgiving Years* (London, 1955).
L. S. Amery, *The German Colonial Claim* (London, 1939).
N. Angell, *The Fruits of Victory* (London, 1921).
N. Angell, *The Defence of Empire* (London, 1937).
Earl of Avon, *Facing the Dictators* (London, 1962).
J. Barnes and D. Nicolson (eds), *The Leo Amery Diaries*, vol. I (London, 1980).
L. Barnes, *The Future of Colonies* (London, 1936).
L. Barnes, *The Duty of Empire* (London, 1935).
L. Barnes, 'The Empire as Sacred Trust', *The Political Quarterly*, 1938.
N. H. Baynes, *Hitler's Speeches*, 2 vols (London, 1942).
E. R. Beck, *Verdict on Schacht: A Study in the Problem of Political 'Guilt'* (Tallahassee, 1955).
N. Bentwich, *The Mandates System*, (New York, 1930).
N. Bentwich, 'Colonies and Mandates' *The Contemporry Review*, 1936.
B. B. Berle and T. B. Jacobs (eds), *Navigating the Rapids 1918–1971: From the Papers of Adolf A. Berle* (New York, 1973).
Earl of Birkenhead, *Halifax* (London, 1965).
J. M. Blum, *From the Morgenthau Diaries: Years of Crisis 1928–1938* (Boston, 1959).
H. N. Brailsford, *The War of Steel and Gold* (London, 1915).
B. Bennett, *Hitler over Africa* (London, 1939).
G. Bonnet, *Défense de la Paix*, 2 vols., (Geneva 1946 and 1948).
F. Borkenau, *The New German Empire* (London, 1939).
P. Bruchlansen, 'German Colonial Propaganda in Africa', *The Contemporary Review*, 1935.
A. Bullock, *Germany's Colonial Demands* (London, 1939).
J. R. M. Butler, *Lord Lothian* (London, 1960).
D. Cameron, *My Tanganyika Service and Some Nigeria* (London, 1939).
Sir Austen Chamberlain, 'Great Britain as a European Power', *International Affairs*, 1930.
W. S. Churchill, *The Gathering Storm* (London, 1948).
Count Galeazzo Ciano, *Ciano's Diplomatic Papers* (London, 1948).
Count Galeazzo Ciano, *Diary, 1937–1938* (London, 1952).
I. Colvin, *Vansittart in Office* (London, 1965).
J. Colton, *Leon Blum: Humanist in Politics* (Cambridge and London, 1966).
T. P. Conwell-Evans, 'Between Berlin and London', *The Nineteenth Century and After*, 1936.
A. Duff Cooper, *Old Men Forget* (London, 1954).
J. A. Cross, *Sir Samuel Hoare*, (London, 1977).
Viscount D'Abernon, *An Ambassador of Peace*, 3 vols (London, 1929).
H. Dalton, *The Fateful Years* (London, 1957).
W. H. Dawson, 'Germany after the War', *The Contemporary Review*, 1917.
W. H. Dawson, 'How Germany Makes Peace', *The Nineteenth Century and After*, 1918.

W. H. Dawson, 'The Fifth Year of the War', *The Contemporary Review*, 1918.

W. H. Dawson, 'The Liabilities of the Peace', *The Fortnightly Review*, 1919.

W. H. Dawson, 'The League and the Peace', *The Fortnightly Review*, 1919.

W. H. Dawson, 'Can France and Germany be Reconciled?' *The Fortnightly Review*, 1922.

W. H. Dawson, 'The Urgency of Treaty Revision', *The Contemporary Review*, 1933.

W. H. Dawson, 'Hitler's Challenge', *The Nineteenth Century and After*, 1936.

D. Dilks (ed), *The Diaries of Sir Alexander Cadogan* (London, 1971).

P. Einzig, *Appeasement* (London, 1942).

F. Ritter von Epp, 'The Claim to Colonies', *Journal of the Royal African Society*, 1937.

S. Erckner, *Hitler's Conspiracy against Peace* (London, 1937).

K. Feiling, *The Life of Neville Chamberlain* (London, 1946).

A. François-Poncet, *Souvenirs d'un ambassade à Berlin* (Paris, 1946).

H. Gaitskell, 'The Politics of Economic Appeasement', *The Political Quarterly*, 1938.

J. L. Garvin, *The Economic Foundations of Peace* (London, 1919).

M. Gilbert, *Plough My Own Furrow* (London, 1965).

I. Greaves, 'A Modern Colonial Fallacy', *Foreign Affairs*, 1936.

R. Guariglia, *La diplomatie difficile* (Paris, 1965).

Earl of Halifax, *The Fulness of Days* (London, 1957).

J. Harvey (ed.), *The Diplomatic Diaries of Oliver Harvey* (London, 1970).

A. Henderson, *The Aims of Labour* (London, 1918).

Sir N. Henderson, *Failure of a Mission* (London, 1940).

A. Hitler, *Hitler's Secret Book* (New York, 1961).

A. Hitler, *Mein Kampf* (London, 1969).

A. Hitler, *Hitler's Table Talk* (London, 1973).

A. Hitler, *Hitlers Politisches Testament: Die Bormann Diktate vom Februar und April 1945* (Hamburg, 1981).

J. A. Hobson, *Imperialism* (London, 1901).

H. V. Hodson, 'Imperial Economic Policy', *International Affairs*, 1935.

H. V. Hodson, 'The Imperial Conference', *International Affairs*, 1937.

J. H. Hofmeyr, 'Germany's Colonial Claims: A South African View', *Foreign Affairs*, 1939.

N. H. Hooker (ed.), *The Moffat Papers. Selections from the Diplomatic Journals of Jay Pierrepoint Moffat* (Cambridge, Massachussetts, 1956).

B. S. Keeling, 'Colonies: The Economic Case Examined', *The Contemporary Review*, 1937.

F. S. Joelson, *Germany's Claims to Colonies* (London, 1939).

G. K. Johannsen and H. K. Kraft, *Germany's Colonial Problem* (London, 1937).

T. Jones, *Diary with Letters* (Oxford, 1954).

J. M. Keynes, *The Economic Consequences of the Peace* (London, 1919).

I. Kirkpatrick, *The Inner Circle* (London, 1959).

R. R. Kuczynski, *'Living Space' and Population Problems*, (Oxford, 1939).

Labour Party, *The Demand for Colonial Territories and Equality of Opportunity* (London, 1936).

R. Lansing, *War Memoirs* (Indianapolis, 1935).

C. K. Leith, 'Mineral Resources and Peace', *Foreign Affairs*, 1938.

Sir F. Leith-Ross, *Money Talks* (London, 1968).

E. Lewin, *The Germans and Africa* (London, 1939).

M. F. Lindley, *The Acquisition and Government of Backward Government in International Law* (London, 1926).

D. Lloyd George, *War Memoirs*, 2 vols. (London, 1938).

Lord Londonderry, *Ourselves and Germany* (London, 1938).

O. Louwers, *Le Problème colonial du point de vue international* (Brussels, 1936).

Lord Lugard, *The Dual Mandate in Tropical Africa* (London, 1922).

Lord Lugard, 'The Basis of the Claim for Colonies', *International Affairs*, 1936.

N. Macauley, *Mandates – Reasons, Results, Remedies* (London, 1937).

Lord Marley, 'The Empire as an Economic Unit', *The Political Quarterly*, 1938.

Sir J. Maynard, 'The Answer to Germany', *The Political Quarterly*, 1939.

G. McDermott, *The Eden Legacy* (London, 1969).

R. J. Minney, *The Private Papers of Hore-belisha* (London, 1960).

H. Nicolson, 'The Colonial Problem', *International Affairs*, 1938.

L. Noël, *Les illusions de Stresa* (Paris, 1975).

P. Orts, 'The Claim for Colonies: A Belgian View', *International Affairs*, 1937.

E. N. Peterson, *Hjalmar Schacht: For and Against Hitler* (Boston, 1954).

O. Pirow, *James Barry Munnick Hertzog* (London, 1958).

H. Rauschning, *Hitler Speaks* (London, 1939).

E. M. Ritchie, *The Unfinished War* (London, 1940).

G. Roberts, *The Nazi Claim to Colonies* (London, 1939).

C. Roden Buxton, 'The Dissatisfied Powers and the World's Resources', *The Contemporary Review*, 1935.

C. Roden Buxton, 'The Government of Crown Colonies', *The Political Quarterly*, 1938.

Royal Institute of International Affairs, *The Colonial Problem* (London, 1937).

Royal Institute of International Affairs, *Germany's Claim to Colonies* (London, 1939).

Round Table, 'The Future of Colonial Trusteeship', 1934.

Round Table, 'South Africa: Nationalism, Nazism and Neighbourliness', (1935).

Round Table, 'Colonial Raw Materials', 1936.

Round Table, 'From Agadir to Nuremberg', 1936.

Round Table, 'Colonial Tariffs and Quotas', 1937.

Round Table, 'The Empire and World Trade', 1937.

Sir A. Salter, *Peace and the Colonial Problem* (London, 1935).

H. Schacht, *New Colonial Policy* (Berlin, 1926).

H. Schacht, *The End of Reparations* (London, 1931).

H. Schacht, 'German Trade and German Debts', *Foreign Affairs*, 1934.

H. Schacht, 'Germany's Colonial Demands', *Foreign Affairs*, 1937.

H. Schacht, *Account Settled* (London, 1949).

H. Schacht, *My First Seventy-Six Years* (London, 1955).

H. Schnee, *The German Colonies under Mandates* (Berlin, 1922).

H. Schnee, *German Colonization Past and Future* (London, 1926).

Sir W. Selby, *Diplomatic Twilight* (London, 1953).

Viscount Simon, *Retrospect* (London, 1952).

G. L. Steer, *Judgement on German Africa* (London, 1939).

E. Staley, *Raw Materials in Peace and War* (New York, 1937).

M. Suetens, 'The Van Zeeland Report', *The Contemporary Review*, 1938.

E. Sutton (ed.), *Gustav Stresemann: His Diaries, Letters and Papers*, 3 vols (London, 1935).

Lord Swinton, *I Remember* (London, 1948).

H. W. V. Temperley, *A History of the Peace Conference of Paris* (London, 1920).

Viscount Templewood, *Nine Troubled Years* (London, 1954).

The Indian Empire Review, 'The British Colonial Empire and the German Claim', (1937).

M. E. Townsend, 'The Contemporary Colonial Movement in Germany', *The Political Science Quarterly*, 1928.

M. E. Townsend, 'The German Colonies and the Third Reich', *The Political Science Quarterly*, 1938.

A. J. Toynbee, *Survey of International Affairs* (London, 1923–).

Lord Vansittart, *The Mist Procession* (London, 1958).

H. G. Wells, *A Reasonable Man's Peace* (London, 1917).

Q. Wright, *Mandates under the League of Nations* (Chicago, 1930).

E. Zimmerman, *The German Empire of Central Africa as a Basis of a new German World Policy* (London, 1918).

5. Historical Works

A. P. Adamthwaite, *France and the Coming of the Second World War* (London, 1977).

P. Addison, 'Lloyd George and Compromise Peace in the Second World War', A. J. P. Taylor (ed.), *Lloyd George: Twelve Essays* (London, 1971).

R. von Albertini, 'Die USA und die Kolonialfrage 1917–1945', *Vierteljahrshefte für Zeitgeschichte*, 1965.

C. M. Andrew and A. S. Kanya-Forstner, 'The French Colonial Party and French Colonial War Aims, 1914–1918', *The Historical Journal*, 1974.

C. M. Andrew and A. S. Kanya-Forstner, *France Overseas: The Great War and the Climax of French Imperialism* (London, 1981).

S. Aster, *1939: The Making of the Second World War* (London, 1973).

C. Barnett, *The Collapse of British Power* (London, 1972).

P. M. H. Bell, *The Origins of the Second World War in Europe* (London, 1986).

E. W. Bennett, *German Rearmament and the West* (Princeton, 1979).

V. R. Berghahn, *Germany and the Approach of War in 1914* (London, 1971).

L. Bisceglia, *Norman Angell and Liberal Internationalism in Britain, 1931–1935* (New York and London, 1982).

H. Bley, *South-West Africa under German Rule* (London, 1971).

A. Bullock, *Hitler: A Study in Tyranny* (London, 1952).

B. Bunting, *The Rise of the South African Reich* (London, 1964).

D. Carlton, *Anthony Eden* (London, 1981).

W. Carr, *Arms, Autarchy and Aggression* (London, 1979).

B. T. G. Chidzero, *Tanganyika and International Trusteeship* (London, 1961).

R. N. Chowdhuri, *International Mandates and Trusteeship Systems* (Amsterdam, 1955).

I. Colvin, *The Chamberlain Cabinet* (London, 1971).

M. Cowling, *The Impact of Hitler* (Cambridge, 1975).

G. A. Craig and F. Gilbert (eds), *The Diplomats*, 2 vols (New York, 1965).

D. Dilks, *Neville Chamberlain: Pioneering and Reform, 1869–1929* (London, 1984).

R. Douglas, 'Chamberlain and Eden, 1937–8', *Journal of Contemporary History*, 1978.

J. E. Dreifort, *Yvon Delbos at the Ouai d'Orsay* (Lawrence, 1973).

H. Duncan Hall, *Mandates, Dependencies and Trusteeship* (London, 1948).

J. B. Duroselle, *La Décadence 1932–1939* (Paris, 1979).

A. Edho Ekoku, 'The British Attitude Towards Germany's Colonial Irridentism in Africa in the Inter-War Years', *Journal of Contemporary History*, 1974.

P. G. Edwards, 'Britain, Fascist Italy and Ethiopia, 1925–1928', *European Studies Review*, 1974.

P. G. Edwards, 'The Austen Chamberlain–Mussolini Meetings', *The Historical Journal*, 1971.

J. T. Emmerson, *The Rhineland Crisis 7 March 1936: A Study in Multilateral Diplomacy* (London, 1977).

E. Eyck, *A History of the Weimar Republic*, 2 vols., (Cambridge, Mass., 1964).

J. C. Fest *Hitler*, (London, 1977).

F. Fischer, *Griff nach der Weltmacht* (Düsseldorf, 1961).

G. Fleming, *Hitler und die Endlösung* (Wiesbaden and Munich, 1982).

L. W. Fuchser, *Neville Chamberlain and Appeasement: A Study in the Politics of History* (New York and London, 1984).

L. H. Gann and P. Duignan (eds), *Colonialism in Africa*, vol. I (Cambridge, 1969).

F. R. Gannon, *The British Press and Germany 1936–1939* (Oxford, 1971).

M. George, *The Hollow Men* (London, 1965).

N. H. Gibbs, *Rearmament Policy* (London, 1976).

P. Gifford and W. R. Louis (eds), *Britain and Germany in Africa* (Yale, 1967).

M. Gilbert, *The Roots of Appeasement*, (London, 1966).

M. Gilbert and R. Gott, *The Appeasers* (London, 1965).

I. Goldblatt, *History of South-West Africa* (Cape Town, 1971).

A. L. Goldman, 'Sir Robert Vansittart's search for Italian co-operation against Hitler, 1933–1936', *Journal of Contemporary History*, 1974.

G. A. Grün, 'Locarno: Idea and Reality', *International Affairs*, 1955.

E. H. Haraszti, *Treaty-Breakers or Realpolitiker. The Anglo–German Naval Agreement of June 1935* (Boppard am Rhein, 1974).

V. Harlow, E. M. Chilver and A. Smith (eds), *History of East Africa*, vol. II (Oxford, 1965).

P. H. S. Hatton, 'Harcourt and Solf: the Search for an Anglo–German Understanding through Africa, 1912–1914', *European Studies Review*, 1971.

M. Hauner, 'Did Hitler want a World Domination?', *Journal of Contemporary History*, 1978.

W. O. Henderson, *Studies in German Colonial History* (London, 1962).

J. Henke, *England in Hitlers politischem Kalkul 1935–1939* (Boppard am Rhein, 1973).

R. Heussler, *Yesterday's Rulers* (London, 1963).

K. Hildebrand, *The Foreign Policy of the Third Reich* (London, 1973).

K. Hildebrand, 'Deutschland, die Westmächte und das Kolonialproblem', *Politik und Zeitgeschichte*, 1969.

K. Hildebrand, *Vom Reich zum Weltreich* (Munich, 1969).

K. Hildebrand, *The Third Reich* (London, 1984).

A. Hillgrüber, *Hitlers Strategie: Politik und Kriegführung 1940–41* (Frankfurt, 1965).

A. Hillgrüber, 'England's Place in Hitler's Plans for World Dominion', *Journal of Contemporary History*, 1974.

A. Hillgrüber, *Germany and the Two World Wars* (London, 1981).

R. F. Holland, *Britain and the Commonwealth Alliance 1918–1939* (London, 1981).

M. Howard, *The Continental Commitment* (London, 1974).

J. Jacobson, *Locarno Diplomacy: Germany and the West, 1925–1929* (Princeton, 1972).

J. Joll, 'The Decline of Europe, 1920–1970', *International Affairs*, 1970.

P. M. Kennedy, '"Appeasement" and British Defence Policy in the Inter-War Years', *British Journal of International Studies*, 1978.

P. M. Kennedy, 'The Logic of Appeasement', *The Times Literary Supplement*, 28.5.1982.

P. M. Kennedy, 'German Colonial Expansion. Has the "Manipulated Social Imperialism" been ante-dated?', *Past and Present*, 1972.

I. Kershaw, *The Nazi Dictatorship: Problems and Perspectives of Interpretation* (London, 1985).

D. O. Kieft, *Belgium's Return to Neutrality: An Essay in the frustrations of Small Power Diplomacy* (Oxford, 1972).

C. P. Kindleberger, *The World in Depression, 1929–1939* (London, 1973).

L. Kochan, *The Struggle for Germany* (Edinburgh, 1963).

R. Kottman, *Reciprocity and the North Atlantic Triangle 1932–1938* (Cornell, 1968).

D. Lammers, 'From Whitehall after Munich', *The Historical Journal*, 1973.

R. Langhorne, 'Anglo–German Negotiations concerning the Future of the Portuguese Colonies 1911–11914', *The Historical Journal*, 1973.

F. M. Leventhal, *The Last Dissenter: H. N. Brailsford and his World* (Oxford, 1985).

N. G. Levin, *Woodrow Wilson and World Politics* (New York, 1968).

R. Logan, *The African Mandates in World Politics* (Washington, 1948).

W. R. Louis, 'The United States and the African Peace Settlement of 1919: the Pilgrimage of George Louis Beer', *Journal of African History*, 1963.

W. R. Louis, 'Great Britain and the African Peace Settlement of 1919', *American Historical Review*, 1965–6.

W. R. Louis, *Great Britain and Germany's Lost Colonies* (Oxford, 1967).

W. R. Louis, 'The United Kingdom and the Beginning of the Mandates System, 1919–1922', *International Organization*, 1969.

W. R. Louis, *Ruanda–Urundi, 1884–1919* (Oxford, 1963).

C. J. Lowe and F. Marzari, *Italian Foreign Policy 1870–1940* (London, 1975).

C. A. MacDonald, *The United States, Britain and Appeasement 1936–1939* (Oxford, 1981).

C..A. MacDonald, 'Economic Appeasement and the German Moderates', *Past and Present*, 1972.

D. Mack Smith, *Mussolini's Roman Empire* (London, 1976).

E. Mantoux, *The Carthaginian Peace* (London, 1946).

G. Martel (ed.), *The Origins of the Second World War Reconsidered: The A. J. P. Taylor Debate after Twenty-Five Years* (London, 1986).

L. W. Martin, *Peace Without Victory* (New Haven, 1958).

W. N. Medlicott, *Contemporary England* (London, 1967).

W. N. Medlicott, *Britain and Germany: The Search for Agreement, 1933–1937* (London, 1969).

W. N. Medlicott, *British Foreign Policy Since Versailles* (London, 1968).

M. Michaelis, 'World Power Status of World Domination?', *The Historical Journal*, 1972.

W. Michalka, *Ribbentrop und die deutsche Weltpolitik 1933–1940* (Munich, 1980).

A. S. Milward, *The German Economy at War* (London, 1965).

A. S. Milward, *War, Economy and Society* (London, 1977).

K. Middlemas and J. Barnes, *Baldwin: A Biography* (London, 1969).

K. Middlemas, *The Diplomacy of Illusion* (London, 1955).

G. Moltman, 'Weltherrschaftsideen Hitlers', in O. Bruner and D. Gerhard (eds), *Europa und Ubersee. Festschrifft für Egmont Zechlin* (Hamburg, 1961).

D. J. Morgan, *The Origins of British Aid Policy* (London, 1980).

W. J. Mommsen and L. Kettenacker (eds), *The Fascist Challenge and the Policy of Appeasement* (London, 1983).

Sir L. B. Namier, *Diplomatic Prelude* (London, 1948).

Sir L. B. Namier, *Europe in Decay* (London, 1950).

Sir L. B. Namier, *In the Nazi Era* (London, 1952).

J. F. Naylor, *Labour's International Policy* (London, 1969).

J. F. Naylor, *A Man and an Institution: Sir Maurice Hankey, the Cabinet Secretriat and the Custody of Cabinet Secrecy* (Cambridge, 1984).

J. Néré, *The Foreign Policy of France from 1914 to 1945* (London, 1975).

J. Nevakivi, *Britain, France and the Arab Middle East 1914–1920* (London, 1969).

I. Nish, *Alliance in Decline* (London, 1972).

A. A. Offner, *American Appeasement: United States Foreign Policy and Germany, 1933–1938* (Cam. Mass., 1969).

R. Oliver and G. Matthew (eds), *History of East Africa*, vol. I, (Oxford, 1963).

A. Orde, *Great Britain and International Security 1920–1926* (London, 1977).

R. Ovendale, *'Appeasement' and the English Speaking World* (Cardiff, 1975).

R. J. Overy, *Goering: 'The Iron Man'* (London, 1984).

R. J. Overy, 'Hitler's War and the German Economy: A Reinterpretation', *Economic History Review*, 1982.

G. C. Peden, *British Rearmament and the Treasury: 1932–1939* (Edinburgh, 1979).

L. Pratt, 'Anglo–German Naval Conversions on the Far-East', *International Affairs*, 1971.

L. Pratt, *East of Malta, West of Suez: Britain's Mediterranean Crisis, 1936–1939* (Cambridge, 1975).

D. Reynolds, *The Creation of the Anglo–American Alliance 1937–1941: A Study on Competitive Co-operation* (London, 1981).

K. G. Robbins, *Munich 1938* (London, 1968).

K. G. Robbins, *Sir Edward Grey* (London, 1971).

E. M. Robertson, *Hitler's Pre-War Policy and Military Plans* (London, 1963).

E. M. Robertson, *Mussolini as Empire-Builder: Europe and Africa, 1932–1936* (London, 1977).

E. M. Robertson, 'Mussolini and Ethiopia: the Prehistory of the Rome Agreements of January 1935', R. Hatton and M. S. Anderson (eds), *Studies in Diplomatic History* (London, 1970).

E. M. Robertson (ed.), *The Origins of the Second World War* (London, 1971).

R. Robinson, J. Gallagher and A. Denny, *Africa and the Victorians* (London, 1961).

N. Rose, *Vansittart: Study of a Diplomat* (London, 1978).

S. Roskill, *Hankey: Man of Secrets*, vol. II (London, 1972).

S. Roskill, *Hankey: Man of Secrets*, vol. III (London, 1974).

V. H. Rothwell, *British War Aims and Peace Diplomacy* (London, 1971).

W. D. Rubinstein, 'Henry Page Croft and the National Party 1917–1922', *Journal of Contemporary History*, 1974.

A. Sauvy, *Histoire économique de la France entre les deux guerres*, vol. II (Paris, 1967).

R. P. Shay, Jnr., *British Rearmament in the Thirties: Politics and Profits* (Princeton, 1977).

G. Schmidt, *England in der Krise: Grundzüge und Grundlagen der britischen Appeasement-Politik (1930–1937)* (Opladen, 1981).

W. W. Schmokel, *Dream of Empire: German Colonialism 1919–1945* (New Haven, 1964).

W. D. Smith, *The German Colonial Empire* (Chapel Hill, 1978).

F. G. Stambrook, 'Das Kind – Lord D'Abernon and the Locarno Pact', *Central European History* 1968.

Z. S. Steiner, *Britain and the Origins of the First World War* (London, 1977).

M. Swartz, *The Union of Democratic Control in British Politics during the First World War* (Oxford, 1971).

R. Tamchina, *The Imperial Conference of 1937*, Institute of Commonwealth Studies, London. Postgraduate Seminar Paper, 13.1.1972.

A. J. P. Taylor, *The Trouble Makers* (London, 1957).

A. J. P. Taylor, *English History* (Oxford, 1966).

A. J. P. Taylor, *The Origins of the Second World War* (London, 1961).

A. J. P. Taylor, *Germany's First Bid for Colonies* (London, 1938).

A. J. P. Taylor, *The Struggle for Mastery in Europe* (Oxford, 1954).

P. M. Taylor, *The Projection of Britain: British Overseas Publicity and Propaganda, 1919–1939* (Cambridge, 1981).

T. Taylor, *Munich: The Price of Peace* (London, 1979).

N. Thompson, *The Anti-Appeasers* (Oxford, 1971).

C. Thorne, *The Approach to War, 1938–9* (London, 1967).

M. E. Townsend, *The Rise and Fall of Germany's Colonial Empire, 1884–1918* (New York, 1930).

M. E. Townsend, *Origins of Modern German Colonialism, 1871–1885* (New York, 1920).

H. Trevor-Roper, 'Hitlers Kregsziele', *Vierteljahrshefte für Zeitgeschichte*, 1960.

H. A. Turner, Jnr., *Stresemann and the Politics of the Weimar Republic* (Princeton, 1965).

J. and A. Tusa, *The Nuremberg Trial* (London, 1983).

J. D. Vincent-Smith, 'The Anglo–German Negotiations over the Portuguese Colonies in Africa, 1911–1914', *The Historical Journal*, 1974.

N. Waites (ed.), *Troubled Neighbours* (London, 1971).

W. K. Wark, *The Ultimate Enemy: British Intelligence and Nazi Germany 1933–1939* (London, 1985).

G. Warner, *Pierre Laval and the Eclipse of Modern France* (London, 1968).

D. C. Watt, 'The Secret Laval–Mussolini Agreement of 1935 on Ethiopia', *Middle-East Journal*, 1961.

D. C. Watt, 'South African Attempts to mediate between Britain and Germany', K. Bourne and D. C. Watt (eds), *Studies in International History* (London, 1966).

D. C. Watt, *Too Serious a Business* (London, 1975).

D. C. Watt, 'Appeasement: The Rise of a Revisionist School', *The Political Quarterly*, 1965.

D. C. Watt, *Personalities and Policies* (London, 1964).

D. C. Watt, *Succeeding John Bull: America in Britain's Place 1900–1975* (Cambridge, 1984).

H.–U. Wehler, 'Bismarck's Imperialism 1862–1890', *Past and Present*, 1970.

H.–U. Wehler, *Bismarck und der Imperialismus* (Cologne and Berlin, 1969).

G. L. Weinberg, 'German Colonial Plans and Policies 1938–1942', W. Besson and F. H. von Gaertringen (eds), *Geschichte und Gegenwartsbewusstsein* (Gottingen, 1963).

G. L. Weinberg, *The Foreign Policy of Hitler's Germany: Diplomatic Revolution in Europe 1933–1936* (Chicago, 1970).

G. L. Weinberg, *The Foreign Policy of Hitler's Germany: Starting World War II 1937–1939* (Chicago, 1980).

B. J. Wendt, *Economic Appeasement: Handel und Finanz in der britischen Deutschland-Politik, 1933–1939* (Dusseldorf, 1971).

Sir J. Wheeler-Bennett, *Munich, Prologue to Tragedy* (London, 1948).

D. Williamson, 'Great Britain and the Ruhr Crisis 1923–1924', *British Journal of International Studies*, 1977.

H. R. Winkler, *The League of Nations Movement in Great Britain 1914–1919* (New Brunswick, 1952).

E. Wiskemann, *The Rome–Berlin Axis* (London, 1966).

A. Wolfers, *Britain and France between the Two World Wars* (New York, 1966).

J. E. Wrench, *Geoffrey Dawson and Our Times* (London, 1955).

6. Theses

A. R. Peters, *Anthony Eden at the Foreign Office 1931–1938* (Keele Ph.D., 1983).

D. T. Rotunda, *The Rome Embassy of Sir Eric Drummond, 16th Earl of Perth, 1933–1939* (London Ph.D., 1972).

Index

343